CICERO'S PRACTICAL PHILOSOPHY

CICERO'S
PRACTICAL PHILOSOPHY

Edited by
WALTER NICGORSKI

University of Notre Dame Press
Notre Dame, Indiana

University of Notre Dame Press
Notre Dame, Indiana 46556
www.undpress.nd.edu
All Rights Reserved

Published in the United States of America
Copyright © 2012 by University of Notre Dame Press

Library of Congress Cataloging-in-Publication Data

Cicero's practical philosophy / edited by Walter Nicgorski.
p. cm.
Proceedings of a conference held in late 2006 at the
University of Notre Dame.
Includes bibliographical references (p. 283) and indexes.
ISBN-13: 978-0-268-03665-2 (pbk. : alk. paper)
ISBN-10: 0-268-03665-9 (pbk. : alk. paper)
EISBN 978-0-268-08763-0
1. Cicero, Marcus Tullius. I. Nicgorski, Walter.
B553.C54 2012
186'.2—dc23
2012003445

∞ *The paper in this book meets the guidelines for permanence and durability
of the Committee on Production Guidelines for Book Longevity
of the Council on Library Resources.*

To Teachers
Who Prepared Me For Cicero,
Led Me to Him, and
Inspired Me to Care

Raymond Windle, S.J. (1928–2010)
J. William Hunt
Leo Strauss (1899–1973)

Contents

List of Contributors	ix
Acknowledgments	xi
Abbreviations	xiii

	Introduction	1
1	Cicero's *De Re Publica* and the Virtues of the Statesman J. G. F. POWELL	14
2	The Fourth Virtue MALCOLM SCHOFIELD	43
3	Philosophical Life versus Political Life: An Impossible Choice for Cicero? CARLOS LÉVY	58
4	Cicero's *Constantia* in Theory and Practice CATHERINE TRACY	79
5	Cicero and the Perverse: The Origins of Error in *De Legibus* 1 and *Tusculan Disputations* 3 MARGARET GRAVER	113
6	Radical and Mitigated Skepticism in Cicero's *Academica* HARALD THORSRUD	133

7   The Politico-Philosophical Character of Cicero's   152
    Verdict in *De Natura Deorum*
    DAVID FOTT

8   Between *Urbs* and *Orbis*: Cicero's Conception of   181
    the Political Community
    XAVIER MÁRQUEZ

9   Cicero on Property and the State   212
    J. JACKSON BARLOW

    Appendix:
    Cicero and the Rebirth of Political Philosophy   242
    WALTER NICGORSKI

Bibliography   283
Index of Citations of Cicero   298
General Index   305

Contributors

J. JACKSON BARLOW is Charles A. Dana Professor of Politics at Juniata College. He has written on Cicero and on American political thought, and is the editor of the forthcoming *Selected Writings of Gouverneur Morris*.

DAVID FOTT is associate professor of political science at the University of Nevada, Las Vegas. He is the author of *John Dewey: America's Philosopher of Democracy* (1998). He is working on a translation of Cicero's *De Re Publica* and *De Legibus* as well as a book on Cicero's political philosophy.

MARGARET GRAVER is Aaron Lawrence Professor of Classics at Dartmouth College, where she specializes in post-Aristotelian moral psychology. She is the author of *Cicero on the Emotions* (2002) and *Stoicism and Emotion* (2009) and is currently working on a translation of Seneca's *Epistulae Morales*.

CARLOS LÉVY is professor of Roman philosophy and literature at the University of Paris-Sorbonne and founder of the Centre d'études sur la philosophie hellénistique et romaine. He is the author of *Cicero Academicus* (1992) and of many studies about Roman philosophy, skepticism, and Middle Platonism, especially on Philo of Alexandria. His last published book is *Les scepticismes* (2008).

XAVIER MÁRQUEZ is a lecturer in political theory in the Political Science and International Relations Programme at Victoria University of Wellington, New Zealand. He is the 2006 winner of the American Political Science Association's Leo Strauss award for the best doctoral dissertation in political philosophy. He recently completed a study of Plato's *Statesman*.

WALTER NICGORSKI is professor in the Program of Liberal Studies and concurrent professor of political science at the University of Notre Dame. He is editor emeritus of *The Review of Politics* and has written and lectured extensively on Cicero's moral and political theory as well as directed summer seminars on the texts of Cicero for the National Endowment for the Humanities.

J. G. F. POWELL is professor of Latin in the department of classics and philosophy at Royal Holloway, University of London. His publications on Cicero include editions of *Cato Maior De Senectute* (1988), *Laelius De Amicitia* (1990), the Oxford Classical Text of *De Re Publica and De Legibus* (2006), and the edited or coedited volumes *Cicero the Philosopher* (1995), *Cicero's Republic* (2001), *Cicero the Advocate* (2004), and *Logos: Rational Argument in Classical Rhetoric* (2007). He is currently working on a new Latin grammar and a study of Latin word order.

MALCOLM SCHOFIELD is Director of Research at the University of Cambridge, where he has been teaching ancient philosophy for nearly forty years. He has published widely in the field, including more than a dozen papers on Cicero's philosophical writings, and is now planning a book on Cicero as philosopher. His latest books are *Plato: Political Philosophy* (2006) and (with Tom Griffith) *Plato: Gorgias, Menexenus, Protagoras* (2009).

HARALD THORSRUD is associate professor of philosophy at Agnes Scott College. He is the author of *Ancient Skepticism* (2009) and "Arcesilaus and Carneades" in the *Cambridge Companion to Ancient Skepticism* (2010).

CATHERINE TRACY received her Ph.D. from the University of Southern California (under the name Catherine Feeley) and is assistant professor and chair of classics at Bishop's University (Canada). Her current research uses Cicero's writing as a window onto popular politics in the late Roman republic.

Acknowledgments

The publication of this volume of essays on Cicero's practical philosophy is indebted to those who helped conceive of the symposium that brought together the scholars whose work is presented here, those who supported and facilitated it, and those who participated either as authors and primary speakers or as commentators. A serious celebration of Cicero as philosopher as a way of marking my retirement as editor of *The Review of Politics* was first raised by W. Dennis Moran, my long-term associate at *The Review* and executive associate editor. I welcomed this idea as a way of more decisively turning my mind and energies back to Cicero, and I received notable encouragement, experienced counsel, and critical financial support from Catherine Zuckert, my successor as editor at *The Review*, and from Gretchen Reydams-Schils, then director of the Institute for Scholarship in the Liberal Arts and my colleague in Notre Dame's Program of Liberal Studies. The Notre Dame Workshop in Ancient Philosophy, of which Gretchen is founding director, also provided financial as well as logistical support all along. Both Catherine and Gretchen contributed as commentators in the course of the symposium, as did other Notre Dame colleagues, namely, Keith Bradley, Edward Goerner, and Michael Zuckert. My colleague Vittorio Hösle presented a major paper on "Cicero's Plato" and participated vigorously throughout the two days of conversation of the symposium. Another colleague, Brian Krostenko, brought his expert knowledge of Latin and Cicero to bear on our discussions, functioning throughout as an ombudsman commentator.

Additional thanks for assistance in funding the symposium goes to The Gladys Krieble Delmas Foundation, Notre Dame's Henkels

Lecture Fund and Ken Garcia, the Nanovic Institute for European Studies, the Devers Program in Dante Studies, the Department of Classics, the Department of Political Science, the Graduate School, the College of Arts and Letters, and the Program of Liberal Studies. Beyond the funding, Henry Weinfield, then chair of the Program of Liberal Studies, and Mark Roche, then Dean of the College of Arts and Letters, gave welcome encouragement in every way possible. I am grateful to my daughter, Ann Nicgorski, Professor of Art History at Willamette University, for her assistance in selecting appropriate iconography of Cicero for the symposium. Administrative details of the symposium were expertly handled as ever by Harriet Baldwin; I was also assisted in these details by then–graduate students Jeffrey Church and Raymond Hain. I am grateful to these and all who helped with the scholarly celebration of Cicero the philosopher that is recalled and continued through this book.

With respect to this book, I am grateful for the cooperation and assistance of the University of Notre Dame Press, specifically to Barbara Hanrahan, who was confident in the significance of this project from the beginning, and to Harv Humphrey and Stephen Little for their professional help in guiding the manuscript to publication. In production I was aided by the expert copyediting of Josh Messner. With the assistance of the Institute for Scholarship in the Liberal Arts, I was able to call on the assistance of S. Adam Seagrave in preparing the bibliography and on that of Genevieve McCabe for the preparation of indices. Finally, I am grateful to the two anonymous reviewers for their helpful suggestions and encouragement. While both reviewers urged me to contribute more in my own name to this volume, I am especially grateful for the suggestion of one reviewer that my 1978 essay on "Cicero and the Rebirth of Political Philosophy" be reprinted here as a way of making it more accessible at this time and as a testimony of the state of Cicero scholarship and regard for Cicero more than thirty years ago. Thank you to *The Political Science Reviewer*, where that essay originally appeared, for granting permission for republication here.

Abbreviations

Abbreviations of the works of Cicero generally follow the standard of *The Oxford Classical Dictionary* (*OCD*). The full titles and abbreviations are also found in the Index of Citations of Cicero at the back of this book.

CD	Augustine, *De Civitate Dei Contra Paganos*
Diss.	Epictetus, *Discourses*
D.L.	Diogenes Laertius
Ep.	Seneca, *Epistulae*
Inst.	Lactantius, *Divinae Institutiones*
M	Sextus Empiricus, *Against the Professors*
NH	Pliny the Elder, *Naturalis Historia*
OCT	Oxford Classical Texts
PH	Sextus Empiricus, *Outlines of Pyrrhonism*
PHP	Galen, *Precepts of Hippocrates and Plato*
SVF	*Stoicorum Veterum Fragmenta*
W	Stobaeus, *Eclogae* (Wachsmuth)

Introduction

The first nine essays featured in this book were presented in initial form at a symposium on Cicero's practical philosophy late in 2006 at the University of Notre Dame. It was an event to mark and, one might even say, to celebrate the renewal of serious interest in Cicero as a thinker that had occurred in the Western world over the previous two generations. Little more than a decade earlier, Jonathan Powell's collection of essays *Cicero the Philosopher* had appeared in Great Britain and sought then to mark the change in regard for Cicero by a presentation of a rich array of European scholarship on various aspects of his philosophical writings. The symposium at Notre Dame brought together a cross section of those who have done significant thinking and research about Cicero as philosopher. A critical edge was not to be sacrificed to celebrating Cicero except, perhaps, in one respect, that being the shared recognition that Cicero was worthy of the renewed serious interest.

The celebrations on both sides of the Atlantic were manifestations that Cicero had much to offer as a philosopher and that his writings withstood serious critical engagement. They were indications that the study of Cicero had finally been liberated from the long shadow

Theodor Mommsen's mid-nineteenth-century critiques of Cicero had cast especially in the Anglo-American scholarly world. They represented some fulfillment of the nearly despairing hope expressed by A.E. Douglas as late as 1965 that there be some movement from the "contempt" for and "neglect" of Cicero's philosophical writings that was the bitter fruit of the previous century.[1] That movement was on the way in the decades that followed. Over that period there was a collective reconsideration and deepening appreciation of Cicero as philosopher. Elizabeth Rawson, a judicious modern biographer of Cicero, reflected this larger development when, upon issuing the second edition of her life of Cicero, she confessed that after ten years of further work on Cicero she found him possessed of "greater intellectual maturity" than most of the thinkers of his time and in fact saw him usually transcending his time. "Closer knowledge of Cicero," she explained, "tends to breed greater appreciation."[2] The scholarly world was coming around to greater esteem for Cicero's philosophical work, to where much of the Western tradition had been prior to the nineteenth century. The republication in the Appendix of my 1978 essay on the state of Cicero studies especially in political science allows a fuller view of where matters stood early in the renewal of the last two generations. It also reminds readers that criticism of Cicero the philosopher was not wholly absent from Western experience before Mommsen's severe judgment.

As a general biographer of Cicero, Rawson's judgment of Cicero's writing and thinking was likely bound up with a judgment of Cicero the man and political actor and leader. Though Mommsen's extension of his negative judgment on Cicero as politician and statesman to his character and his philosophical writings is abrupt, careless, and seemingly lacking in engagement with those writings, Cicero himself seems to have wanted to be judged as a whole, though, to be sure, he wanted to be judged fairly. He looked at his life and writings as one fabric, the latter as but another form of his action for the long-term well-being of his political community. He would not have welcomed praise based on a distinction of his philosophical writings from his political efforts or, for that matter, on a separation of his style from his substance. The importance of overall consistency to Cicero, especially in his public actions, is highlighted and explored in Catherine Tracy's essay in this volume.

It is, however, a sensible and thus understandable tendency, especially with respect to Cicero given all the controversies surrounding his life and achievements, that one be able to assess his practical politics a failure or disappointing in some ways and still embrace as significant the substance of his philosophical writings, that one be able to see him as a master of Latin prose and the supreme orator and yet think that he used these talents in political efforts that were on the whole not admirable. In this spirit and even still in Mommsen's nineteenth century, J.S. Reid protested that the severe judgment of Cicero the philosopher that he frequently encountered was based on "wholly insufficient grounds." Reid attributed the "unfairness" in judging Cicero to scholars who having "learned to despise his political weakness, vanity, and irresolution, make haste to depreciate his achievements in philosophy, without troubling themselves to inquire too closely into their intrinsic value."[3]

It is important to remind ourselves of the almost incredible range and frequently regarded excellence of Cicero's overall achievements. In the light of these, it is no surprise to find that he was for so many during the Renaissance the ancient model of what we have come to take as the Renaissance man. His major achievements were sixfold: as orator, as student and scholar of the art of rhetoric, as lawyer and legal theorist, as statesman, as philosopher, and finally as a very active and revealing correspondent.[4] As remarkable as is the range of his achievements, even more surprising to most is the extensive written record of these that we still possess.

In a sense, Cicero's orations are both first and last among his achievements. First, because through his oratorical ability he initially gained public notice and positioned himself for elevation to public office. They are last for Cicero because they remain today the most acclaimed and least controversial of Cicero's achievements. We now have the texts of some fifty-eight orations by Cicero, some polished toward perfection and never actually delivered. His oratorical achievement seems clearly to be the fruit of the art of rhetoric coupled with his natural talent. He began to study the art at least as early as his adolescent years. His masterful achievement in that art was recorded in seven books of his, the chief being his three-book dialogue *De Oratore*. This work and all the other of his rhetorical writings but one appeared in the last thirteen years of his sixty-three years of life and after his formal political service was completed, after, in other words, he had held the highest office in Rome and had already begun to suffer from decisions he made in that office and from the overall condition of faction-ridden Rome in those last days of the Republic.

Like the study of the art of rhetoric, so the study of law. Observing law's leading practitioners and thinking about its foundations in the very nature of things was a discipline to which Cicero submitted from his earliest years. First, his father it appears, then Cicero himself, held a conviction that rhetorical ability coupled with legal knowledge and skills would equip one to elevate oneself on the stage of Roman politics. Cicero in the courtroom represents then one of the two major venues for his oratorical ability as well, of course, for his legal knowledge and skills. His interests and achievements in this sphere as well as his deep probing of the foundations of all true law are represented in his dialogue *De Legibus*.

The law then, like the art of rhetoric, was first taken up as a necessary piece of equipment for the life of political leadership, of statesmanship. Cicero's achievement as political leader and statesman was indeed one of his significant accomplishments. He held all the major offices in the Roman Republic at the earliest possible age, including the highest elective office, that of consul. Assessment of how he led and governed has often turned on how one thinks about his struggle for the Republic over against the emerging popularly based tyranny of Caesar.

Cicero's achievement in philosophy is, of course, the basis for the scholarly renewal this volume celebrates. Cicero turned with a much-remarked-upon intensity to philosophical writing in the last dozen years of his life, after he had held the office of counsel and was suffering the recriminations just noted. In that time, from approximately 55 B.C. to his December death in 43 B.C., he wrote at least fourteen works of philosophy, eleven of which we possess substantially intact. While his love of philosophy and recognition of its importance was evident from his earliest years, his turn to philosophy in late life was for him a way to serve the Republic's possible future when the emerging tyranny and violence of Roman politics was closing the forum and courts to his oral eloquence.

It is fair to Cicero and necessary to completeness at this point to add a word about Cicero the letter-writer. Remarkably and again like no other ancient thinker in quantitative terms, Cicero has left more than nine hundred letters between himself and friends and family, allies and enemies, associates in business and those with philosophical interests. In the material of these letters, we have in effect the first autobiography. These letters are not, of course, a polished whole book as is Augustine's *Confessions*, but in these letters the soul and struggles of Cicero are bared to view, sometimes embarrassingly so. He confesses his weaknesses and matters of confusion; he explains his intent and his efforts in constructing certain of his written texts, including the dialogue of special importance to this volume, *De Re Publica*. So the very human Cicero at the center of his heroic-like accomplishments is brought before readers.

Besides the issue of fairness in how one handles disappointment with one or another of the many facets of Cicero's talents and achievements, there is the prudential consideration for some of not wanting to take on at once all or many of the controversies surrounding Cicero and thus necessarily a number of those regarding the complex politics of the late Roman Republic. This understandable desire to distinguish aspects of Cicero's life and achievement seems to have brought Leo Strauss to a very interesting question. Strauss appears at one point to want to bracket and set aside Cicero's concrete political judgments and actions while appreciating his philosophical work, in this instance appreciating the political defense of philosophy that constitutes an important theme of that work. Strauss had compared Cicero's political action on behalf of philosophy to Plato's and then observed that this political action has nothing in common with Cicero's actions against Catiline and for Pompey.[5] In the very same essay, Strauss wonders whether the separation of the high politics of defending philosophy from ordinary politics has been too successful in the West. It seems that Strauss is concerned that philosophy's defense in a certain way can give rise to a philosophy and science unrelated to the citizen's and statesman's horizons of political engagement, of necessary decisions about the good. Rather, active political life and leadership may appear simply as forms of data to be explained in a science of politics, if not the science of psychology, both in the service of a comprehensive philosophy or science of humankind. Strauss's wonder then may allow us to understand better why Cicero's distinctively *practical* philosophy has often seemed alien and even unphilosophical to the dominant strains of philosophy in the post-Enlightenment world.

However much Cicero's political actions are seen as related or unrelated to his philosophical work, there is an overlap in the methodology that students of each are now, in a period of greater respect for Cicero, drawn to follow. It is the caveat that one must pay close attention to Cicero's own words, and we have, indeed, many words of his in various genres to which to attend. Early in the shift on Cicero in the last couple of generations, W.K. Lacey began his historical study of Cicero's role in the late Roman Republic with such sensible advice. "Cicero's biographers," he wrote, "must begin with Cicero himself. How much of his testimony they believe, and which parts, will make them produce differing interpretations, but Cicero must himself always be consulted first about what he thought of the situation in the Roman *res publica*."[6] As to Cicero the philosopher and this specific volume, J.G.F. Powell opens his essay here describing what he is doing (and I would add, what is happening in this volume as a whole) as in accord with the emphasis of recent times, namely, as an effort "to interpret Cicero on his own terms." Margaret Graver, another contributor here, cannot be seen to deny this emphasis even as she attends here and in much of her other work to significant sources that Cicero appears to have utilized. Graver, early in her essay, remarks that "we do not necessarily deny Cicero's intellectual agency when we grant that many of the arguments he employs have a significant philosophical prehistory." In fact, Graver can be said to illustrate in her piece how knowledge of certain sources and teachers of Cicero can further our understanding of what he means in expressing his distinctive agency. Earlier in introducing her translation and commentary on the *Tusculans* (Books 3 and 4), she had noted her commitment to follow Cicero's "argument on its own terms," for he is "well-informed about his subject through many sources, oral and written, that are now lost to us, and his treatment is both intelligent and relatively impartial."[7]

The privileging of Cicero's own words and thoughts in seeking to interpret him is more than the offspring of the new respect for him; it is the fertile basis for comprehending Cicero much better than at times in the past and in turn for a much greater sense of how he has contributed and yet can contribute to our own thinking. The scholarship assembled here and developed from that basis makes clear again that, as T.P. Wiseman once remarked, Cicero matters. Writing well into this period of a Ciceronian renewal as he reviewed scholarship on Cicero the political leader and philosopher, Wiseman observed that "Cicero matters not just to classical scholars" but because his political career "for all its failings and compromises stood for the rule of law against the rule of force," and he matters because he gifted us with "a literary corpus that effectively defined our civilization's concepts of *humanitas* and the liberal virtues. Mommsen was wrong," continued Wiseman. "We need to read Cicero's lesson; Caesar's is all too familiar."[8] Whether or not the effect of Mommsen's shallow depreciation of Cicero still lingers as Christian Habicht and others have suggested, there is no basis for anything like a triumphal retaliation or an uncritical reverencing of Cicero.[9] To act so would be, at the least, to be forgetful that if Homer nods at times, surely the busy and passionately engaged Cicero does and possibly in ways more significant than a casual slippage. Present in the Notre Dame symposium was a celebration of the space and air for scholarly balance and with it a contribution to the growing rediscovery of the riches in thought and action of one of the truly remarkable figures in our Western tradition.

Cicero's achievement, of course, transcends the conventional disciplinary lines, lines that too often have walled off various communities of scholars and their discourse from each other. The Notre Dame symposium sought to bring into conversation specialists in political theory, ancient philosophy, classics, history, Latin, and Roman literature. One of the delights of the meetings here was the confessed mutual discovery of the significance and quality of work focused on Cicero being done outside of one or another's specific community of discourse. Notre Dame's celebration of the renewal of Cicero studies sought also to contribute to building some bridges over the gaps in direct contact between different generations of Cicero scholars and between European and American Ciceronians. It was also an effort to pay specific attention to Cicero's practical philosophy and thus to bring scholarly illumination to bear on a dimension of Cicero's thinking that has been especially valued by the educated public down through the years and that arguably might provide the key to a greater understanding of the coherence of Cicero's overall philosophy.

A few words follow about this concept of "practical philosophy," which gave title to the symposium as it does to this book. "Practical philosophy" is understood in the sense that is usually found in Aristotelian studies, namely, to refer to moral and political philosophy. In the case of Cicero and his writings, this translates into his *De Re Publica*, *De Legibus*, *De Finibus*, and *De Officiis*, his primary writings on political community, law, the ultimate good, and moral duties. These texts and their primary topics should not be taken as narrowly and exclusively definitive of the range of concerns that might and often do enter Cicero's practical philosophy. Room must be made for his extensive writings on the art of rhetoric, the chief of which he explicitly draws into the orbit of his philosophical work (*Div.* 2.4). His concern with the divine, with epistemological issues, and with competing analyses of the human soul are among matters that are necessarily encountered in pursuing with Cicero, likely with any serious inquirer, those large entry questions of moral and political philosophy, namely, what is the good and genuinely happy life and how are our communities to be rightly ordered. In fact, such issues as seem outside the practical sphere appear within the very "practical" texts of Cicero just named and point us to the relevance of others of his writings. There is no surprise in this. Important philosophical questions are all interrelated, and they all will arise in any careful and thorough effort at trying to make sense of the human condition.

Cicero above all seeks to make sense of that condition in order to find guidance for action. He is insistent that philosophy bear this fruit of giving moral direction and is drawn to judge philosophies on the basis of whether and how persuasively they do this (*Fin.* 1.11; 2.51; *Off.* 1.4–5). He associates practical philosophy and its priority among all learning with the Socratic orientation to which he gave the most memorable and classic formulation in describing Socrates as bringing philosophy down from the heavens and into the homes and everyday lives of people (*Tusc.* 5.10–11; *Brut.* 31). If Aristotle gives us the concept of practical philosophy, Cicero is its most enthusiastic and purest devotee among ancient thinkers. It distorts Cicero's thinking, however, to believe that he does not appreciate inquiry for inquiry's sake or the delightful pleasure of the philosophical life for its own sake. Duty, nonetheless, does not allow such indulgence in the lives of the most talented, most of the time. Yet one of the fruits of the chapters here by Carlos Lévy, Jonathan Powell, and Harald Thorsrud, each with a different primary focus, is that they, notably in their pointing to *De Inventione*, lead readers to appreciate that Cicero's philosophical interests are not casual or simply incidental to the practical life; rather, they are serious, long-standing, and broad interests, not limited to practical philosophy.

There seems, however, to be great potential significance to attending more to Cicero's own practical orientation in philosophical inquiry. His engagement in political practice might then be seen less as a philosophical distraction and more of an advantaged perspective, a view that Cicero himself held not only of himself but also of certain major figures in Rome's earlier history, like Scipio Africanus Minor. The practical orientation could then be the key to discerning more clearly what is Cicero's distinctive contribution to the Platonic-Aristotelian tradition of the Academy that he appears to embrace and revere. The practical orientation and what assurance comes with it might well be the key to understanding how Cicero understands his own philosophical foundation and thus a way to finding coherence in Cicero's overall philosophical thinking (*Div.* 2.2; *Fin.* 4.14).

Everywhere in the troubled modern world there are publically spirited citizens with whom Cicero's appeal to ethical need along with commonsensical rational responses would seem to resonate. The practical assurance or certitude that emerges from his mix of rich moral and political experience and philosophical skepticism can itself be appealing amid the confusion of disabling modern skepticism and the fog of so much of postmodern thinking.

In this larger picture or set of concerns, this volume presents nine illuminating studies of certain texts and topics at the heart of Cicero's practical philosophy. Properly, then, the volume focuses initially on *De Re Publica*, Cicero's first philosophical writing save, perhaps, for his somewhat philosophical earlier writings on the art of rhetoric. That the four classic virtues are highlighted in the first two essays, those by Powell and Schofield, can serve to remind us of their foundational role in Cicero's moral philosophy, a role clearly articulated in

De Officiis, Cicero's last philosophical writing, which appeared in the year before his death.

Powell finds the imprint of the virtues as an organizing basis for the gap-ridden *De Re Publica.* His chapter, self-confessedly speculative in some ways, makes even more convincing the critical role of the virtues in Cicero's thinking and makes even more incumbent on modern interpreters of Cicero to formulate his specific voice and argument in the context of discussions about virtue ethics. Powell couples his long experience working with *De Re Publica* and other texts of Cicero with his recent fresh examination and critical rethinking of Cardinal Mai's Vatican manuscript of *Re Publica* to provide the interpretation offered here.

Malcolm Schofield, characteristically one might say, takes on likely the most vexing problem in Cicero's treatment of the virtues and among the most important problems bearing on his practical philosophy, namely, the nature and high status of the fourth virtue, *moderatio,* or temperance, as commonly expressed in Cicero. He brings not only his well-established expertise in Hellenistic philosophy and Stoicism in particular to this challenging task but also his proven aptness at close critical reading well-informed by a mastery of the subtleties of the original language. He takes us through an inquiry on *decorum, honestum,* and *verecundia* as aspects of what the fourth virtue is and how it is functioning with respect to the other virtues and in human community. Schofield leaves us with a better appreciation for the coherence of Cicero's treatment of the four virtues and the critical role of reason in Cicero's understanding of them.

Carlos Lévy's work on Cicero has been distinguished by his uncovering a view of the unity and coherence of Cicero's overall philosophy, even being able to integrate into that understanding Cicero's skepticism and *Academica.* In his chapter in this collection, he brings fresh insights marked by notable subtlety to one of the large themes and points of tension in Cicero's life. This is Cicero's fundamental and seemingly anguished ethical choice between the active political life and the philosophical life. Though this fundamental issue is highlighted in the prologue and early pages of *De Re Publica,* Lévy's focus is on other sources, such as the correspondence with Atticus, *Pro Sestio,* and *De Fato,* as he explores Cicero's personal struggle with the issue.

In portraying how Cicero slides to one side or another under the pressure of specific contexts and opportunities, Lévy's study invites a reading that relates this basic tension and choice to the more general concern of Cicero, also anguished, for consistency and sensitivity to appearances that Catherine Tracy highlights in her contribution to the volume. Employing a wide selection of Cicero's texts, including orations and close scrutiny of key terms of Cicero, Tracy not only explores the long-standing issue of the "two Ciceros"—Cicero the political actor and Cicero the writer of ennobling philosophical treatises—but also *constantia* within each side of that basic divide.

Emotions and the control of reason are clearly involved not only in Cicero's fundamental choice, highlighted by Lévy, but also in what Cicero and earlier thinkers on morality like him, especially the Stoics, regarded as bearing on the choices of all humans. Understanding how error and moral wrong come about is a part of better understanding human nature and human agency. That the seeds of virtue are implanted by nature and bound up with the human's inclinations turns out to be part of an important tradition before Cicero appropriates it to this thinking. Margaret Graver's contribution here as well as much of her other work is a reminder of how necessary it is to assimilate well Cicero's *Tusculan Disputations* into any effort to grasp the overall coherence of Cicero's moral and political philosophy.

Consistency again appears as an issue with respect to Cicero's skepticism. Catherine Tracy finds, in fact, that Cicero's skeptical allegiance, along with its entailed adaptable posture, is in tension with his attachment to *constantia*. Harald Thorsrud, endeavoring here to find a consistent position in Cicero's various expressions of his skepticism, works out a lucid portrayal of the specific nature of that skepticism as essentially a "mitigated" skepticism. Thorsrud shows in the course of his essay how that specific mitigated skepticism impacts on and is impacted by Cicero's practical philosophy. Like Graver as noted earlier, Thorsrud illustrates how attention to key sources of Cicero can help in understanding the very text of Cicero himself, in this case, his *Academica*.

David Fott, too, is interested in this skepticism and how it bears on Cicero's political philosophy. He looks at this issue, however, not in terms of two directly related items but through these concerns meeting in Cicero's resolution for himself of the debate over the gods, their existence and nature, which he presents in *De Natura Deorum*. Fott has brought fresh eyes to an examination of this vexing text and the varied interpretations of its conclusion. He highlights the problem of a dogmatic skepticism and Cicero's apparent sophistication in confronting this. For many in his time and through the years, how Cicero resolves the question of the divine's existence and possible role in our lives is critical to an adequate teaching about the law and the obligations of humans to their political communities and one another.

Central topics for Cicero's political theory are treated in the essays by Xavier Márquez and J. Jackson Barlow. Márquez provides a crucial and necessary inquiry into Cicero's model for a political community (*res publica*), how it stands with respect to those of his Greek predecessors in political theory, how Rome and her history impacts on that model, and how translatable it is to the modern nation-state. What then did Cicero think about the political community's responsibilities with respect to property? Was a true political community, suggested by Cicero as a kind of property of a people, simply to protect absolutely and unqualifiedly property rights? If Cicero thought this, was he so inclined simply as a representative of an advantaged class, as some have suggested? Barlow addresses such questions in the course of a chapter that reveals Cicero's treatment of property to be more sophisticated and complex than has generally been thought. Barlow anchors his interpretation in the role justice plays in Cicero's thinking and brings readers back to the foundational function of the four virtues in Cicero. As with Schofield's piece, Barlow provides an important new perspective on an aspect of *De Officiis*.

My remarks here have been, in each case, but one perspective on the significance of these scholarly essays and are intended above all to constitute an invitation to engage them directly in the rest of this book. Some readers will find the essay republished in the Appendix a helpful starting place in approaching this collection, for it reviews the life of Cicero and his varied interests and accomplishments and probes the reasons for the relative neglect of his philosophical writings in recent times. It gives special attention to how Leo Strauss and Eric Voegelin engage Cicero in the course of their leading efforts to renew the study of classical political philosophy in the second half of the twentieth century. Thus it used the term "rebirth" in two senses, one to refer to Cicero's return to and reworking of the political philosophies of his great Greek teachers and the other to refer to how Cicero was treated in the revival of classical political philosophy in the twentieth century.

NOTES

1. Douglas, "Cicero the Philosopher," 164ff.
2. Rawson, *Cicero*, vi.
3. Reid, *Academica of Cicero*, 9–10.
4. For a more chronological and biographical narrative of Cicero's achievements, see Appendix, Nicgorski, "The Rebirth," 240–49.
5. Strauss, "Restatement on Xenophon's *Hiero*," 127.
6. Lacey, *Cicero and the End of the Roman Republic*, v.
7. Graver, *Cicero on the Emotions*, viii.
8. Wiseman, "The Necessary Lesson," 648.
9. Habicht, *Cicero the Politician*, 5, 121–22 n. 29.

1

Cicero's *De Re Publica* and the Virtues of the Statesman

J. G. F. POWELL

In dealing with a fragmentary philosophical text such as Cicero's *De Re Publica*,[1] it is more than usually difficult to perform the basic tasks of scholarly interpretation: to characterize plausibly the main lines of argument and the structure of the exposition, to notice the deployment of recurring themes, to examine the relationship to any literary models and precursors, and to come to a view on the overall persuasive purposes of the work. Even with texts that survive complete, there can be a good deal of debate and disagreement about that kind of issue. What hope, therefore, for a text of which at the most reliable estimate only about a quarter survives in total and what does survive is heavily weighted toward the first half of the work? Any attempt to take the broader view risks being dismissed as hopelessly speculative. However, for this occasion I am prepared to take the risk and make the attempt. I shall try to stay clear about where the boundary lies between interpretation of what is there in the text and speculation about what is not there. I should also make clear at the beginning that while I address in part the issue of Cicero's relationship to Plato,[2] I am not by and large attempting to unravel the sources of Cicero's ideas but rather—in tune with the overall direction of Ciceronian scholarship in the last twenty years—to interpret Cicero on his own terms.

I start with one of the more out-of-the-way testimonia for Cicero's *De Re Publica*. This comes from the late-antique but by no means unintelligent commentary of one Grillius[3] on another work of Cicero, the *De Inventione*. Grillius is commenting on a passage of the prologue to that work (1.4) in which the young Cicero sets out a view of the relationship between oratory and politics. He refers to a work that he calls Cicero's *politia*—evidently what we know as the *De Re Publica*—for a characterization of the statesman, or *rector rei publicae*. (Clearly the word is *rector*, not *rhetor* as one branch of Grillius's manuscript tradition has it; the error is understandable in a work otherwise on rhetoric.) This phrase occurs notoriously in a number of places in the text of the *De Re Publica* and has been the subject of a good deal of controversy. As Heinze showed in 1924,[4] the *rector rei publicae* is not a king or a dictator, nor necessarily a person with supreme political authority, nor a kind of precursor of the Augustan *princeps*: these interpretations, popular until recently, are misunderstandings. It is not the name of a political office or position at all; this was clear to Heinze and to Krarup.[5] There has not, however, always been clarity as to what it does designate.

The solution for which I have argued[6] is that it is simply the name of a profession or occupation, that of the statesman or politician. Confusion has arisen from the fact that, like many such terms, it can be used either in a relatively neutral, factual sense or in an idealistic, value-laden sense: as for example "poet" may be used as a general categorization of anyone who writes verses or as a term of praise (especially in phrases like "true poet") for the finest practitioners of the art. Sometimes our own language provides us with a choice between different terms for the ordinary and for the ideal: thus run-of-the-mill practitioners of politics tend to be called "politicians," while we reserve "statesman" for those we admire. In Latin there was no easy way of making this distinction, nor indeed was there a convenient Latin word or phrase for either concept until Cicero invented his *rector rei publicae*. It will not, however, surprise us to find that Cicero mostly uses the phrase to refer to an excellent or ideal practitioner of the political art, just as the word *orator* in the rhetorical works (especially *De Oratore* and *Orator*) more often than not refers to an excellent or ideal orator.

Now Grillius happens to preserve for us a description of Cicero's ideal statesman, almost certainly not in Cicero's own words but in a close enough paraphrase to enable us to see the main lines of the concept. According to Grillius, Cicero said *rectorem rei publicae summum virum et doctissimum esse debere, ita ut sapiens sit et iustus et temperans et eloquens, ut possit facile currente oratione animi secreta ad regendam plebem exprimere. Scire etiam debet ius, Graecas nosse litteras, quod Catonis facto probatur, qui in summa senectute Graecis litteris operam dans indicavit quantum utilitatis haberent.*

This gives the politician a number of qualities both moral and intellectual, as well as educational attainments. First he is described as in general *summus vir et doctissimus*, an imprecise characterization but one that would surprise many politicians both ancient and modern. We should not weaken our reading of *doctissimus* and make it appear to mean no more than "well educated," *non illiberaliter institutus* as the Scipio of Cicero's dialogue puts it in 1.36. The onus of proof would be on anyone who maintained that *doctissimus* did not here have its full sense of "highly learned" in intellectual matters. And if Cicero himself really said anything like this, he was aligning himself firmly with Plato in the debate over whether statesmen needed to be intellectuals.

Next, the general characterization is explicated by reference to a list of individual qualities of character and intellect. The statesman is to be *sapiens*, wise; *iustus*, just; and *temperans*, temperate, self-controlled, or orderly in behavior. These are three of the canonical four Platonic cardinal virtues; and I think it likely (for reasons that will become clearer in due course) that this is not to be attributed to the schematizing tendencies of late antiquity as they may be manifested in Grillius's commentary but to Cicero himself. The remaining cardinal virtue, that of courage, is missing from the list; instead, the stress is placed on eloquence as a characteristic of the statesman. Eloquence doubtless has a special relevance to the passage of *De Inventione* that Grillius is expounding but was not necessarily imported here by Grillius: it could also have been part of Cicero's picture. Speaking out does sometimes require courage, and the two concepts no doubt overlapped in Cicero's mind; the ideal statesman of *De Re Publica* is a complement to the ideal orator of *De Oratore*.

The Cardinal Virtues in the First and Second Books of *De Re Publica*

The Prologue and Opening Discussion

In general, Cicero's interest in the four cardinal virtues needs no demonstration: to go no further, they constitute the structuring principle of his last work of moral philosophy, the *De Officiis*. Furthermore, they play an important part in the argument of Cicero's overt model in the *De Re Publica*, Plato's *Republic*. To find them in the *De Re Publica* would not, therefore, be in the least surprising, and I think the only reason their role in that work has not attracted attention is that nobody has been looking for them there. In fact, once one starts to look for them, they come into relief with an unexpected degree of prominence, occurring either individually or in combination at various key points of the work. Of course, I do not mean to say that whenever a Roman author mentions wisdom or courage he is automatically recalling the Greek cardinal virtues. It is the combination of the four, or at the very least of three out of the four, that is significant. But once one has found them together in combination in a text such as the *De Re Publica*, one may then begin to suspect that mentions of the individual virtues, even when not immediately found in combination, may still contribute to a larger picture. The case for Cicero's involvement, in this text, with the idea of the four virtues is a cumulative one: the reader therefore must be both patient and on the alert for details that otherwise might be taken for granted.

I propose first to examine the references to wisdom, justice, temperance, and fortitude—and to virtue in general—in the surviving parts of *De Re Publica*; and secondly to suggest a hypothesis as to the part the four virtues may have played in the overall argument of this work. This hypothesis can never, of course, be proved, except by the unanticipated discovery of a complete text some time in the future, but I hope at least that it may take its place among the recognized possibilities. After all, the three most puzzling questions about the fragmentary text of Cicero's *De Re Publica* must surely be these: First, what was in the lost sections of the text? Second, what was the overall message? And third, what relation did it bear to Plato's *Republic*? The hypothesis I shall propose seems to me to add significantly to our ability to answer all three of these questions, although the answers it provides are not always tidy or schematic.

We start in the prologue to Book 1 with *virtus* in general. The extant text begins some way into the prologue, and we have little evidence as to what was in the lost initial section except for a fragment preserved in Nonius about the duty we owe to our country as to a parent.[7] The continuous portion of the text plunges us into the middle of a series of standard examples of Roman political and military excellence, which are summarized (1.1) in the statement that nature has implanted in mankind a *necessitas virtutis* that overcomes all the temptations of pleasure and idleness. Obviously, this is the concluding section of an argument against the partisans of the quiet life—one may think in particular of the Epicureans—and *virtus* is identified, in traditional fashion at this point, with the virtues of the active statesman and soldier, that is, native courage and primitive morality. Cicero then continues with the point that *virtus* is not just an "art" that can be possessed in the form of theoretical understanding without being practiced but consists entirely in action (he reverts to the idea in later philosophical works: *Off.* 1.19, *virtutis laus omnis in actione posita est,* in the context of a caution against letting enthusiasm for academic research take one away from public business; *Nat. D.* 1.110, the Epicurean god cannot have virtue since he does nothing). As well as countering Epicurean notions of *ataraxia*, the present passage opposes cognitivist accounts of virtue like the Socratic or Stoic, which risk being reduced to the position that virtue is knowledge of the right thing to do irrespective of whether one actually does it.

According to Cicero (and the point recurs again at the very end of the work in the "Dream of Scipio"), the most important arena for virtuous action is politics, which is characterized as the achievement in practice, not just in theory, of those things that the philosophers "shout about in their corners" (*in angulis personant*), a phrase seemingly taken from Callicles' attack on philosophers in Plato's *Gorgias* (485d). In other words, politics is the practical embodiment of the ethical principles established by philosophers; and the supreme form of politics turns out to be that which is practiced by the lawgiver, that is, the *nomothetes* of Greek tradition, *eis... a quibus civitatibus iura descripta sunt*. Lawgivers are responsible for both explicit law (*leges*) and custom (*mores*) (*Rep.* 1.2), and from them derives a whole range of essential features of human civilization: religious attitudes (*pietas*) and practices (*religio*); the common law of humanity (*ius gentium*) and the particular law of the Roman state (*ius civile*); plus a range of individual virtues listed as follows: *unde iustitia fides aequitas? unde pudor, continentia, fuga turpitudinis, appetentia laudis et honestatis? unde in laboribus et periculis fortitudo?*

This rhetorical tricolon with anaphora of *unde* quickly gives away its underlying structure: the first clause lists justice and its kindred virtues of trust and fairness; the second, the virtues of self-regulation, that is, temperance;[8] and the third, fortitude. In other words, the activity of the lawgiver is responsible for the existence of three of the four Platonic virtues; the missing one this time is wisdom, which is not long in coming as an attribute of the lawgivers and statesmen themselves (1.3 *eos qui his urbibus consilio atque auctoritate praesunt, eis qui omnis negoti publici expertes sint longe duco sapientia ipsa esse anteponendos*). This also makes explicit for the first time the distinction between practical and theoretical *sapientia* and Cicero's preference for the former over the latter. Furthermore, it is to be noticed (the point will recur later) that the development of justice, temperance, and bravery or endurance in human societies is not supposed to come of itself by the light of nature: it is the result of the activities of particular individuals who, nevertheless, are obeying a natural urge toward virtuous action. When we come to consider the prologue to Book 3 we shall see more clearly stated there the theory that humankind has natural, unformed impulses toward virtue, which must be perfected by means of cultivation, education, and intellectual endeavor.

At the end of 1.3, this part of the argument is summed up: the will to improve the conditions of human life is stated to be a natural one; political activity is presented in what must be admitted to be a highly idealistic light, of making the life of men "safer and better resourced" (*tutiorem et opulentiorem*) and of always having been the preferred activity of the best men (*optimi cuiusque*). Here the life of the politician is already being presented in the guise of Cicero's ideal statesman whose attributes are laid out in more detail in the course of the work; in the phrase "making human life safer," there is also a nuance of the politician as guardian and protector of the community that again we shall see developed later (esp. 2.51, *quasi tutor et procurator rei publicae*) and in connection with which it is easy, though not perhaps at this stage imperative, to recall Plato's *Phylakes*, "Guardians."

Cicero's argument so far has succeeded in inflecting what was doubtless a common popular prejudice against the impractical preachings of philosophers toward a more positive view of the way in which the principles of philosophical ethics can be put to work. Philosophers have the right ideas but are ineffective in making the bulk of the people follow them (1.3), whereas the legislator and politician equipped with philosophical principles can create a political system that will ensure that those principles are followed in practice. In this context Cicero turns on its head a saying of the Academic philosopher Xenocrates, who said that philosophy enabled people to do the right thing of their own accord rather than because the laws compelled them to do it: Cicero's view is that the lawgiver is preferable to the philosopher, because the former does not rely on the hazardous process of intellectual persuasion but makes sure people do the right thing whether they want to or not. Yet Cicero does not imply that the lawgiver is less of an intellectual than the philosopher; rather, the reverse is implied, that one who has both the theoretical understanding and the means to apply it is actually better as an intellectual (*ipsa sapientia*, 1.3, already quoted above) even than the philosopher.

The next section (1.4–8) is a refutation of the counterargument that political life is troublesome and dangerous, which Cicero says to be a matter of little consequence for men of courage (*fortibus viris*), using mainly the example of his own consulship and exile. Section 1.9 deals with the further objection that politics is a dirty business and that a wise man (*sapiens*, twice in the paragraph) stands little chance against corrupt opponents or the madness of the crowd; to which he replies that for good and brave men (*bonis et fortibus et magno animo praeditis*) there can be no better reason to take part in politics than to make sure that one does not have to be subjected to wicked rulers or allow the body politic to be torn apart by them. Here the virtue of courage is presented as a prerequisite for becoming a good statesman, and in fact the stress on the risks and dangers of politics only serves to emphasize this.

The *sapiens* is again the focus of attention in the following section (1.10–11), which has little trouble in refuting the position apparently held by some philosophers that the wise man would not take part in politics as a matter of course but would offer his services in an emergency. Cicero points out that this is an impractical attitude, since one cannot necessarily help in an emergency unless one already has the political standing to do so; one cannot suddenly take the reins in a difficult situation if one has no experience of governing in normal times. Even if this were possible, Cicero continues, one should at least take the trouble to learn the art of politics in case one may sometime have to use it. He has no doubt that there *is* an art or science of politics, a *scientia rerum civilium*, which can and ought to be learned by one who claims to be *sapiens*, not merely a knack learned by practice and experience. It is in Greek terms a *techne* or *episteme*.

Already by the end of this prologue (which he admits is long and elaborate, 1.12), it has become clear to the alert reader precisely how much Cicero has digested of Greek thought on these matters; and in the final paragraph the appeal to the authority of the Greeks becomes explicit. The so-called Seven Wise Men (*sapientes* again) were actually politicians and legislators; the "men who have most authority among the most learned," who did not themselves take part in government but wrote and researched a great deal about politics, are not named, but it is obvious who they are: Cicero is thinking primarily of Plato and Aristotle. Cicero, with studied modesty, claims an implicit advantage over all these because he had not only mastered the theory but also had experience of the practice of politics: Plato and others were *in disputationibus perpoliti* but achieved nothing practical, while the Seven Sages had commendable practical experience but were primitive in their modes of exposition.

Cicero, then, has established himself as an ideal expositor; and with that, he turns to the setting of the dialogue, which is to take place between Scipio Aemilianus and his friends and is set at the Latin

Games of 129 B.C. I have suggested elsewhere[9] that the choice of these characters is significant in several ways: not just because they represent an idealized earlier generation of Roman politicians, and certainly not primarily because their charmed circle represents an escape from current problems; it is absolutely clear that the Roman Republic is in as much turmoil at the dramatic date as it was at the time of writing. Rather, as becomes even clearer in the prologue to Book 3, they are themselves exemplars of the kind of enlightened statesman that Cicero recommends as his ideal, and they display the requisite combination of intellectual gifts and interests with intense practical concern for politics and, in the case of Scipio and some of the other families represented, military glory. They represent a time when Roman political life did indeed appear to be in the hands of more than usually educated men with easy access to the thought of Greek theorists such as Polybius the historian or Panaetius the Stoic: in other words a time when, for a short period in the history of the Republic, philosophers had actually seemed to become politicians (if not actually kings) and vice versa. Yet the fragility of their enlightened rule is strikingly shown in the dialogue itself and in its setting: the ominous portent with which the discussion begins, Laelius's allusions in Book 3 to the impending downfall of the Republic caused by the divisive activities of such men as Tiberius Gracchus, and the consciousness (reinforced in the concluding narration in Book 6) that Scipio, the hero of the dialogue, will soon be found murdered in his bed.

The first section of the dialogue, apart from its scene-setting function, also works as an illustration of the contrast between theoretical and practical intellectual activity. The starting point is the portent of the double sun, which could be interpreted either as an astronomical phenomenon to be investigated scientifically or as a symbol of political dissension. Scipio first mentions Panaetius as an exemplar of scientific acumen but prefers the approach of Socrates, who abandoned natural science for the study of morals and politics, incidentally dealing concisely with the "Socratic question." Scientific interests are attributed also to the younger Roman interlocutors—Tubero, Philus, and Rutilius—and these in due course elicit from Scipio himself a paean of praise for science and philosophy (1.26–29). Laelius enters (1.18–19), himself playing the part of Socrates in trying to bring the conversation down to earth; Philus, in Stoic mode, points out the interconnection of celestial and earthly phenomena and illustrates this with an account of the usefulness of understanding the cause of eclipses and predicting them: not least the political usefulness of such a rational explanation in dispelling superstitious fear (1.23–25). Cicero is, of course, being self-consciously literary in making his Roman characters take on debating roles associated with particular well-known Greek philosophers or schools, in a kind of masquerade. Some readers might think this artificial, but it is one of the ways Ciceronian dialogue works.

All of this discussion centers implicitly and sometimes explicitly on the question of what is meant by *sapientia*, wisdom. Scipio's philosopher has everything within his power not by quiritary right but *sapientium iure* (1.27); he despises all things merely human and thinks them inferior to wisdom (1.28). He cultivates intellectual activity as the distinguishing mark of humanity and engages in politics only from a sense of duty. Against this high intellectual conception of *sapientia*—which, as I argued in my 1996 article,[10] represents an idealistic strain, but not the only one, in Cicero's own thought—is set the practical wisdom of Laelius, himself named *sapiens*, who points to the practical wisdom of the Roman legal expert Sextus Aelius Paetus Catus (*catus* meaning "clever" or "acute") and stresses that knowledge of the political arts is the *praeclarissimum sapientiae munus maximumque virtutis vel documentum vel officium* (1.33). Scientific speculation has had its due and politics shown its place in a much larger scheme of things, a topic that will be reverted to at the very end of the dialogue in the "Dream of Scipio"; but attention is now focused on the kind of wisdom that will enable us to be of practical use to our own community.

The Discussion of the Constitutions; Good and Bad Rulers

What then is political "wisdom," or *sapientia*? In the first place, it is Greek political theory, but (1.36) this will not provide all the answers: rather, we are explicitly offered Greek theory interpreted in the light of historical and particularly Roman experience. The definition of *res publica* itself, as Malcolm Schofield has shown,[11] is a Roman one dependent on the Latin meaning of the word; and in discussing the theory of constitutions, Cicero's Scipio lays on one side the complications of the Polybian cyclic theory of constitutions in favor of a simpler evolutionary model, supposed to be instantiated in the history of the Roman republic itself. Both these developments may be seen as notable signs of Ciceronian independence of thought, yet his theory of constitutions is straightforwardly based on the Greek philosophical tradition. Furthermore, his analysis of the advantages and disadvantages of the different possible constitutions provides another context for the cardinal virtues to surface.

For Cicero—as for Plato, Aristotle, Polybius, and others—there are three simple forms of constitution, monarchy, aristocracy, and democracy. A good monarchy is one in which the king is *aequus et sapiens* (1.42) or *iustissimus . . . sapientissimusque* (1.43): just and wise, two of the Platonic virtues. A good aristocracy can rule *summa iustitia* (1.43) and can display *virtus* in general (1.52) but especially in the fact that it *servit . . . nulli cupiditati* (i.e., is temperate). The characteristic feature of a good democracy is *aequabilitas* or *aequitas*, and especially equality before the law (1.49), and this is a form of justice (though in Scipio's view an imperfect one, 1.53). Thus good monarchy is strong on justice and wisdom; good aristocracy possesses justice and temperance and may also surpass monarchy in regard to wisdom, on the basis that a number of heads are better than one (1.55; cf. also the beginning of Book 2); good democracy is characterized by a form of justice and also by self-control (*moderatior*, 1.65) but tends to be weak on wisdom. If these forms of constitution lose their characteristic virtues, they turn into their corresponding corrupt forms. A king becomes a tyrant by becoming unjust (1.65, cf. in more detail 2.50–51); a minority government that oversteps the limits of self-control and acts with *audacia* is a *factio* (oligarchy), not an aristocracy; a democracy that loses its self-control and abandons itself to *licentia* becomes an instance of mob rule and can also (as in Plato) produce a tyrant (1.68), the most unjust form of ruler.

The opposite of the tyrant is the wise politician/statesman, *tutor et moderator rei publicae, prudens*, and so on: a wider category than that of the good monarch, since it includes good democratic leaders as well. The task of political wisdom, according to Cicero, is not only to understand the classification of constitutions but also to be able to see changes coming and to predict them (1.45 *quos [orbes et circuitus] cum cognosse sapientis est, tum vero prospicere impendentes . . . magni cuiusdam civis et divini paene est viri*). Both Platonic and Polybian theory and Roman experience are taken to show that the simple constitutions are highly subject to change, but once one has reached a situation in which elements of the three simple constitutions are mixed together, change is no longer so likely. In addition to the *aequabilitas* it shares with democracy, the mixed constitution has added stability (1.69), and change does not happen except through great faults in the leading citizens or rulers (*non ferme sine magnis principum vitiis evenit*).

The evolution of the mixed constitution at Rome is demonstrated at length in the historical discussion in the second book of the dialogue, which need not concern us in detail. The ultimate message of this is partly that Rome in fact has the best possible kind of constitution; but it is not only that. It is also, as I hope to have shown elsewhere,[12] that even though Rome has had and still has a constitution of the best possible kind, it is at risk precisely because of great faults in the rulers. Ultimately, it is the good qualities of the rulers that for Cicero determine the survival of the state, and the downfall of a state (however good a constitutional system it has) is the result of their bad ones (*vitia*, which is incidentally Cicero's standard translation of *kakia*, the opposite of *aretē*—hence our word "vice" as opposed to "virtue"). Hence the need to answer the question: What constitutes a good ruler? Or in other words: What virtues of character and intellect does the good ruler need to have? To this I shall return, observing at this point only Cicero's characterization of the work in a letter as *de optimo civitatis statu et de optimo cive* (*QFr.* 3.5.1). The perception of the logical connection between the virtues of the statesman and the good condition of the state is, I suggest, one of the keys to understanding Cicero's overall argument.

So far, then, in the first two books, examples of the virtues and vices have appeared on at least three levels. First, the different types of constitution display characteristic virtues (if good) or vices (if bad). Second, the moral condition of individuals (e.g., kings, aristocrats, popular leaders, or rulers in a state with a mixed constitution) can cause changes in the *constitutio* or *status rei publicae* (the condition of the republic). Here the inadequacy of the translation "constitution" becomes very apparent, since such a development can happen without any change that we would call constitutional: injustice in a king produces tyranny, intemperance in an aristocracy or democracy produces oligarchy or mob rule; and a mixed constitution of the Roman kind, though it is more predisposed toward stability, nevertheless will fail to survive if the rulers display "great vices" (presumably of all these kinds). Third, the proper understanding of these matters is a form of wisdom or knowledge (*sapientia* or *scientia*) to which one can aspire both as a political theorist and as a practical politician. The ideal politician, indeed, must also be a theorist, someone who knows how politics and politicians work in the abstract and can put that knowledge to use, that is, precisely the sort of Roman politician that, Cicero claims, is instantiated in the characters and indeed in the author of the *De Re Publica*. These three points are reasonably straightforward and not at all difficult; indeed, the chief risk they run is that of oversimplification. Still, this is not an inappropriate harvest of ideas from the first third of a philosophical dialogue that overtly started from absolute first principles. We shall expect these ideas to be developed and built on in the remaining two thirds. The trouble is that at this point the text becomes a great deal more fragmentary, and attempts to divine Cicero's train of thought become increasingly speculative. At this point it will be convenient to stand back from the text for a moment and try to judge on grounds of general probability what Cicero *might* have been saying.

Virtues in the Community and in the Individual

It is not perhaps so surprising that the characterization of the "best form of state" (*optimus civitatis status*) should be formulated partly in terms of standard notions of virtue. The idea of "goodness" in general is regularly unpacked by ancient thinkers, especially in the Platonic tradition, with reference to one or more of the canonical "virtues" or "excellences," *aretai* or *virtutes*. Thus a good person or community must be good because of his, her, or its possession of particular excellences such as justice, temperance, and so on. But there is often an element of sleight-of-hand in this kind of reasoning when applied to political theory. The ancient *virtutes*, as indeed their Latin name implies, were on the whole primarily qualities of individual human beings. It is from the start an open question in what sense wisdom, or self-control, or courage can be predicated of a collectivity of human beings, though answers of various kinds can be proposed. An exception, perhaps, is justice, which is primarily a quality that belongs to the interactions between one individual and another. Cicero was evidently aware of this difference between justice and the other virtues. Two fragments of Book 2 (my frr. 8 and 9) make this clear: *iustitia foras spectat et proiecta tota est atque eminet* and *quae virtus praeter ceteras totam se ad alienas utilitates porrigit atque explicat*. Indeed, these isolated fragments can make sense only on one hypothesis: that Cicero was making a distinction between justice, which "looks outside" and "offers itself to the interests of others," and the other virtues which do this to a lesser degree or not at all. They must come from a context, in other words, in which the topic of enquiry was virtues in general.

The ancient philosophical tradition clearly saw no problem with attributing justice to a whole community. Plato did so in the *Republic*, Aristotle in the *Politics* (1253a), and Polybius in his section on constitutional theory (6.47). Similarly, in modern times, we are very happy to talk about something we think we can identify as a "just society." Furthermore, our concept of a "well-ordered society" approaches closely to what an ancient author might have meant by attributing *sōphrosynē* or *moderatio* to a community. However, the notion of a "wise society" or a "brave society" might cause both the ancients and ourselves more difficulty: What precisely would it mean? It might mean, in the ideal, a society all of whose members were wise or brave, but this would risk appearing unrealistic: the most that one could hope for in practice would be that the general ethos of the society or its leadership encouraged bravery or wisdom in its citizens. History could produce a few examples of societies that plausibly could be characterized collectively in this way. Yet this way of thinking is notably absent from *De Re Publica*. The Spartans, for example, or the Romans of the regal period or early Republic might be seen as providing an exemplar of collective bravery. However, in the case of the early Romans, Cicero prefers to emphasize their primitive ferocity (e.g., 2.26–27; no idealization here of the "brave days of old"), and Spartan military morale figures not at all in the extant parts of *De Re Publica*. Similarly, Athens might in more conventional literary contexts be projected as the home of "wisdom," but in *De Re Publica* Cicero (good Platonist that he is in this context) stresses only the unbridled nature of its democracy or its lapses into tyranny under Pisistratus or the Thirty (e.g., 1.44). It is not that Cicero was unaware of these conventional collective representations of Athenian wisdom or Spartan or Roman bravery; he draws upon them amply elsewhere. But for one reason or another, for the purposes of his argument on the best condition of society he is having nothing to do with them.

Plato in the *Republic* famously solved the problem by speculating that wisdom, courage, and temperance belonged not to the whole community but to particular parts of it: wisdom to the Guardians, courage to the military class, and temperance to the ordinary citizens. There is no sign of anything quite like this neat schematic distribution of virtues among the social classes in Cicero's text; indeed, there is no real sign of anything like Plato's tripartite division of social classes in the first place. Cicero has only the simple two-way division of aristocrats and populace. Where Cicero does agree with Plato, however, is in the notion that justice (given favorable conditions) can be found diffused throughout the whole community because it concerns the proper relations between the different parts of the community. Cicero was certainly preoccupied, to the same degree as Plato if in a different way, with the notion of justice and its role in society, and it is to his discussion of justice in Book 3 that we must now turn.

The Lead-In to the Justice Debate

The Role of the Statesman

The fragmentary last section of Book 2 leads into this topic, and it is most frustrating that we do not have a complete text at this point, though Augustine's summary helps to some extent. Section 2.66 points toward a less historically based, more abstract definition of the "best condition of the state" that is to be elucidated by means of an "image drawn from nature" (*naturae imago*). But the text breaks off before we can get any idea of what this image was, and there is probably nothing to be gained from speculation.[13] When the text resumes (and there is not even any clarity as to how long the gap was), we are again on the subject of wisdom, and specifically the wise individual. Here, indeed, we get a kind of image drawn from nature: the wise (*prudens*) politician is compared to an elephant-driver who keeps a great beast under control, in the same way the politician controls the minds of human beings (note: minds, not, as a reader of Plato might have predicted, passions or appetites). Then there is another gap, and the role of the wise politician is now being discussed. He is to be constantly engaged in self-education[14] and self-criticism; he is to set an example for others. Above all, his task is to preserve *concordia* in the state, the meaning of which is illustrated by the musical metaphor of harmony; and this, Scipio says, cannot be achieved without justice.

Justice, then, is something the wise statesman has somehow to *produce*: the statesman, who possesses the virtues in himself, is supposed by his political efforts to engender them in the community. Indeed, that is the main purpose of his existence. The point is made again, and more explicitly, in a passage Cicero himself happens to quote (to the disadvantage of contemporary Roman politicians) from the lost Book 5.[15] There he provides a teleological definition, very Socratic in its imagery, of the role of the statesman, here called *moderator rei publicae*: *Ut enim gubernatori cursus secundus, medico salus, imperatori victoria, sic huic moderatori rei publicae beata civium vita proposita est, ut opibus firma, copiis locuples, gloria ampla, virtute honesta sit. Huius enim operis, maximi inter homines atque optimi, illum esse perfectorem volo.*[16] The statesman's role is to ensure that the citizens' life is happy: not only in terms of material resources, wealth, and reputation but also in its possession of that *virtus* that is needed to make it truly a *beata vita* in philosophical terms.

The Prologue to Book 3

It is evident from Augustine (*CD* 2.21.29) that Scipio at the end of Book 2 expanded a little on the advantages of justice in the state and that he was then interrupted by a question from the interlocutor

Philus, who asked for more careful discussion of the issue in view of the common idea that states could not be governed without injustice. This evidently alluded to the arguments of Thrasymachus and Glaucon in the *Republic* that were developed further by Carneades and set out in Philus's speech in the third book.

Yet the dialogue on justice does not immediately proceed. The third book (more precisely, the second pair of books) is introduced by a second authorial prologue, where the focus is again on *sapientia*, or wisdom. This prologue is very fragmentary and has not hitherto appeared in editions in anything resembling a coherent form. The traditional order of fragments is, of course, the one adopted by Cardinal Mai in the *editio princeps* of 1820. It was clearly in some points conjectural, but it has remained unchallenged until now. Renewed inspection of the manuscript has satisfied me that the order of the fragments needs to be changed and that a fragment wrongly attributed to Book 5 needs to be restored to its place in this context. A much more satisfactory reconstruction of the argument is possible as a result.

The basic theme of the prologue is an account of the origins of civilization that in some respects recalls the myth of Plato's *Protagoras*. A quotation in St. Augustine (*Contra Iulianum* 4.12.60) probably belongs near the beginning: it remarks that Nature has been not a mother but a stepmother to humans, bringing them forth into life in a state of weakness: *corpore nudo fragili et infirmo, animo autem anxio ad molestias, humili ad timores, molli ad labores, prono ad libidines*, but with a divine spark of intelligence buried in them.[17] Whether this is to be understood phylogenetically of primitive mankind, or ontogenetically of the human baby, is not entirely clear, though the wider context (and, if it be granted, the reminiscence of the *Protagoras*) points to the former. Section 2 describes the expedients invented by some feminine subject who turns out to be *Mens*, mind (but whether human or divine mind is not clear from this fragmentary extract), to make life more bearable: forms of transport to counteract the natural slowness of human progression, language, writing, arithmetic, and astronomy—the last, incidentally, with a strong nod in the direction of Plato, where number is said to be the one thing (in human life) that is immutable and eternal. The next fragment is the one that previous editions attribute to Book 5 but that more naturally belongs here. It bears no attribution to any particular book in the palimpsest, but its script is that of scribe "B," which is otherwise found only in Book 3, and its style and subject-matter are entirely consonant with those of this prologue. Civilization has now progressed to the stage of forming communities, in which "the best men" (*optimi*) seek praise and honor, avoid shame and dishonor, and are deterred from wrongdoing not so much by laws as by the quality of *verecundia*, which was given to human beings by Nature. This seems to reflect *aidos*, which according to Protagoras in Plato's dialogue was given to men by Zeus, along with justice, not as an optional specialty like medicine or carpentry but (to use modern academic terminology) as a core subject to be attempted by all candidates. At this point the statesman (*rector rerum publicarum*), in the guise of the legislator, takes over where Nature left off and devises all the institutions necessary for a developed civilization.

Then there is a gap. When the text resumes, Cicero is again comparing philosophers with statesmen (good ones) and arguing that they both foster the beginnings put in place by Nature (*aluerunt naturae principia*). But while philosophers do so by words and theories (*verbis et artibus*), statesmen do it by laws and institutions (*institutis et legibus*). He argues, probably here with an eye on the Stoics, against those who restrict the use of the word *sapientes*: he says that even if these statesmen were not themselves wise, nevertheless they put into practice the principles discovered by the wise (*sapientium praecepta et inventa coluerunt*) and deserve the highest honors for that reason. He remarks on the large number of good statesmen that must have existed in order to bring to birth all the various political communities of the world that have survived down the centuries to his own time, even if there was only one master legislator per community. Then another gap, after which Cicero reiterates once more that, while all credit is due to philosophy, there is also such a thing as political science: *ratio civilis et disciplina populorum, quae perficit in bonis ingeniis id quod iam persaepe perfecit, ut incredibilis quaedam et divina virtus exsisteret.* Best of all, Cicero continues, is the combination of natural intelligence, sound education, and the study of philosophy, which was to be found in Scipio and his friends who are the characters in the dialogue. But if one has to choose between the two paths of wisdom, the life of the philosopher in retirement may be happier, but that of the politician (illustrated by Roman heroes such as Manius Curius) is more praiseworthy.

Rearranged this way, this section turns out to be both coherent in itself and consistent with what Cicero previously said about *sapientia*. He has now established what perhaps he could not say so convincingly at the beginning, before the discussion of Books 1 and 2: political science is a proper subject, or *ratio* (as exemplified by that discussion). One can argue about whether it is really *sapientia* in the strict sense, but at least it is a kind of practical wisdom, or *prudentia*; and every successful community provides evidence that exponents of it have existed in the past. This argument is very reminiscent of the view attributed by Seneca (*Ep.* 90) to Posidonius that advances in civilization have been due to the activity of *sapientes*. Indeed, Cicero's account of Roman history in Book 2 has already supported that view, since at each point he is keen to point out the wisdom of those who successively contributed to the making of the Roman constitution. As I have pointed out elsewhere,[18] this is necessary for his wider purposes: if the growth of Roman institutions was due to an inevitable historical process, it might be equally inevitable that they should in time decline, and so it might be impossible to do anything about the problems of the Republic. But if the creation of the Republic was due in the first place to human wisdom, human wisdom in turn could recreate it.

Justice and Temperance in Books 3 and 4

The mention of Scipio, Laelius, and Philus in 3.5 clearly signals the end of the prologue and the resumption of the dialogue between those characters. The debate on justice, thus introduced, was one of the most famous parts of the dialogue in antiquity, and although there are many gaps in our text of it, including the almost complete loss of Laelius's speech, nevertheless we know the main lines of the discussion from the summaries in Lactantius and Augustine. Again, as with the prologue, I have rearranged the manuscript pages and have presented the text for the first time in a form that coheres with Lactantius's account of the argument.[19] The climax of Philus's speech, of which we have part at 1.24 Ziegler = 1.18 Powell, involved a contrast between *sapientia* and *iustitia*. Wisdom, said Philus, meaning enlightened self-interest, leads to success, while justice always leads to failure. Lactantius (*Inst.* 5.16.12–13) adds that he divided justice into two kinds, political (*civilis*) and natural. Political justice was a form of wisdom but was not justice; natural justice was certainly justice but was a form of stupidity.

Our knowledge of Laelius's reply is very incomplete, but we know that it was based on the theory of natural law. He argued that states could not be governed without justice. The only true laws are just ones; unjust laws are not laws at all; justice is not "the interest of the stronger" (Augustine, *CD* 2.21.46). It is naturally just for some to command and others to obey; there are different kinds of ruling appropriate to a king, a master of slaves, or a father of a family (19.21.42–49): here Laelius sounds very Aristotelian (cf. *Politics* 1252a, 1254b, 1255b). Slavery may be either just or unjust; there are just wars and unjust wars; Rome expanded not through greed but by defending its allies. True justice is based on nature and is desired for its own sake. The reward of virtue is honor; the bad consequences of injustice cannot be avoided. In a state, injustice leads to ruin. At the end of the speech, Laelius expresses the fear that the injustice of Tiberius Gracchus, in neglecting the rights of the Latins and allies, will cause the downfall of the Republic. It will be observed that throughout this debate both Philus and Laelius are concerned with justice between communities as well as with justice within them.

The next continuous section of text from Book 3 is part of a dialogue in which Scipio carried further the idea that justice was essential in government, since only justice can ensure that a *res publica* accords with its definition as *res populi*, the property of the people (as we might say, a "commonwealth" is truly a community in which wealth is held in common). A state that is unjustly governed, whether a tyranny, or oligarchy, or a disorderly democracy, is not truly a *res populi* and therefore is not a *res publica* at all. This part of the argument is reflected in Augustine (*CD* 2.21.47–66). In the following and last remaining section, Scipio seems to be arguing that, on the other hand, there can be good government in a monarchy, an aristocracy, or a democracy provided that justice is present. At all events he seems to have reverted to the idea of justice as largely a matter of the internal relations between the different sections of the community.

How the discussion of justice ended is unknown, but it is reasonable to assume that it coincided with the end of the third book. In the fragmentary Book 4 the discussion has turned to a different set of topics: there are fragments concerning the education of the young, the control of morality and expenditure, the political process, funeral rites, the rejection of Plato's views on property, the role of poetry and drama, and the calendar. What can be made of this miscellany? If there is a common theme running through all these fragments, it must be that of order in society: the discussion is about the political and social institutions necessary to produce what a Roman would have called a *bene morata civitas*, or a society with good customs and morality. This is generally agreed among scholars.[20] But a well-ordered society is, in Greek terms, nothing other than a society characterized by *sōphrosynē*, or temperance. I wonder, therefore, whether it would be too much to suggest that as the subject of Book 3 was justice, so that of Book 4 was temperance, these being the two of the cardinal virtues that can clearly apply to communities as well as to individuals. Furthermore, Book 4 seems to end (though my new placing of these fragments is admittedly speculative—traditionally they are placed at the beginning) with an allegory of temperance: the mind's control over the body and the rational principle's control over the universe.

The Fifth and Sixth Books

The final pair of books, 5 and 6, started with another prologue, from which all we have is a passage of twenty or so lines quoted by St. Augustine (*CD* 2.21.71–95). But this is enough to show that Cicero was very explicit about the contemporary reference of his dialogue. Having shown in the course of the previous discussion that a state without justice was no state and that the collapse of a state must be due to the faults of its rulers, he now squarely blames himself and his contemporaries for the fact that they have retained only the name of *res publica* and lost the substance through their own fault and not because of some chance. Cicero quotes the famous line of Ennius—*moribus antiquis res stat Romana virisque*—and this doubtless facilitates the transition between the preceding discussion of *mores* and what is to follow, which focuses on the character of the individual politician. Book 5 is the source of the fragment already quoted on the function of the *moderator rei publicae*, to ensure a happy life for the citizen body. The only pages of the palimpsest to survive from this book concern the statesman's need for legal knowledge, not in a detailed professional sense but in the sense of knowledge of the general principles of law that are necessary in order to be just; and this ties in with Grillius's statement that according to Cicero the politician had to know the law. Beyond that, we have no secure indications of the way Book 5 and the greater part of Book 6 were laid out, and it is at this point that I move into the realm of speculation.

One of our sources for fragments of the *De Re Publica* is the late antique linguist Nonius Marcellus. Of his ninety-five quotations from the text, some coincide with passages that are otherwise preserved, while others are so corrupt that hardly any sense can be made of them. Among the clearer of them is a definition of *fortitudo* quoted from Book 5 (fr. 7 in my OCT) and an etymological definition of *prudentia* from Book 6 (fr. 1). At first sight it may seem rash to base any deductions on these two seemingly random quotations. But I am not so sure. These are not in fact quite random survivals but passages quoted as grammatical examples by a writer who does not otherwise preserve many quotations from Books 5 and 6, preferring in general to cull his material from the earlier, doubtless more familiar books. Hence one might conjecture that they were well known, perhaps even among the best-known passages from those books. But why should definitions of the virtues have attained this degree of familiarity? Perhaps, for a lexicographer such as Nonius, just because they were definitions; a number of his quotations from elsewhere in *De Re Publica* are also of this type. But perhaps also because they were not merely incidental but performed the function that definitions usually do perform in philosophical discussions, that is, the elucidation of concepts of major significance. Did Books 5 and 6 perhaps concern themselves with *fortitudo* and *prudentia* as major themes?

More can be gained from a closer look at the latter quotation. It runs as follows: *Totam igitur exspectas prudentiam huius rectoris, quae ipsum nomen nacta est ex providendo.* The context of this must have been a discussion of political foresight (reverting to the point made in Books 1 and 2 about the necessity of foreseeing political changes), and *totam igitur exspectas* suggests (a) that we are about to have a comprehensive discussion of the statesman's *prudentia* and (b) that this discussion has been prepared for and is expected as part of some larger structure.

I first thought that Book 5 might have been entirely devoted to *fortitudo* and Book 6 to *prudentia*, so that Books 3 to 6 would follow a simple fourfold scheme: justice in 3, temperance in 4, courage in 5, and wisdom in 6. However, unfortunately for this simple scheme, it does not seem to fit the evidence of the fragments of Books 5 and 6. I therefore came up with an amended hypothesis: that Cicero made (in terms of the structure of his argument) a clear distinction between the two of the four virtues that were proper to the community, that is, justice and temperance, and the complete quartet of virtues that could be shown by the individual. The discussion of the *rector rei publicae* in the fifth and sixth books would then itself have been structured around some kind of rhetorical division based on all four virtues. On this hypothesis, Book 5 could have contained the discussion of individual justice (the virtue mentioned in the surviving passage on knowledge of the law) and of courage (which we know to have been defined in that book, cf. above; two other fragments, my frr. 8 and 9, also seem to be relevant to a discussion of courage). Temperance could well fit in Book 6 given the reference to the dangers of *libidines* in my fr. 5 (frr. 6 and 7 could also be placed there). And I guess that the discussion of the statesman's *prudentia*, the most important virtue, would form the fourth and concluding division.

There have been other attempts to divine the structure of Books 5 and 6. Büchner, for example, supposes that Book 5 was devoted to the characterization of the *rector* and that the theme of Book 6 was the "statesman in a crisis." Zetzel thinks that the odd-numbered books were more theoretical, the even-numbers more practical, and thus extrapolates a principle of organization that he sees quite correctly in the pair of books 1 and 2 and much more dubiously in 3 and 4. It is difficult to see very clear evidence in the surviving fragments for either of these speculations as to the arrangement of material in 5 and 6.[21]

A further advantage of my reconstruction, as pointed out at the Notre Dame Symposium by Carlos Lévy, is that it makes Cicero's approach in *De Re Publica* eminently Ciceronian, picking up themes already adumbrated in *De Inventione* in Cicero's youth and returned to again spectacularly in *De Officiis*. (A four-virtue structure may perhaps also be divined in the *Cato Maior de Senectute*: the first section of the argument dwells on the wisdom of the old in political and intellectual affairs, the second on the need for the old to maintain their due (i.e., just) position in society, the third on temperance in the pursuit of pleasure, and the fourth on courage in facing death.) In the crudest terms, the classical virtues could be used as a mechanical structuring device in ordering the rhetorical *topoi* of encomium; but the precedent of Plato's *Republic* showed that they could also be used for profounder reflections.

After the statesman had been characterized in this way, it would remain only—again following Plato's *Republic*—to set out the rewards of virtue, both in this life (my frr. 8 and 9) and in the life to come (the "Dream of Scipio"). In commenting on the "Dream," Macrobius quotes part of the introductory dialogue, in which Laelius complained that no statue had been erected of Nasica, the killer of Tiberius Gracchus; to which Scipio responded that the real rewards of political virtues were not statues or triumphs but something fresher and longer lasting (*stabiliora et viridiora*), that is, the rewards of immortality. These rewards are said quite explicitly by Macrobius to be reserved for *bonis rerum publicarum... rectoribus*, that is, good statesmen (echoing the text of the "Dream" itself, 6.13 Ziegler = 6.17 Powell). And beside this phrase Macrobius uses another wording to characterize those who are destined for heaven: *qui rem publicam cum prudentia iustitia fortitudine ac moderatione tractaverint*. This is the nearest we get to an explicit indication that Cicero's discussion of the *rector rei publicae* was structured around the four Platonic virtues. This could perhaps be taken for a purely conventional rhetorical enumeration of virtues by Macrobius as commentator. But F. Solmsen[22] had already interpreted it as indicating that Cicero himself "endowed his 'rector' or 'princeps' with the four Platonic virtues," commenting further that "the four virtues are not among the Platonic dogmas which the Neo-Platonists were anxious to revive." Solmsen further points to a passage of Augustine that, though his hypothesis that this is a verbal allusion to *De Re Publica* falls short of proof, could well reflect in some way a Ciceronian definition of *sapientia* or *virtus*: *prudenter discernit, gerit fortiter, cohibet temperanter iusteque distribuit* (Augustine, *CD* 19.20). In view of what else has by now been uncovered regarding Cicero's interest in the virtues, it is very strongly tempting to assume that Macrobius's characterization of the *rector* reflects Cicero's own description and possibly summarizes the *divisio*, whose presence I have suspected in Books 5 and 6.

Summary and Conclusion

The virtues turn up in *De Re Publica* at the following points.

1–2 Prologue	Primitive *virtus (fortitudo)* exhibited in defending the state. *Temperantia, iustitia, fortitudo* have their source in good legislation. *Sapientia* of legislator. *Fortitudo* and *sapientia* impel one to political participation. *Sapientia* of philosophers vs. that of statesmen. The two combined in Cicero (ideal author).

1 Dialogue	Politics and its place in the universe:
	The *sapientia* of the scientist/philosopher.
	The virtues of the constitutions:
	    Good monarchy has *sapientia* and *iustitia*.
	    Good aristocracy has *sapientia, iustitia, temperantia*.
	    Good democracy has *iustitia (aequitas), temperantia*.
	Sapientia of political scientist who can foresee changes.
	Mixed constitution more stable, can collapse because of vices of rulers.

2	Illustrates in practice theoretical principles of Book 1. At the end, the statesman is *prudens*, exercises control (*moderatio* = *temperantia*), and creates *iustitia* in society.

3–4 Prologue		Origins of civilization. *Sapientia* of philosophers vs. that of statesmen. The two combined in Scipio, etc. (ideal characters in the dialogue).
3 Dialogue:		*Iustitia* shown to be essential in society. The consequences of injustice—the rewards of virtue. States can collapse through injustice.
4:		*Temperantia (moderatio)* in society. Possibly at the end, an allegory of *temperantia* that presents the mind controlling the body and the rational principle controlling the universe.
5–6 Prologue		The decline of Rome through the faults of its rulers (Transition to the virtuous statesman).
5 Dialogue		*Iustitia* and *fortitudo* in the individual statesman.
6		*Temperantia* and *prudentia* in the individual statesman.
6 End		"The Dream of Scipio": The rewards for the individual statesman who has shown all four virtues. The place of human communities in the universe. "Strive on."

If it is true that the four virtues are both a recurrent theme and, especially in Books 5 and 6, a structuring device in Cicero's dialogue, it becomes obvious that we have here an important thematic link between Cicero's *De Re Publica* and its Platonic model. But of course Cicero's dialogue is no mere imitation of a single model, and his treatment of the virtues is in one important way un-Platonic: he does not insist on the exact parallelism between the virtues in the individual and the virtues in the community. Instead, his discussion of the community in Books 3 and 4 focuses on the two virtues appropriate in that context, that is, justice and temperance; the complete quartet emerges only when discussing the individual statesman in Books 5 and 6. And the fact that he probably discusses justice and temperance all over again under that heading suggests that he saw some difference, as Aristotle and Polybius did but Plato did not, between the type of justice or temperance that an individual can display and the type that can exist in a community.

What then of Cicero's overall message? What was his diagnosis of the problems of the Roman Republic of his time and what were his proposals for curing them? For that must clearly be what was uppermost in his mind when writing. The answers may be set out briefly in the list that follows. Put generally like this, they may seem banal, but in the first place, they may not have been so banal from a Roman Republican point of view (the concept of a professional politician, for instance, might have seemed quite novel), and in the second place, we cannot really judge without having a full text of the last three books, in which he presumably must have set out their detailed application.

- The Roman Republic was in a terrible mess.
- It was not the Republican constitution that was at fault; Rome had a constitution of the best possible kind, and the problems were caused by the failings of individuals.
- It would do no good to try to establish one-man rule: a dictator of the Sullan variety would be likely to turn out as a tyrant, not an ideal monarch.
- It was necessary for the best minds of Rome to apply themselves to politics, not to retire and study philosophy.
- One should strive for justice both within society (cf. Cicero's political watchword *concordia ordinum*) and in dealings with foreign communities; this did not involve abandoning the Roman Empire (which Cicero regarded as natural and just), but it did involve government by consent and not by terror.
- Legislation was necessary to promote order and discipline in society and to educate the next generation.
- Politics was a science that needed to be learned and treated as seriously as any other profession; besides political theory, the politician had to be master of several arts including at least law and rhetoric.
- The excellence of character required of the politician was to be analyzed and exhibited under the four classical Platonic headings.

- As appears from the passage just before the "Dream of Scipio," the wise statesman should sometimes follow the Graeco-Roman tradition of tyrannicide and resort to assassination, and will be rewarded in heaven for doing so.

This last may come as rather a disappointment after the rational good sense of the rest; but it reminds us that the author is, after all, Cicero, who defended the murderer of Clodius around the time when *De Re Publica* was receiving its final touches and whose name is alleged to have been invoked by Brutus, seven years later, at the moment of the assassination of Caesar.

NOTES

1. Where there is the possibility of doubt, I cite from both my own Oxford Classical Text and Ziegler's Teubner edition, which was for a long time standard. Translations: Sabine and Smith, *On the Commonwealth*—still useful; Rudd and Powell, *The Republic and the Laws*; Zetzel, *On the Commonwealth and On the Laws*; a new translation by Fott is in preparation. Commentaries with bibliography: Büchner, *Cicero, De Re Publica: Kommentar*; Zetzel, *Cicero: De Re Publica, Selections*. Full treatment of the fragments in Heck, *Die Bezeugung von Ciceros Schrift De Republica*. References to older literature are collected in Ziegler's edition and in Schmidt, "Cicero 'De re publica,'" as well as in Suerbaum, "Studienbibliographie."
2. A starting point in this area is provided by Long, "Cicero's Plato and Aristotle." I expect in due course to publish a fuller investigation of Cicero's use of Plato's *Republic* in *De Re Publica*.
3. Edited most recently by Jakobi.
4. Heinze, "Ciceros Staat."
5. Esp. Krarup, *Rector Rei Publicae*, 152. "Ciceros rector rei publicae er ikke en mand, der er udstyret med nogen formel magtstilling.... Det er den ypperste romerske vir nobilis, idealiseret gennem den græske tænknings teoretiske diskussioner." This formulation is not fully reflected in Krarup's English summary.
6. Powell, "The *rector rei publicae*."
7. There are seventeen leaves missing from the palimpsest at the beginning, equivalent to just over ten pages of the OCT text. Previous editions have located a number of fragments in this initial lacuna, but only two can be placed there with anything approaching certainty; the rest I have had to banish to the *incerta* and *dubia*.

8. Büchner, *Cicero, De Re Publica: Kommentar*, 81, identifies these as "Roman virtues" and says they are different from the Greek "philosophically defined" virtues but does not make it in the least clear where the difference lies. It is surely most likely that the Roman tendency to claim *pudor, continentia*, etc. as Roman traits had already gained momentum precisely under the influence of Greek notions (philosophical or not) such as *aidōs, sōphrosynē*, and *encrateia*: for Polybius, for example (6.47), the test of a legal system was whether it made the private lives of citizens *hosious kai sōphronas* and the common character of the community *hēmeron kai dikaion*; this assessment must therefore be implicit in Polybius's judgement that the Roman system was particularly good.

9. Powell, "Second Thoughts on the Dream of Scipio."

10. Ibid.

11. Schofield, "Cicero's Definition of *Res Publica*."

12. Powell, "Were Cicero's Laws the Laws of Cicero's Republic?"

13. Büchner, *Cicero, De Re Publica: Kommentar*, compares Rep. 3.36 Z = Aug. *CD* 19.21 *exemplum naturae*, which is about the divine mind ruling the universe; cf. also my remarks below on the end (or beginning) of Book 4.

14. I assume that the reading *instituendo* is correct, versus Mähly's ("Zu Cicero de re publica") conjecture *intuendo*.

15. This is the self-quotation in *Att*. 8.11.1. The passage that follows has been traditionally placed at *Rep*. 5.8.

16. Translation of this key passage by N. Rudd: "The aim of a ship's captain is a successful voyage; a doctor's, health; a general's, victory. So the aim of our ideal statesman is the citizens' happy life—that is, a life secure in wealth, rich in resources, abundant in renown, and honorable in its moral character. That is the task which I wish him to accomplish—the greatest and best that any man can have."

17. Readers of extant Latin know this idea best from Pliny the Elder, *NH* 7.1–5. Almost certainly Pliny will have got it from Cicero, although it is impossible to see how much in the passage is Ciceronian and how much elaborated by Pliny himself.

18. Powell, "Were Cicero's Laws the Laws of Cicero's Republic?"

19. For the details see my OCT preface, ix–xi. The failure of the text in its traditional arrangement (that of Mai's *editio princeps* of 1820) to cohere with Lactantius's summary was already noticed by Ferrary, "Le discours de Philus."

20. See, for example, Zetzel, "Citizen and Commonwealth."

21. See also my reservations about Zetzel's proposed structure in my review of his commentary, Powell, "Review of Zetzel," 249.

22. Solmsen, "New Fragments of Cicero's *De Re Publica*," 423–24 with n. 2; see also Krarup, "Rector Rei Publicae," 115 (Danish), 196 (English).

2

The Fourth Virtue

MALCOLM SCHOFIELD

This essay is a study of a marriage between two ways of conceptualizing *officia*, our duties or obligations, as what the morally "fine" or the virtues require of us, or as what is incumbent upon us on account of the roles or characters we play in life—our *persona* or *personae*. The text in which the harmonization of these two different approaches to *officia* is attempted is Book 1 of Cicero's *De Officiis*. The author of the enterprise was very probably the second-century B.C. Stoic Panaetius, on whom Cicero avowedly depends in Books 1 and 2 (*Off.* 3.7). More specifically, the attempt at harmonization is made in the long section of Book 1 (*Off.* 1.93–151) devoted to discussion of the fourth virtue in *De Officiis*'s version of the canonical quartet of cardinal virtues: introduced as the *decorum* (1.93: I shall translate as "appropriate," but a really satisfying English equivalent has proved elusive; *decorum* is what both *is* and *looks* just right).

As the major modern commentary says, the arrangement and interconnections between the various elements of the *decorum* section of *De Officiis* 1, and the criteria for inclusion and order of topics, are "not easy to grasp."[1] There is not much difficulty in getting from the text a general sense of what Cicero means by *decorum*. But a coherent and precise philosophical understanding has proved hard to achieve. I think Panaetius's theory of the *prepon*, the Greek term Cicero renders as *decorum*, is a powerful and extraordinarily ingenious and resourceful piece of philosophizing. My aim is to show that and how it is. It is my conjecture that the theory was devised as the solution to a set of interlocking problems. The acceptability of the conjecture will depend on whether it makes better sense of the anfractuosities of the text than has been achieved by commentators to date.

My argument will move through five stages, considering in turn virtue, *decorum*, the incorporation of *decorum* into the theory of virtue and the *honestum* (morally fine), *decorum* as both the fourth of the cardinal virtues and virtue in general, and *verecundia*, the untranslatable quality "between respect and shame"[2]—"modesty" is as good as I can do—in which *decorum* is said to exert its maximum force. To keep the complexities of the material manageable I have gone for maximal concision and concentrated on the essentials. Reference to bibliography is likewise sparing.[3]

Virtue

The variety in surviving accounts of the theory of four virtues in the Hellenistic Stoa indicates vigorous debate about the way they should be conceptualized and defined.[4] But there is always a contrast between understanding or knowledge (*phronēsis*) and *sōphrosunē*, which in Cicero's Latin becomes *moderatio* (or *modestia*) *et temperantia*. One way of putting it would be to say that knowledge or understanding is what you need for a grasp of what your duties are, what you should or should not do, whereas *sōphrosunē* is what enables you in the light of that knowledge to choose or refuse what you should (Zeno's formulation) or to keep your impulses settled or firmly established (a later formulation).[5] The spheres of knowledge special to courage and justice are then demarcated as enduring what you should and as making allocations or distributions as you should. The virtues are standardly listed in that order. *Sōphrosunē* has no special status.

In Cicero's *De Officiis*, the Stoic theory of four virtues has been radically reshaped, thanks presumably to Panaetius (see especially *Off.* 1.11–17). At its core is now the notion of reason as what above all else distinguishes humans from other animals and of the different impulses whose dynamic and regulation is due to reason: for society with other humans (the province of justice), for the pursuit of truth whether practical or more theoretical (the sphere of understanding and wisdom), and for an independence and largeness of outlook that rises above the merely human (which characterizes *magnitudo animi*, replacing or reconceptualizing courage). The behavior required of someone whose impulses have been properly shaped by the *honestum*—that is, by what is morally fine—is what will constitute our *officia* as rational animals. Book 1 of *De Officiis* accordingly sets out the basic obligations of justice and *magnitudo animi* in the general terms one would expect of an approach to its subject so determinedly foundational.

Sōphrosunē is now set to play a special role as the fourth virtue (the expression is taken from *Tusculanae Disputationes* 3.17: on which more in due course). Since its particular province is impulse, it is implicated on that account in the spheres of each of the other three virtues, in fact in all behavior, every word and deed. Characteristic of it is an aversion to doing or saying or thinking anything gratuitously injurious to another, or anything precipitate in judgement, or anything that might appear unmanly, formulations I take not from *De Officiis* itself but from the earlier account of the virtues in the anti-Epicurean Book 2 of Cicero's *De Finibus*, a more concise and more sharply focused version of the same Panaetian theory (*Fin.* 2.45–47).[6] In short, *sōphrosunē* gives a person a settled aversion to doing or saying or thinking anything that would be inconsistent with the impulses characteristic of the other three virtues. In that sense the conception of it depends on the other three—it "follows" from them and is "dependent on" or "constructed from" them (*aptum*: *Fin.* 2.47). It has at once a particular sphere (aversion to improper impulse) and a generic character making it hard to distinguish from virtue as such—consistency across the entire range of human behavior through life: the Stoics defined virtue in general as "consistent disposition" (e.g., D.L. 7.89).

Decorum

To develop an account of what our duties are within the framework of a theory of the virtues conceived in Panaetian terms is to articulate them in the light of human nature itself at its best. Starting from the notion of the *decorum*, or what is "appropriate," is on the face of it to begin from more local and more variable considerations. The basic idea, as Cicero explains it in his *Orator*, is that as differences in fortune, rank, position, and age, and again place, time, and audience, require different styles of thought and expression in oratory or poetry, so they do in life—in actions as well as words. What is appropriate depends on subject matter and on *personae*, the roles or characters of speaker and audience. This is a topic, he tells us, that philosophers discuss at length under duties, *not*, by contrast, when they are arguing about what is morally right, for there is no variation there. A related contrast is then drawn between the verbs *oportere* ("it is obligatory") and *decere* ("it is appropriate"). To use *oportere* is to indicate "perfection" in a duty: something that must be done always and by everybody. Using *decere* says that it is fitting and in accord with occasion and *persona*—and, presumably, is the expression applicable when one is talking about duties in the ordinary sense (*Orat.* 70–74).[7]

The *decorum* section of Book 1 of *De Officiis* contains a famous theoretical treatment of *personae*, usually attributed to Panaetius (*Off.* 1.100–121).[8] Some of its subsequent illustrative material fits the program for a philosophical discussion of *officia* that Cicero has adumbrated in the *Orator*. For example, duties of the young differ from those of the old, those of magistrates from those of citizens: they have different *personae* (*Off.* 1.122–24). And as the *Orator* stressed, facial expression, gesture, and gait are important in *decorum;* so space in the *De Officiis* section on *decorum* is given over to the topic (*Off.* 1.130–33, 145–46). Even where the theorization of *personae* in *De Officiis* goes beyond anything detectable in *Orator*, much of it accords with the general conception of *persona* in the earlier work, as when it proposes (*Off.* 1.119–21; cf. 108–9) that what is *decorum* for someone depends on the *persona* expressed in their entire choice of what life to lead, and that in turn is heavily influenced by the *persona* that fortune brings (e.g., someone who suffers from poor health cannot play the same kind of role as someone whose health is robust), and especially by the *persona* that nature endows a person with (e.g., open or more devious).

Reflection on the requirements of the virtues is not rendered irrelevant. Both magistrate and private citizen, for example, need to consider from the vantage point of their different *personae* what duties of fair treatment they have towards others (*Off.* 1.124). Guarding against indulging the passions and appetites is something particularly important for adolescents (*Off.* 1.122); but in the discussion of *personae* there is no attempt to represent the need for *sōphrosunē* as pervasive in the *decorum*. Nonetheless the heuristic for determining *officium* is quite different from that suggested by the theory of the virtues. There we start with general consideration of what fine behavior to others or of what the pursuit of truth (for example) requires. *Personae* theory, by contrast, makes the *persona* or *personae* of particular individuals or types of individual the starting point for determining one's *officium*, although one then has to ask oneself what virtue requires of one in that role. Consistency in the performance of every undertaking and in the conception of every plan in accordance with our *persona* is what will make thought and action appropriate (*Off.* 1.125).

Persona, *Decorum*, and Virtue

Different though the approaches to determining *officium* through consideration of the *honestum* (what is morally fine) and of *persona* may be, the *decorum* section of Book 1 of *De Officiis* makes a striking attempt to harmonize them. It does this primarily by complementary adjustments to virtue theory and to *personae* theory.

The basic adjustment is to *persona* theory. The *De Officiis* account makes a distinction quite absent from the *Orator* discussion of *persona* in its account of the *decorum*. It distinguishes between *personae* due to nature and *personae* due to fortune and circumstance and to our own choice. More crucially and radically, as well as the difference in *persona* that we acquire through natural variations in temperament and mental ability, or again in physique, the *De Officiis* theory proposes that humans share a common *persona* due likewise to nature: "arising from the fact that we all have a share in reason and in the superiority by which we surpass the brute creatures" (*Off.* 1.107). Making a *role* out of our shared humanity obviously stretches the notion of a *persona* to the limit.

The innovation is clearly designed to bring *persona* theory within the framework of the treatment of the virtues developed in the opening section of Book 1 (*Off.* 1.11–17: see Section 2), whose stress on the impulses of reason as what make human nature superior to the animals is echoed by the formula I have just quoted. If when we consider how to behave in accordance with our *personae*, we need primarily to have regard to our common rational human nature *as a persona* (cf. *Off.* 1.97–98), then that is tantamount to a requirement to make the *honestum* and the demands of the virtues guide our decisions and behavior. As Cicero comments straight after he has enunciated the formula, from the *persona* constituted by our natural superiority to the beasts "all *honestum* and *decorum* is drawn, and the method of determining *officium* is discovered" (*Off.* 1.107). That approach to the conduct of life is now conceived as implicit in the *persona* that makes us what we are.

There are complementary adjustments to *decorum* theory, which in *De Officiis* as in *Orator* is the context within which conceptualization of *personae* is located. *Orator* had distinguished between *oportet* ("it is obligatory") and *decet* ("it is appropriate"). *De Officiis* is at pains to insist that it is impossible to drive a wedge between what is *decorum* and what makes the highest demands on us: "Its force (*vis*) is such that it cannot be separated from what is morally fine (*honestum*)—whatever is appropriate is fine, whatever is fine is appropriate. It is easier to grasp than to explain what the difference is between 'fine' and 'appropriate'" (*Off.* 1.93–94). When Cicero comes to give a general definition of the *decorum* involved in all *honestas*, he does so in terms which at once replicate the treatment of the distinctiveness of human rationality developed in the opening section of Book 1, and mirror the account of our common natural *persona* that will follow. It is: "What accords with the excellence of a human being just where human nature differs from that of other living beings" (*Off.* 1.96). Cicero goes on to support the thesis that according with[9] human excellence is key to the notion of *decorum* by appealing to the poets' assumption that choice of language and behavior has to fit *persona*: "*est enim digna persona oratio*" (people applaud when "speech is worthy of the *persona*," *Off.* 1.97). However whereas in poetry appropriateness has to be judged in each case by the poet, our *persona* as humans, excelling all other living things, is assigned by nature itself.

This is plainly a revisionist account of what it is for behavior to be appropriate. It sets the bar very high. One might wonder what room is left for behavior in accordance with any of the other three *personae* to count as "appropriate" at all.[10] Cicero does something to deal with the problem when he discusses the second of our four *personae*: the one constituted by our individual nature. He suggests that attaining the high ideal of *decorum* in the sense he has defined will be facilitated by following individual natural bent (provided that involves no vice), even if the pursuits of someone with a different natural bent might be better or more serious. "There is no appropriateness," he says, "if nature opposes and fights against it" (*Off.* 1.110); "the thing most appropriate for each of us is what is for each of us most his own" (*Off.* 1.113). And indeed the entire section on individual natural *persona* is devoted to arguing in these terms the merits of living within its limitations (*Off.* 1.111–14).

The concession that other pursuits might be better could suggest that this is a recipe for a second-best life. That is in a way true, in a way not. When Cicero goes on to stress the importance of consistency in life as a whole, and between individual actions alike, as something you might jeopardize if you copied someone else's nature and ignored your own (*Off.* 1.111), we recall that consistency in life is the Stoic goal and virtue "consistent disposition." There is nothing better than consistency: "When someone has adopted a plan of life entirely in accordance with his own nature (assuming it is not a vicious one), let him then maintain constancy—that, most of all, is what appropriateness consists in (*decet*), unless perhaps he comes to realize he has made a mistake in choosing his type of life" (*Off.* 1.120). If we may extrapolate to appropriateness in non-natural aspects of *persona* too, nothing is going to count as the *decorum*—whether we consider doing what fits our own individual nature or employing the right style in oratory or conversation ("we must work at all these things, if in everything we are seeking what is appropriate [*decet*]," *Off.* 1.133)—unless it is not merely consistent with itself and with the circumstances in which we find ourselves but consistent also with the demands of the *honestum*. In other words, consistency with our common natural *persona* is what ultimately determines whether consistency in any of the other *personae* meets the standard of the *decorum*.

On the other hand, Cicero envisages that one person will naturally develop good qualities another does not: that would not be true of the Stoic sage. His concluding remarks under the heading of individual natural *persona* are revealing:

> We shall, therefore, exert ourselves above all in those things to which we are most suited. But if necessity has on occasion pushed us towards things for which we have no natural talent, we shall have to apply all possible care, preparation and diligence to be able to perform them, if not appropriately, with as little inappropriateness as possible. Nor should we strive so much to acquire good qualities that have not been given us, as to avoid vicious ones. (*Off.* 1.114)

Here the point about the uneven distribution of good qualities is repeated. And it is coupled with the thought that approximation to the ideal of consistency is the most that we may be capable of, given the exigencies of "necessity."

Decorum as the Fourth Virtue

So far *De Officiis*'s redefinition of *decorum* and *persona* gives a way of subsuming the *personae* approach to determining our *officia* under the general theory of the virtues, as established dispositions for acting on the rational impulses that mark us out as human beings. But it gives no basis for making *decorum* itself *one* of the virtues, with its particular sphere regulation of impulse. *Decorum* as first introduced is close to being equivalent to *honestum*: what is morally fine in general (*Off.* 1.93–94). However, *De Officiis* now distinguishes two uses of *decorum*: the generic (defined as above in the previous section), and a narrower one that is represented as a species of the generic, subordinated to it.[11] The *decorum* in this narrower sense is "what accords with nature in such a way that moderation and restraint are apparent in it, along with the style characteristic of a free person" (*Off.* 1.96). In other words, *decorum* more narrowly defined specifies the kind of fine behavior particularly associated with *sōphrosunē*, or moderation and restraint.

What reason is there for associating the notion of *decorum* more particularly with this kind of behavior? Cicero has an answer prepared. When he turns to the *officia* dictated by the *decorum* in general, he claims that its greatest *force* is apparent in the part of virtue he is currently discussing, that is, the fourth virtue: moderation and restraint (*Off.* 1.100). Something he says a little earlier may help to explain what he means by the claim and why he makes it. The *decorum* of a mind, he says, "shines out" (*elucet*) in a person's life and "arouses the approval of those with whom the life is lived because of the order and constancy and moderation of every word and action" (*Off.* 1.98). In other words, consistent moderation in *all* of a person's behavior is what gives *decorum* its greatest impact, particularly, Cicero will add, where that is manifested in *verecundia*, respect for others (*Off.* 1.99). It is not just that it *is* appropriate; no less importantly, it *looks* right. Zeno of Citium had propounded the thesis that "character can be known from appearance (*eidos*)" (D.L. 7.173), and that remained a Stoic conviction. Stoic materialism took states of character to be bodies, and as bodies in some sense perceptible (Stobaeus, *Eclogae* 2.64.18–23).[12] Ethical attractiveness—the manifestation and so impact (*emphasis*) of virtue—is, for example, something Epictetus thinks of as particularly characteristic of someone who lives the Cynic version of the Stoic life (*Diss.* 3.22.86–92).[13]

Cicero says that *decorum* of this more specific and arresting kind "is observed in each single kind of virtue" (*Off.* 1.98; cf. 1.96: it "pertains to the individual parts of *honestas*"). Commentators have been puzzled by these remarks and have wondered whether there is something wrong with the text, presumably because they do not see how one part of virtue can show up in another. From Dyck in his commentary, we learn of an attempt as long ago as 1864 to emend the text at 1.96 to *ad singularem partem honestatis*: "to *an* individual part of *honestas*."[14] In their translation, Griffin and Atkins adopt this correction to the text,[15] and assume some parallel correction at 1.98, although as Dyck says, "it strains credulity to suppose that this text, too, has been corrupted independently." Winterbottom leaves the text as it is in both places but exclaims in despair: *"delirat Cicero."*[16]

Not a bit of it. Reference back to our discussion of *De Finibus* 2.47 (p. 45 above) suffices to show what Cicero means when he says that specific *decorum* shows up in each single kind of virtue and why given the theory he is right to say it. The wise person dreads precipitate judgement; the just person does not have the effrontery to injure anyone by an insolent word or deed; the large-spirited person shrinks from doing or saying anything unmanly. Here Cicero stresses precisely the way the order and restraint (*ordo et moderatio*) characteristic of the fourth virtue gets exhibited in the consistent practice of each of the first three cardinal virtues.

In his discussion of the virtues in the next work he composed after *De Finibus*, the *Tusculanae Disputationes*, Cicero makes it the special function of the fourth virtue to rule and settle the impulses of the soul, and to preserve a moderated constancy (always opposing uncontrolled desire) in everything (*Tusc.* 3.17). But he has already emphasized that it "includes (*complexa est*)" the three virtues of courage, justice, and prudence. He adds at once that this is a feature common to the virtues and familiar to students of Stoicism: "all are mutually connected and bound together" (something likewise emphasized in the opening treatment of the virtues in *De Officiis*: *Off.* 1.15). The passage in which this discussion is set (*Tusc.* 3.16–18) expends a lot of energy on finding a good Roman name for the fourth virtue. Perhaps surprisingly (and certainly uniquely in his philosophical writings), Cicero opts for *frugalitas*, which he wants us to take not in the usual narrow sense of "being economical," "good control of resources." But the point (assisted by the echo of the cognate adjective *frugi* [cf. *Tusc.* 4.36] when applied as a sobriquet of the great L. Calpurnius Piso) is to indicate that the fourth virtue is more than just one virtue among others. It is goodness in general, or rather goodness in general viewed as "good control inhibiting impulses such as fear, greed, and impetuosity." Something very similar is true of the treatment of the fourth virtue in *De Officiis* too.[17]

The preferred name for the fourth virtue in *De Officiis* is, of course, not moderation or restraint, nor yet *frugalitas*, but *decorum* (*Off.* 1.93). The opening section of Book 1 explains why this should be so. It is because the fourth virtue is the morally fine as exhibited in a fourth kind of rational impulse: humans are the only animals (human uniqueness is particularly emphasized at this point) who have a feeling and an attraction for order, for what is appropriate (*quod deceat*), for measure in word and deed. Just as we appreciate beauty and harmonious construction in things visible, so nature and reason prompt us still more strongly to maintain beauty, constancy, and order in our plans and our actions (*Off.* 1.14).

The moderation and restraint of someone who shrinks from irrational impulses disturbing or threatening psychic order are the features of the fourth virtue that may sometimes make its distinctiveness most apparent to the rest of us. But what powers moderation and restraint in the virtuous person is now understood as the rational impulse to order and consistency, which is actually an impulse to *decorum* understood quite generally. As such it is a superordinate impulse to virtue—consistent disposition—in general. It is not surprising that when Seneca came to ask how we get an understanding not of the particular virtues but of virtue itself, he clearly found his answer in Cicero's account of the fourth virtue: "What reveals it to us is its order and beauty (*decor*) and constancy, and the harmony of all actions with each other, and a greatness that carries itself above everything" (*Ep.* 120.11). This is why the *decorum* is not just the fourth but the crowning virtue in *De Officiis*'s presentation of the theory of virtues.

Verecundia

Cicero claims that *decorum* achieves its greatest impact where it is manifested in *verecundia* (*Off.* 1.99). *Verecundia* is given striking prominence throughout his extended treatment of *decorum* at *Off.* 1.93–151. At the very outset he identifies the fourth virtue—"the one remaining part of *honestas* (moral fineness)"—as that where "*verecundia* and what one might call a sort of polish exhibited by a life" is to be seen, before adding that this is where *temperantia et modestia* are located (*Off.* 1.93). Cicero's treatment of the *officium* of the fourth virtue effectively begins with advice on control of impulses, the need for judiciousness—and with illustrative material focused on *verecundia*: we are to ensure that even when we jest "something of the light of an upright character may shine forth (*eluceat*)" (*Off.* 1.103). After the exposition of *persona* theory is complete, the entire final sequence of the *decorum* section (*Off.* 1.126–51) is given over to detailed advice about the behavior to be expected of *verecundia*—including, I shall argue, the final paragraphs on occupations *not* suitable for the style of life expected of a free person (*Off.* 1.150–51).

The main argument of the subsection begins with nature, and the claim that it has hidden those parts of the body that look ugly and dishonorable: human *verecundia* (modesty) imitates nature. Dismissive treatment of the Cynics then frames the rest of the main discussion (*Off.* 1.128, 1.148: *Cynicorum ... ratio tota ... est inimica verecundiae*). The chief programmatic statement occurs at *Off.* 1.143: "We have for some time been speaking of those virtues which pertain to *verecundia* and to the approbation of those with whom we live (cf. 1.98), and it is what is appropriate to these that we should now be discussing."

There is no hint in the earlier treatments of the fourth virtue in *De Finibus* (2.47) and *Tusculanae Disputationes* (3.16–18) that in *verecundia* it achieves its most important expression. The obvious inference is that this development is due to the importation of *persona* theory into conceptualization of the virtue. Once again we should recall how Cicero appeals to the way the poets make the notion of *persona* key to their model of the *decorum* (*Off.* 1.97–98). In suggesting that our "role" as humans is given us by nature—we are to play the part of constancy, moderation, restraint, and modesty—he adds (I think in explication of *verecundia*, modesty): "and this same nature teaches us not to be careless in the way we behave towards other men" (*Off.* 1.98). In other words, just as an actor has to manage the way he presents the character he is playing, so modesty involves managing the impression we create on others. Only if we do that properly will we be achieving the order in our behavior for which nature has given us the impulse. Only then will our virtue "shine out" and "arouse the approval of those with whom life is lived because of the order and constancy and moderation of every word and action."

Is the fourth virtue's reorientation toward *verecundia* indicated by anything in the definition of special or subordinate *decorum*? To supply just such an indication is presumably the point of the inclusion in it of reference to "the style characteristic of a free person" (*cum specie quadam liberali*: *Off.* 1.96). In his discussion of the definition,

Dyck says: "Surely the emphasis on *moderatio et temperantia* is all that is needed to indicate the tendency of this virtue."[18] Wrong: *moderatio et temperantia* capture neither its external orientation nor the management needed to achieve the right impression that is crucial in *verecundia*, which, as we have seen, is a quality no less important than *moderatio et temperantia* in the characterization of *decorum*. Early in the long *verecundia* section (*Off.* 1.126–51), preoccupation with "style" or "appearance" (*species*) quickly becomes apparent (*Off.* 1.127). Here is the tone set: "Let us follow nature and avoid anything that shrinks from the approval of eyes and ears. Let our standing, our walking, our sitting and our reclining, our countenances, our eyes and the movements of our hands, all maintain what I have called *decorum*" (*Off.* 1.128). When after discussion of modes of speech and style of accommodation Cicero turns at last to the substance of action—what rather than how—he reiterates the importance of governing impulse and of appropriate judiciousness and once again emphasizes the need to take care to control "what pertains to the style and standing (*dignitas*) of a free person" (*Off.* 1.141; cf. 1.103).

Cicero's implicit contrast throughout is with the expectations one might have of a slave or of a slavish character. Translators sometimes make him talk of a "gentleman" rather than a "free" person. And it is certainly true that the style of behavior he goes on to recommend in the detailed prescriptions of the *verecundia* section sound like nothing so much as etiquette for the few Roman grandees left surviving the disintegrating republic. Slavish behavior for Cicero encompasses a great deal that in other societies would be regarded as perfectly compatible with the proper conduct of a free citizen, notably when it comes to the list of occupations he regards as unsuitable (crafts, tax collecting, banking, retail, trade—except perhaps when on a large scale: *Off.* 1.150–51).[19] We can agree that Cicero's highly restrictive notion of the style of freedom is dramatically culture-specific. Nonetheless, a style of freedom is what it suggests. To quote Robert Kaster (writing about Roman republican culture more generally), *verecundia* "animates the art of knowing your proper place in every transaction and binds the free members of a civil community."[20]

Cicero's prescriptions for *verecundia* are emphatically not mere etiquette, nor does his treatment of *decorum* represent the awkward imposition of an aesthetic category onto ethical subject matter, as commentators have complained. Cicero is writing as a Roman citizen to other Roman citizens of his own class, not least, of course, the addressee of *De Officiis*, his son Marcus. So his prescriptions are naturally not universalizable as they stand, and none the worse on that account. More importantly, they are not universalizable *in principle*, except where he talks in the most general way about our duties to others as citizens and as members of the human race (*Off.* 1.149: a striking example of *decorum* within the sphere of another virtue: justice). How you manage the impression you make on others and what impression it should be depend both on who you are and on who the relevant others are. If contemporary moral philosophers were to be asked to specify for us the behavior appropriate to a consideration for others rooted in modesty, they would rightly cast it in terms often highly specific to the world as it is in the early twenty-first century, terms unavoidably more complex than Cicero's, given the multicultural societies we live in now.[21]

NOTES

I would like to express my gratitude to Walter Nicgorski for the invitation to contribute to this book and to the colloquium that generated it. A revised version of the original paper was subsequently delivered to a conference in Oxford to celebrate the life and work of Peter Brunt (March 2007): I thank Alan Bowman and Teresa Morgan for inviting me. Thanks also to participants on both occasions for their oral reactions, and to Christopher Gill for written comments. The present version has since been substantially redrafted.

1. Dyck, *A Commentary on Cicero, De Officiis*, 239.
2. The formula is derived from Kaster, *Emotion, Restraint, and Community in Ancient Rome*, chap. 1.
3. Dyck's commentary supplies a great deal of background information of all sorts (see also the helpful introductory material in Griffin and Atkins, *Cicero: On Duties*). His treatment of the *decorum* section of Book 1 of *De Officiis* suggests that Cicero's handling of the topic is in many ways and for various reasons full of confusion. My response is to try bringing out its power and coherence in essentials.

4. For a useful selection of texts see Long and Sedley, *The Hellenistic Philosophers*, section 61. For some discussion of the earliest Stoic debates, see Schofield, "Ariston of Chios and the Unity of Virtue."

5. "Impulse," here as elsewhere, translates Greek *hormē*, or Cicero's Latin equivalent *appetitio* (e.g., *Off.* 2.18). For discussion of the Stoic theory of impulse, focused on some key texts, see Long and Sedley, *The Hellenistic Philosophers*, section 57. Impulse is the psychological mainspring that Stoics make responsible for any and every form of animal motivation.

6. So Dyck, *A Commentary on Cicero, De Officiis*, 85.

7. I am grateful to Brian Krostenko, participant in the Notre Dame Colloquium, for alerting me to the importance of this text for my theme.

8. A helpful discussion is Gill, "Personhood and Personality."

9. The expression I translate "according with" (*consentaneum*) here is the same word Cicero uses to explain *decere* when elaborating his *persona* theory at *Orator*, 74.

10. For some pertinent discussion, see Gill, "Personhood and Personality," 177–94.

11. Dyck (*A Commentary on Cicero, De Officiis*, 246) suggests that despite Cicero's explicit assertion that the relationship is subordination of species to genus, he is wrong about that. But provided we take "what accords with nature" in the definition of specific *decorum* as shorthand for the formula defining generic *decorum* ("what accords with the excellence of a human being just where human nature differs from that of other living beings"), there is surely no reason to question Cicero's thesis.

12. See Schofield, *The Stoic Idea of the City*, 31–32, 112–18.

13. A revisionist interpretation of Cynicism, certainly as Cynicism is viewed by Cicero at *Off.* 1.128, 148. For discussion, see Schofield, "Epictetus on Cynicism."

14. Dyck, *A Commentary on Cicero, De Officiis*, 247.

15. Griffin and Atkins, *Cicero: On Duties*, 38 n. 2.

16. Winterbottom, *M. Tulli Ciceronis De Officiis*, 39.

17. My thanks to Margaret Graver for drawing my attention to the relevance of this passage in *Tusculanae Disputationes*.

18. Dyck, *A Commentary on Cicero, De Officiis*, 247.

19. The sort of list a Plato or an Aristotle might have constructed: for discussion of its provenance see Brunt, "Aspects of the Social Thought of Dio Chrysostom," 26–34.

20. Kaster, *Emotion, Restraint, and Community in Ancient Rome*, 27.

21. Appiah (*Cosmopolitanism*) perhaps gives a flavor of how contemporary *verecundia* might look.

3

Philosophical Life versus Political Life

An Impossible Choice for Cicero?

CARLOS LÉVY

The ways of life in antiquity have been the subject matter of many studies.[1] Some of these studies are focused specifically on the case of Cicero, who is indeed especially interesting since he presents a fine example of the assimilation of philosophical themes into a different society from the one out of which those themes had arisen. We shall not dwell on the works we evoked, but we shall rather question something that seems obvious. Indeed, to one looking back, it seems self-evident that Cicero could never have devoted himself to a theoretical life. It is precisely this idea of an absolute impossibility that comes to light in the title of the chapter J.-M. André has devoted to our author: "Cicero and the Drama of the Impossible Retirement."[2] What is the nature of this "impossibility"? The solution does not appear very clearly throughout the works we have read. If one is content with raising the issues of anthropological and sociological strains, two examples that move in opposite directions spring immediately to mind. First, the example of Lucilius, who though a knight was a poet influenced both by the Stoicism of Panaetius and by the New Academy of Clitomachus. Although this was before Cicero's time, he had decided to stay away from the *cursus honorum* and devote himself to literature and to increasing his fortune.[3]

The second example is Atticus, who chose to lead a life of leisure in conformity both with his material interests and his philosophical ones. Cicero himself, in the *Pro Cluentio*, will pay a vibrant tribute to the life *tranquilla et quieta* of the *equites* (*Clu.* 153). Our task therefore shall be to understand this "impossibility" by showing how Cicero has continually evolved through the ways of justifying his choice or, more exactly, his absence of choice.

A Matter of *Voluntas*

As a starting point, we shall take a sentence from a letter to Atticus, dating from 5 December 61 B.C. The letter is devoted mostly to the deterioration of the relationship between Quintus, Cicero's brother, and Atticus, with regard to which Cicero expresses his affection for his friend. We are especially interested in the following sentence: "I am thoroughly persuaded of your disinterestedness and magnanimity, and I have never thought that there was any difference between you and me, except our choice of a career. A touch of ambition led me to seek for distinction, while another perfectly laudable motive led you to honorable ease."[4]

What does this sentence mean exactly? Let us leave aside the fact that Cicero is in an emotionally difficult situation where he is caught between his family and Atticus. He tends to put himself down and to give emphasis to Atticus's choice. We should note that the organization of the life of an individual depends on his *voluntas*, which takes on two forms in the sentence: a passionate form, *ambitio*, and a reflective form, *ratio*, which is associated with *otium*, perhaps alluding thereby to the rational calculation of the drawbacks and advantages of a given situation, which is the basis of Epicurean ethics. In this letter, the duality of will and judgement features in the first line: "He has continually changed his mind—*varietas voluntatis*—and wavered in his opinion and judgement."[5] This duality is taken up again, further in the letter, with regard to Atticus's decision not to go to Asia: "so the fact that you are not with him cannot be attributed to your quarrel and rupture, but to your choice and plans—*voluntate ac iudicio tuo*—already fixed."[6] In other words, the choice of life depends on a still-mysterious power, *voluntas*, that can be either in contradiction with reason or in harmony with it. If we look at the only theoretical work written before this letter, the *De Inventione*, we can see that *voluntas* is very present in it,[7] appearing like an enigma that the orator must decipher in order to perceive the intentions of the accused or of the legislator. If we acknowledge, at least as a hypothesis, this anthropological fact, how then is the Ciceronian choice of life approached and thought through? How is it justified with regard to the poles of either contradiction to or harmony with respect to reason?

A Foundational Experience and Cicero's Enthusiasm for Philosophy

Meeting Philo of Larissa

Perhaps we can start from the beginning. Cicero tells us in his *Brutus* (306), that in 88 B.C., when Philo of Larissa, the last scholarch of the Academy, took refuge in Rome, he followed his teaching with unwavering enthusiasm: "Filled with enthusiasm for the study of philosophy, I gave myself to this instruction."[8]

The *totum* indicates that in this philosophical commitment, there is a unification of potentially discordant functions. As if he anticipated the possible objection—namely, "Why then did you not become a philosopher?"—Cicero adds that his enthusiasm was all the greater because the legal system seemed to have been definitely brought to a halt due to the turmoil in Rome at that time. Of course, this is not a contemporary testimony but a reconstruction from memory of something that had happened forty years earlier. Nevertheless we can take note of the distinction made between the great pleasure he took from philosophy (*summa delectatione*) and the world of law, referred to by the term *ratio*, which however, in the sentence, does not designate individual reason but legal organization. Thus on the one hand, there is an attraction attributed to enthusiasm (*studium*) and to intellectual pleasure (*delectatio*), and on the other, a reality that is the law, which, at least as far as it is a signifier, is placed on the side of reason. Let us add that the sentence emphasizes the importance of the context in which this reaction to philosophy occurs by specifying its function: the fact that the law-courts were inactive did not determine the nature of the reaction to philosophy but enabled his enthusiasm to have a more constant intensity (*commorabar attentius*). Furthermore, the expression *totum ei me tradidi* is strong enough for us to understand that the interest for the teaching went hand in hand with an admiration and a great fondness for the teacher.

The Three Possibilities

If we acknowledge that this experience was fundamental, and there is no reason to think that it was not, we must also acknowledge that it led Cicero to ask himself the question not only in the traditional terms of theoretical life, practical life, or mixed life—to which we shall return—but also in the following way:

> (A) Whether to be Philo, that is to say, not only a philosopher but also a teacher of philosophy. Philo's case was interesting with respect to Cicero's other teachers in that, after having had important intellectual and institutional power, as scholarch of the Academy, he had re-created in Rome a much more immaterial power that, through his words, he held over the young Romans. At the same time, his disappearance left vacant the most prestigious of successions, the successor to Plato. The state of abandonment of the Academy comes back as a leitmotiv in Cicero's late treatises. Cicero, the *homo platonicus*, who was called in his youth *Graikos kai scholastikos*,[9] likely must have wondered whether he was not himself the last successor of Plato, since the legitimacy of his other Academic master, Antiochus of Ascalon, had divided the institutional structure of the Academy in opposing Philo.
>
> (B) Whether to live a life in which philosophy would be present though not in the foreground, but how so.
>
> (C) Or to live only a practical life.

Exploring Cicero's Options

Methodological Remarks

The first hypothesis was, for the young Cicero, unacceptable or perhaps even unthinkable, since the *mos maiorum* had established in the preceding decades what contradicted Roman *dignitas*. The expulsion of Greek philosophers and rhetoricians and the sanctions enforced by Crassus on the *rhetores latini*, accused of forming an *impudentiae ludus*, had illustrated the rejection by the Romans of a Latinization of the educational system established in the Greek world.[10]

Besides, the other role models of his youth, Anthony and Crassus, had shown, at least if we go by the *De Oratore*, that the interest in Greek culture could be secured within the respect for tradition. Crassus, conceptually the boldest of the two, makes philosophy part of the training of an orator, though he treats culture according to a political model: *imperium* belongs to eloquence, and philosophy is a province, the richest, the most interesting one, subject to this *imperium*. Crassus is not only an outstanding orator but also a traditionalist with mighty intuitions, for whom the Roman imperialistic pattern must be applied even to the world of culture. As for Anthony, he acknowledges philosophy to be, at most, an interesting but passing distraction. These two characters, whom Cicero admired so much in his youth, represent at least a part of his own personality. However, we shall see that the fascination for the professorial model will continue to be present in Cicero and will manifest itself with great brilliance in the last part of his life, though he does not carry out its ultimate consequences, that is, become a scholarch. The third hypothesis, on the other hand, had become impossible due to the intensity of the interest he had felt in his encounter with the philosophers. When he writes in the *De Natura Deorum*: "It is precisely when it seemed least the case that I devoted myself the most to philosophy," and he adds, "I consider that, both in my public life and in my private life, I have put into practice the prescriptions of reason and of the education I have had,"[11] he thus expresses in a manner we may judge as hyperbolical what for him was an indisputable reality, namely, that he had been decidedly impressed by philosophy. So we are faced with the problematic (B).

The passage from the *Brutus* explains how he had been filled with enthusiasm for philosophy and why this enthusiasm had not been disrupted by public life. But it still does not enable us to understand explicitly why he did not choose a philosophical life, at a distance from the forum, with or without teaching. It is significant that the first Ciceronian text, the *prooemium* of the *De Inventione*, should be a legitimization of the life engaged in politics, and thus it is relevant to look at this text in detail.[12]

The First Prooemium *of* De Inventione

De Inventione should be dated from 88 B.C., if we go by a literal interpretation of Cicero's own indication that he had written this treatise when he was a *puer adulescentulus* (*De. Or.* 1.5). Since it is possible that he used this expression not so much for historical accuracy but more to present this treatise, which he considered quite mediocre, as a "youthful indiscretion," we could place it, as G. Achard has, as late as 84 to 82 B.C.[13]

Whatever the solution to this problem may be, we find ourselves necessarily in a period in which Cicero was still directly under the influence of the teaching of Philo of Larissa, who had undertaken, surprisingly for a scholarch of the Academy, to teach both rhetoric and philosophy. He went to the extent of dealing not only with the *quaestiones*, that is, the general subjects, but also with the *causae*, the particular causes.

The *prooemium* is presented as a *thesis*, in other words, one of those "double edged discussions, which offer the possibility of copiously arguing both sides of a general issue" (*De Or.* 3.107). The issue at hand is to know whether eloquence is the cause of more good than evil for individuals and for nations. This two-part choice is itself completed by a two-part observation: experience and personal memories show that very eloquent men have been the cause of much evil to the greatest states, whereas historical and literary testimonies reveal that, in a distant past, eloquence has played a positive role in the history of the relations between nations.

The solution to this contradiction is immediately given. It is reason itself (*ratio ipsa*) that is summoned to dictate the solution through the definition of a criterion of choice, namely, utility: wisdom without eloquence is not useful to cities, whereas eloquence without wisdom is most of the time harmful and, in any case, is never useful. The citizen, armed both with philosophy and rhetoric, will be *utilissimus atque amicissimus*. This solution is logically acceptable only if we acknowledge that the association of eloquence and philosophy is located in the distant past, whereas eloquence on its own is placed in the recent past. That is to say, the positioning of the problem and the proposed solution assume considerations about the decadence of the times.

Where we would expect an immediate recollection, we are given a myth, one that takes up the sophistic theme of the miserable beginnings of humanity but in an utterly unusual way, with a few Platonic echoes that we shall not dwell on here. Neither shall we dwell on the reasons why we think that this is not a myth of Isocratic origin. But it does seem important to underline that this is truly a myth, that is to say, that it has only a relative truth. In order to claim that the man who enabled the move from the wild to the civilized life was both eloquent and wise, Cicero uses the verb *videtur*, which is used again to speak of the period in which eloquence was beneficial.[14] *Veri simillimum* is used to speak of the process of decadence that results in having, on one side, at the head of the *res publica*, eloquent but cynical men (*temerarii atque audaces*), whereas the most talented men retire in *otium*.

Let us note that, once again, the pair *voluntas/ratio* is at the heart of the myth. In order that cities may subsist, their inhabitants must accept, *sua voluntate*, to obey the orders of another, and this may happen only if the governors make use of eloquence so as to communicate what they have discovered thanks to reason (*ea quae ratione invenissent*). This education of the will is presented to us as the means of moving on to a state of law through the renunciation of violence of those who possessed physical force. Eloquence is, in such a context, that which enables us to rationalize the will.

The connection between the myth and the *mos maiorum* takes place when Cicero, after having spoken of the chronologically indeterminate period in which wisdom and eloquence were each practiced separately, speaks of the great personalities of the *mos maiorum*, of Cato and Scipio Aemilianus and Laelius, presented as paradigms of *virtus*.

It is obvious that this text, though it is allegedly the study of the two terms of an alternative, actually aims to legitimize the solution that consists of engaging in political life. Its demonstrative value is, from a logical point of view, rather weak. The problematic points are:

(1) The awkward joining up of a myth and a historiographical ambition that does not give precise chronological specifications.

(2) The confusion over *sapientia* between a general sense (the human qualities of an individual, such as those of the three great Romans mentioned above) and a more technical sense, such as in the first paragraph where two of the three parts of philosophy are dealt with, namely, logic and morals. Cato, Scipio, and Laelius were not unlearned people, but Cicero evokes only their *virtus* and *eloquentia*, not their philosophical knowledge. For this reason, he later says: "It is eloquence which brings to the State a host of advantages, at least if wisdom, which regulates all things, comes with it."[15] The criterion of this wisdom is rather vague.

Actually, the text does not offer any choice but aims at showing that one must be engaged in public affairs, make use of eloquence, and possess a political science (*civilis quaedam ratio*) in which philosophy is included. But the means for this are very vague indeed. We note at *Inv.* 1.8 that Cicero condemns the pretension of Hermagoras of assigning to the orator questions such as: "Is there a good other than virtue?" or "Are the senses trustworthy?" The distinction between rhetoric and philosophy is therefore necessary at first, in order to enable their association at a later stage.

In fact, it seems as though the mimetic attitude Cicero could have developed out of admiration for Philo was repressed in favor of an attitude more in conformity with the *mos maiorum*, which will have as a result his establishing as role models the great men of the tradition. Those men to whom he will give a role in the *De Oratore* and the *De Re Publica*.

The image of what could be the necessarily complementary pairing of speech-action with culture-wisdom is found in the *Pro Archia*. The *litterae* can fill in only the moments in which the activities of the city are suspended. They have a double function: they allow a restoring rest after the tension (*contentio*) of the forum, but they also enrich eloquence, which is thus all the better put at the service of others.

Concerning the question left unanswered by *De Inventione*—namely, the question of the relation between innate *prudentia* and *sapientia* one acquires through philosophy—some specifications are given here. Cicero affirms that his own moral qualities were formed thanks to the precepts and the examples he found in books. He does not deny that certain individuals could have by nature superior moral qualities (*excellenti animo fuisse et sine doctrina*),[16] but he claims that even in such cases, *doctrina* enables one to surpass oneself. Cicero justifies himself by putting a high emphasis on the productivity of culture—productive of pleasure and productive of ethics—which never, at any point, threatens the only kind of life considered most worthy of a true citizen: the political life.

The Attraction of the Life of *Otium*

The Desire of Otium

In the period from *De Inventione* to the year 59 B.C., there is no lack of texts in which the expression of a temptation to the life of *otium* surfaces, but it never goes beyond a pious wish. Thus, in the *Pro Murena*, Cicero says that the torments he is confronted with in public life have often made him envious of the calm and tranquillity of those who have distanced themselves from all ambition. In contrast to what can have been claimed, this is not necessarily an "oratorical trick."[17] All the terms used by Cicero to describe himself refer either to reasoning (*iudicarem*) or to affections (*adfectus, miserari*), but none of them make reference to *voluntas*. These therefore are merely thoughts that do not lead to the will of changing lives. This is asserted explicitly in the *Pro Sulla*, contemporaneous with the *Pro Murena*, where Cicero says that the occasions in which he will have been useful to the country will give him the right to ask for a *honestum otium* and that he prefers, however, to continue to devote himself to the country. *Voluntas* is present in this text through the use of the verb *postulo* but only in order to show that, far from being engaged in a process of choice-making, his will is intensely involved in serving others.[18]

Regarding what J.-M. André has called "the crisis of 59," how is the problematic issue of making a choice presented? Most certainly, the change of the political situation, characterized by the instauration of the first triumvirate, did not enable Cicero to set out the problem of the *bioi* in the same terms as at the time of the *Pro Archia*.

Two Interesting Letters

The letter to Atticus, 2.5, dated from April 59 B.C., is a letter of desire, which is very different from will.[19] Cicero desires to travel to Alexandria and to the rest of Egypt (*cupio Alexandriam reliquamque Aegyptum visere*). He desires to give up all his activities and devote himself entirely to philosophy, that is, returning to the situation he was in when he was following the teachings of Philo. The verb *volo* is used in a past supposition (*vellem*), that is to say, that there never is a real commitment to a choice, but rather the issue is treated at the level of desires and ideas that are circulating *in animo*.[20] What is the reason for this incapacity, which he describes himself as *levitas*, if we follow the emendation suggested by Muret?[21] It is because, despite his queries, he remains profoundly attached to political life, convinced as he is of the rightful cause of the *optimates*, which, though seriously undermined, is perhaps not utterly lost.

The letter to Atticus, 2.16, probably the most famous of the letters concerning the question of the ways of life, dated from May 59 B.C., seems to mark the passage from desire to a decision, since the famous passage starts with a *statui*. In effect, Cicero seems this time really to be choosing between practical life, symbolized by Dicaearchus, and theoretical life, symbolized by Theophrastus—or more exactly, he seems decided to establish a "harmonious balance" between the two types of life. He would thus find his inspiration from Antiochus of Ascalon who, as is said by Augustine, distinguished between three types of life: the first, given to contemplation; the second, devoted to the management of human affairs; and the third sees "one type and the other harmoniously associated." Antiochus, says Augustine, preferred the mixed way: "of these three ways of life—indolent, active, mixed—it was the third way he was want to privilege. That was the opinion and the teaching of the old Academics, according to what Varro claims, on the words of Antiochus."[22]

Things are, in actual fact, much less simple. Let us note first of all the irony that has Dicaearchus, the theorist of the active life, presented as the *familiaris* of Atticus the Epicurean, whereas Cicero, the political man, declares himself the *amicus* of Theophrastus, philosopher of the theoretical life.[23] Furthermore, there is no real choice made by Cicero, but rather he observes that he has done all that he had to do for the *praktikos bios* and that, acquitted from that obligation, he can move on to the other type of life.

Finally, what is said of the two lives does not go in the direction of a harmonious conciliation within a *bios miktos* but rather sets an opposing relation between the two, since he says that he should never have distanced himself from the theoretical life. The sentence *respicio nunc ad hanc familiam* presents a real problem of identification. The demonstrative of the first person and the prefix *re-* would suggest that Cicero is alluding here to Academic philosophy in a version inspired by Antiochus, in other words, the version that associates the Academy to the Lyceum and would thus enable a recovery also of Theophrastus. However, the sentence presents itself in such a form that it would suit Epicureanism even better, supporting thus the association with Atticus in the next sentence. In fact, rather than with too specific philosophical identifications, the sentence should be interpreted as a nostalgic recalling of the period, so well evoked at the beginning of Book 5 of *De Finibus*, where Cicero and Atticus attended the philosophical schools in Athens, the one attending the classes of Antiochus and the other those of Phaedrus.

A New Theory of Otium*: The* Pro Sestio

Before the two great theoretic works, the *De Oratore* and the *De Re Publica*, the *Pro Sestio*, delivered in March 56 B.C., constitutes a more in-depth line of thought about the ways of life than anything Cicero had written earlier. In contrast to the confused mythico-historical time of *De Inventione*, the *Pro Sestio* delineates a kind of eternity of the *Urbs* (*duo genera semper in hac civitate fuerunt*)[24] and distinguishes between two categories of political men: those who flatter an undifferentiated mass (*multitudo*) and those who are at the service of the *optimi*, a category defined on purpose in an extremely vague manner, since it covers the *principes consili publici* as well as freedmen, as long they were morally irreproachable people and with a salutary economic situation. Obviously, in such a text Cicero could not mention philosophers or amateurs of philosophy, a category sociologically far too small within the Roman society. But of course a man like Atticus entered in this definition of the *optimi*. Thus, if philosophy is never explicitly mentioned, philosophy is present and not only through the famous expression *otium cum dignitate*.

First, the politician is assigned a *propositum*, the term with which Cicero in the *De Finibus* translates the word *telos*.[25] This *propositum* is further said to be *optabile*, a term that appears also in the definition of *telos*. This *telos* can simply be the object of a contemplation (*intueri*) and of a strong aspiration (*volunt*), but it is not made to stay purely theoretic. We find in the idea that the *propositum* is carried out only through the action of those who act (*qui efficiunt*), an anticipation of the famous expression of *De Re Publica*: *virtus in usu sui tota posita est*.[26] The difference lies in that, in *De Re Publica*, *otium* is condemned as belonging to the philosophers who proclaim *in angulis*, principles that are merely verbal.[27] The *Pro Sestio*—if we set aside the violent attack against the Epicurean *otium* that Piso would be defending (*Sest*. 23)—defines, on the contrary, a double-leveled policy, as it is the case in Stoicism, *mutatis mutandis*, with Stoic double-leveled ethics: one level for the relative, with the *officium*, and one for the absolute, the *honestum*. Just as in Stoic ethics, what makes the difference is not a dual reality but rather the attitude toward one and the same reality, namely here, the *otium cum dignitate*.[28] All of the *optimi* wished for a peaceful society, one that would function according to hierarchy, but the best of the best are those who insure that this is carried out for the whole of society and not only for themselves. In addition, the expression *membra tueri*, used to designate what the *summi viri* must protect, appears in the Antiochian version of *oikeiōsis* in Book 5 of *De Finibus*.[29]

The Stoic idea that the moral qualities of an individual cannot be dissociated from the preservation of the organism, both individual and collective, is therefore very much present in this text of rhetorical character. The comparison with Stoicism nevertheless has its limits. Cicero's line of argument avoids here the main criticism made of the Stoics, namely that of determining a goal that in itself was not good but the choosing of which was in conformity with the good.[30]

In order to avoid the objection of circularity, the Stoics had developed complex strategies (which do not need to be examined in detail here). On the contrary, for Cicero, it is obvious that the *otium cum dignitate* is to be sought because it constitutes a good in itself. The forces involved in revolutionary agitation (*motus conversionesque rei publicae*, in *Sest.* 99) are not, according to him, forces of change but rather forces of death that would not hesitate to bring about a universal conflagration: *communi incendio malint quam suo deflagrare*. By assimilating the *optimates* to survival in the dignity of society and the *populares* to the violent destruction of that society, Cicero does not make any room for choice, since it is nature that dictates that choice. For the Stoics, the living being at birth seeks life instinctively, but in moral life, that life is but a preferable indifferent. The political considerations Cicero has concerning society are a mixture of these two aspects.

Probing further into the causes of the commitment either to the side of the *populares* or to the side of the *optimates*, we find a certain number of philosophical themes. The *populares* are to the social body what passion is to the individual. At least two of the Stoic passions are mentioned with regard to them: fear (*propter metum poenae*) and desire (in the form of the desire of money). Most of all though, at least as far as a certain number of them is concerned, they represent *furor insitus*, madness deeply settled in the soul, which shall be theorized over in the *Tusculans* (*Tusc.* 4.26–27).

The *optimates*, who engage in the fight for the *otium cum dignitate* and who take upon themselves the *voluntas populi* (*Sest.* 122) in order to carry it out, do so in the name of the social *oikeiōsis* in the revised Ciceronian version but also in the name of a rational recompense, since they are rewarded by honors and glory, a theme Cicero develops in the *De Officiis* and the *De Gloria*. Not only must we participate in the fight for the *otium cum dignitate*, but it is also in our interest to do so. It is the rhetorico-political version of the identification between the *honestum* and the *utile*, argued for notably in *De Officiis*. The fight between the two groups, between the *popularis cupiditas* and the *consilium principium*, is the social expression of the confrontation between reason and desire (*Sest.* 104). But never does Cicero put forward a choice that would be comparable to Hercules' choice, placed between vice and virtue. Cicero prefers to turn the political categories of *populares* and *optimates* into ontological categories.

It does not seem that the *De Oratore* and *Re Publica* actually modify the themes developed in the *Pro Sestio*. For sure, in the second dialogue Scipio undermines in very strong terms the conception of glory, which is defended in the discourse: "Never has a man's reputation lasted very long; it gets buried once those who had made it die, and it fades out as the next generation forgets it" (*Rep.* 6.25). However, the affirmation that a virtuous action should be performed for itself and not for the sake of fame, together with the suggestion to scorn the *humana* and to contemplate the *caelestia*, does not in the least imply an evolution toward theoretic life (*Rep.* 6.20). The way that leads to the sky is not the way of philosophy but rather the way forged by political action. Cicero says that this is the vastest of fields of action for the practice of the virtues. And yet the ideal remains that of adding to an exceptional nature and to brilliant political actions the *adventicia doctrina*, which comes from Socrates (*Rep.* 3.6). This time, true enough, the choice is set out in the form of a *bivium*, and the use of the potential subjunctive (*sin sit diligenda*) shows there is no *a priori* exclusion. But nothing is left to uncertainty: *haec civilis laudabilior certe est et inlustrior* (*Rep.* 3.6).

Philosophy in the Public Service

Everyone knows that the *otium honestum* will impose itself on Cicero as an alternative not to political life, from which he was at that point removed, but rather to *desidia*, to which Caesar's dictatorship could have forced him.[31] Everything or almost everything has been said about his wish to give Rome a great philosophical literature, the illusion of being able, in spite of everything, to play a role in the *res publica* thanks to his political reasoning (*Fam.* 9.2.5) or even thanks to an influence on Caesar, as the *Pro Marcello* shows. His recognition of the new situation goes together with his justifying the *otium litteratum*. This takes up the theme of legitimate cultural leisure after having led an existence intensely devoted to the *res publica*. He knew only too well that the *dignitas* that came with this *otium* was but apparent and depended merely on the benevolence of Caesar. We will examine the resurfacing of the temptation to be Philo, that is, not only to be a philosopher but also a teacher of philosophy. We shall distinguish on this point three cases: the first case concerns the *Academica*, the *De Finibus*, the *De Natura Deorum*, and the *De Divinatione*; the second case is the case of the *Tusculans*, and finally the third, that of the *De Fato*.

In the first group of works, Cicero, while declaring his passion for philosophy and his wish to create a philosophy in the Latin language, cannot for obvious reasons of *decus* give a representation of his authority in his dialogues. He is, as it were, an amateur more enlightened than others who holds discussions with his friends with equal or almost equal dignity. This did not go without consequences for the very economy of the dialogue: the universal suspension of assent was in perfect harmony with the social constraint according to which, in such discussions, there should be neither a winner nor a loser. When the participants of the *Lucullus* or the *De Natura Deorum*—to name but the two most clear examples in my judgment—part company, there is no disgrace on any side, no one is considered as the keeper of truth, and there are only criss-crossed preferences. In the *proemia* to these books, Cicero tries to show the continuity between his public life and *otium*, since in both cases he acts in the interest of the *res publica*. Philosophical authority is addressed to the whole of the Roman people, and for this reason we remain, from a certain point of view, in the domain of public activity.

The Tusculans

The *Tusculans* indicate the first attempt to come out of this situation. In this work, through a certain number of more or less distinct signs, Cicero shows that he takes on his function as a teacher not abstractly, in relation to the whole of the Roman people, but in the sense of the Greek academic institution. This is made manifest by his using the expression *scholas Graecorum more* (1.7), by his use of the verb *ambulo*, which obviously refers to the space of the *peripatos* of the Greek schools,[32] and most of all by the fact that the second dialogue is placed under the patronage of Philo of Larissa, of whom Cicero tells us that he had, at different moments of the day, given classes of philosophy and rhetoric. This staging of the villa of Tusculum as a Roman school of philosophy implied nevertheless a constraint, namely, that the interlocutor be anonymous, since it would have been mortifying to present one of the *familiares* from the villa as a mere *discipulus* of Cicero, listening to long demonstration and being allowed to intervene only very briefly. In the *Disputationes*, Cicero presents himself thus as the scholarch of a school the students of which have been made anonymous, precisely because it was impossible to carry out completely a process that made the metaphor of the lawsuit—so very present in the preceding dialogues—give up its place to a reality that originally was absent from his own world: the philosophical school. It is also in the *prooemium* to Book 2 of this work that the famous verse from Ennius's *Neoptolemus*—saying that he would like to do some philosophy but not much, since he did not wish to devote himself entirely to it—is contradicted by Cicero in favor of a total commitment to philosophy.[33]

Let us mention an interesting variant reading that is rather revealing of Cicero's state of mind:

- De Or. 2.156: *ac sic decrevi philosophari potius, ut Neoptolemus apud Ennium, nam omnino non placet.*
- Rep. 1.30: *ait philosophari velle sed paucis; nam omnino non placere.*
- Tusc. 2.1: *philosophari sibi ait necesse, sed paucis; nam omnino non placere.*

In the first two quotations, the verbs *decrevi* and *velle* are, in a certain sense, counterbalanced by *omnino non* and *paucis*. In the second *Tusculan*, the *necesse* of Neoptolemus is transferred onto Cicero himself (*necesse mihi quidem esse arbitror philosophari*), which allows him to avoid the use of a verb expressing volition. Through this sort of *lapsus calami*, philosophical life is first a constraint for which it was possible subsequently to find certain justifications.

De Fato *as Test Case*

The *De Fato* seems to make for a middle course between the two preceding situations. As in the dialogues of the first group, Cicero is having a discussion with a high-placed personality of Roman politics, and the discussion is placed under the auspices of the Academy. The main difference, emphasised by the author himself, lies in the fact that the *disputatio in utramque partem* is replaced by the method of *contra propositum disserere*, already used in the *Tusculans*. If we were to believe Cicero, this change of method would be due only to a *casus*, probably the chance arrival of Hirtius at his home who had, so to speak, asked Cicero for some lessons in philosophy. To place a book about destiny under the sign of *casus* was already a veiled reference, announcing the philosophical hue as it were, namely, that human actions are not controlled by destiny. But it seems to us that we must go further in the analysis in order to understand what is at stake in the confrontation of these two characters. In comparison to the very controlled boldness of the *Tusculans*, *De Fato* seems to present a sort of intermediary solution. Cicero takes it upon himself to be the master; the reference to Philo of Larissa, however implicit, is nonetheless obvious. The disciple, this time given a name, Hirtius, gives signs of having attended rhetoric classes, but then he is precisely a private disciple, and this is not an institutional school (*Fam.* 9.16.7). In other words, the situation of master-disciple is the result of a mutual agreement between the two characters and not an institutionalization of the dialogue. It will take until the Sextii for the Romans to carry through the process undertook by Cicero and for them to dare to open a real philosophical school.[34]

The choice of Hirtius, *consul designatus*, together with Pansa for the year 43 B.C., must now be explained. On reading the many references to Hirtius in the correspondence, he appears—leaving aside the probably overdone praise given to him in the seventh *Philippic*[35]—as someone Cicero tries, though without great expectations, to steer to his own side. In May 44 B.C. he writes to Atticus: "Cassius, as for him, asks me, implores me insistently to make out of Hirtius the best possible of citizens. Is he sound of mind? A colorist (cannot whiten) coal."[36] In the correspondence, the effort consisting in making Hirtius behave differently from his natural way of behaving or from his past habits is presented as an undertaking that is both necessary and risky: "They want me to make Hirtius better; I am trying to and he is very good when he speaks, but he lives with Balbus who is also very good when he speaks."[37]

Taking these elements into account, the *De Fato* is anything but a treatise detached from its times. It is written at a time when the situation seems particularly uncertain: *quid futurum sit plane nescio*, Cicero will write shortly after. In such a confused situation, the attitude of the consuls who will hold office from 43 B.C. is an essential element. Pansa seems to have been won over to the side of the murderers of Caesar, but Hirtius hesitates. What makes an individual act this way or that at a given moment? What is the power of his will? Such are the questions at the center of the *De Fato*. I have tried to show, with regard to the *Academica*,[38] that the philosophical discourse worked in it as a metapolitical text with respect to the situation created by Caesar's dictatorship. It is no different in the *De Fato*: the situation has changed but not the aims of the philosophical discourse, which leads the reader to reflect on themes that, in the correspondence or in discourses, were immediately expressed. The philosophical dialogue transfers into the domain of conceptual expression the following question: "Can a human nature that is black as coal whiten?" The correspondence answers "no" with regard to the particular case of Hirtius, whereas the *De Fato*, referring to Carneades, insists on the utter autonomy of the will. This concept, the importance of which we have seen throughout Cicero's considerations about the choices of life, finds thus at the end of Cicero's career an argument in the direction of the greatest freedom, yet without throwing much light on its relation to the intellect. Better than the *Tusculans*, the *De Fato* shows how difficult it was for him to isolate his philosophical activity from political issues. In any case, it was easier for him to emphasize the autonomy of will than to give a clear account of the use he made of it.

The results of this overview are disparate. Cicero gave himself all the conceptual means to think out a choice he never really wanted to make. Most probably the fascination that the great names of the Roman past held for him, the firm belief that he had an important role to play in the survival of the *res publica*, and his passion for honors all together prevented him from detaching himself from the public life whose negative aspects he otherwise saw with great lucidity. From this point of view, it is his correspondence that enabled him freely to express that part of himself that could not be put in the foreground—if only when the circumstances made political life impossible—and that presumably enabled him to lessen the contradiction. The fact that—in spite of all the hardships, the disappointments, and the consciousness of his ability to serve the *res publica* in giving it a philosophy in Latin—he still can have written, in the beginning of the *De Officiis*: "It is against duty that one's studies should divert one from the management of public affairs,"[39] goes to show, if it still were necessary to show, that the profound belief in the superiority of practical life over a purely theoretical life never really left him.

NOTES

1. Kretschmar, *Otium, studia litterarum*; Grilli, *Il problema della vita contemplativa*; Barwick, *Das rednerische Bildungsideal Ciceros*; André, *L'otium dans la vie morale*; Boyancé, "Cicéron et la vie contemplative"; Müller, "Das Problem Theorie-Praxis."
2. André, *L'otium dans la vie morale*, 279–334.
3. Zucchelli, "L'independenza di Lucilio."
4. *Att.* 1.17, 5: *neque ego inter me atque te quicquam interesse umquam duxi praeter voluntatem institutae vitae, quod me ambitio quaedam ad honorum studium, te autem alia minime reprehendenda ratio ad honestum otium duxit.*
5. *Att.* 1.17, 1: *magna mihi varietas voluntatis et dissimilitudo opinionis ac iudicii Q. fratris, mei demonstrata est ex litteris tuis.*
6. *Att.* 1.17.7: *ut quod, una non estis, non dissensione ac discidio vestro sed voluntate ac iudicio tuo factum esse videatur.*
7. *Inv.* 1.3, 24, 55, 56, 70, 92, 102; 2.4, 24, 35, 52, 64, 67, 90, 92, 94, 96, 97, 99, 101, 105, 107, 137, 139, 140, 143, 145, 161, 163, 166.
8. *Brut.* 306: *totum ei me tradidi, admirabili quodam ad philosophiam studio concitatus, in quo hoc etiam commorabar attentius—etsi rerum ipsarum varietas et magnitudo summa me delectatione retinebat—quod tamen sublata iam esse in perpetuum ratio iudiciorum videbatur.* See also Brittain, *Philo of Larissa*, 296–343.
9. Robinson, *Eight Great Lives*, 5.
10. *De Or.* 3.94. See the commentary of A.D. Leeman in Leeman, Pinkster, and Wisse, *Cicero*, De oratore libri III, 304–6.
11. *Nat. D.* 1.6–7: *Nos autem nec subito coepimus philosophari nec mediocrem a primo tempore aetatis in eo studio operam curamque consumpsimus et, cum minime videbamur, tum maxime philosophabamur, quod et orationes declarant refertae philosophorum sententiis et doctissimorum hominum familiaritates, quibus semper domus nostra floruit, et principes illi Diodotus, Philo, Antiochus, Posidonius, a quibus instituti sumus. Et si omnia phlosophiae praecepta referuntur, ad vitam, arbitramur nos et publicis et privatis in rebus ea praestitisse, quae ratio et doctrina praescripserit.*

12. On this text, see Barwick, "Die Vorrede zum zweiten Buch"; Giuffrida, "I due proemi del *De inventione*"; Alfonsi, "Dal proemio del *De inventione*"; von Albrecht, "Cicéron : Theorie rhétorique et pratique oratoire"; Schmitz, "Rhetorik in Praxis und Theorie,"; Lévy, "Le mythe de la naissance."

13. Achard, *Cicéron: De l'Invention*, 5–10.

14. *Inv.* 1.3: *Ac mihi quidem hoc nec tacita videtur nec inops dicendi sapientia perficere potuisse, ut homines a consuetudine subito converteret et ad diversas rationes vitae traduceret. Age vero, urbibus constitutis, ut fidem colere et iustitiam retinere discerent et aliis parere sua voluntate consuescerent ac non modo labores excipiendos communis commodi causa, sed etiam vitam amittendam existimarent, qui tandem fieri potuit, nisi homines ea quae ratione invenissent eloquentia persuadere potuissent?*

15. *Inv.* 1.5: *Nam hinc ad rem publicam plurima commoda veniunt, si moderatrix omnium rerum praesto est sapientia: hinc ad ipsos, qui eam adepti sunt, laus, honos, dignitas, confluit.*

16. *Arch.* 15. On this writing, and especially on glory as a reward of political action, see Narducci, *Cicerone e l'eloquenza romana*, 3–18.

17. *Mur.* 55: *Nam cum saepe antea, iudices, et ex aliorum miseriis et ex meis curis laboribusque cotidianis fortunatos eos homines iudicarem qui, remoti a studiis ambitionis, otium ac tranquillitatem vitae secuti sunt.* "Oratorical trick" is the phrase of Joly, *Le theme des genres*, 159.

18. *Sull.* 26: *Ego, tantis a me beneficiis in re publica positis, si nullum aliud mihi praemium ab senatu populoque Romano nisi honestum otium, quis non concederet. . . . Quid si hoc non postulo? . . . si voluntas mea, si industria, si domus, si animus, si aures patent omnibus.*

19. André affirms, *L'otium dans la vie morale*, 295: "la volonté affichée n'aura été qu'une velléité." But Cicero, very precise in the choice of words, did not use *voluntas*!

20. *Att.* 2.5.2: *Vide levitatem meam. Sed quid ego haec, quae cupio deponere et toto animo atque omni cura* φιλοσοφεῖν? *Sic, inquam, in animo est; vellem ab initio, nunc vero, quoniam quae putavi esse praeclara, expertus sum quam essent inania, cum omnibus Musis rationem habere cogito.* The manuscripts give *videle evit-*, or *videte civit-*, or *videte vitam*. In any case, it is interesting to note how the *vellem* is reduced to a simple *cogito* at the end of the sentence.

21. Muret, *Opera Omnia*, t. III, 106.

22. *CD* 19.3: *ex tribus porro illis vitae generibus, otioso, actuoso et quod ex utroque compositum est, hoc tertium sibi placere adseuerat. Haec sensisse ac docuisse Academicos veteres Varro adserit, auctore Antiocho, magistro Ciceronis et suo.* See on this point, Müller, "Βίος Θεωρητικός bei Antiochus von Askalon und Cicero." There is a seeming difference between the testimonies of Augustine and Cicero on Antiochus; see Bénatouïl, "Le débat entre stoïcisme et platonisme."

23. *Att.* 2.16.3: *Nunc prorsus hoc statui, ut quoniam tanta controversia est Dicaearcho familiari tuo cum Theophrasto amico meo, ut ille tuus* τόν πρακτικὸν

βίον *longe omnibus anteponat, hic autem* τόν θεορητικόν, *utrique a me mos gestus esse videatur. Puto enim me Dicaearcho adfatim satis fecisse; respicio nunc ad hanc familiam quae mihi non modo ut requiescam permittit, sed reprehendit quia non semper quierim. Quare incumbamus, o noster Tite, ad illa praeclara studia et eo unde discedere non oportuit aliquando revertamur.*

24. *Sest.* 96: *Duo genera semper in hac civitate fuerunt eorum qui versari in re publica atque in ea se excellentius studuerunt; quibus ex generibus alteri se popularis, alteri optumates et haberi et esse voluerunt.*

25. *Fin.* 3.22. We find also *conservatis . . . fundamenta ac membra*, in *Sest.* 99. The verb *conservare* is used to express the *oikeiōsis* in *Fin.* 4.41. On *oikeiōsis*, see Radice, *Oikeiōsis*.

26. *Rep.* 1.2: *Nec vero habere virtutem satis est quasi artem aliquam, nisi utare; etsi ars quidem, cum ea non utare, scientia tamen ipsa teneri potest, virtus in usu sui tota posita est.*

27. Ibid.: *usus autem eius est maximus civitatis gubernatio et earum ipsarum rerum quas isti in angulis personant reapse non oratione perfectio.*

28. On this expression and its Aristotelian nuances, see Boyancé, "*Cum Dignitate Otium*," and Lacey, "Cicero, *Pro Sestio*."

29. *Fin.* 5.40: *ut sensus quoque suos eorumque omnem appetitum et si qua sint adiuncta ei membra tueatur.*

30. See Long, "Carneades and the Stoic Telos," and Soreth, "Die zweite Telosformel des Antipater von Tarsos."

31. *Brutus* 9: *in portum non inertiae neque desidiae, sed oti moderati atque honesti.*

32. *Sedens aut ambulans*, and *ambulantibus* in *Tusc.* 2.10. On these *disputationes*, see Lévy, "L'âme et le moi dans les *Tusculanes*."

33. *Tusc.* 2.1: *Ego autem, Brute, necesse mihi quidem esse arbitror philosophari (nam quid possum, praesertim nihil agens, agere melius?), sed non paucis ut ille.*

34. On the Sextii, see Lana, "La scuola dei Sestii."

35. *Phil.* 7.12.2: *Sed animi viris corporis infirmitas non retardavit.*

36. *Att.* 15.5.1: *Cassius vero vehementer orat ac petit ut Hirtium quam optimum faciam. Sanum putas?* ὁ γναφεὺς ἄνδρακας.

37. *Att.* 14.20.4: *Quod Hirtium per me meliorem fieri volunt, do equidem operam et ille optime loquitur, sed vivit habitatque cum Balbo, qui item bene loquitur.*

38. Lévy, *Cicero Academicus.*

39. *Off.* 1.19: *cuius studio a rebus gerendis abduci contra officium est.*

4

Cicero's *Constantia* in Theory and Practice

CATHERINE TRACY

Cicero's interest in philosophy was both theoretical and practical. He wrote extensively on the philosophical schools of his day and also related his own practical circumstances to the philosophical views that he held.[1] The extent to which his theoretical philosophical affiliations affected his practical and political behavior is a subject that interested Cicero himself, as it has also interested many of his critics and admirers. Cicero often argued, in particular, that he preferred the freedom of thought allowed by the anti-dogmatic skepticism of Philo of Larissa's Academy to such philosophies as Epicureanism and Stoicism.[2] This skepticism allowed the weighing of the relative merits of any course of action without obedience to a dogmatic set of principles, and the making of decisions based on what seemed, according to the available evidence, to be most probably true. The discovery of new evidence could, therefore, cause one to change one's mind and behave in a manner that contradicted the previous decision.

Cicero often claimed to follow this skeptical approach. But in practice Cicero was guided by his determination to justify his earlier decisions and actions. Regardless of his theoretical philosophical freedom, Cicero the politician considered that *constantia*, which he generally uses to mean "firmness" or "consistency," was essential to his political and public appeal. Public statements that he may originally have made in response to specific exigencies he later tried not to contradict, even when circumstances or context had changed. This may have been a pragmatic response to the demands of his electorate, who would not support a vacillating and unreliable magistrate, but Cicero's concern to achieve *constantia* was more than just pragmatic. His correspondence, combined with references in his speeches and treatises, show that the achievement of *constantia* became a guiding moral and philosophical principle for him that overrode his theoretical belief in skepticism.

The extent to which Cicero was influenced by the desire to appear consistent is best seen in the conflicting demands of his populist and elite audiences: Cicero had to please both, and his efforts to do so without too obviously contradicting himself show the value he laid on public *constantia*. More direct evidence of Cicero's concern with *constantia* is shown in the numerous references in Cicero's correspondence, especially in his letters to Atticus, to his anxiety on the subject: Cicero's desire to appear consistent, though often unattained, frequently influenced his actions despite Atticus's more cautious advice. Cicero's stated adherence to the skeptical philosophical stance—that inconsistency might be justified if changed circumstances warranted it—was, in fact, a veneer that imperfectly covered Cicero's more practical and entrenched belief: that the appearance of public consistency was necessary for a *homo novus* to succeed in politics.

Cicero's Populism

It is sometimes assumed that Cicero's more populist statements were expressed for purely pragmatic electoral reasons, since they seem, in sentiment at least, to contradict his attempts in other contexts to fit himself into the inner circle of the ruling class. But his populist rhetoric, though clearly required by the context of the *contio*, should not be dismissed as irrelevant to the rest of Cicero's career. Indeed, a comparison of Cicero's populism with statements from more elite contexts shows that Cicero did not freely contradict himself. If Cicero used populist rhetoric for immediate pragmatic ends, he did not subsequently disregard what he had said just because the context had changed. This was a society, after all, in which verbal contracts were binding, especially when there were witnesses to prove the contract.[3] The statements that Cicero made in *contio* speeches that verbally raised the *populus* up to supreme authority in the state were not easily said and then easily forgotten—at least not by Cicero.

Cicero's speeches *De Lege Agraria* 2 and 3 are good examples of this sort of populist language. These speeches, addressed to crowds of ordinary Romans on the subject of agrarian reform, have been described as Cicero's worst descent into insincerity. Cicero is against agrarian reform (we know this from his letters as well as from these speeches), and most people assume that the *populus* should have been in favor of it; but Cicero persuades his audience to dismiss the bill while giving the crowd clear assurances of their wisdom and authority. Commentaries on Cicero's *De Lege Agraria* have tended to describe Cicero's popular stance as duplicitous: E.J. Jonkers's opinion, for example, is that "Cicero misleads the people. True, he did say in the senate that he wished to be a *popularis* consul, but there he meant this word to be interpreted in a sense pleasing to the senate."[4]

Nicolet assumes that Rullus's agrarian bill risked seriously embarrassing Cicero, since he would be compelled to show himself to the *populus* as one who was opposed to the people's real interests.[5] If Rullus's bill was intended as a trap for Cicero, his populist rhetoric proves that he was not so easily caught.[6] He gives the people, in return for their voting down the bill, a public statement of, and commitment to, their mastery of the republic, the empire, and their consul. Cicero repeatedly states that this agrarian bill will enslave the *populus Romanus* by setting up the decemvirs—the board of governors who were to oversee the land redistribution—as masters over them.[7] He has always been, and will always be, a consul *popularis*, or so he claims (2.7; 2.9).

Cicero manipulated the meaning of *popularis* (usually translated as "populist") so that he could use it both in the *contio* and in the senate and end up by pleasing both audiences.[8] Cicero's word-play does not, however, imply that the word *popularis* had no meaning; rather, the reverse is true. It is clear from Cicero's critical comments that he could still use *popularis* with a negative connotation in the senate as seen, for example, in his arguments for Caesar's continued command in Gaul when he suggests that the *popularis* menace must be bribed to prefer senatorial praise (*Prov. Cons.* 38). Cicero's self-designation as *popularis* was potentially risky because of the very fact that he used it as a criticism of others; he makes it clear that *popularis* is a red flag for the senate, unless he redefines the word appropriately. His self-description as a *popularis* before the *multitudo* in this speech on the agrarian law is therefore an important statement of his position and his relationship with the crowd.

This sort of public commitment to the popular cause appears in all of Cicero's extant *contio* speeches.[9] His speech on the Manilian law, his first *contio* speech, begins with his flattering (though possibly true) statement that the crowded forum, which he had always deemed the most impressive location for action and the most distinguished for speaking (*Leg. Man.* 1) has nevertheless been closed to his talents due to an early devised plan of his not to address the crowd until his rhetorical talents were honed and worthy of such an audience.

Similar compliments appear in the *In Catilinam* 2, when Cicero claims that he is fundamentally committed to the plight of the urban poor: "I must either live with [the urban poor whom he is addressing] or die for them" (2.27), managing cleverly to contrast himself with Catiline by describing this villain as simultaneously one of "the have-nots eager to take from those who have, and [one of] those who have so much that they can afford luxuriant lifestyles inaccessible to the average member of the urban plebs," as Habinek notes.[10]

In Cicero's speech *Post Reditum ad Populum*,[11] he depicts the hierarchy of Roman politics with the *populus* firmly at the top, and himself as the people's servant who deserves to suffer "eternal retribution if" he says, "I had ever put my own plans before your [the *populus*'s] welfare" (1). Even in his last extant *contio* speech, the sixth *Philippic*, Cicero tells his audience that he owes everything to them in return for their having raised him, a *homo novus*, to every honor, and that he is appropriately grateful (6.17).

Fulsome praise of the *populus Romanus* appears also in some of Cicero's forensic speeches which, it is likely, were attended by members of the urban *populus* and thus needed to be aimed at a larger audience than just the jury. Cicero's fragmentary speech *Pro Cornelio de maiestate*, given in 65, is a particularly good example of this, since in this speech Cicero recites approvingly all the increases in popular power that had been gained within historical memory, including "the Porcian law, origin of rightful freedom; the Cassian law, by which the legality and authority of ballots was established; the other Cassian law, which confirmed the judgments of the people" (78). Squires's commentary says that "the occasion [of Cornelius's trial] attracted a huge attendance"; hence Cicero's need to appeal to the ordinary members of the *populus*.[12] Usually these kinds of statements are dismissed as unimportant, inserted by Cicero into his popular speeches as a basic courtesy to his audience, but not meant seriously.[13] Nevertheless, Cicero made these statements and published them in their written version at some point following the speech. I discuss later Cicero's awareness that recording his speeches in written form committed him to certain public stances.

At this point, however, it is interesting to consider Cicero's discussion in *De Amicitia* 61 on the evils of using complimentary, but insincere, language—that is, flattery—for personal or political gain. It is through the mouthpiece of Laelius that Cicero makes these comments, but it is probable that the opinions are Cicero's own.[14] Admittedly he is talking about the *blanditia* (translated variously as "flattery," "compliments," or "charm") and *assentandum* (also translated as "flattery," but having the literal sense of "agreeing" or "saying 'yes'") of *cives*, which in this context refers to powerful men who may be able to provide political benefits.[15] With these powerful men, however, the use of flattery is, Laelius says, shameful. He acknowledges that *fama* and the *benevolentia* of one's fellow citizens ought not be neglected as a "weapon" (*telum*) for getting things done but that to achieve popularity by means of vain compliments and flattery is *turpe* (*Amic.* 61). What differentiates flattery from honest speech is that flattery is temporary (and, of course, untrue, though that is harder to prove). And flattery (*adulatio, blanditia, assentatio*) is, Laelius says later, "a vice belonging to those who are unreliable and deceitful, who would say anything for the sake of pleasing, and nothing for the sake of truth" (91).

For members of the Roman ruling class, such as Cicero, what might be immoral behavior toward a politically powerful *amicus* would not, necessarily, have been so toward the general populace. In a pair of letters that he wrote to Atticus in May or June of 46 (about two years prior to his publication of *De Amicitia*), Cicero claims that he does not use flattery. This is specifically with reference to Atticus, and Cicero implies that either he or Atticus might be capable of stooping to the flattery of someone less intimate.[16]

Although, as indicated earlier, Cicero deliberately obfuscates his various meanings of the word *popularis*, his overall use of the word sustains the idea that he considered pleasing the *populus Romanus* by empty compliments to be disreputable. In Cicero's speech in defense of Sestius, he embarks on a long discussion on what is meant by the terms *optimates* and *populares*, and though he ends up defining *populares* so that it can have a pro-senatorial (and hence meritorious) meaning, he makes it clear that the general and automatic assumption is that a *popularis* politician would ignore the will of the senate, the authority of the *boni*, and the established practices of the ancestors, and would aim solely at pleasing "the ignorant or impetuous multitude" (140). This is opposed to one of Cicero's initial definitions of the term *optimates*, which denotes deliberately unpopular politicians who, according to Cicero, "worried that they had said something wrong on the rare occasions when they received public applause" (105).

Cicero generally implies, therefore, that making complimentary but untrue statements to any audience for the sake of political gain is not something to which he would stoop. That Cicero made many complimentary statements to the Roman people might, therefore, have showed him up as hypocritical, unless he could claim the statements to have been true. A method by which Cicero might have avoided charges of flattery and pandering to the popular will could, therefore, have involved Cicero's showing, by his subsequent behavior, that his public statements had not been made lightly.

Cicero's Concern to be Consistent

This idea—that a reputation for *constantia* was politically important, and that Cicero tried not to belie previous public statements by contradictory speech or action—suggests that he tried to apply a practical solution for the particular handicap of a *homo novus*. For Cicero, however, *constantia* became more than just a useful political tactic. This section of this paper documents both Cicero's expressed concern to be seen to be consistent, and incidences of his attempts, whether successful or unsuccessful, to uphold previously expressed political or moral stances. The pressure that Cicero put on himself to maintain *constantia* suggests that it was a deeply held philosophical principle for him, and one that overrode his skeptical justifications for changing his mind.

Cicero may have made some of his more populist statements in order to gain immediate political power with the Roman *populus*, but his attempts not to contradict these statements later, and in different contexts, are examples of this desire to appear consistent. One topic that might have prompted contradictions between populist and elite rhetoric is that of the Gracchi, populist heroes, who were generally deemed by the elite to have been responsible for ending the unquestioned supremacy of the senate. Jean Béranger has argued that Cicero shows a surprising consistency in his attitude to this contentious topic despite differing audiences. Not that Cicero does not adapt each Gracchan reference to his setting, writes Béranger, but that regardless of the circumstances, Cicero maintains a stance of admiration for the brothers' qualities even if he also regrets some of their political actions.[17] What is significant with respect to Cicero's references to the Gracchi is how his opinion of especially Tiberius Gracchus's disloyalty (as Cicero saw it) to the republic was not hidden from popular audiences. While Cicero refers to the Gracchi frequently in speeches to the *populus*, he does not praise them in ways that contradict his less favorable Gracchan references to elite audiences.

The speech in defense of Gaius Rabirius (the uncle of Postumus) shows how Cicero could praise the Gracchi without contradicting his opinion, clearly expressed elsewhere, that both the Gracchi had been justly killed by the republic (a united one, as he implies). In this speech before the *populus*, Cicero manages to disparage his opponent Labienus by contrasting him with the far more admirable Gaius Gracchus, asking "how great a gulf do you then suppose to be fixed between you and him?" (*Rab. Post.* 14). Nevertheless, this praise of Gaius Gracchus is only explicitly explained as being due to his commendable devotion to his elder brother. Cicero applauds Gaius's *pietas, animus, consilium, opes, auctoritas,* and *eloquentia* without praising his policies. His praise of Tiberius Gracchus consists only in that he left such a great loss (*desiderium*) among the *populus Romanus*.

By contrast Cicero freely condemns the populist hero Saturninus, calling him *hostis populi Romani*. His job in delivering this speech is, of course, to defend one of Saturninus's murderers and the innocence of his client apparently needs to be supplemented by arguments that the crime, if he had committed it, would have been no crime in fact. Could Cicero afford to make this attack on a populist hero because his populist statements elsewhere, which he showed he would not contradict, gave him some credit with the *populus*? Or did the hierarchical voting procedure of the *comitia centuriata* (if indeed this was the speech's setting)[18] give Cicero more leeway for risking the anger of the *populus*? That some members of the audience were angry at his criticism of Saturninus is shown by Cicero's claim to be unmoved by it (18). At any rate, while Cicero is free in his condemnation of Saturninus, his careful praise of the Gracchi shows that, though he would play the Gracchan card to please his popular audience, he would not actually commit to an opinion he could not maintain to the senate.

This is further seen by comparison with the ways in which Cicero referred to the Gracchi when his audience was a select elite. While by no means necessarily expressing his true opinions, they show, at the least, the stance Cicero felt would be acceptable. They do not fundamentally differ from his pro-Gracchan comments to the *populus*. In his dialog *Brutus,* Cicero describes Gaius Gracchus as "a man of the most outstanding talent and passionate zeal, and well taught from boyhood," than whom no one "was more filled with such productive eloquence" (125). These compliments do not, of course, imply any liking for Gracchus's political activities. These are excused only as far as they show great *pietas* and grief at the death of his brother Tiberius. Tiberius Gracchus, on the other hand, has no such justification, and Cicero's references to him in the *Brutus* are far more critical, saving only that he admires his oratory for he wishes aloud that Tiberius had been as good at acting in the republic's interests as he was in speaking (103).

It is clear that there is some difference of emphasis in Cicero's Gracchan comments, depending on the intended audience. But it is also clear that Cicero does not usually contradict himself on the subject. That is, before the *populus* he praises Gaius Gracchus's talents as well as his devotion to his brother and shows his awareness of his popular appeal. His praise of Tiberius is simply that he was loved by the people. But he does not, in the *Pro Rabirio Perduellionis Reo*, praise the brothers' political acts. Therefore it is no contradiction for him to do the same to an elite audience, even though his lack of praise for their politics is there changed into actual criticism.

Cicero's reflections on the *leges tabellaria* show even more strongly that even if he adjusted the emphasis of certain populist statements when addressing an elite audience, he did not fundamentally contradict them. In *De Legibus* 3.33–39, Cicero confronts the issue of the secret ballot when he depicts himself, his brother Quintus and his friend Atticus discussing the best set of laws that they can envision for the republic. Cicero's modified approval of the secret ballot is contrasted with Quintus's dismay at the loss of power the secret ballot brings about for the upper classes. Cicero's response is a rather confusing qualification of the secret ballot, whereby it is secret from everyone except the few *optimates* who, Cicero implies, are automatically above bribery or intimidation. The fact that Cicero thinks, or claims to think, these incorruptibles are so easily identifiable shows either an unlikely naiveté or an attempt to please his aristocratic readership by an appearance of trustful admiration. Nevertheless, Cicero is defending the (modified) secrecy of the ballot against what was probably the standard aristocratic anti-ballot stance.[19] He explains that the secret ballot is necessary in order the keep the *populus* happy: "let the people have its ballot as a badge of liberty" (3.39) and "my law gives the appearance of liberty while keeping the authority of the respectable and eliminating an occasion for dispute" (3.39).

This defense of the ballot laws was not likely to have been as pleasing to the *populus* as his more vehement defense in the *Pro Cornelio* mentioned above, but the two statements are fundamentally similar. Quintus's initial response, on the other hand, to Marcus Cicero's argument that oral voting was best but unfortunately not practical suggests that the opinion that would have most pleased Cicero's intended (that is, a fairly elite) audience would have been a plain statement of opposition to secrecy in elections. He does not do this, however, perhaps because he genuinely believed that secret voting was a good thing (not improbable), but surely also because he had previously made public statements in favor of the ballot laws.

Cicero's treatise on *officia* forms another example of his apparent attempt to rationalize the political behavior that had brought him so much electoral success, and furthermore shows how Cicero's attempts to seem consistent were rooted in his practice of oratory. Speaking in his own voice with advice to his son, Cicero discusses how one should behave and what constitutes virtue. Virtue, in this treatise, tends to be the behavior expected of a wealthy elite that need not depend on trade or manual labor for survival (*Off.* 1.150). Yet despite this ideal of independence, Cicero does not despise the politician's attempts to appeal to the *multitudo* upon whom he depends for votes (2.31). In spite of his elite stance of anti-populism, Cicero had had to work very hard at gaining popular support. Now in this philosophical treatise he does not ignore or deny that he has craved (and still craves) popularity, but rather justifies it as consistent with the approach of a virtuous man.

His method of defending a man's desire to accrue popular support is that the true *populus* (to be distinguished from the false *populus* that causes all the trouble) is clear-sighted enough to evaluate correctly his genuine worth. Nevertheless, Cicero was keenly aware that an orator had to work at presenting a convincing image in order that even the *verus populus* might correctly identify him as worthy of election. Politicians, that is, have to act a part. Cicero's *De Oratore* repeatedly shows that the art of speaking involves acting a part that is not one's own, but Michelle Zerba argues that Cicero cannot really admit to the artificiality of the role.[20] References to the orator's practice of simulation are countered by Cicero's insistence (whether in his own character or not) that simulation nevertheless comes to be a reflection of the orator's real character. In the *De Officiis*, Cicero hints that the show he might have put on simply to cause the *populus* to believe that he was worth voting for becomes a reality because of having initially played a role. If this is a true insight into Cicero's political tactics, then he could not later contradict his earlier populist rhetoric, but, in order to show *constantia*, would have had to justify it within elite contexts as well.

Cicero's letters to Atticus give us the clearest insights into his anxiety over political and public self-presentation, and are particularly interesting when the concerns he discusses in letters relate to his political actions. Cicero refers repeatedly to the importance of *constantia*[21] both as regards his own and others' conduct. What he has publicly claimed to be important becomes a stance, he tells Atticus, he feels constrained to maintain.

When Cicero becomes governor of Cilicia in mid-51, for example, he writes frequently to Atticus how determined he is that his term should be exemplary for *iustitia, abstinentia,* and *clementia* (*Att.* 6.16.3). He writes with pride that he is keeping himself and his staff on so strict a budget that the Cilicians are put to no private or public expense on his account. He indeed succeeded so well in achieving a reputation for justice among the Cilicians that he had to sooth the wrath of the province's previous governor, Appius Claudius, who complained that he was made to look bad by contrast (*Att.* 6.1.2).

Early in his governorship Cicero states that he was behaving with such rectitude for the sake of his reputation, even if he may not have intentionally wished to tarnish his predecessor's. He writes to Atticus that he was only forbearing from the natural greed of a provincial governor for the sake of *fama* and *gloria*. At the beginning of his term as governor he wrote warning Atticus that his ανεξιαν (which, according to Shackleton Bailey, must have meant "abstinence" or "incorruptibility")[22] could only be maintained for a year, and that if, as Cicero was hoping Atticus could prevent, his governorship should be extended, he would likely be discovered after all as *turpis* (5.11.5). It is significant that by the middle of his term as governor Cicero writes to Atticus that his virtuous behavior gives him simple pleasure for its own sake, regardless of the *fama* it happens to be producing for him (6.20.6). The probability that Cicero's honorable behavior as governor of Cilicia was due initially to his desire to seem good does not preclude the truth of his later statement that he genuinely delighted in knowing himself to be virtuous.[23] It is, indeed, one of the arguments of this chapter that though the achievement of *constantia* began for Cicero as a pragmatic move, it came to hold a fundamental place in Cicero's motivations as a good in itself.

That Cicero chose his governorship as an occasion on which to display such exemplary behavior is particularly interesting when examined in the light of his Verrine speeches twenty years earlier. Then

Cicero took on the unpopular (unpopular, at least, with the senatorial class)[24] role of prosecutor and gave an impassioned account of the horrors of living under the rule of a corrupt and unjust governor like Verres. The amount of money Verres took from the wealthy provincials and the means he used to acquire it makes fascinating reading, but the fact that Cicero personally investigated Verres' crimes, and exposed and publicly deplored them, may have some relevance to Cicero's own behavior as Cilician governor. It is an example of Cicero wishing to and succeeding in behaving in a manner consistent with his publicly professed opinions. He wished to maintain Atticus's good opinion of himself, and also clearly wished to show himself as honorable to the world.[25]

Cicero made his concern to live up to his reputation even more explicit in other letters. Especially when his actions would be perceived by those who had heard him previously state certain principles, Cicero specifically adjusted his actions to suit his previous statements. In the Spring of 59, for example, Cicero has been thinking of going to the games at Antium because his daughter Tullia wished to go (*Att.* 2.8.2). However, he changes his mind, in spite of his fondness for Tullia, because of what people might say if they heard of his going. He has publicly defined himself as a serious man and thinks that going to the games will make him appear the opposite. "Please admire my consistency. It's not a good idea for me to watch the games at Antium. It would be somewhat unbecoming, when I'd like to avoid the suspicion of all extravagance, to appear openly as an absurd and self-indulgent tourist" (*Att.* 2.10).

At another point he confronts the contrast between personal safety and public consistency and writes that he thinks he has achieved both ends. "So measured is my whole approach" he boasts "that I display consistency (*constantia*) as regards the republic, while in my private affairs I use a certain care and caution" (*Att.* 1.19.8). Similarly he refers to the need he feels to show a consistent face to the world (when worrying about his alliance with Pompey): "for I shouldn't withdraw from my dignified position," he writes to Atticus (*Att.* 1.20.2).[26] That sometimes he did withdraw from his dignified position does not change the fact that he worried about the consequences of doing so. Cicero considered that inconsistency was both unprincipled and made him liable to criticism and ridicule.

A far more serious event shows again how constrained by his previous public statements Cicero felt himself to be. In the year 49 B.C., Cicero wrote frequently to Atticus about whether or not he ought to join Pompey in the war with Caesar. Then Cicero thought the safe decision was not to commit himself, since Caesar seemed far more likely to win. In a letter to Atticus written March 4th he writes that he is torn by the conflicting demands of caution and honor, and, though caution has so far prevented him from joining Pompey, the fear of what people would think of him for not acting in accordance with *officium* is a very real concern for him: "I'm in torment, and have been tormented for a long time, worrying about where my duty lies. Caution prompts me to remain here, but making the crossing is considered to be more honorable. Sometimes I would prefer that many should think me to have acted incautiously than for a few to think me to have acted dishonorably" (*Att.* 8.15.2).

The question of what people (in this case the *optimates* or *boni*) are saying of Cicero's indecision (or *cunctatio*, as he himself terms it, *Att.* 9.1.3) arises many times in the letters of this period. Though Cicero keeps pointing out that these supposedly respectable men in fact are selling themselves to Caesar (*Att.* 8.16.1) and are not themselves *boni* after all (*Att.* 9.1.2), it seems that Cicero's previous statements of dedication to the cause of Pompey—and his equating of Pompey with the safety of the republic—have made it very difficult for him to waver like this without giving rise to harsh criticism at the upper class *convivia* (*Att.* 9.1.3).

His letters to Atticus from 49 are what particularly expose Cicero's concern to maintain an appearance of *constantia* in his relationship with Pompey. It is not really a genuine sense of loyalty that torments Cicero, since Pompey has not always behaved in a way that would deserve loyalty from Cicero. Rather, it is Cicero's fear of what will be said about him that most motivates him in this instance. He does not always admit this: at one point Cicero tells Atticus that he has decided to play the good citizen and go to join Pompey, claims that his determination to do so is due entirely to his sense of obligation to Pompey, and says that he is influenced not at all by the opinions of the *boni* nor even of the *causa*, which has been badly and timidly conducted (*Att.* 9.1.4). Yet he returns repeatedly to the subject of what the *boni* are saying, and Shackleton Bailey's commentary argues that Cicero "knew that his obligation to Pompey was not in reality a very powerful argument, at least not in Atticus's eyes, and therefore puts it forward most emphatically when he is most averse to the course indicated."[27] Cicero, that is, was genuinely concerned with how his inactivity might look, and since these disapproving *boni* were themselves in Rome—not with Pompey—their expectation that Cicero should be more actively working for Pompey than they themselves implies that Cicero had set himself up as a more voluble supporter of Pompey than had they.

Cicero's position in the civil war posed an extraordinary difficulty for him. His vacillation about joining Pompey is no more to be despised than his appreciation of the dangers. His anxiety is only recognizable because he recognized it himself and tried honestly to deal with it.[28] Atticus's advice and Cicero's fears for his own safety worked to keep Cicero from committing to Pompey's side in the struggle. Yet the fear of what people would say about him, compounded with his own desire to appear consistent, continually prompted Cicero to disregard Atticus and caution. Cicero, thus, was influenced by his previous public commitment eventually to act on his stance of dedication to Pompey's and (as was usually claimed) the republic's cause. As he later asked the senate (in the context of Marcus Antonius's challenge to senatorial authority) "is anything more dishonorable to individuals and especially to the entire senate than inconsistency, irresponsibility, fickleness?" (*inconstantia, levitate, mobilite*, Phil. 7.9). Cicero wished to be politically and morally consistent in upholding his previously espoused republican principles even if it went against his personal safety.

Thus the letters to Atticus, which, of the Ciceronian corpus, bring us the closest to Cicero's personal thoughts,[29] show that Cicero was concerned with maintaining a reputation for consistency. Similarly, some of his speeches show that he assumed his public audiences, both senatorial and popular, also considered consistency to be important in a politician. His discussion of the same subject in his treatise *De Officiis*, however, adds a more complicated dimension to Cicero's interest in it. Despite Paul MacKendrick's identification of the Stoic Panaetius as Cicero's source for this discussion,[30] the subject was clearly one that appealed to Cicero for his own reasons. "Consistency (*aequabilitas*),"

Cicero says, "in one's whole life as well as in individual deeds" (*Off.* 1.111) must be considered essential. He continues by claiming that someone can achieve this *aequabilitas* only by being true to his own nature, rather than introducing discrepancies in behavior by trying to imitate others. This is an interesting statement of Cicero's. It goes beyond what is found in the letters and speeches (which simply show that consistency was important to Cicero) and gives a partial explanation for why Cicero might have had such an interest in maintaining a consistent appearance. Someone who seems to be consistent, the comment in *De Officiis* implies, must be displaying an honest reflection of his true character. Since Cicero rarely claims to fall short of his philosophical ideals, we must assume from this comment that Cicero would prefer, if possible, to claim that the various political stances he took throughout his career were true to his philosophical principles, and not merely temporary postures assumed in order to achieve an immediate end.

Constantia as a Pragmatic Political Tactic

Displaying a consistent front was a politically pragmatic tactic for a Roman politician. At least in Cicero's evaluation (and he was probably correct about it), Romans noticed when their politicians appeared merely to be imitating others, and thus displaying contradictory behavior, for the sake of temporary political gain. The public and senatorial trust would tend, therefore, to be transferred to a politician whose consistent actions seemed to reflect his true character, since it would thus seem more possible to estimate that politician's future behavior. A Roman politician, after all, was not elected for any campaign promises he might make in the modern sense. He was not elected, that is to say, in order to accomplish specific political goals. Rather, he was elected because he seemed to be the kind of person who, by his very nature, would be useful to the electorate. The *Commentariolum Petitionis*, a treatise on seeking office written for Cicero likely by his brother, suggests that a candidate would try to avoid making specific political statements during a campaign,[31] and that a consul would be elected because he appeared to be useful, generous, and reliable.

Cicero's stance for *constantia* can, therefore, be seen as purely strategic, and indeed Cicero implies this at various times. One such example appears in his speech in defense of P. Cornelius Sulla (relative of the dictator), where he attempts to explain why he, who had acted so forcefully against the Catilinarian conspiracy, is now defending someone allegedly connected with the affair. He makes the interesting statement that if his original stance as defender of the republic against the dangerous Catiline had been a result of chance political circumstances (which he naturally denies), he would not now allow the fortuitous nature of such a success to be publicly known by taking an opposite stance: "Wouldn't I be mad to act in such a way now that would make the actions I took for all our safety seem to have been done more by chance and good luck than by virtue and good planning?" (*Sull.* 83).

More specific references to the seeming artificiality of Cicero's political roles appear in *De Officiis* (written in 44) and in *De Oratore* (written in 55). In *De Officiis* Cicero makes the comparison between the politician's choice of behavior to the actor's choice of role, but by stating that even the actor cannot act a part foreign to his nature he rescues the orator from the charge of artificiality. "Each man should recognize his own good and bad qualities" (*Off.* 1.114), he argues, so that, as an actor avoids the types of roles he knows he cannot play well, the good man should try to select a *res* (which here seems to imply a career path, or even a public persona) in life to which his qualities best suit him. In this very practical approach to ruling Cicero may again have been reflecting the ideas of the Stoic philosopher Panaetius.[32] John Dugan describes Cicero's "model for the self" as "consisting of a series of personae or 'masks,'" which, interestingly, suggests the idea of *imagines* set up by Cicero for Cicero to live up to.[33]

The notion of role-playing is only gently hinted in the first book of *De Officiis*, but it is more strongly implied in the second book. Cicero recalls a saying of Socrates, observing that as "Socrates used so admirably to say, the closest—and, as it were, the quick route—to glory is to be if possible what you would like to be thought to be" (2.43). Glory, Cicero argues, will be short-lived if a man tries to win it merely by *simulatio, inani ostentatio* and by lying words and facial expressions. So those words and facial expressions must become real.

Though Cicero implies that acting the role of a virtuous man is impossible unless the virtue is genuine, it is clear that he assumes the act can often precede, or temporarily substitute for, the reality.

Narducci notes that Cicero's complaint to Atticus, in a letter of 20 January 60 B.C., shows that Cicero normally felt compelled to hide his true self from others, Atticus being the only person to whom he could be unguarded.[34] But he is not really, as Narducci claims, longing for a life free from pretense; rather he is acknowledging the need for one relationship that is outside the political game. Within the political sphere Cicero argues for the need to create, and then to uphold a consistent public persona. "The most important thing is that we be the men we would like to be thought to be" Cicero states, although "certain maxims must be laid down so that we may most easily seem to be what we actually are" (*Off.* 2.44).

In *De Oratore* the character Antonius says that the emotion and manner of speaking should be such that "the speech, as it were, may express the character of the speaker" (*ut quasi mores oratoris effingat oratio*, 2.184). The verb *effingere* literally means "to form or fashion," and it is tempting to interpret Antonius's remarks as meaning that the giving of the speech helps to fashion the character of the orator. "The notion," John Dugan has argued, "that Cicero's self is the consequence of his speeches dovetails with the essential equivalence in Roman thought between a speaker's words and his self—*talis oratio, qualis vita*."[35]

These passages certainly suggest that Cicero theoretically viewed his role as an orator as artificially put on for the purposes of political gain. Michele Zerba argues precisely this, describing Cicero as "more Machiavellian than Machiavelli, for the author of *The Prince* and the *Discourses* is not a deceiver at second remove."[36] Cicero, she argues, shows in *De Oratore* that he is aware of the fraud involved in acquiring and exercising power, but still attempts to conceal that awareness by claiming that he and other admired orators pretend to be good men, but also are good men. While it is true that Cicero sometimes depicts himself as deceptive in this way, his opinions elsewhere suggest that he was himself unwilling to accept an orator's role that entailed artificiality and temporary postures. If Cicero was "a deceiver at second remove," he was also deceiving himself. Especially when taken in conjunction with Cicero's wish of acting in accordance with his reputation, it is more plausible that, if his political persona was a role that he put on in order to satisfy his ambition, he did not consider it likely or desirable that he should ever put off that role. Furthermore, there is little evidence that Cicero had as much control over his own decision-making as he might sometimes claim.

Constantia as Cicero's Philosophical Belief

For Cicero, indeed, the concern to play a consistent role went beyond the merely pragmatic. His response to the first real blow to his political career shows that he sincerely believed that, had he consistently behaved in accordance with a strict code of behavior, he could have prevented his exile. Exile came as a bitter blow to him. His letters of the time show that he found life away from Rome, and especially from the Roman political scene, nearly unendurable.[37] He naturally blames Clodius, the instigator of the *interdictio aquae et ignis* (against anyone who had unlawfully put Roman citizens to death) and eventually he levels blame at Pompey and others whose compliance had failed to prevent his exile. "My rivals, not my enemies, have ruined me," he writes bitterly to Atticus in June of 58 (3.9.2). At first, however, he rages futilely against his own inept handling of the affair. In a letter to his wife Terentia written on 29 November 58, Cicero, in deep despair, shows how upsetting he finds his own inconsistency toward his principles: "Nothing" (he writes) "was more pitiful, more dishonorable, or more unworthy of myself than what I did" (*Fam.* 14.3.1). Having failed to negotiate safely a dangerous and complicated political situation, Cicero shows, initially, his underlying belief in the idea that if he had behaved in a manner consistent with his principles he could have avoided exile. Cicero took the politically useful stance of *constantia* more seriously than a cool pragmatist might have done.

Indeed, Cicero's desire to be consistent became so ingrained that he could use it against himself in order to commit himself to some action or other. He knew that writing things down committed the writer to a particular stance, or else risked embarrassment, and Cicero used this fact deliberately to create traps for his own potential inconsistencies.

Cicero comments at various times on his belief that written statements are commitments to which the author will be held accountable. In his speech of 66 B.C. in defense of Cluentius, Cicero shows that he saw written records of public speeches as at least harming the speaker when later contradictions were noted. On this occasion Cicero is faced with the embarrassing task of explaining why he is now taking the opposite side from that which he apparently took in a related case some years before. The story of Oppicianus's prosecution of Cluentius for having poisoned Oppicianus's father involved Cluentius's having prosecuted Oppicianus's father on a similar charge of poisoning nearly ten years previously. Then the elder Oppicianus had been convicted, but the corruption of the jury became so incontrovertibly known in Rome that it was generally held that Oppicianus had after all been innocent. As Cicero mentions in *Pro Cluentio* 138, he too had expressed his opinion that the elder Oppicianus had been unjustly convicted by Cluentius's false prosecution, and this makes his current defense of Cluentius appear inconsistent. Rather than deny what cannot be denied (although he claims not to remember his earlier and unfortunate statement himself, apparently it did not appear in written form, and so could be denied more easily), he discusses the subject of inconsistencies and their consequences. He refers to the practice of the great orator Marcus Antonius, who never wrote down any of his speeches for fear of giving his opponents the opportunity of comparing his contradictory statements (*Clu.* 140). Cicero dismisses such behavior as futile: "as though people could only remember what one has said or done if it was written down!" (*Clu.* 140).[38] But he does not deny the unfortunate consequences of being caught in a contradiction with a previous statement.

Cicero, unlike Antonius, published his speeches very willingly and probably very soon after their delivery.[39] While this practice was no doubt due in large part to Cicero's assurance that his speeches were well worth recording, it shows that he did not expect, in general, to be able to deny authorship later. He does not, for instance, ultimately deny his contradiction in the *Pro Cluentius* but instead employs distraction tactics, and, as one of several strategies, tries to defend his right to change his mind upon examination of further evidence (142). This last effort matches Cicero's theoretical adherence to Academic skepticism, but was obviously not convincing enough, in Cicero's mind, to stand on its own.

In the *Brutus* Cicero makes a comment that suggests he saw the writing down of a speech to be specifically useful as an aid to consistency. At 216–20, Cicero is criticizing the poor memory of the orator Gaius Scribonius Curio, who published a tract against Gaius Julius Caesar that involved several discrepancies. That Curio should have forgotten the details of his story even when he could reread the tract as many times as he liked, showed, as Cicero has Brutus exclaim, his flaws as an orator. But for the purposes of this discussion, Cicero's comment gives further evidence for his views on avoiding inconsistency.

It is difficult, of course, to ascertain for how long a spoken commitment was remembered by the audience. But thanks to Cicero's practice of publishing so many of his speeches, we do have evidence for the power of written speech on its author. It is not that, once written down, Cicero considered any statement he may have made to be binding upon him; it is quite clear that he was never so rigid. But Cicero felt that a written statement became a commitment the breaking of which would be embarrassing for him.

A letter to Atticus, for instance, presents an example of the importance Cicero assigned to his published writing. In this letter, written in Thessalonica on 17 July 58, Cicero refers to the fact that he had at some point written a scurrilous speech against Curio in revenge for an attack against himself. He immediately regretted it and tried to suppress it, but now Atticus writes that it is nevertheless being circulated. In this letter Cicero reports that he is going to try to claim that the speech is a forgery, since it was written "more carelessly than his others" (3.12.2). "The problem that the *In Curionem* posed to Cicero shows the unintended perils of textual fixity," writes Dugan,[40] for though this was a situation that Cicero would have liked to avoid, he did not normally expect to regret what he had published.

This case shows that Cicero expected to have to abide by his words, as long as they were known and known to be his. The *amicitia* between Cicero and Curio apparently hinged on the existence or non-existence of this written speech, and if Cicero could deny authorship of this speech, then his relationship with Curio, which had otherwise been amicable, would remain good. That is, the publicity of this speech made it into something to which Cicero had to respond, and a successful denial of it would make the animosity between himself and Curio, which did in fact occur, no longer a reality.

Cicero considered, therefore, that written commitments were powerful. So much so, indeed, that on occasion he deliberately used written commitments to try to limit his future actions. Cicero's desire to be seen as acting consistently caused him, in the year 56 B.C., to commit himself in writing to supporting Caesar. He tells Atticus that he used writing to prevent himself from subsequently changing his mind. Cicero's relationship to Caesar is in fact a good example of his inconsistency, for he disliked Caesar's politics, feared his power, was flattered by Caesar's attempts to win him over, was compelled by prudence to give Caesar his support, and rejoiced after Caesar's murder.[41] But Cicero's anxiety about his wavering is good evidence for his wish to be seen to fulfill his own publicly stated commitments.

In a letter to Atticus written in the late spring of 56, Cicero refers to having written a παλινῳδία[42] in order to commit himself irrevocably to his new alliance with Pompey and Caesar. He writes to the disapproving Atticus: "For heaven's sake! I wished to commit myself to this new alliance so that I wouldn't be able to slide back to those whose ill-will towards me doesn't diminish even when they ought to pity me" (4.5.2).

From this comment we can see that Cicero knew himself to be quite capable of changing his mind on a political stance, but less so when he had made a public statement as to his stance. The punishment for backsliding, as Cicero depicts it here, would come both from the recipient of the commitment (Caesar, in this case) and from those members of the political elite who would hear, or possibly read, Cicero's commitment and criticize him should he back away from it.

Cicero's relationship to Caesar in particular was, of course, embarrassingly full of *inconstantia*, *levitas*, and *mobilitas*. Whatever may have been this palinode expressing his loyalty to Caesar, by allying himself with Caesar Cicero was contradicting his previous public stance against him, and as soon as he could, Cicero once more resumed his anti-Caesarian stance. This evidence of *inconstantia* is also, however, evidence for Cicero's enormous anxiety about it. Christian Habicht describes Cicero's inconsistency toward Caesar, saying that "he felt the contempt shown to him by his peers and he was covered in shame."[43] It is easy to see that Cicero was in an impossible situation. Caesar was too powerful to stand against, yet Cicero had publicly tried, and just as publicly failed, to do just that.

Cicero's *Inconstantia*

Cicero's reactions to his own inconsistency in this and other situations are further evidence for his anxiety on the subject, and therefore evidence that *constantia* was more than merely a pragmatic political tactic. In speaking, in mid-56, to the senate *De Provinciis Consularibus*, Cicero tries to justify the shameful fact that he had been brought to heel by the combined efforts of Pompey and Caesar. In a senatorial debate on the Campanian land, Cicero had recklessly challenged the triumvirs' wishes. His evaluation of their power proved to have been inaccurate, and he found this out as soon as he had made his opposition public. Caesar and Pompey worked on him and persuaded him to return to his acquiescent and indeed supportive role. He absented himself from further discussion on the Campanian land debate and committed himself publicly as Caesar's supporter by making a speech in favor of extending Caesar's term in Gallia Cisalpina and Transalpina.

This speech is laden with Cicero's desperate attempts to explain his recent about-face. Cicero's self-justifications show that a significant segment of his audience thought that he should be Caesar's enemy because of the latter's role in Cicero's exile. More simply, they considered (as he implies in this speech) that Cicero's previous attitude toward Caesar had been uncooperative, though not publicly hostile, and that his current support of Caesar showed an unprincipled inconsistency unworthy of a good man. Cicero, in fact, cannot deny any of these accusations—presumably since his past behavior was well known to his audience. Indeed, it is fairly obvious that Cicero's contradictory Caesarian policies caused a great deal of talk and criticism in Rome, as Magnus Wistrand has discussed.[44] But though being faced with Caesar's superior power has caused him to contradict himself, this speech makes it clear just how embarrassing

Cicero found his predicament. He tries first to claim that the good of the republic must come before any personal enmity and produces *exempla* of great politicians of the past who likewise had mended a personal quarrel for the sake of the republic. Tiberius Gracchus, father of the famous tribune, protected his longtime enemy Lucius Scipio from imprisonment, Cicero points out, because the honor of the empire, which would have been harmed by Scipio's disgrace, was too important (*Prov. Cons.* 18). Gracchus attained "great praise" for this, as did Marcus Lepidus for reconciling with his enemy Marcus Fulvius when he deemed it beneficial for the republic for them, who had been elected censors, to cooperate (*Prov. Cons.* 21). Other historical examples follow, showing that Cicero sees his inconsistency as undeniable and awkward but hopes to convince people that it is justifiable if seen in the right light.

Cicero's supplementary self-defense shows even more convincingly how insupportable he finds a reputation for inconsistency (and how little he expects anyone to accept his claims that changing one's mind is the act of a wise man). His change of tack with Caesar is, after all, consistent with his previous behavior, he argues. On the one hand his loyalty to the state (which his reconciliation with Caesar apparently demands) has always been fundamental to his actions, and so the trifling shift of attitude toward Caesar is unimportant compared with his unswerving love of the republic (*Prov. Cons.* 23). Cicero's apparent inconsistency turns out, after all, to be consistent.

On the other hand, even his attitude toward Caesar has not really changed in spite of appearances (the speech continues). Cicero's previous rejection "firmly indeed, and very vigorously" (*constanter quidem et fortiter certe*, *Prov. Cons.* 41) of so many flattering offers from Caesar are evidence of Cicero's strictness of principle and his unwillingness "to turn aside from his general position" (*Prov. Cons.* 41). The argument is that Cicero's past conduct, noted for its admirable consistency, must be taken as evidence that his current behavior is equally principled.[45]

There are other, less serious incidents in Cicero's career where his lack of *constantia* is made clear. He was also prepared to lie about minor details.[46] But while the boasts he made of his *constantia* show how much he wished to be seen in this light, the anxiety he expressed when he had so publicly failed to be consistent show this no less.

Furthermore, the likelihood of his *inconstantia* being obvious to the political world affected his anxiety over it. The embarrassment of being publicly caught out in an inconsistency was very real for Cicero, as his reaction to that accusation (referred to above) in his speech *Pro Cluentio* shows. But even more interesting is the fact that, within the same speech, he expresses both his concern to excuse his inconsistent behavior as well as a comment (which accords well with the approach of Academic skepticism) that justifies his having changed his mind.

He first insists that his job as an orator allows him to say what is expedient to the occasion regardless of his own opinions: "Anyone who thinks that we [orators] have maintained our real opinions in law court speeches wildly mistakes the matter" (*Clu.* 139). It was, he argues, his job as prosecutor (and he is probably referring to his prosecution of Verres) to present the best case, and that included referring disparagingly to the honesty of the jury in that ten-year-old conviction of the elder Oppicianus. But then he attempts to distract attention from himself by telling of another orator, Lucius Crassus, whose response, when faced with his own inconsistencies in court, had been not to justify them but to make a counterattack on his opponent with accusations of unthriftiness: "Actually in this sort of situation I'll happily follow the lead of Lucius Crassus, a most eloquent and intelligent man, when he was defending Gnaius Plancus against the prosecution of the vigorous and shrewd speaker Marcus Brutus. Brutus brought forward two readers whom he made recite contradictory paragraphs by turns" (*Clu.* 140).

It is at this stage that Cicero mentions that Marcus Antonius had refused to write any of his speeches down for fear of being caught in an inconsistency. Inconsistency is thus shown to have been an embarrassment to which distraction tactics were the only effective response.

Cicero ends his string of excuses with a point that fits in well with his theoretical philosophical approach: he claims that the inconsistencies were in fact due to his own opinion changing after hearing better evidence. "If I were to confess that I have now investigated Aulus Cluentius's case, but that in the past I sided with popular opinion, who could really blame me?" (*Clu.* 142).

This excuse, and the comment at 136 about the right of orators to say whatever is best for their chosen argument, coincides with his skeptical philosophical stance as stated, for example, in his *Tusculanae Disputationes*. In response to the speaker known as "A," who has pointed out a possible contradiction in *De Finibus*, the speaker called "M" (which may stand for *Magister* or Marcus but who is certainly Cicero) rejects any notion that he ought to be held to his previous statements. "Indeed, you are presenting me with sealed records and calling to witness something I said or wrote at another time. Use that method with others, who argue according to set rules: we live in the moment; we say whatever strikes our minds as probable, and so we alone are free" (*Tusc.* 5.33).

Cicero says he considers himself to be free to change his mind and to contradict earlier statements. But even in this section of the *Tusculanae Disputationes*, the context of this skeptical assertion is a discussion of *constantia*. Cicero has argued that "philosophers should be examined not by their individual statements but by their continuity and consistency" (*Tusc.* 31). Cicero does not really experience the "freedom" from the constraints of *constantia* that he claims to have.

Returning to the *Pro Cluentio*, it is notable that Cicero's claim (that no one could object to his changing his mind) is only one of many, sometimes contradictory, excuses for *inconstantia*. A similar point is notable also in his *De Provinciis Consularibus* as discussed above. This suggests that either he does not consider it a sufficient excuse on its own or that he knows his audience will not—or that both these options are true.

Most probably it was Cicero, more than his audiences, who fundamentally could not justify the skeptical approach (that changing his mind was morally acceptable). Our primary evidence for the consequences of Cicero's *inconstantia* is his own reaction to potential public outrage, and it is impossible to know whether Cicero was being seriously criticized or if he was exaggerating the criticism through his fear of it. But Cicero's shame on the subject of his own inconsistency was at least as powerful a deterrent as actual gossip. And it is the evidence of this shame that suggests Cicero's concern for *constantia* was more than merely a pragmatic political strategy.

It is, for example, unclear how much if at all Cicero's concern for *constantia* was shared by Atticus or any of his political competitors, or even if there were concrete consequences for inconsistent behavior.

In a letter of April 59 B.C., Cicero expresses his outrage at Caesar's blatant contradiction of a previous action. It was Caesar's decision in March as *pontifex maximus* that had allowed Clodius to be adopted (by "a man twenty years of age, or even less" according to Cicero in *Dom.* 34) into a plebeian family in order to allow him to run for tribune of the plebs, and now he was denying that he ever supported the adoption (*Att.* 2.12.2). Caesar seems, as far as we know, to get away with this contradiction. People talked and criticized, but Caesar was in the exceptional position of having so much power from so many sources that what might have injured Cicero left Caesar unharmed (although perhaps it was outrageous behavior like this that provoked his murderers to their eventual violence). T. P. Wiseman asserts that *homines novi* could not afford to be consistent because of their need to find allies wherever they could,[47] but Cicero did not expect to be able to behave with such blatant inconsistency as Caesar did in the case of Clodius's adoption. Shackleton Bailey, in his commentary on Cicero's letters to Atticus, wonders how Caesar could have denied his involvement in the adoption and points out that the original proposal had been "carried at three hours' notice instead of the legal twenty-four days," as though that might mitigate Caesar's later denial.[48] Cicero, at any rate, seems to think Caesar's denial of a public act incredible.

It is clear, however, that Cicero assumed that his friends and political rivals did share his concern. Cicero and Atticus regularly discussed the subject of virtue in their letters to each other, and, though Atticus seems often to have separated principle from practical behavior without qualm, Cicero considered such pragmatism in himself to be shameful and certainly bad for his public image. He ensures, as far as he can, that his practical behavior either fit consistently into his created self-image or that his philosophical ideas explain and justify the practical deeds of his past. And Cicero seems to use Atticus as a judge for his (Cicero's) behavior even when Atticus's pragmatism falls short of Cicero's idealism.

Cicero claims, for instance, that Atticus's imagined face is always before his eyes whenever he is considering his duty or his reputation, yet in *Ad Atticum* 6.2.8 he expresses his shock that Atticus should urge him, when he is governor of Cilicia, to appoint the villainous Scaptius as prefect and allow him to use mounted troops to extract money from certain of the provincials. "You, Atticus, who usually praise my integrity and discrimination?" (6.2.8), Cicero exclaims, and asks how he would ever be able to read or even touch the volumes of his own *De Re Publica* that Atticus has been praising so extravagantly if he did what Atticus was asking of him (6.2.9). He ends by reprimanding Atticus for caring too much for Brutus (who had apparently asked Atticus to use his influence on Cicero in this matter)[49] and not enough for Cicero himself. Whether the issue is care for his moral integrity or for his public reputation is difficult to judge. Regardless of whether or not Atticus would have criticized Cicero for inconsistency, Cicero acts as though he would, or ought to, and accordingly tries to live up to the reputation he has built for himself.

Atticus, however, seems generally to have expressed the voice of caution, against which Cicero's concern for *officium* and people's opinion occasionally struggles. Cicero writes as though Atticus's advice sprang from considerations of honor rather than from practical concerns. Five years later, for instance, Cicero refers to Atticus as usually being his Cato, in the sense of acting (as Shackleton Bailey puts it) as "Cicero's optimate conscience,"[50] even though this particular circumstance involves Cicero's reprimanding Atticus for failing to play the Cato role consistently (*Att.* 16.7.4). But in general Atticus's advice tends toward pragmatism rather than principle. Though Atticus may sometimes have argued that Cicero should join Pompey abroad if certain circumstances should arise, when the conditions are met, Atticus generally seems to have tried to persuade Cicero not to commit himself. If Cornelius Nepos's biography can be trusted, Atticus's whole approach to life was to achieve *tranquillitas* (*Att.* 6.5) by practicing a studied neutrality. This was very far from Cicero's approach.

· · ·

This chapter has attempted to show how seriously Cicero took the notion of *constantia*, that is, of maintaining the appearance and actuality in his later behavior consistent with his earlier behavior including his public words. I have made no attempt to claim that Cicero succeeded in being consistent. Rather, the argument is that the concern to achieve *constantia* was for Cicero a fundamental motivator in his political career and one in apparent tension with his stated adherence to Academic skepticism.

I suggest that the reason for Cicero's particular interest in achieving *constantia* was due to his lack of a famous ancestry, which made him so aware of the need to make himself appear reliable in other ways. This theory is supported by Cicero's references to the importance he and all Roman politicians attached to their reputations. For example, in the speech he gave arguing that he, and not Caecilius, should take on the prosecution of Verres, he claims that since he (Cicero) already has a good reputation he is bound to try to maintain it. "There is no greater security for the republic than that those who prosecute someone else should be as concerned for their glory, their honor and their reputations as those who are prosecuted are concerned for their political status and their fortunes. And so the people who have acted most conscientiously and thoroughly as prosecutors are also those who believed that they themselves were risking their reputations" (*Div. Caec.* 71).

Cicero thus claims that he is constrained by public opinion to act honorably in this prosecution, whereas Caecilius "has nothing to lose if he fails" (*Div. Caec.* 71). In Cicero's case, however, "the Roman people have many hostages" to his honorable behavior, that is, his dependency on them for political success, and his hard-won reputation (72).

James May uses this reference to show how important *ethos* was in Roman oratory; the character of the speaker acting as proof of his truthfulness.[51] My argument is not fundamentally different from May's, but it places the emphasis less on *ethos* as a means of persuasion, and more on Cicero's need to maintain his reputation of reliability and consistency so that he can use it convincingly in political oratory. The implication is that a man with a well-established reputation—whether it be due to a distinguished ancestry or to his own previous political actions—can be counted on not to tarnish that reputation by indulging in corruption or any other disreputable behavior.

A similar notion is implied in Cicero's *Pro Sulla* (given in 62), when he is trying to show that his defense of a man accused of involvement in the Catilinarian conspiracy is consistent with his successful vilification of Catiline in the previous year. Naturally, his client is innocent, argues Cicero, and proof of this is found in the fact that he, the man whose actions against the conspiracy had saved the republic, has agreed to defend Sulla (*Sull.* 83).[52] The argument is circular and similar to his self-explanation in *Provinciis Consularibus*: Cicero may seem to be acting inconsistently now, but the proof that his current actions concur with his previous behavior is the very fact that Cicero does not behave inconsistently.

Cicero's emphasis on *constantia* was a response to the particular handicap under which a *homo novus* acted. In Roman tradition, a man took more than just his name from his famous ancestors. The great grandson of Cato the Censor, for instance, was assumed to carry on some of the qualities of his forebear, and the fame of the Scipiones was political capital for the younger members of the family, even for Scipio Aemilianus, who acquired the name Scipio only by adoption. Susan Treggiari argues that the peculiarly Roman assumption that a man would be like his ancestor was based only partly on a vague idea of genetic determinism and more on the idea that a man would be trying hard to fulfill this expectation in the minds of the voters.[53] Scipio Aemilianus, after all, took the Scipio name from his adoptive father, but he took his adoptive grandfather's cognomen Africanus only after having captured Carthage, winning the title on his own merits yet obviously connecting his merits with those of his adoptive family. If the Roman people felt they could expect the son of a Scipio to follow a certain political pattern, they were sometimes not disappointed.

Cicero's ancestors were undistinguished and unknown to the Roman people. He had no *imagines* in the usual sense, and so he had to convince the voters that they could rely on him to act in a certain way. John Dugan argues that Cicero created *imagines* out of his literary and oratorical predecessors, just as Marius had claimed his war trophies and battle scars as *imagines*.[54] Dugan's argument shows how Cicero tried to create an authoritative place for himself in the eyes of his fellow literary elites. My argument supplements this by showing how Cicero also tried to justify his authority with his non-literary, political audience by creating precedents of his own reliability within his previous public words and actions.

NOTES

1. As he wrote in the *Academica*, "Indeed, I myself employ this wholehearted devotion to philosophy to keep my life on a consistent track, as far as I am able" (*Acad.* 1.7).

2. For a brief discussion of Cicero's links with Academic skepticism, see Powell and Thorsrud in this volume. For an interesting discussion of Cicero's rejection of the Younger Cato's dogmatic adherence to Stoicism at the expense of necessary political compromise, see Stem, "Cicero as Orator and Philosopher."

3. The prosecutors in Archias's citizenship trial, for example, tried to argue for the inadmissibility of verbal testimony, but Cicero successfully showed that the written records (which had been destroyed) were not necessary to demonstrate proof when human witnesses of Archias's citizenship were present (*Arch*. 8). Shane Butler suggests that Cicero was innovative in relying as much as he did on written records in his forensic speeches (Butler, *The Hand of Cicero*, 12–13), and as Elizabeth Meyer discusses, even in the third century A.D. the arguments of jurists suggest that oral contracts were the norm, for which written contracts were merely a record (Meyer, *Legitimacy and Law in the Roman World*, 260–62).

4. Jonkers, *Social and Economic Commentary*, 59. T. Rice Holmes, back in 1923, put it even more harshly when he wrote that "the three [*De Lege Agraria*] speeches, and especially the second, should be studied by all politicians who aspire to become proficient in the art of misrepresentation" (Holmes, *The Roman Republic and the Founder of the Empire*, 249 n. 2).

5. Nicolet, *Le métier de citoyen*, 388. Sumner, following Syme and Carcopino, argues that the bill was never in fact meant to pass but was proposed only for the sake of showing up Cicero's claim to be *popularis*: Sumner, "Cicero, Pompeius, and Rullus," 576; Syme, *Sallust*, 99; Carcopino, *La République romaine*, 664.

6. Morstein-Marx considers the second and third *De Lege Agraria* speeches to be one of two instances only when contional rhetoric seems to have changed the course of a piece of legislation, bringing what appeared to be an easily passed bill to defeat. Morstein-Marx, *Mass Oratory and Political Power*, 190.

7. The references to "kings" and "masters" to describe the decemvirs are repeated multiple times throughout the second speech, at 2.6.15; 2.10.24; 2.11.29; 2.6.15; 2.13.32; 2.14.35; 2.21.57; 2.28.75; 2.34.93; 2.8.21; 2.9.22; 2.23.61.

8. The bibliography on what was meant by *popularis* and its supposed opposite *optimas* (or its more common plural form *optimates*) shows that Cicero's attempt to use the term both as a self-descriptive compliment and as a vilification of others has resulted in some confusion. See on this topic: Achard, "Langage et sociéte"; Badian, "*Optimates, Populares*"; Burckhardt, "Optimates"; David, "Eloquentia *popularis* et conduites symboliques"; Ferrary, "*Optimates* et *Populares*"; Hellegouarc'h, *Le vocabulaire latin*; Mackie, "*Popularis* Ideology and Popular Politics"; Meier, "Populares"; Seager, "Cicero and the Word *Popularis*." This confusion was deliberate on

Cicero's part in order that he could present a consistent front to his two types of audience.

9. The extant *contio* speeches comprise the following list: *Pro Lege Manilia* (66 B.C.), the second and third *De Lege Agraria* speeches (63), *In Catilinam* 2 and 3 (63), *Post reditum ad Populum* (57), *Philippicae* 4 (44), and *Philippicae* 6 (43). The *Pro Rabirio Perduellionis Reo* (63) may also have been delivered at a *contio*, or, as has usually been assumed, at a popular trial before the *comitia centuriata*. See Tyrrell, *A Legal and Historical Commentary*, 39–40, on this point.

10. Habinek, *Politics of Latin Literature*, 74.

11. Also sometimes called *Post Reditum ad Quirites* or *Cum Populo Gratias Egit*.

12. Squires, *Asconius Pedianus, Quintus*, 97.

13. Commentaries on Cicero's *contio* speeches rarely discuss his praise of the audience, as though such compliments were simply necessary embellishments but not real commitments.

14. There is good justification for interpreting Laelius as Cicero's spokesperson here partly because of the similarity of these arguments with Cicero's opinions expressed in other treatises and partly because of Cicero's obvious admiration for the real Laelius. In particular, Cicero's offer in a letter to Pompey to be his "Laelius" shows that Cicero identified himself with this *sapiens* (*Fam.* 3.3 [or 5.7.3]).

15. Habinek argues that candor, and the absence of flattery, in *amicitia* was typically practiced by a social inferior to a socially superior *amicus*, though the social gap would not have been vast (Habinek, "Towards a History of Friendly Advice").

16. *Ad Atticum* 12.3.1 reads: "I think you [Atticus] are the one person less prone to flattery than I—or if either of us does ever use flattery it is towards someone else. Between ourselves certainly there is no flattery." The following letter (*Att.* 12.5c) repeats Cicero's assertion that he does not use flattery (or at least not to Atticus): "You know that I never flatter."

17. Béranger, "Les jugements de Cicéron," 762.

18. There is some doubt as to whether the speech *Pro C. Rabirio perduellionis reo* was given at the *comitia centuriata* or at a *contio*. See Tyrrell, *A Legal and Historical Commentary*, 39–40, for the argument that it was a *contio* speech. Andrew Lintott points out that the procedure for criminal trials conducted in assemblies (in the *comitia centuriata* for capital cases) involved initial debate in succeeding *contiones* with the final vote conducted in the assembly. Cicero's speech may, therefore, have been given in the official arena for debate (the *contiones*) rather than just preceding the vote in the assembly (Tyrrell, *A Legal and Historical Commentary*, 68–69).

19. See Yakobson on his argument (against Hall and Gruen) that the aristocracy was very opposed to the ballot laws.

20. Zerba, "Love, Envy, and Pantomimic Morality."

21. The term *aequabilitas* has similar connotations. According to Gordis (*The Estimates of Moral Values*, 82), the word *gravitas* can also be seen as equivalent.

22. Shackleton Bailey, *Cicero's Letters to Atticus*, 3:104.

23. If virtuous behavior done for reasons of *fama* is not considered truly virtuous, as has been suggested (Rawson, *Cicero*, 180), then Cicero's behavior cannot be so called. But such an interpretation oversimplifies human motives.

24. As Cicero points out in the *De Officiis*, it is the role of defense lawyer that brings *gloria* and *gratia* (*Off.* 2.51). In the Verrine speeches Cicero tries to cast himself as essentially speaking for the defense, since it is the Sicilians who have suffered and who will continue to suffer if Verres' case does not lead to a conviction (*Verr.* 2.2.179).

25. Such strictness of principle, however, was applicable only to his own actions. Cicero's defense of three other men charged with gubernatorial corruption shows a certain amount of tolerance for Roman rapacity in the provinces (*Font.*, ca. 70, *Flac.*, 59, and *Scaur*, 54). Cicero's ability to argue in *utramque partem* has been analyzed, especially in the cases against Verres and for Flaccus, in Vasaly's *Representations*, 191ff. His defense of governors accused of corruption does not involve stated approval of corrupt behavior but rather a denial that corruption took place (his use of negative ethnic stereotyping may imply that corruption would have been justifiable against such disreputable provincials, but explicitly Cicero uses it to disparage the quality of the provincials' testimonies).

26. See also *Att.* 2.3; 2.4; 2.5; 2.7; 2.18; 2.19; etc. for similar examples.

27. Shackleton Bailey, *Cicero's Letters to Atticus*, 4:360. Shackleton Bailey also writes in the introduction to his volumes of Cicero's *Letters to Atticus* that "A man who gives a bad reason for doing what he knows he ought is excusing his own reluctance" (1:42).

28 Anthony Trollope's passionate response (*The Life of Cicero*, vol. 1:15–16) to Mommsen's and De Quincey's charge of cowardice is justified. "Their authority" he wrote in 1880, "they have always found in [Cicero's] own words. It is on his own evidence against himself that they have depended—on his own evidence, or occasionally on their own surmises. When we are told of his cowardice, because those human vacillations of his, humane as well as human, have been laid bare to us as they came quivering out of his bosom on to his fingers!" For Cicero to have been so influenced by what the *boni* would say about him does not, for all we know, make him any different from the rest of the Roman political elite who did not happen to leave hundreds of letters written unguardedly to close friends. Brunt, indeed, speculates that "in his prolonged hesitations and final plunge Cicero was not altogether an unrepresentative figure" (Brunt, "Cicero's *Officium*," 32).

29. Even these letters, of course, must not be seen as entirely reliable windows into Cicero's soul. Catherine Steel comments on the issue of reliability in the *Ad Atticum* letters: "while Atticus was a valued confidante precisely because he was not a member of the Senate, and thus in no way a political rival or competitor, Cicero must have been aware that he was a close and valuable friend to others who were senators. Absolute frankness is not to be expected" (Steel, *Reading Cicero*, 89).

30. MacKendrick, *Philosophical Books of Cicero*, 254–55.

31. The treatise urges Cicero: "all the same, there must be no politics in your campaign, either in the senate or in popular meetings" (13).

32. Narducci, *Modelli etici e società*, 158.

33. Dugan, *Making a New Man*, 6.

34. Narducci, *Modelli etici e società*, 162.

35. Dugan, *Making a New Man*, 2.

36. Zerba, "Frauds of Humanism," 238.

37. On 29 April 58 B.C., he writes to his wife, daughter, and son, for instance, that "there has been no error on his part, except that he did not [choose to] lose both his life and his prestige together" (*Fam.* 14.4.6). In general, Cicero's reaction to his exile is that it is a fate worse than death and that his decision to flee rather than risk death had been an unfortunate one.

38. A disingenuous comment, if Cicero really had taken a vocal (but not written) stance on the injustice of the elder Oppicianus's conviction and was now trying to imply that he had made no such statement!

39. On this topic, see William C. McDermott, "Cicero's Publication of His Consular Orations," who argues that Cicero published his consular speeches, and probably his others as well, as soon as was practical after delivering them. As to how closely the published versions imitated the oral deliveries, that is a question that can never be fully answered. While it is unlikely that there was complete parity between the oral and written versions (Steel, *Reading Cicero*, 22), it is probable that Cicero would have avoided significant changes unless in exceptional circumstances.

40. Dugan, *Making a New Man*, 52.

41. In a letter to Decimus Brutus, for example, in December 44 B.C., Cicero refers to Caesar's assassination as a deed "which is the greatest in human memory" (*Fam.* 11.5.1).

42. This may have been his speech *De Provinciis Consularibus* in support of Caesar's command in Gaul, according to the commentary in Shackleton Bailey, *Cicero's Letters to Atticus*, 2:185.

43. Habicht, *Cicero the Politician*, 57.

44. Wistrand, *Cicero Imperator*, 125.

45. Catherine Steel has pointed out a similar situation in Cicero's letters to exiled Pompeians in 46 B.C. (Steel, *Reading Cicero*, 99). These letters, notably *Fam.* 4.7 and *Fam.* 7.3, are ostensibly letters of consolation and

support but include clear evidence of Cicero's attempts to justify his own reconciliation with Caesar. He found it embarrassing to have to explain why his support of Pompey had fluctuated and how he could now condone his own moral betrayal of the Pompeian cause.

46. An example of a minor contradiction that Cicero made appears in *Phil.* 2.2, when he implies that Antony has accused him of involvement in the murder of Clodius. He responds by arguing that, since no one accused him of this at the time, it is implausible for Antony to lay such a charge at his door now. But Cicero was lying about there having been no accusation against him eight years before. In his speech in defense of Milo, written but not delivered (at least, not delivered in the same form) in 52 B.C., Cicero refers to the fact that some people suspected him of involvement. "Evidently," he writes, "some despicable and depraved men were calling me the bandit and murderer" (*me videlicet latronem ac sicarium abiecti homines et perditi describebant, Mil.* 47). If the speech *Pro Milone* was not originally delivered orally, this fact may have encouraged Cicero to hope that none of his enemies would notice the contradiction and publicize it. And the length of time that had passed between the delivery of the *Philippics* and the death of Clodius must have dulled people's outrage at the murder. Perhaps, in fact, the comparative unimportance of the lie allowed it to remain unchallenged, or prompted Cicero to take the risk of its being noticed. Interestingly, Catherine Steel suggests that, in the case of the *Pro Milone*, Cicero took the unusual step of publishing a version of a losing speech because he wished to use it as evidence for his political constancy (Steel, *Reading Cicero*, 117). Pompey was, it was generally thought, in favor of Milo's conviction, and Cicero's defense of Milo was evidence that Cicero could consistently sustain his hostility to Clodius despite Pompey's influence.

47. Wiseman, *New Men in the Roman Senate*, 173.

48. Shackleton Bailey, *Cicero's Letters to Atticus*, 1:375.

49. Brutus, in fact, was ultimately the creditor in this disreputable provincial debt, hence his involvement, much to Cicero's distaste. See Rawson, *Cicero*, 178.

50. Shackleton Bailey, *Cicero's Letters to Atticus*, 1:51.

51. May, *Trials of Character*, 37–38.

52. See Goodwin, "Cicero's Authority," 40–41. She argues that the speech hinges on Cicero's *auctoritas*, that "Cicero claims right at the beginning of the speech that his authority is sufficient to support an acquittal." This is, it appears, the same thing as saying that since he put an end to the conspiracy, he could not be defending a man guilty of taking part in this conspiracy.

53. Treggiari, "Ancestral Virtues and Vices," 156.

54. Dugan, *Making a New Man*, 12, 41, and throughout.

5

Cicero and the Perverse

The Origins of Error in *De Legibus* 1
and *Tusculan Disputations* 3

MARGARET GRAVER

I am here concerned with what we might call the problem of the perverse in Cicero's ethics. Briefly put, the problem is this. Though presenting himself as a skeptic in some matters, Cicero does not wish to give up on the concept of a divinely conferred human nature. He strongly favors a cosmology in which all events are arranged for the good by an organizing principle called Nature, whether or not "Nature" is conceived as a benevolent divine person, and he is inclined to believe that both individual human beings and societal groups are endowed by Nature with the very capacities we need in order to behave rightly and fulfill our function as rational animals.[1] He therefore needs to provide some explanation for how it is that people fail to become exemplars of wisdom and virtue living together in perfect societies. Why do we ever stray from the path that nature lays before our feet? Referring to this difficulty, Cicero repeatedly employs language of "sparks" or "seeds," which are implanted by Nature in every human being and have the potential to develop into the virtues but which at some point we manage to extinguish, thwarting our own prospects of happiness.

An important piece of background for this discussion is to be found in Book 6 of Plato's *Republic,* 490a–93b. There Socrates sets out to explain how it is that the philosophic nature, though endowed at birth with deep insight and various virtues, is nearly always corrupted (*diollutai*) and made vicious. Every growing thing, he says, requires proper nurture, and the more powerful it is, the more danger there is that deficiencies in its upbringing will make it spectacularly bad. Similarly, the psyche that is best by nature does not grow to excellence if it is sown among the "sophists" but is instead corrupted by their teaching. Even worse than private sophists are the people in the assembly, whose noisy shouts of approbation and disapprobation "resounding and redoubling from the rocks" overwhelm any private instruction the young person may have received and impart to him their own debased opinion of what actions are honorable or shameful. And it is from the crowd that the sophists themselves have learned their version of wisdom, studying their values as the keeper observes the rages and whims of a large and powerful beast. Either way, it is by transmission from the vagaries of the multitude that error and vice are instilled where nature had imparted only virtue.

Of particular interest is Plato's concern for the corruption of the best and brightest and his awareness of the seductive power of audience response. These are observations to which the class-conscious Cicero, with his long experience in public speaking, could not help but respond. But it is also notable that Plato does not regard the problem of perversion as a *universal* problem of human development. It is at this point that Cicero's handling of the issue will diverge from his. For one who holds that Nature's full benevolence extends to every human being, it is of limited use to say that the potentially virtuous psyche goes astray because corrupted by others. Before there can be transmission of error, there has to be something to transmit. It is therefore necessary to provide a further account of perversion that has explanatory force even in the absence of transmission, in the child brought up under ideal conditions without contamination from others.

We will see here that Cicero offers such an account in at least two of his works. In both the works named in my title he speaks first of a kind of confusion that arises in the immature mind as it attempts to sort out impressions that may be misleadingly similar. Then in addition he refers to false values imparted by caregivers and by the surrounding culture. Through both of these causes, we come to identify the wrong objects—pleasure, money, power, and reputation—as goods that we should pursue when in fact ethical conduct should be the object of all our deliberations. Once fully understood, Cicero's two-part answer to the problem of perversion will emerge as a particularly interesting part of his philosophy, both for its own sake and as an illustration of his manner of working with and through older systems of thought. For we do not necessarily deny Cicero intellectual agency when we grant that many of the arguments he employs have a significant philosophical prehistory. In this instance, he takes his cue from a strikingly similar two-part explanation of error that was propounded by the third-century Stoic Chrysippus of Soli. I indeed mean to suggest that the lines of inheritance are clear enough to enable us to draw upon Cicero in reconstructing certain elements of Chrysippus's position.[2] But for all its Stoic provenance, the explanation Cicero gives is also meaningful within his own system of thought.

De Legibus 1: Extinguishing the Sparks

Let us first consider in somewhat more detail the passages in which Cicero presents his position. The earlier of the two is in Book 1 of *De Legibus*. While the problems of dating that work are well known, its ties to *De Re Publica* are much in evidence, and it is probably safe to consider *De Legibus* 1 as belonging to the earliest phase of Cicero's serious thinking about ethics.[3] The book aims to show that the origin of all codes of law lies not in convention but in an untutored awareness of fairness and justice that is shared by all human beings.[4] Cicero is vehement in defending this claim, and yet he does not mean to say that all people actually behave justly or even know what justice is. The claim about human nature is in fact quite minimal: it is only that humans possess, even without teaching, a kind of "initial and inchoate intelligence" that favors the development of justice in each person. This *prima et inchoata intelligentia*, also referred to in the plural (*intellegentiae*), is not "intelligence" in our sense of the word, and it is not what Cicero calls *intelligentia* in *De Finibus* 3.21, that is, a full-scale concept. Rather it is a natural endowment that equips us in some way to form the concepts out of which justice is built.[5] The process by which one comes to understand justice is therefore self-starting, but its success is not guaranteed, for humans in general are also subject to perversion (*depravatio*) through "customs and [false] opinions," first mentioned in section 29.[6] It is this perversion that produces the great differences among us, for considering only our innate rational capacities, we are all much the same; "there is no dissimilarity within the species."[7]

Even though perversion drives us apart, there is also some similarity in the kinds of perversions that occur. There are certain types of objects that regularly lead us astray, and these turn out to be surprisingly few in number.

> For all people are also attracted to pleasure, which has something in it similar to what is good by nature even when it is an inducement to shameful conduct. For it so delights us by its smoothness and sweetness that it is construed as something healthful, through an error of the mind. It is by a similar misunderstanding that people flee death as being a dissolution of nature and pursue life as preserving us in the state in which we are born. Pain is considered to be one of the worst evils both because of its sharpness and because it is seen to accompany destructions of our nature. And there is a resemblance between moral excellence and glory, which is the reason why those held in honor are regarded as fortunate and those in disgrace as unfortunate. (*Leg.* 1.31–32)

Cicero names just six objects people mistakenly regard as goods and evils: pleasure and pain, death and life, honor and disrepute. Each of these is closely associated with an object we might more appropriately seek or avoid: pleasure is associated with health, pain with bodily harm; life with the preservation of one's natural state and death with its dissolution; honor with moral excellence and, by implication, disgrace with moral turpitude. For ease of reference, we may represent these in tabular form:

proper objects	*associated objects*
health	pleasure
bodily harm	pain
preservation of natural state	life
dissolution of natural state	death
moral excellence	honor
moral turpitude	disgrace

The objects in the left-hand column are ones for which we have a natural affinity or disaffinity. Nature actually favors our pursuit or avoidance of these: the phrase "sparks of the virtues," appearing later in the paragraph, refers to our innate preference or dispreference for them.[8] For those on the right, he will not concede this. Our apparently universal tendency to pursue or avoid these objects is only the result of their association with the proper objects.

But how exactly does this association bring about error? Cicero twice speaks of the confusion in terms of a resemblance between one thing and another. Pleasure, he says, "has something similar" to what is good by nature. Glory, also, is said to resemble moral excellence (*honestas*). However, the language of resemblance is not entirely transparent. Ordinarily, we think of resemblance as a sharing of properties: to perceive a resemblance is to observe the same properties in two distinct objects, each of which is already fully conceptualized. That is not quite what is happening in this case, where the relevant concepts are still in the process of formation. The immature mind is engaged in a delicate process of sorting its experiences into kinds (*genera cognovit*, 1.27). We would expect that it fails to draw a distinction rather than blurring an existing distinction. If it mistakenly construes pleasure as something healthful, it ought not to be because it perceives a resemblance between two things so much as that it fails to recognize that there are *two* objects before it.

We can find the explanation expressed in just this way in what Cicero says about the confusion between pain and the destruction of our nature. Pain, he says, is thought to be an evil both because of its sharpness and because it is seen to accompany (*videtur sequi*) destructions of our nature, that is, instances of harm to our natural constitution.[9] Being injured is not at all the same thing as being in pain, yet because pain does regularly accompany injury, it is easy for the undeveloped mind to assume that it is the pain itself that is to be avoided. Hence the difficulty of persuading a child to accept some necessary but painful medical treatment. With greater experience of the world, the child may come to realize that there are two object types to be kept straight—those that cause pain and those that harm the body—and to regard these things in different ways. Until then, the frequency with which these co-occur will be misleading. Likewise, pleasure comes to be understood as a distinct object type from that which promotes health, and good or bad reputation as distinct from reputable or disreputable conduct. Even life itself—that is, the mere continuance of one's existence as an animate organism—is to be distinguished from a proper object, the preservation of one's natural state or (as we might say it) of one's wholeness as a person. A mature person does not necessarily believe that death is to be avoided at all costs.

The subject of perversion comes up again a few pages later in *De Legibus*, in section 47. At this point Cicero is arguing against the relativist position in ethics. It is wrong, he says, to assume, just because moral issues engender differences of opinion while the objects of sense do not, that the senses are reliable but morality has no basis in nature. Our conflicting and generally mistaken understanding of moral concepts can be explained without appeal to relativism, as a result of various forces that skew our intellectual development.

> For our senses are not perverted by the parent, the wet-nurse, the teacher, the poet, the stage, the agreed-on view of the many. Our minds, though, have every snare laid against them, either by those whom I just listed, who take us when we are young and inexperienced and give us whatever shape and color they wish, or by that one that is deeply implicated in every one of our sensations, namely pleasure, an imitator of the good yet in reality the mother of all evils. Corrupted by her enticements, we do not properly perceive those objects that are good by nature, because they lack this sweetness and this itch.

The first part of this later explanation differs from the earlier passage in that it appeals to cultural transmission, operating through the agency and by implication usually through the verbal messages of other human beings: "the teacher, the poet, the stage, and the agreed-on view of the many" operate upon us verbally. But here, too, Cicero finds it necessary to name a cause that might pervert our ethical development even independently of transmission. When he speaks again of pleasure as "an imitator of the good," he is beginning again on his earlier explanation in terms of misleading impressions.

Tusculan Disputations 3: The Hall of Mirrors

It is striking to compare these portions of *De Legibus* with the treatment Cicero gives to the perversion theme some years later, in the preface to Book 3 of the *Tusculan Disputations*. The context is now quite different. The *Tusculan Disputations* are primarily concerned with the experience and nature of the individual, and the harm done by false values is here chiefly that they give rise to painful and disturbing emotions. But the particular problem to be solved is essentially the same. Again Cicero is seeking to maintain the beneficence of our native endowment in the face of what might seem like overwhelming evidence to the contrary. The skewing of our values was never a foregone conclusion: although we were endowed at birth with only the smallest beginnings of mental capacity, "the tiniest sparks of understanding," these if not perverted would be sufficient to enable us to grow into beings both virtuous and wise. "Seeds of the virtues," he says, "are inborn in our characters, and if they were allowed to mature, nature itself would lead us to perfect happiness."[10] It therefore becomes necessary to explain how it is that those sparks are extinguished, overwhelmed by our "wrongful habits and beliefs." This occurs in the first place through the influence of associates, the list of whom is identical to that given in *De Legibus* 1.47: the wet-nurse, the parent, the teacher, the poet, the public. Each of these is described, with emphasis given especially to the last. It is when we meet with society at large, says Cicero, that we "become thoroughly infected with corrupt beliefs, and secede from nature absolutely."

But the explanation is not yet finished, for the ultimate origin of perversion has not been identified. Cicero therefore proceeds to a second mode of explanation, although he makes no effort to mark it as such. He observes that while children in the course of development are influenced mainly by the opinions of others, there are also certain people who have made up their minds for themselves what is to be valued. These people are intellectual leaders, though misguided ones; the rest of us merely acquiesce in their judgment. It seems also that they are political leaders, men perhaps like Cicero himself, for their interest is specifically in civic and military honors: "As a result, we think the meaning of nature best understood by those who have made up their minds that public office, military commands, and the glory of popularity are the best and most honorable goals a person can have" (3.3). And it is mistakes concerning honor and glory that will be the principal target of the explanation. Desires for money and pleasure will be mentioned at the end of the passage, but only summarily: if the erroneous pursuit of glory can be explained, these will follow in its train.

Themes of honor and glory have complex ramifications, of course, in a Roman political context; Cicero treated them a number of times in his works and seems to have invested them with considerable personal significance.[11] Here, though, the topic is handled with particular sophistication. Those who are called "the noblest among us" have come to an erroneous conclusion about glory through failure to sort through a double set of distinctions. A false glory, also called "popular acclaim," is to be distinguished from true glory, and the latter must still be kept distinct from moral excellence and the right actions in which it is displayed.

> These things attract the noblest among us, so that even as they pursue that genuine distinction which is the one chief aim of their nature, they spend their lives in great emptiness, chasing not a solid figure of virtue but only a shadow-shape of glory. For real glory is a solid thing, clearly modeled and not shadowy at all: it is the unanimous praise of good persons, approval sounded without bias by those who know how to judge excellence of character. It is, as it were, the reflection or echo of such excellence, and there is no need for good men to disown it, since it is the regular accompaniment to right actions. But there is another sort of glory, which pretends to imitate the first, and which is rash and

ill-considered, frequently praising misdeeds and faults. This is popular acclaim, which offers a perverted caricature of the beauty that belongs to true distinction, and people are blinded by it, so that they do not know where to find or how to recognize the fine things they desire. (*Tusc.* 3.3–4)

The relation between true glory and excellence of character is somewhat like the relation we observed in *De Legibus* between pain and bodily harm: the one regularly accompanies the other. With this pair, though, the connection is especially reliable, for true glory is praise spoken by the wise, knowledgeable observers who can be counted upon to dispense approval on exactly the right occasions and in exactly the right degree. Thus true glory is a concomitant or "regular accompaniment" (*comes*) to appropriate actions.[12] This implies that justified praise never merits avoidance, as Cicero also says: any state of affairs in which such praise is heard is also an object worthy of pursuit. The difficulty, it seems, is that the undeveloped mind identifies the wrong feature of appropriate acts as making them worthy of choice. Rather than valuing those acts as being in accordance with nature, it values them as being praiseworthy; in effect, it values the praise itself.

This opens the door to further error. For praise coming from ordinary observers might be virtually indistinguishable from the praise that would be spoken by a person of perfect understanding, if one happened to be present. The words spoken might be the same, and they might be spoken with the same inflection and ring of sincerity. Only one who had the wise person's own sensitivity to the epistemic state of others would be in a position to assess the mind of the speaker and determine whether he speaks from knowledge. Putting it in real terms (since actual wise persons are rarely to be encountered), we might say that even where the praise a young person receives is justifiable, one whose concept of the good is not yet fully formed will have no reliable way to distinguish such praise from that which is accorded to misdeeds and faults. It is therefore very unsafe to draw any inference from the praise of the fallible multitude to one's real merits. But this is a risk the young progressor will invariably have to take.

The imagery is worth dwelling on. Real glory is "a solid thing, clearly modeled." We are meant to think of statues in bronze or terracotta, but solid as it is, real glory is itself only a "reflection or echo" of something yet more substantial.[13] Popular acclaim, in turn, is a shadow cast by true glory, a shadow of a reflection, as it were. Those misled by it find themselves pursuing only shadows, and distorted shadows at that, "perverted caricatures" that trick our vision and leave us blundering around in the dark of our own blindness. The multiple image-original relations recall Plato's Allegory of the Cave in Book 7 of the *Republic*, where ordinary people compete for honors while striving to identify regularities in the progression of shadows cast by statue-like images of people and animals. The allusion is highly appropriate, for Cicero's theme is closely related to the question being treated in this portion of the *Republic*, that of "our nature in its education and lack of education" (*Republic* 7.514a1). But Cicero's account of the specific features of human conduct to be explained, and the particular way he configures his explanation, do not find their antecedents in the *Republic* passage. Another intellectual influence is at work.

The Twofold Cause of Chrysippus

We can trace a much closer analogue for Cicero's treatment of the perversion theme in Stoic texts as early as the hymn of Cleanthes in the middle part of the third century. In the hymn we find Cleanthes asserting strongly that under the rule of Zeus the universe as a whole is designed to produce good outcomes, including good outcomes for the human species. At the same time, he is concerned about humans' tendency toward moral error. Rather than cooperating with Zeus's benevolent purposes, people pursue their own "bad ends," which are of three kinds:

> witless, they act for various bad ends,
> some in contentious zeal for glory,
> others disorderly, bent upon gain,
> others for ease and bodily pleasures.

The regularity with which we pursue these mistaken aims is attributed by Cleanthes simply to "witlessness" and failure to see and hear the universal law. People indeed long to possess good things but misconceive where they are to be found.

Note again that the difficulty confronting the providentialist is not so much that people fail to get the right answer as that our wrong answers follow certain predictable patterns. Error in general need not present a problem, since one might posit a course of intellectual development in which correctness of view comes only with maturity. But if people exhibit marked tendencies to err in certain particular ways, then their errors begin to look suspiciously like design characteristics of the species. Some further explanation is required.[14] Cleanthes' hymn does not say anything further on this score, but Cleanthes' intellectually powerful successor Chrysippus of Soli did address the problem, as we shall see.

As a means of entry into the Chrysippan explanation it is helpful first to consult the outline summary of Stoic ethics by Diogenes Laertius. Diogenes writes, "The rational animal is corrupted sometimes by the persuasiveness of things from without, sometimes through the teaching (*katēchēsis*) of our associates. For the starting points which nature provides are uncorrupted" (7.89). Two causes are named for our perversion: first the persuasiveness of "things from without" and second, the teaching of one's associates. Nothing is said, in this barebones summary, about how these causes work. It is reasonable to suppose, however, that "things from without," if they are persuasive, must be impressions coming in propositional form from our environment and that the teaching of our associates comes by repeated verbal messages: *katēchēsis*, the word that later became *catechesis* as in religious instruction, is literally a dinning of something into one's ears. And we have every reason to think that the "starting points which nature provides" are the same "starting-points toward virtue" that Cleanthes compared to half-lines of poetry, "worthless when incomplete, but worthwhile [or righteous, *spoudaioi*] when completed."[15] According to other sources, these consist in our natural preferences for physical well-being, understanding, and the company of others. They are not virtues in themselves, nor even fully formed concepts, but they point us in the direction of virtues that we may develop as we mature.[16]

The dual explanation of moral error is explicitly linked by Galen to Chrysippus's *On Emotions*. Galen quotes Chrysippus's treatise in order to criticize his claim that children have a natural orientation toward moral excellence.[17] If that were true, says Galen, then faults could never arise from within but only from without, whereas what we actually observe is that even if children are reared in good habits and properly educated, never seeing or hearing any example of fault, they still go wrong sooner or later. Chrysippus himself admits this but thinks he has adequately explained the phenomena when he says (and here Galen seems to be quoting his exact words) that "the cause of perversion is twofold: one comes about through transmission from many people, the other through the very nature of things."[18] The phrase "through the very nature of things" is hopelessly vague; it is shortly to be restated, however, as "the persuasiveness of impressions," the same cause as is named in Diogenes Laertius. The terms "perversion" and "transmission" also match exactly with our other source.

Galen also indicates something of how Chrysippus developed his view, for as part of his critique he insists that Chrysippus has not explained why all the following occur: (1) pleasure gives us the persuasive impression that it is a good; (2) pain gives the persuasive impression that it is an evil; (3) we hear the many praise those who have had statues put up of them and are persuaded this is a good thing; (4) we hear defeat and dishonor spoken of as bad and are persuaded of this.[19] It is not entirely clear from this whether (3) and (4) are meant to be examples of persuasiveness or of transmission. It is significant, though, that Chrysippus not only listed the same two causes as are later found in Cicero but also gives at least some of the same examples.

A more comprehensive statement of the Chrysippan position can be found in a late source, a Latin commentary on Plato's *Timaeus* by a scholar named Calcidius, writing somewhere around 400 A.D. Calcidius's knowledge of the relevant Stoic doctrine is impressive: he supplies clear Latin equivalents for the terms "corruption" (*diastrophē*), "transmission" (*katēchēsis*), "the twofold cause" (*dittē aitia*), and "the circumstances themselves" (*auta ta pragmata*), language that is not preserved either in Cicero or in Seneca.[20] This suggests that he has access to material derived from the same Chrysippan treatise used by Galen. He may not have consulted that work himself; it is likely, though, that he worked closely with earlier *Timaeus* commentaries that supplied him with good information.[21]

Calcidius states clearly that what Stoics call "the twofold cause" is meant to explain how false values become established among people whose nature is to pursue the good. He describes this twofold cause as follows:

> This arises both from things themselves and from the transmission of rumor. For the very experience of being born involves some pain, because one is moving from a warm and moist place into the chill and dryness of the surrounding air, and as a remedy for this the midwife provides a warm bath and swaddling to recall the womb, to ease the young body with pleasant sensation and quiet it. Thus ... there arises a kind of natural belief that everything sweet and pleasurable is good, and that what brings pain is bad and to be avoided. Older children learn the same thing from the experience of hunger and satiety, and from caresses and punishments.
>
> As they mature, they retain this belief that everything nice is good, even if not useful, and that everything troublesome, even if it brings some advantage, is bad. Consequently they love riches, which are the foremost means of obtaining pleasure, and they embrace glory rather than honor. For humans are by nature inclined to pursue praise and honor, since honor is the testimony to virtue. But those who are wise and engaged in the study of wisdom know what sort of virtue they ought to cultivate, while people do not know about things and so cultivate glory, that is, popular esteem, in place of honor. And in place of virtue they pursue a life steeped in pleasures, believing that the power to do what one wants is the superiority of a king. For humans are by nature kingly, and since power always accompanies kingship, they suppose that kingship likewise accompanies power.... Similarly, since the happy person necessarily enjoys life, they think that those who live pleasurably will be happy. Such, I think, is the error which arises "from things" to possess the human mind.
>
> But the one which arises "from transmission" is a whispering added to the aforementioned error through the prayers of our mothers and nurses for wealth and glory and other things falsely supposed to be good, and a disturbance from the bogeys which frighten young people very much, and from comfortings and everything like that. Yes, and think of poetry, which shapes the minds of older children, and of the impressive productions of other authors! How great an influence concerning pleasure and suffering do they convey to the novice mind!

What about painters and sculptors? Do they not deliberately lead the mind toward sweetness?[22]

Unlike Galen, Calcidius admits that the Stoics have provided an explanation for what it is that makes pleasure, riches, and the like so appealing to people, without their being good in fact and independent of transmission. All these objects have a tendency to co-occur with objects that one is indeed inclined by nature to pursue. The warm bath and swaddling clothes ease and quiet the newborn body; they would count, then, as restorative of the natural constitution. But most restorative experiences are also pleasurable, and it is hardly surprising if the infant fails to realize that drinking milk or taking a bath is to be pursued qua healthful rather than qua pleasurable. The same can be said of an older child's experience of nourishment or of a parent's embrace. Because these things do provide pleasure, it is easy for a mind that has not yet formed the requisite concepts to assume that it is the pleasure itself that has value rather than the benefit to the natural functioning of our bodies and family units. Some epistemic confusion is practically inevitable; it is "a kind of natural belief" and yet not a true belief.

The account of pleasure as a concomitant or by-product (*epigennēma*) of activities that restore one's natural constitution is familiar to us already from another fragment of early Stoic thought.[23] Less familiar is the apparent implication that other objects mistakenly valued similarly supervene on one's natural goals. This is most clearly stated in the sentences on power and what Calcidius calls "kingship." Part of our native endowment is a predilection for mastery, which motivates us to assume control over our surroundings. But not every exercise of power is a manifestation of the human being's proper controlling role. Rather, power supervenes on that role just as pleasure supervenes on the flourishing condition.

Where honor and glory are concerned, there is an additional level of confusion to be sorted out. Humans are by nature inclined to pursue praise and honor, for honor, says Calcidius, is "the testimony to virtue": it has a reliable connection to virtuous action and for that reason constitutes a legitimate object of choice. But humans frequently make the mistake of cultivating another form of praise that is here called "glory," or "popular esteem," deceived apparently by the resemblance between justified and unjustified praise. Thus popular esteem stands at two removes from the real source of value: honor is derived from virtue, and popular esteem is then confused with honor.

The extra attention devoted to the topic of reputation is in keeping with the interests of Stoics in the early period. Separate definitions were given for honor (*timē*) and for repute (*doxa*): honor, we learn from the Stobaean summary, is a genuine good restricted to the virtuous, while repute merely a preferred indifferent.[24] Cleanthes is said to have composed a short treatise on each.[25] Calcidius's report helps to bring out the significance of the distinction within the developmental story. As the young person matures, he or she is expected to begin to value praiseworthy behavior for its own sake, no longer being deeply concerned for reputation, though still perhaps pursuing it as a preferred indifferent. But that new understanding of what behavior is praiseworthy has been derived largely from observations of what behavior commonly tends to be praised. During the period when one's own concepts of justice and integrity are still in the process of formation, there is no way to correct mistakes in this area. It is an inherently risky procedure.

Once the spontaneous cause of error is in place, the transmission from person to person happens quite easily. There was in the earlier paragraph no implication that the midwife acts improperly in bathing and swaddling the baby. Error in that case arises spontaneously, from babies' misinterpreting what happens to them. Here, by contrast, the caregiver is already in error, and the child has only to absorb and remember her values. Most false beliefs are transmitted verbally, from the "whispering" of those who pray in the child's hearing for the supposed blessings of wealth and reputation, or from tales of bogeymen intended to frighten the child into good behavior. Poetry and drama, mainstays of education in antiquity, are deeply implicated. So also are the visual arts, though these must convey their messages through symbolism or other non-linguistic means of representation.

Reception and Reconfiguration

Neither in *De Legibus* 1 nor in *Tusculan Disputations* 3 does Cicero make any explicit attribution of these arguments to Chrysippus or to the Stoic tradition. In the earlier work, he presents his view as a kind of consensus of mainline Greek philosophers, including the Old Academic Speusippus, Xenocrates, and Polemo, the followers of Aristotle and Theophrastus, Zeno of Citium, and Zeno's follower Aristo (1.38). It would spoil the rhetoric of his broad-based philosophical appeal if he were to admit that portions of his discussion are in fact derived from just one of the schools listed. In the passage in *Tusculan Disputations* 3, he follows his usual convention for book prefaces and addresses the reader in his own voice, as if in the *parodos* of an Aristophanic comedy. Again it would be inapropos for him to reveal just at this point that not all of the ideas expressed are of his own devising.

That at least some of his ideas do originate in the Stoa may nonetheless be suspected even without taking into account the correspondences we have seen here. An alert reader will note a covert reference to Stoicism in *De Legibus* 1.36, when Marcus compares his own procedure to that of "philosophers—not those old ones but the ones who have, as it were, set up philosophical workshops," who will not argue broadly but insist upon presenting separate arguments that justice exists by nature.[26] Moreover, the Stoic provenance of important ideas in the discussion can be identified by close verbal echoes among attested fragments of Chrysippus's *On Laws*.[27] Neither is the preface to *Tusculan Disputations* 3 entirely Cicero's own composition. It is in fact quite unlike most Ciceronian book prefaces in that it takes up a philosophical problem rather than merely reflecting on the act of writing philosophy. And there is, again, a clear echo of a known fragment of Chrysippus's *On Emotions* in the preface immediately before the passage we have studied.[28] When we see, as well, that in both works Cicero makes extensive use of a distinctive explanation that is attested for Chrysippus, we cannot but conclude that he here relies heavily, though tacitly, on his knowledge of that author. This knowledge may well have been gained directly from reading the treatises in question, though he had benefited also from the oral instruction of Diodotus and others and retained much in his prodigious memory.

With that said, we should also be sensitive to the ways he may have adapted or extended his Stoic inheritance. It is instructive to compare the above passage from Calcidius with the two versions given to us by Cicero. Calcidius's Latinity is notably deficient, but the contrast between the two extends further than matters of language and style. Calcidius proceeds in a simple, rather pedestrian way, attending to each element of the explanation in sequential fashion and bringing out as best he can the meaning of such phrases as "twofold cause," "transmission of rumor," and "the things themselves." Cicero, by contrast, chooses not to make use of any terms immediately recognizable as Stoic—for while *corruptela* in *Leg.* 1.33 is a fair equivalent for *diastrophē*, it bears no special emphasis in its context. Instead, he focuses his accounts on points that are of interest to him: in *Leg.* 1.31–32, the substitution of false for true values; in *Leg.* 1.47, the corruption of opinion by a sequence of authority figures; in *Tusc.* 3.2–4, the especially pernicious influence of honor and glory. In the passage from the *Tusculan Disputations*, moreover, he uses language that calls to mind the earlier handling of the perversion theme by Plato in the *Republic*. Not only does he draw upon the imagery of the Cave narrative, with its multiple shadows and reflections, but he also retains the emphasis of Plato's more direct treatment of the issue in Book 6, when he speaks at length of the effect of popular acclaim on those who are noblest among us. The Platonic echoes do not seem to have been in Chrysippus's version; at least if they were they do not survive in any discernible way in Calcidius or any other Stoic source. Most probably, Cicero has added them himself.

Cicero's own philosophy is a tricky thing to get hold of. Because of the depth and range of his intellectual interests, venturing into many works that no longer survive for our scrutiny, and because of the cautious stance he adopts with his public, refraining from any definite assertion on many of the subjects he treats, it is usually very difficult to say what he himself thought on a given issue. If we are ever to catch his elusive mind at work, it will be in the way he negotiates the tensions among (at least) four intellectual motives. First of these is his perception, influenced apparently by Antiochus, that an insightful reading will find much common ground between the ethics of Plato (and Plato's early or dogmatic followers) and that of the Stoics generally. The second is his conviction that it is in the public interest to uphold what he considers the mainline virtue tradition in Greek philosophy as represented by those just named. The third is his intense admiration, partly on aesthetic grounds, for the dialogues of Plato and his desire to make similar use of his own literary talent. But fourth, and closest to the ground, is his personal experience of a career in politics, of the instability of reputation and the internal effects of the constant effort to maintain it. In his handling of the perversion theme we see all four of these at work. The Stoic explanation has provided Cicero with a basis for argumentation, but the form that argument assumes is distinctively Ciceronian.

NOTES

I wish to thank the participants in the Notre Dame conference for their responses to the earlier version of this paper, and Walter Nicgorski for encouragement to recast it in its present form.

   1. See for instance *Rep.* 1.2–3, 1.41; *Leg.* 1.16–19, 24–25; *Tusc.* 1.40–42. I give fuller treatment to the nuances of his theological position in Graver, "Cicero's Philosophy of Religion."
   2. This portion of the argument is presented also in Graver, *Stoicism and Emotion*, 149–63, which gives a more comprehensive treatment of the Stoics' intellectual position.
   3. Dyck, *A Commentary on Cicero, De Legibus*, 5–6, effectively counters arguments that have been proposed for a later date.
   4. For the broader issues see Schofield, "Two Stoic Approaches to Justice"; Mitsis, "Natural Law and Natural Right"; and Striker, *Essays in Hellenistic Epistemology and Ethics*, 209–20.
   5. *Leg.* 1.27: "Now, since it is god who has begotten and adorned the human being, wishing humans to take precedence over all other things, let it now be clearly understood (without exhaustive discussion) that human nature goes on its own beyond that point, and, even without instruction, starting from those things whose kinds it has conceived through its initial and inchoate intelligence, consolidates and perfects its rationality all by itself." Concept-formation is indicated in the phrase "whose kinds it has conceived" (*genera cognovit*); the "initial and inchoate intelligence" precedes and promotes this. Consequently the *intelligentiae* are not themselves concepts formed through experience. It seems to me most natural to take them as equivalent to the *aphormai* in Diogenes Laertius 7.89. They might, however, be equivalent to the Stoic 'pre-conceptions' (*prolēpseis*), depending on how that term is interpreted; see note 16 below.
   6. Reading *vanitas* with the MS; see Dyck, *A Commentary on Cicero, De Legibus*, 146.

7. *Leg.* 1.30: *nullam dissimilitudinem esse in genere* (the rendering is by Zetzel, *On the Commonwealth and On the Laws*, 116).

8. For the metaphors, compare *Fin.* 5.18, 5.43; *Tusc.* 3.2; *Rep.* 1.41; and note also *Rep.* 1.3.

9. The translation given here (making *dolor* the subject of *sequi*) is more in accordance with Latin idiom than the rendering preferred by Zetzel and Keyes, making *interitus* ("destruction(s)") the subject and inferring *eum* (i.e., "pain") as object.

10. *Tusc.* 3.2. For a more detailed explication of the passage, see Graver, *Cicero on the Emotions*, 74–78, 206–7.

11. See especially Long, "Cicero's Politics in *De Officiis*," and compare *Fin.* 2.48–49; *Tusc.* 1.109–10, 2.63–64; *Off.* 1.65.

12. Despite *Fin.* 3.24, the term "right actions" (*recte facta*) need not refer in this context to the Stoic *katorthōmata*. The right actions here are performed by ordinary persons on the basis of judgments that are the same in content as the wise person would make. Thus in Stoic terms they are simply "appropriate actions" (*kathēkonta*).

13. Compare *Tusc.* 1.109: "Although glory is not pursued for any intrinsic reason, still it follows virtue like a shadow."

14. This issue is identified by Striker, *Essays in Hellenistic Epistemology and Ethics*, 253, as a serious defect in the Stoics' naturalistic account of human development, on which see further Brunschwig, "The Cradle Argument"; Engberg-Pedersen, *The Stoic Theory of Oikeiosis*; Frede, "On the Stoic Conception of the Good"; and Inwood, *Reading Seneca*, 271–301.

15. Stobaeus 2.7.5b8 [Long and Sedley, *The Hellenistic Philosophers*, 61L].

16. On the *aphormai* and on Cicero's report of this doctrine in *Fin.* 3.16–21 and *Off.* 1.11–14, see Graver, *Stoicism and Emotion*, 151–53, 246–47; and Jackson-McCabe, "The Stoic Theory of Implanted Conceptions."

17. According to Galen, the same criticisms had already been expressed by the earlier Stoic Posidonius. Further information on Posidonius and on possible connections between his views and those of Cicero may be found in Graver, *Cicero on the Emotions*, 215–23, and *Stoicism and Emotion*, 75–76; see also Gill, "Personhood and Personality"; and Tieleman, *Chrysippus' On Affections*, 198–207.

18. Galen, *PHP* 5.5.14. It is made quite clear in *PHP* 5.4.5–17 that the Chrysippan work being criticized is indeed *On Emotions*.

19. *PHP* 5.5.14–15, 19–20; cf. 5.5.21, quoting Posidonius.

20. For Seneca's knowledge of the topic, see *Ep.* 94.53–54; 115.8–14; 118.7–11. In his case it is possible that the knowledge is derived from Cicero.

21. Among earlier commentaries on the *Timaeus* were some written by authors familiar with Stoic thought: Crantor, Posidonius, Calvenus Taurus, and Galen. But the surviving evidence is meager; see Reydams-Schils, *Demiurge and Providence*, 207–10; and Sedley, "Plato's *Auctoritas*." I differ from

Reydams-Schils on the role of Posidonius in the transmission. Chrysippus's own treatise was still widely available for consultation in at least the second century A.D., whereas that of Posidonius seems to have been little known; at least it is not mentioned by authors other than Galen. The value of the Calcidius material for understanding Chrysippus's view is urged also in Tieleman, *Chrysippus' On Affections*, 133–38, 161–62.

22. Calcidius, *On the Timaeus of Plato* 165–66 (= *SVF* 3.229); text in Waszink, *Timaeus*.

23. D.L. 7.86: "As for what some say, that it is toward pleasure that the first impulse of living things comes about, they deny it. For they say that pleasure, if indeed it occurs, is a by-product when [the animal's] nature all of itself seeks out and obtains the things that are fitted to its constitution."

24. Stobaeus, *Ecl.* 2.7.7e (83W), 5l (73W), 11i (103W). The standard Stoic definition for *timē*, given in Stobaeus (2.7.11i, 103W) and in Alexander of Aphrodisias (*On Fate* 35 = *SVF* 2.1003), connects it with virtue as Calcidius does: *timē* is "evaluation as worthy of reward," with "reward" being "the prize for virtue that does good works."

25. D.L. 7.175.

26. Zetzel, *On the Commonwealth and On the Laws*, 118 n. 45, is wrong to refer this to "philosophers up to Plato's time." "Old" is Cicero's marker for the late-fourth-century Academy, and "workshop" must be the organized Hellenistic schools. For the argumentative rigor of the Stoic school, cf. *Fin.* 4.5–6.

27. On the sources of *De Legibus* 1, see Dyck, *A Commentary on Cicero, De Legibus*, 49–52; Ferrary, "Statesman and Law," 67–68. In addition to a general similarity of themes and outlook, there are close similarities of language at 1.18 and 1.33; cf. *SVF* 3.314 (Marcianus) and 3.310 (Proclus).

28. The Chrysippan passage is quoted by Galen in *PHP* 5.2.22–24. For further exploration of Cicero's sources in this portion of the *Tusculan Disputations*, see the appendices to Graver, *Cicero on the Emotions*.

6

Radical and Mitigated Skepticism in Cicero's *Academica*

HARALD THORSRUD

Throughout his philosophical dialogues, Cicero characterizes the Academic method as a mitigated skepticism: certainty is beyond our reach, but by arguing pro and contra, one is able to draw out and give shape to the truth or its nearest approximation (*Acad.* 2.7). Given the consistency with which Cicero practices and defends this method, it is surprising that he also appears to endorse an incompatible, radical skepticism in the *Academica*: certainty is beyond our reach, and we must suspend judgment regarding any matter on which we cannot be certain. To do otherwise would be rash and foolish (*Acad.* 2.113, cf. 2.67, 2.78).

On several occasions Cicero points his readers to his Academic books for an explanation of his philosophical allegiance.[1] So it would be confusing, to say the least, if he were defending a view of the Academic method in the *Academica* that he fundamentally disagrees with elsewhere. The alternative I argue for is that the supposedly radical skepticism Cicero endorses is actually consistent with his usual position of mitigated skepticism.

Mitigated Skepticism and the Fallible Sage

Before turning to the evidence for radical skepticism, we should consider the character of Cicero's mitigated variety. Woldemar Görler has persuasively argued that Cicero's allegiance remained unchanged throughout his life.[2] He accounts for the apparently dogmatic tone in the dialogues of the 50s (*De Oratore*, *De Re Publica*, and *De Legibus*) as a matter of focus and not philosophical allegiance. "There was always an antagonism in Cicero. He strongly wished to believe in certain doctrines (or dogmata): immortality of the soul, existence of God, self-sufficiency of virtue, and so on. But from youth on, he was a skeptic, knowing well that none of this could ever be proved."[3] So the middle dialogues exhibit the more epistemologically optimistic side and the later dialogues the more cautious side; nonetheless they are two sides of the same coin.

These aspects of Cicero's character are reflected in his view of Academic philosophy. Cicero is forthright about the human epistemic predicament: just as it is supremely honorable to discern the truth, it is shameful to approve what is false as if it were true.[4] His competing desires to avoid error and believe the truth feature prominently in his earliest as well as his latest expressions of allegiance to the Academy.[5]

As the only means of acquiring ever-closer approximations to the truth, Cicero must have thought the Academic method the best route to wisdom as well. He could hardly have offered it up to his fellow Romans as preferable to every other school if he thought otherwise. This is especially the case given Cicero's view of the great benefit he was providing his fellow Romans by encouraging them to engage in Academic philosophy.[6] So for Cicero, the road to wisdom is paved with cautious opinion.

Does it follow that wisdom itself is compatible with holding mere opinion? If not, if wisdom requires infallibility, then argument pro and contra will never get us there, for in the end all we will have is closer, though still fallible, approximations. Thus progress must come in degrees, if it comes at all.

Cicero thinks (at least sometimes) that the same is true in the ethical context also. In *De Finibus*, he remarks that those who studiously pursue virtue gradually diminish their errors and vices (*Fin.*

4.65). This remark is specifically aimed at the very different, Stoic account of moral progress. For strictly orthodox Stoics the completion of this progress is marked by a sudden and complete transformation from ordinary human being to extraordinary sage. It is as if one finally emerges from the water and is able to breathe. Drowning in one hundred feet of water is no different from drowning in only two if you cannot make it to the top. In the same way, all vice is equally vicious. Just as one cannot be more or less drowning while deprived of oxygen, one cannot be more or less vicious.

What makes the qualitative transformation into sagehood possible is the existence of a certain kind of impression about which one cannot be mistaken. According to the Stoics, everyone receives such *kataleptic* impressions, but the sage alone has developed his sensory and cognitive equipment so that he is able to assent only to these and never to any others. Because of the firmness of the sage's character, he is never even tempted to perform an immoral action. But if it were not possible to be certain regarding the empirical world, he could never arrive at moral certainty either. As strict empiricists, the Stoics believe that all of our knowledge originates in experience. Any uncertainty in that experience will be inherited by the higher-order judgments we make regarding what is morally valuable.

While there is a great deal more to be said about this, it is sufficient for our purposes to note that in order for an impression to be *kataleptic*, it must be such that it could not arise from what is not the case. The Academics aimed to show that this condition could never be met. They assembled two kinds of counterexamples. First, we may imagine two objects that are so similar no one can tell them apart (e.g., twins, eggs, imprints made in wax, and so on, *Acad.* 2.84–87). Even granting a high degree of skill at differentiating such objects, Cicero contends that the possibility of mistaking one thing for another always remains. Second, we can imagine richly detailed and vivid but false impressions that arise from madness, drunkenness, or other abnormal mental states (*Acad.* 2.88–91). Such impressions give us no indication themselves that they are false, once again assuring our fallibility.

By virtue of these arguments, Cicero thinks he has shown that the Stoics fail to defend adequately their account of knowledge. As long as they cannot rule out the possibility of such errors, they cannot assert that anyone is ever able to identify an impression as *kataleptic*. But if it is unclear whether anyone could acquire the disposition to assent only to *kataleptic* impressions, it is unclear whether anyone could become a Stoic sage.

On at least five different occasions, Cicero (or his Academic spokesman) remarks that there never have been any real life Stoic sages.[7] However, in one of these passages Cicero expresses more than a grudging admiration for this apparently unattainable ideal. In *De Amicitia* (18–19), he claims that even though the Stoics may be right, they discuss the topic of friendship and moral goodness with too much precision or subtlety and with too little concern for common practice, that is, for communal standards for the use and application of these terms.[8] At this point in the discussion, Laelius is not able, or at least willing, to reveal the flaws in the Stoic arguments, but he does not accept their view that no true friendships have ever existed because no truly good, that is, virtuous human beings, have ever lived. He prefers the more moderate view that true friendships, though exceedingly rare, have existed among those who have attained some degree of the moral goodness that is available to human beings: "Those who so act and so live as to give proof of loyalty and uprightness, of fairness and generosity; who are free from all passion, caprice, and insolence, and have great strength of character . . . let us consider good, as they were accounted good in life . . . because in as far as that is possible for man, they follow Nature, who is the best guide to good living" (*Amic.* 19).[9] He even offers the Stoics a compromise: let them keep their invidious and obscure usage of the term wisdom (*sapientia*) as long as they will grant that some people have achieved a real goodness that falls short of this ideal. They decline the offer. But this clearly indicates that Cicero (via his character Laelius) allows for two distinct conceptions of wisdom: one, a lofty, unattainable ideal, and the other, an expression of the best that real human beings can achieve.[10]

The distinction between actual and ideal virtue also appears in the opening remarks to *De Officiis* 3. In that book Cicero discusses cases in which what appears to be expedient conflicts with what is morally right. The goal of this discussion is to illustrate the general rule that what is truly expedient never conflicts with what is morally required and vice versa. As the Stoic sage would have no need of seeing this principle illustrated, the discussion is aimed at the rest of us who fall short of Stoic virtue. Cicero's ultimate goal is to encourage us to perform more consistently the morally right actions we non-sages are capable of performing. The Stoics called these "mean duties" (*kathēkonta*, which Cicero translates *officia*). When these actions are performed from the perfectly virtuous disposition of the sage, they take on the character of perfect duties (*katorthōmata*).

But Cicero thinks that no living person has ever developed the disposition of perfect wisdom. So when he refers to the courage or justice of real Roman heroes, he does not mean for us to understand these as *perfect* models of virtue. They achieved only a semblance and likeness to wisdom (*similitudinem quondam ... speciemque sapientium*, *Off.* 3.16). Nonetheless, Cicero refers to these real-life exemplars as good men, *boni* (e.g., *Off.* 3.62, cf. also 3.31), a term the Stoics reserve exclusively for their ideal sage (D.L. 7.100). And he clearly thinks their moral achievements have greater significance than the orthodox Stoic would allow.[11]

Regulus is one of those that Cicero would have us consider wise and courageous (*Off.* 3.99–115). The legend Cicero retails is that after Regulus had been captured by Xanthippus, he was sent back to Rome to negotiate an exchange of prisoners, being sworn to return to Carthage if he should fail. Knowing that the Carthaginian prisoners were extremely dangerous enemies of Rome, he argued against their release in the Senate. Once he convinced the Senate that this was in the best interest of the State, he returned to face torture and death in Carthage rather than betray his oath. This story is offered as a striking instance of an apparent conflict of expediency and moral obligation. Regulus could not have failed to see that staying in Rome with his family and friends appeared to be in his own best interest. But Cicero praises him for placing the good of the state first, and more importantly for seeing that his real interest lies in preserving his oath.

In what sense did Regulus *see* that his real interest coincides with his moral obligation? Cicero does not offer any account of his hero's mental states. But he appears to have had this kind of case in mind earlier in the *Academica* when he has Lucullus draw some unacceptable consequences from the Academic position of *akatalēpsia*.

> Suppose their constancy [of the sage] didn't depend on any apprehension or knowledge. Then I'd like to know where it does come from,

and how; and why the good man resolves to endure every torture or be wracked by intolerable pain rather than give up on an appropriate action or his word.... It's impossible for anyone to value impartiality and fidelity so highly that there's no punishment he would refuse in order to maintain them, unless he has given his assent to <impressions> that can't be false. (*Acad.* 2.23)[12]

In other words, Regulus would never have done what he did if he were not completely certain that it was in his true interest to be tortured to death. If his actions stemmed from an irrational or fanatic conviction, we should not find him admirable. But of course, other options are available. Regulus may have been moved by a profound and rational, though fallible, conviction. Indeed, what all of Cicero's real-life ethical models have in common is a deeply held conviction that virtue alone is good and vice evil, or short of that, at least that the good of virtue so far outweighs all other goods as to make them morally insignificant (*Off.* 3.33). But none of these real-life sages, as far as Cicero is concerned, could have had certain knowledge that their *praecepta* are true.

To sum up, Cicero maintains that there is a kind of wisdom that is attainable and a kind that is not. Since he thinks that even the most careful and responsible judgment of probable truth may always turn out to be wrong, that is, that deception is an inescapable part of human life, it follows that the attainable type of wisdom must be compatible with it. The real life sage will have thoroughly considered and defended opinions, the ideal one will not.

What to Do with Cicero's Infallible Sage and Radical Skepticism

Given his general and marked preference for mitigated skepticism, we may reasonably expect to find Cicero agreeing with Philo's view in the *Academica* that the sage will sometimes hold opinions. But he emphatically does not.

Cicero reports a disagreement between Philo and Clitomachus regarding the proper interpretation of Carneades, specifically whether he thought the sage would assent to something unknown. The two options emerge in the form of related arguments Carneades used against the

Stoics. Assuming he had shown that the Stoic requirements for an impression to be *kataleptic* can never be met, he sometimes argued this way, following Arcesilaus (*Acad.* 2.67).

> (A) If the sage assents (to something unknown) he will hold an opinion. The sage will never hold an opinion (he is infallible). Therefore, the sage will never assent to anything (since there is nothing worthy of his assent).

And he sometimes argued this way (*Acad.* 2.78, 67, 59).

> (B) If the sage assents (to something unknown) he will hold an opinion. The sage assents (to something unknown). Therefore, the sage holds opinions (and is fallible).

Neither of these options is acceptable to the Stoics. Since they thought that assent is necessary for action, (A) would render the sage impassive. And they had to reject (B) because they thought that assenting to what is unknown is foolish and blameworthy (M 7.157), and thus that the sage would never opine (D.L. 7.121). Again, for the Stoics, opining is a moral as well as an epistemic failing.

Cicero agrees with Clitomachus in maintaining that Carneades granted the sage will have opinions only for the sake of refuting the Stoics and not because he approved of this view himself (*Acad.* 2.78, 67). But more importantly, Cicero affirms that the sage will hold no opinions (*Acad.* 2.66). He even goes to the trouble of reassuring us that he is not merely saying this to suit the occasion but that he genuinely, openly believes it (*Acad.* 2.113).

Well then, which is it? Does Cicero believe the sage will have opinions or not? In the next section, I will consider and reject the notion that he changed his mind on this issue. For now I would like to propose a charitable and economical resolution: he believes the ideal Stoic sage will have no opinions, and he believes the actual sage will have opinions.

Clitomachus interprets Carneades' arguments as dialectical, so he employs the Stoic concepts of *sage* and *opinion*. These concepts are apparent in Lucullus's outrage at the thought that the sage will ever have opinions, that is, that he will ever transgress (*opinaturum id est peccaturum*, *Acad.* 2.59). As long as Cicero accepts the Stoic view of wisdom and opinion (dialectically, for the sake of refutation), he is quite right to agree with Lucullus: the ideal Stoic sage never opines.

Philo and Metrodorus, by contrast, do not interpret Carneades' arguments as dialectical. So it is open to them to provide different interpretations of wisdom and opinion, allowing the real life sage to have carefully considered and thoroughly defended opinions.

It is consistent for Cicero to agree both with Clitomachus's interpretation of Carneades' dialectical strategy (A) and with Philo's positive development of Carneades' arguments as well (B). The shortcoming of this view is that it dissolves the disagreement that Cicero reports between Clitomachus and Philo into a simple equivocation on *opinion* and *sage*. But in that case, why does Cicero bother to take sides in a non-existent dispute?

I have no answer to this question. But Cicero never explicitly refers to this disagreement elsewhere. In this instance when he does, he drops it as quickly as he raises it (*sed id omittamus*, *Acad.* 2.78). On the other hand, the coherence of Cicero's account of Academic methodology hangs in the balance. If it can be avoided, we should not attribute to Cicero both the defense of mitigated skepticism and the infallibility of the sage in the very dialogue in which he defends his Academic allegiance.

It is clear that Cicero sometimes uses the concepts of *opinion* and *wisdom* in the Stoic sense and sometimes in his preferred Academic sense. For the most part we have to rely on the context to determine which it is. For example, when he announces that he is a great opinion-holder (*Acad.* 2.66), he is referring to the results of his application of the Academic method; these are the opinions he has deemed *veri simile*. And he takes a good deal of pride in his self-appointed status as *magnus opinator*.[13] As far as he is concerned, his opinions are not the reckless transgressions a Stoic might take them for.

On the other hand, his disavowal of wisdom in the same passage must be understood within the dialectical context. He is disavowing *Stoic* wisdom: "[I guide my thoughts] by more easily accessible principles, not ones refined almost to the vanishing point. As a result, I err or wander farther afield. But it's not me, as I said, but the wise person we are investigating. When these [less precise] impressions strike my mind or senses sharply, I accept them, and sometimes even assent to them (although I don't apprehend them, since I think that nothing is apprehensible). I'm not wise, so I yield to these impressions and can't resist them" (*Acad.* 2.66). Cicero's intellectual roaming refers to his cherished Academic freedom. So it is not simply a synonym for error, and he is not simply critical of his fallibility. The interpretative crux is the distinction between the "more easily accessible principles" and those "refined almost to the vanishing point." The analogy he draws is between these two kinds of principles and constellations that are used in navigation. Cicero prefers the Septentriones, the brighter and hence more easily seen constellation. It appears earlier in the evening and shines throughout the night. The other constellation is the Cynosure. This one is composed of the same number of stars but is smaller and more difficult to see. Phoenician sailors prefer this constellation because it enables them to steer a more direct course (*Acad.* 2.66, *Nat. D.* 2.104–6).

The analogous distinction between principles is this. One type is extremely difficult to employ. Indeed, they are quite hard to make out in the first place. Yet if one were able to grasp them, he would be infallible, going directly to the truth in each case. The other type is far more evident, though less precise. They are more readily available and ultimately more useful for those who lack the ability to grasp the first type. But it does not necessarily follow that they are a mere second best. Since Cicero has the Stoic sage specifically in mind in this passage, the analogy breaks down when we realize there are no principles corresponding to the Cynosure, or at least none that anyone can actually employ. And so, in fact, we are all left to navigate by the Septentriones, that is, *probabilia*. This anticipates Cicero's later assurance that Academics simply do away with what never existed and leave what is sufficient for life (*Acad.* 2.146).

Furthermore, when Cicero presents views of Clitomachus on how the sage will live and act while suspending judgment (*Acad.* 2.99–104), it appears that the portrait is of an actual and not a merely possible sage. Even your (Stoic) sage, he says to Lucullus, will make use of the same merely probable or convincing impressions that ours does (*Acad.* 2.99, 105). If he were arguing dialectically at this point, there could be no reason for introducing an Academic sage. Living prudently in accordance with *probabilia* is what we must all strive to do, not just the Stoics.

Dogmatic and Skeptically Appropriate Assent in the *Academica*

In Cicero's view, to follow *probabilia* is to adopt fallible beliefs, even for the sage. Cicero paraphrases at length from the books of Clitomachus in order to show how the sage operates while suspending assent.

> The wise person is said to suspend assent in two senses: in one sense, when this means that he will assent to nothing entirely;[14] in another, when it means that he will restrain himself even from giving responses showing that he approves or disapproves of something, so that he won't say "yes" or "no" to anything. Given this distinction, the wise person accepts the suspension of assent in the first sense, with the result that he never assents [entirely]; but he holds on to his assent in the second sense, with the result that, by following what is persuasive wherever that is present or deficient, he is able to reply "yes" or "no." (*Acad.* 2.104)

So there are two kinds of positive attitudes the sage might take toward objects of potential assent, (i.e., propositions associated with impressions): an unreserved assent and a more qualified, or restrained, approval.

A mitigated skeptic will agree that we should withhold assent in some sense. At the end of the dialogue, Catulus puts the point this way: "While I don't think that anything is apprehensible, I still reckon that the wise person will assent to something he hasn't apprehended— that is hold opinions—but in such a way that he understands that it is an opinion and realizes that nothing is apprehensible. So, while I accept[15] that universal *epochē*, the other Academic view, that nothing is apprehensible, has my vehement approval"[16] (*Acad.* 2.148). In order for Catulus to accept universal *epochē*, it must be possible to withhold assent (in some sense) and yet also assent in the fallible manner he describes. What renders assent skeptically appropriate on this view is that he does not take himself to know what he merely believes to be true. So Catulus would identify dogmatic assent as a double judgment: one judges that *p* is true, and then also that one knows *p* is true. These need not be distinct. The second judgment may be understood more simply as the manner in which one assents to the truth of *p*. In any case, one may avoid dogmatic assent by not taking himself to know that what he assents to is true. (We should not think this is an easy task—a hard-won awareness of his ignorance is precisely the advantage Socrates enjoyed over everyone else.)

The outstanding question is whether and how these two kinds of assent described by Catulus (= Philo) differ from those described by Clitomachus. It is likely that they share the same conception of dogmatic assent. Clitomachus describes this as "assenting entirely," which I take to mean "without any reservation," that is, with no hesitation or doubt as to the truth of what one assents to. Catulus similarly sees dogmatic assent as taking something to be true along with the confidence that one knows it is true.[17] The Academic sage inquires "with the fear of forming *rash opinions* and the thought that things are going wonderfully for him if he finds something truth-like in questions of this sort" (*Acad.* 2.128). On this interpretation, the Herculean labor that Carneades accomplished was to throw out opinion in the Stoic sense of the term along with the associated vices of rashness and obstinacy (*Acad.* 2.109).

Regarding skeptically appropriate assent, Catulus describes a consciously fallible judgment that takes the form "*p* is probably true" or "*p* resembles the truth," and Clitomachus describes a positive attitude that merely allows the sage to say yes or no to the impression. One widely accepted view of the latter is that it is passive and truth-indifferent. That is to say, when the Clitomachian sage assents, he does not assent to an impression *as true*; he is utterly indifferent to whether it is true or false, or even whether it is probably true or false. Unlike Catulus's (or Philo's) fallible sage, this one merely finds the impression subjectively convincing—it seems right, good, and so on—but as to whether it really is, he has no view whatsoever.[18]

Such a position is evident in the account of skeptically appropriate assent by Sextus Empiricus. Like the Academics, Sextus does not see his attack on dogmatism and the resulting *epochē* to threaten ordinary life: "attending to what is apparent, we live in accordance with everyday observances, without holding opinions—for we are not able to be utterly inactive" (PH 1.23).[19] The basic idea is that the skeptic may yield to, or go along with, appearances in a passive sense. Such yielding, which Sextus describes as a kind of assent (PH 1.193), does not result in holding an opinion, since it is merely a passive acquiescence in the way things appear; it does not commit him to any view about the way the world really is. When he feels heated or chilled, hungry or thirsty, he goes along with these impressions in seeking the appropriate remedy (PH 1.13).

Sextus differentiates this Pyrrhonian view of acquiescing in appearances with Clitomachus's and Carneades' view of going along with things that are plausible (*pithanon*). The fundamental difference is found in the two senses of *peithesthai*: "It means not resisting but simply following without strong inclination or adherence (as a boy is said to go along with his chaperon); and it sometimes means assenting to something by choice and, as it were, sympathy (as a dissolute man goes along with someone who urges extravagant living)" (PH 1.230). Pyrrhonists simply yield without adherence and without deliberately choosing to yield. Carneades and Clitomachus, by contrast, yield in accordance with a strong wish and strong inclination. Thus the main difference, as Sextus sees it, is that Academics actively and deliberately accept and prefer certain impressions, whereas Pyrrhonists allow themselves to be guided without actively choosing among their impressions or preferring one to another.

Some scholars have discounted these claims on the grounds that Sextus either misunderstands the dialectical character of Carneades' *pithanon* or that he is unduly concerned to brand the New Academics as crypto-dogmatists. They may be right. But it is a mistake, I believe, to import this view to Cicero's understanding of the Clitomachian passages in the *Academica*. To do so, we would have to say that prior to the *Academica*, he maintains the sage is guided by cautious, fallible judgments; and then in the *Academica*, he maintains that the sage withholds judgment in the absence of certainty but is guided by a passive, truth-indifferent acquiescence to how things seem; and then after the *Academica*, he reverts to his original view. We might appeal to Cicero's intellectual freedom as an Academic to account for such a radical shift (cf. *Tusc.* 5.33). But again: such an exercise of intellectual freedom would undoubtedly confuse the reader looking for the promised explanation of Cicero's affiliation in the *Academica* (*Nat. D.* 1.11; *Tusc.* 2.4; *Div.* 2.1).[20] Also, if wisdom consists in eliminating all opinions, the mitigated skepticism that Cicero defends even in the preface to the *Academica* would be counterproductive.

Unfortunately, the relevant passages in the *Academica* (especially 2.99–104) do not themselves provide adequate detail to settle this issue—neither the question of what Cicero understood by this type of assent nor what Clitomachus understood by it. We are never told explicitly what relation, if any, *probabilia* (= *ta pithana*) are supposed to have to the truth, and we are never told whether skeptically appropriate assent is active or passive. Even when Cicero describes convincing impressions as *similia veri* (*Acad.* 2.99, cf. 2.108) and says that many things seem true to the sage (*Acad.* 2.101), we need not infer that assent to such impressions requires a judgment of probable truth. One may just notice that such and such appears true without committing himself to it actually being true, though I must admit I find highly obscure the notion of taking something to be convincing but not taking it to be probably true.[21]

Similarly, Cicero never comments on whether skeptically appropriate assent requires any active engagement with or choice among impressions. We find that the sage will use whatever strikes him as persuasive (*Acad.* 2.99), but such reliance could simply describe what the sage in fact does, automatically as it were. So too: "anything that induces in him a persuasive impression without any impediment will move him to act" (*Acad.* 2.101). In this regard, it is notable that Clitomachus maintained that for those who suspend judgment, "there are still impressions of the kind that excite us to action" (*Acad.* 2.104).

These and other passages suggest the kind of picture we find in a passage from Plutarch's *Against Colotes* (1122A–F). Plutarch reports Arcesilaus's argument that the first two elements in the Stoic account of human action, impression and impulse, are sufficient to initiate action; the third element, assent, is not necessary. In particular, we need not assent to an impression of something appropriate or desirable in order to experience an impulse; at least sometimes, impulse arises directly from our impressions and compels us to act. Thus we may suspend judgment—that is, refrain from assenting—and yet remain active.

On the other hand, we also find in Cicero's account of Clitomachus's view that the whole structure of the sage's life will be governed in this way (*Acad.* 2.99) and that the sage will deliberate about what to do on the basis of persuasive impressions (*Acad.* 2.100). It is hard to believe that Cicero could think passive acquiescence in how the world appears could produce an admirably structured life. Further, "if a question be put to [the sage] about duty [*de officio*] ... he would not reply in the same way as he would if questioned as to whether the number of stars is even or odd" (*Acad.* 2.110).[22] Clearly, it would not do for Regulus merely to acquiesce in what seems to be his duty. As Cicero describes this, it is a momentous judgment, and one, we should add, that is rendered all the more poignant given the fact that he could be mistaken about where his duty lies.

If we are to determine what Cicero thinks about *probabilia* in these passages on the basis of what he says elsewhere, we will be compelled to say that following *probabilia* is just another expression of mitigated skepticism. Nothing in his paraphrase of Clitomachus prevents us from doing so, and preserving the coherence of Cicero's account of the Academy, as well as his usage of the term *probabilitas* in the *Academica*, encourages us to do so.[23] It would be quite surprising for Cicero to use such an important term within the same dialogue to indicate a fallible criterion of truth on some occasions (e.g., *Acad.* 2.7) and then to indicate a purely subjective or truth-indifferent persuasiveness on others.[24]

To avoid these problems we should say that there is little, if any, real difference between the skeptically appropriate assent described by Catulus and that described by Clitomachus, at least as far as Cicero is concerned.[25] Replying "yes" to an impression may be understood as accepting it as convincing, that is, judging that it is probably true. Cicero's real-life sage is able to avoid the rashness and obstinacy of dogmatic assent while nevertheless holding firm to his fallible conviction.

This interpretation makes the best sense out of the sage's acceptance of the conclusion that Cicero would have us accept as well: nothing is apprehensible (*nihil posse percipi*). Antiochus argued that the Academics hold this as their principle (*decretum* = *dogma*) and are committed to its truth in such a way that should allow for no doubt (*Acad.* 2.28–29). In the absence of the Stoic criterion of truth, the Academics provide a different criterion on the basis of which we should accept some impressions and reject others. Antiochus apparently thought that the Academics' willingness to teach this method to others requires that they claim at least to have grasped that the Stoic criterion is a fiction and that their alternative is the right one. Otherwise, they should not be so willing and eager to teach others what they themselves do not claim to know.

Regardless of the merits of Antiochus's objection, it is striking that in his response, Cicero agrees in attributing *decreta*—that is, *dogmata*—to the sage. "As if the wise person has no other principles and could live his life without principles! But just as he holds those as persuasive rather than apprehended principles, so with this one, that nothing is apprehensible" (*Acad.* 2.109–10).

It is certainly possible that the Academic sage arrives at the notion that nothing is apprehensible on the basis of repeatedly seeing the Stoics fail to defend their view adequately. So it is possible that this *decretum* is not the result of a conscious attempt to determine which position is most defensible or likely to be true. However, this simply does not fit the overall picture of the *Academica*. At least part of Cicero's motivation in writing this dialogue is to explain the grounds for his methodological preference and to encourage others to adopt it as well. So he must have thought that the arguments he reports are adequate to sway a reasonable reader to the view that nothing is apprehensible. This *decretum* is held or assented to in just the same way as the sage holds (or assents to) *probabilia* in general. Thus, for Cicero, there is no important difference between Clitomachus's and Philo's views of the skeptically appropriate kind of assent. Both involve a conscious weighing of the rational merits of alternative views and a deliberate as well as fallible judgment of truth. This is the best explanation for the otherwise puzzling fact that Cicero quite happily relies on both Philo and Clitomachus in defending mitigated skepticism.

NOTES

I am very grateful to the National Endowment for Humanities for awarding me a Faculty Research Award for the Spring semester of 2006 during which time I wrote the first draft of this paper.

1. *Nat. D.* 1.11; *Tusc.* 2.4; *Div.* 2.1; *Off.* 2.8.

2. Görler, "Silencing the Troublemaker," argues against Glucker's thesis in "Cicero's Philosophical Affiliations" that Cicero changed his philosophical allegiance twice: first, after taking on a prominent role in Roman politics, he moved from the New Academy of Arcesilaus and Carneades to the more dogmatic views of Antiochus, and then he moved back to the more skeptical position in his encyclopedic burst of dialogues written between 46 and 44 B.C.

3. Görler, "Silencing the Troublemaker," 112.

4. *Acad.* 2.66: *ut hoc pulcherrimum esse iudico, vera videre, sic pro veris probare falsa turpissimum est.* Brittain translates: "approving falsehoods *in the place of* truths" (*On Academic Scepticism*, 38). This suggests that what Cicero thinks is *turpissimum* is the fact that one believes what is false; i.e., holding false beliefs is most shameful. But in my translation of this phrase, what is *turpissimum* is adopting the attitude towards one's beliefs that is only justified when they are true; i.e., holding false beliefs in the way one should hold true beliefs is most shameful. This difference will become important later.

5. *Inv.* 2.9 and *Off.* 2.7, respectively; cf. also *Acad.* 2.7–9.

6. *Div.* 2.1–2; *Fin.* 1.10; *Nat. D.* 1.7. We should not ignore the fact that Cicero wrote his dialogues for the ruling class and not for the general public, for whom he had considerable contempt—see *Att.* 2.1.8, where he describes the people of Rome as the dregs of Romulus (*Romuli faece*). But neither should we make too much of this fact either. Despite his contempt for "the dregs," he took seriously his obligation to govern in their interests as well. He prides himself in several letters on his just dealings with the public as governor of Cilicia (e.g., *Att.* 7.1.6).

7. *Fin.* 4.65; *Div.* 2.61ff., 3.14–16; *Amic.* 18; and *Nat. D.* 3.79. The Stoics themselves were reluctant to acknowledge any actual sages. For further discussion see Brouwer, "Sagehood."

8. Cf. *Off.* 2.35: When I call some men brave, others good and others wise, I am speaking in the popular sense and not in the precise sense employed in philosophical disputation.

9. *Amic.* 19 (Falconer, trans).

10. Cato is just the sort of person that Laelius (and Cicero) would have us consider good, though not perfectly so. Cicero thinks highly of Cato's unwavering moral convictions and considers him a genuinely virtuous man. But he also thinks Cato's constancy needs to be tempered by the humanizing effect of practice and experience. Cato needs to learn that within the limitations and imperfections of real human life, the inflexible and severe principles of Stoic ethics are out of place. In short, Cicero thinks Cato's virtue is real, but it is not, contrary to what Cato may think, the product of his Stoic training (cf. *Off.* 1.112, 3.15–16; *Fin.* 4.61; *Att.* 1.18, 2.1; *Mur.* 60–66). See Stem, "Cicero as Orator and Philosopher" for further discussion and a convincing defense of the propriety of using the *Pro Murena* passage as evidence for Cicero's philosophical and political views.

11. We also find this distinction between a kind of virtue that is attainable and a kind that is not in the *Tusculan Disputations*. In the second book, Cicero argues that we must counter the belief that pain is an evil with the view that virtue alone is good and vice evil (2.44–46). The chief expression of virtue is the mastery of the lower, irrational part of the soul by the rational part. Insofar as the Stoics maintained that the soul is homogeneously rational and unified, they would never describe the attainment of virtue in terms of the domination of a lower irrational part of the soul. So a few paragraphs later, when Cicero refers to the character of the *perfecta sapientia* as described by philosophers (2.51), he is thinking either of earlier Academics or of some unorthodox Stoics. Although he remarks that we have never seen a living example of this perfect wisdom, he goes on to list some famous Romans who endured every imaginable pain rather than fail to fulfill their obligations, and a bit earlier he had referred to the wisest Greeks (*sapientissimus Graeciae*) who similarly endured great pain without crying out (2.48).

12. This and all subsequent translations from the *Academica* are by Brittain, *On Academic Scepticism*, unless otherwise indicated.

13. See Görler, "Cicero's Philosophical Stance," 37–38. *Opinator*, as Rackham notes in his translation, "is coined to suit the pretended self-deprecation of the speaker" (introduction to *De natura deorum, Academica*, 550, fn. a).

14. *uno modo, cum hoc intellegatur, omnino eum rei nulli adsentiri*. The translation "he will assent to nothing entirely" is preferable to Brittain's "he won't assent to anything at all." Following Reid, (*Academica*, 300), and Bett, ("Carneades' Distinction," 15), we should take the adverb *omnino* as directly modifying the verb, i.e., qualifying the sense in which the sage will assent to nothing rather than modifying the object of the verb, *nulli rei*.

15. Although the text is not corrupt, many emendations have been proposed. Brittain canvasses these proposals and concludes that the correct reading "can only be determined by the context and philosophical sense of the passage" (Brittain, *On Academic Scepticism*, 80 n. 13). I am following Reid, (*Academica of Cicero*, 348) in retaining the original *comprobans* yielding Catulus's acceptance of universal *epochē*. I have modified Brittain's translation accordingly. The full defense of this choice depends on the overall coherence and success of my interpretation of Cicero's position.

16. Just prior to this remark, Catulus says that he is returning to his father's judgment. Mansfeld, "Philo and Antiochus," argues that Catulus had defended Philo's Roman position in the now-lost portion of the dialogue that was named for him. It seems equally likely that his newfound approval of mitigated skepticism is the result of being swayed by Cicero's arguments leading up to that point.

17. Augustine confirms this interpretation of dogmatic assent. "The Academics call what can incite us to act without assent 'plausible' or 'truth-like.'

Now I say 'without assent' inasmuch as we don't hold the opinion that what we do is true, or think that we know it, and yet we do it nevertheless" (*Acad.* 2.26, translation by King, *Against the Academics and the Teacher*, 49).

18. Burnyeat, for example, argues that Philo compromises the originally radical skepticism of Clitomachus and Carneades by allowing for tentative, fallible beliefs. He maintains that the sort of opinion that Philo ascribes to the sage "is as different from ordinary Stoic *doxa*, which is always foolish and blameworthy, as it is different in its vehemence from Clitomachean non-assent" ("Antipater and Self-Refutation," 305). Brittain develops the most detailed account of this position (*Philo of Larissa*). He argues that Philo held three distinct philosophical positions: first the original, radical skepticism of Clitomachus and Carneades, then the mitigated skepticism endorsed by Cicero virtually everywhere except in the *Academica*, and finally the moderate dogmatism of the infamous Roman books. However, Glucker's examination ("The Philonain/Metrodorians,") of the evidence in his extensive review of Brittain makes it seem unlikely that Philo ever occupied a distinctive "middle" position. See further: Allen, "Academic Probabilism and Stoic Epistemology," Bett, "Carneades' Distinction," Bett, "Carneades' *Pithanon*," Frede, "The Skeptic's Two Kinds of Assent," and Striker, "Sceptical Strategies."

19. This and all subsequent translations are from Annas and Barnes, *Outlines of Scepticism*.

20. The notion that Cicero defends a different version of the Academy in the Academic books also ignores the passages in that very dialogue in which Cicero reaffirms his commitment to mitigated skepticism. He tells us, for example, that he is defending the very same doctrines that Antiochus had studied with Philo (*Acad.* 2.69). And we may infer from Lucullus's exposition that what Antiochus had studied was a moderate fallibilism. For example, Lucullus remarks that the Academics get quite worked up by the claim that what is probable, or resembling the truth, provides a criterion of judgment both in day-to-day life and in philosophical investigation (*Acad.* 2.32). Lucullus also accuses the Academics of concealing their views (*sententia*) as if they were something shameful. And he challenges "Cicero" to reveal what truths have been discovered by the Academics as a result of their arguments pro and contra (*Acad.* 2.60). Judging by Cicero's response to this challenge, he does not think that Lucullus has misrepresented the Academic position. "You also want to know whether I agreed that the truth could have been discovered in the many centuries since those early philosophers, given the great number of intellects seeking it with such perseverance. I will deal with what has been discovered a bit later, and make you the judge of it" (*Acad.* 2.76). Unfortunately Cicero never gets around to this. But the fact that he invites Lucullus to sit in judgment would make no sense if these discoveries were not held to be true or at least likely to be true.

21. The separation of judging something as plausible or convincing from judging it as probably true leaves us with no answer to the question: Why does one find *p* convincing? Sextus never describes his passive acquiescence to appearances as finding something convincing, so he need not bother with this question.

22. *Acad.* 2.110 (Rackham, trans).

23. It is necessary to offer some explanation for what may appear to be Cicero's rejection of the view of the sage that Catulus offers at the end of the dialogue (*Acad.* 2.148). What Cicero says is that he does not entirely reject it (*nec eam admodum aspernor*). This is an ambiguous phrase—although it suggests at least some reluctance it may be taken as a qualified acceptance. Compare the off-hand remark, "I don't think that's half bad." He does seem to contrast Catulus's view with Hortensius's assessment, "Away with it [assent]," calling the latter the proper view (*propria sententia*) of the Academy. However he also says virtually the same thing regarding each view, *habeo*, to Catulus's and *teneo*, to Hortensius's. I submit that this passage is not decisive either way. There probably were some differences between Clitomachus and Philo on the proper understanding of skeptically appropriate assent, but given the lack of evidence we can only speculate as to what these might have been. Whatever the differences were, Cicero does not feel compelled to choose between them.

24. On the use and meaning of the term *probabilitas* in Cicero's dialogues, see Glucker, "*Probabile, Veri Simile*, and Related Terms."

25. In his commentary, Reid (*Academica of Cicero*, 348 n. 2) provides a similar interpretation. He maintains that Catulus's distinction is the same distinction we encounter at *Acad.* 2.104, which he takes to be between withholding assent in theory and in practice. The theoretical *epochē* "arises when a man absolutely refuses to pronounce any opinion whatever; the second [practical sort] when he merely guards himself from saying what would imply absolute certitude" (300 n. 1).

7

The Politico-Philosophical Character of Cicero's Verdict in *De Natura Deorum*

DAVID FOTT

"The Cosmos is all that is or ever was or ever will be."[1] Those words begin *Cosmos*, the widely hailed book by the eminent scientist Carl Sagan. Sagan made great contributions to our thinking about the universe by applying to it the method of modern science. That method required him to be open to new suggestions about the cosmos and skeptical of received wisdom about it. Sagan would not have accomplished so much as he did without having that openness and skepticism to a great degree. The opening words of *Cosmos*, however, are as dogmatic as anything one would hear from a religious fundamentalist. How could Sagan have *known*—as opposed to *assumed*—those words were true? Modern science cannot tell us about anything outside the cosmos, but it does not follow that nothing outside the cosmos exists, or did exist, or will exist. Sagan took a leap of faith in making his claim. It is reasonable to surmise he took it because according to modern science, whatever exists is assumed to be not only intelligible but also predictable. The fact that Sagan opened his book with that boast illustrates how difficult it is for skeptics (as to some extent modern scientists are) not to become dogmatic, especially on the most important questions.

That point is the central message of Cicero's dialogue on theology, *De Natura Deorum*, and the answer to a puzzle he leaves for us at the end of the work. The dialogue occurs among three characters representing the approaches to theology of three philosophical schools: Epicurean, Stoic, and New Academic.[2] Epicurus's teaching on theology was based on Democritus's doctrine that the universe consists of atoms in a void, moving with no inherent purpose. We know that gods exist, Epicurus said, because all people believe in them, but the gods are also made of atoms, and they do not intervene in the mechanical workings of the universe. Stoic theology was also materialistic but focused on the divine mind (which consisted of matter as fire, aether, or air) as the ultimate reality. The affirmation of a single divine mind was held to be consistent with the existence of many gods. Stoics affirmed the providential care of gods for the universe and for humans in particular.

By contrast, the Academy—which had been founded by Plato and to which Cicero subscribed more than any other school—took a critical stance toward all philosophical and religious questions. It sought to avoid dogmatism on those matters, on the conviction that certainty is unavailable to humans. According to Cicero, the school maintained "not that nothing seems true, but . . . that false sorts of things are joined to all true things by such a similarity that there is no definite mark in them for judging and assenting. From this it stands out that many things are probable; although they are not thoroughly comprehended, nevertheless because they have a sort of distinguished and bright appearance a wise person may regulate his life" (*Nat. D.* 1.12). To be an Academic was to subscribe to a method, not to any substantive conclusions. In another work Cicero refers to "that true and elegant philosophy, conducted by Socrates" (*Tusc.* 4.6). For Socrates, who wrote no treatise or dialogue we know of, philosophy is not a doctrine advanced by a school or a set of fixed conclusions; it is a way of life, the pursuit of wisdom, the striving after knowledge of the whole. That Cicero understands philosophy in this way is further supported by his claims that he pursued philosophy from his youth and that "I have philosophized the most when I have least seemed to be doing so" (*Nat. D.* 1.6). That remark is an obvious reference to the long periods of his life spent as a politician and a lawyer; it seems to indicate he sees philosophy as a continuous pursuit that does not require the constant reading and writing of philosophical works. Still more evidence for the view that Cicero sees philosophy as a way of life is found in his statement, "I will hold to the ordinance of no single teaching as if I were bound to laws that I must obey in philosophy; I will always seek what is most probable in each matter" (*Tusc.* 4.7). He seeks what is most probable since the truth itself lies "hidden in obscurity" (*Orat.* 237). Cicero does not take the next, postmodern step of denying that truth exists, for to do so would be dogmatic. The truth may be obscured, but it does not follow that a person's thought is so bound by his situation (such as time and place) as to be incapable of moving toward truth.

Because the Academy taught only a philosophic method and not any substantive conclusions, adhering to that school was compatible with political duties that implied certain substantive conclusions—such as the public office of augur, which involved divining the gods' will on a range of social and political matters. Both Cicero and Gaius Aurelius Cotta, the Academic spokesman in the dialogue, were augurs. Cotta has a thin line to walk, then, as he seeks to rebut the Epicurean and Stoic arguments without denying the existence of gods.

Book 1 features the presentation of Epicurean theology by Gaius Velleius and its refutation by Cotta. Book 2 is entirely devoted to the defense of Stoic theology by Lucilius Balbus—a sign that Cicero takes Stoic theology more seriously than Epicurean. In Book 3 Cotta attacks Stoic views. Cicero depicts himself as having been present during the conversation, but he is mainly silent in the work—with the major exceptions of setting the stage in a prologue and of pronouncing his verdict at the end. In the prologue he observes that the variety of theological views constitutes a reminder that philosophy begins in ignorance, and that the Academy has been prudent to withhold its assent in uncertain subjects (*Nat. D.* 1.1). Many readers have found it all the more surprising, then, when at the end of the work Cicero the Academic declares in his own voice that "Cotta's argument seemed truer to Velleius," while "to me Balbus's argument seemed nearer the appearance of truth" (*Nat. D.* 3.95).³ That verdict leaves the Stoic two removes from the truth, according to Cicero. But what more would one expect an Academic, who speaks of probability, to admit? What is puzzling is that Cicero sides with the Stoic at all.

In attempting to determine why he does so, I run the risk of violating Cicero's own instructions, or what can be called his principle of silence: "Those who ask what I feel about every subject do so with more curiosity than is proper; for what should be sought in arguing is not so much the weight of authority as the weight of reason" (*Nat. D.* 1.10). I ignore the first part of his warning, but only as a step toward respecting the second part.

Review of Secondary Sources

Thinkers of the caliber of Augustine, Voltaire, and Montesquieu attempt to come to grips with Cicero's writing on theology in different ways.⁴ Augustine renders the most specific judgment of those three when he accuses Cicero of giving an insincere verdict: Cicero actually agrees with Cotta, and both men are atheists who hide their own views for the public good.⁵ Voltaire calls the work "perhaps the best book in all antiquity."⁶ One may make an educated guess that Voltaire agrees with Augustine that Cicero is an atheist. In an early essay Montesquieu writes, "What a pleasure to see him, in his book *On the Nature of the Gods*, make all the sects pass in review, confound all the philosophers, and mark each prejudice with some stain! Now he fights against these monsters; now he makes sport of philosophy. The champions whom he introduces destroy themselves; that one is confounded by this one, who finds himself beaten in turn. All these systems disappear one before another, and there remain, in the reader's mind, only contempt for the philosophers and admiration for the critic."⁷ It is unclear whether Montesquieu thinks each of the three philosophers in the dialogue—including Cotta—shows prejudice and whether Montesquieu has contempt for all three of them.

A survey of recent scholarship reveals no consensus as to why Cicero sides with the Stoic arguments. Some scholars have agreed with Augustine. For example, Arnaldo Momigliano wrote, "The inescapable conclusion a reader was bound to draw from the end of the *De natura deorum* was that Cicero, with all due precautions (for which cf. 3.95 [i.e., where Cicero announces his verdict]), intended to be negative" about the gods' existence.[8] He continued, "The *De natura deorum* had paid lip service to the traditional values of Roman religious tradition, including *auspicia* [i.e., the taking of auspices to divine the gods' will], but had been a rigorous denial of the possibility of demonstrating the existence of the gods."[9] Whatever Momigliano may have meant by "precautions," he did not think Cicero means to signal even the likelihood of the gods' existence when he favors Balbus.

John Glucker took an opposite view to Momigliano's, based on the setting of the dialogue between 77 and 75 B.C. He concluded that Cicero's pro-Stoic verdict was sincere because Cicero was a dogmatic Old Academic at the time.[10] Glucker's thesis was decisively refuted by Joseph G. DeFilippo's observation that Velleius calls Cicero an ally of Cotta, the skeptical New Academic (*Nat. D.* 1.17);[11] and by the lack of evidence that Cicero ever preferred the Old to the New Academy.[12] Yet DeFilippo arrived at a similar interpretation to Glucker's: Cicero dogmatically believes that a person's conduct, and hence more broadly religious and political traditions, can be rationally justified—unlike Cotta, who supports Roman politico-religious tradition despite believing that it cannot be rationally justified.[13] Like Glucker, DeFilippo considered Cicero's verdict sincere. Along the same line, P. G. Walsh asserted (without argument) in the introduction to his translation that Cicero's "judgement of what was probable ... was swayed by his sense of Roman piety."[14]

One scholar apparently unable to decide on Cicero's sincerity was Arthur Stanley Pease, who edited the Latin text. Pease had earlier written an article in which he took issue with Augustine's thesis: First, if Cicero was concerned to avoid a charge of atheism or to maintain public confidence in the official religion, he would not have published the dialogue.[15] Second, the absence of printing meant that the work would have a limited distribution. But Pease also rebutted the claim that Cicero is truly inclined toward Stoicism: Cicero claims to side not with Stoic principles, but with Balbus's specific arguments.[16] Pease argued that Cicero's purpose is "descriptive," even "encyclopaedic," rather than didactic.[17] According to Pease, Cicero wants to appear impartial, knows that the Academic position is liable to be misunderstood as dogmatic atheism, and has divided sympathies on the merits of the argument because he agrees with much of Stoic philosophy.[18] "To suppose, then, that he really accepts the Stoic's *disputatio* [i.e., argument] is, I think, wrong; it is the positive convictions which lie beneath it to which ... his assent is inclined."[19] That statement of Pease's militated against his earlier recognition that Cicero endorses Balbus's arguments, not Stoic principles or convictions. Pease argued more consistently in the introduction to his edition of the text, in which he wrote nothing even similar to that last quotation.

Following partly in Pease's footsteps was Philip Levine, who agreed that the purpose of the work is primarily descriptive.[20] Cicero wants to protect the Academy from a reputation for atheism, Levine maintained; but Levine also claimed that at the end of the work Cicero "is, in fact, revealing his private verdict on the philosophic question."[21] Just two pages after defending Cicero's sincerity, however, he wrote, "Whether or not the statement [in favor of Balbus's arguments] reflects his own true sentiments on the subject is controversial, and the question need not be treated here."[22] If a scholar writing in a prestigious journal committed such a blatant self-contradiction over the space of a few pages, we can be fairly confident that the problem is daunting.

According to Levine, when Cicero pronounces a verdict at the end of the work, he violates his own principle of silence from the beginning of the work.[23] Such a principle "constitutes, in effect, an attempt to emphasize the descriptive character of such philosophical writing, and the objectivity gained thereby better serves his purpose of acquainting his fellow countrymen with the views of the different Greek schools of philosophy."[24] But the conflict that Levine saw between beginning and end is absent. In his prologue Cicero observes that most people have said that gods exist; and that view, Cicero remarks, is the one "that most appears to be true and to which we all come, led by nature" (*Nat. D.* 1.2). Cicero judges at the beginning of the work, as well as at the end.

Moreover, it is highly doubtful that Levine and therefore Pease were correct about the main purpose of Cicero's principle of silence. As we have seen, Cicero himself says he wants his readers to follow the force of the argument, not merely to observe a diversity of views. *Pace* Pease and Levine, Cicero says he wants to be didactic, not merely descriptive; he wants his readers to think for themselves.[25] Elsewhere he provides an equally clear link between his principle of silence and the goal of instructing his readers: he claims to be following Socrates in order "that I might conceal my own sentiment, raise up others from error, and in every argument seek what most appears to be true" (*Tusc.* 5.11). For Cicero to announce his verdict without giving a reason is the best way for him to accomplish all of those goals simultaneously; arousing readers' curiosity is the best way of urging them to think for themselves.

Pease remarked that Cicero makes a show of his freedom from dogmatism, suggesting he is not really using that freedom to search for wisdom.[26] Pease and Levine neglected that the Academic search for probability was a quest, a striving—especially on an issue where what one believes tends to have a great effect on how one lives. To those who cared about the subject of religion—the vast majority of his readers—Cicero would have appeared a trivialist if he had written a work in which he showed an indifference to the truth of the matter.

Another line of scholarship, which comes closer to the thesis that I will maintain, was represented by John Valdimir Price. Like Augustine, Price saw irony in Cotta's affirmation of the gods' existence.[27] Price described Cotta as "usually bluff, almost dogmatic in his scepticism," without linking any specific statements of Cotta's to that bluffness or near-dogmatism. But in Price's view, Cotta's rigidity does not mitigate his success against his opponents. On that last point I will disagree with Price.

Setting of the Dialogue

An interpretation of a dialogue must reflect an awareness of the form of the work. A dialogue differs from a treatise in that the former uses dramatic details to advance a teaching, so to ignore the details is to miss the teaching. Cicero wrote both philosophical treatises and philosophical dialogues. In almost all of the dialogues he is quite specific as to the dramatic date, location, and characters involved. In

De Natura Deorum, however, he is not very specific as to any of those matters. The dramatic date can be narrowed only as far as sometime between 77 and 75 B.C., between his return from studying philosophy and recovering his health in Greece, on the one hand, and, on the other hand, his departure for his quaestorship in Sicily.[28] In other words, the dialogue comes at a time between Cicero's need for study and his need for action. Perhaps that is what he wants us to infer, because in his prologue he summons his audience to deliver a verdict on the question of the gods; he uses language one would expect to see a lawyer use to a jury (*Nat. D.* 1.13–14). Cicero seems to be emphasizing the urgency of deciding theological matters. The location of the discussion is Cotta's home, but we are not told whether it is his villa in the country or his house in the city.[29] Two of the three characters (excluding Cicero), Velleius and Balbus, are completely unknown other than what Cicero writes about them; Cicero does refer to Velleius as a senator (*Nat. D.* 1.15).[30]

It is possible, if not likely, that Cicero published *De Natura Deorum* without having edited it to his full satisfaction.[31] Whether he would have been more specific about the date, location, or characters if he had further revised it can never be known. It seems likely that his vagueness about those matters has a specific purpose, especially when taken in connection with his principle of silence: to encourage his readers to pay attention to the argument, not ancillary matters, on this profoundest of subjects.

Cotta versus Epicureanism

In Book 1 Velleius, the Epicurean spokesman, argues for the existence of gods based on the universal or nearly universal belief of all mankind, a belief he calls "innate" (*Nat. D.* 1.44). Also innate are the beliefs that the gods are eternal and happy. Such gods, he continues, are passionless, fit for human reverence but not fearsome, anthropomorphic but not truly corporeal, and grasped by means of a stream of images in the mind, not by the senses. The gods created and administer the world, but they are happy because they remain in quietude; their administration occurs through nature, through the motion of an infinite number of atoms in an immense void. The true god is he whose happiness lies in his own enjoyment. The gods create no trouble for themselves and wish to create none for others.

Cotta, the Academic skeptic and augur, then replies to Velleius. The difficulty of the task confronting him stems from the conflict between those two aspects of his life. That difficulty is evident from two remarks at the beginning of his speech. First, he confesses that "in almost all things, but most of all in matters of natural science, I say what is not the case more quickly than what is the case" (*Nat. D.* 1.60). The word I have translated "matters of natural science" (*physicis*) refers to the field under which the philosophers' inquiries concerning the gods came; they studied the gods through a study of nature. Cotta implies, surprisingly to a modern way of thinking, that he is surer of himself when speaking of ethics than of natural science. We must remember that Cotta does not subscribe to positivism, with its fact-value distinction that still—despite unanswered attacks from Friedrich Nietzsche and postmodernists—infects the thinking of many natural and social scientists, as well as some scholars in the humanities. Ethics is a subject that no thinking person can ignore. It poses a question that each of us faces every day: What should I do with my life? And every day we see the consequences of the choices we make, which help us to revise our thinking about what is good and bad (and even, perhaps, our thinking about the importance of consequences for ethics) and make it impossible for us to live without strong opinions on some ethical questions. Natural science, by contrast, involves more remote matters. In neither ethics nor natural science, however, does Cotta claim to have certainty. Thus his remark is one of a good Academic skeptic.

But Cotta's second remark seems not to be skeptical: "I, myself a priest, who think that the public ceremonies and religious observances must be maintained in a most holy manner, would like to be persuaded on this primary point, that gods exist, not only as a matter of opinion but also plainly as the truth. For many disturbing things present themselves, so that now and then there seems to be none [i.e., no god]" (*Nat. D.* 1.61). When Cotta voices a desire to have "the truth" about the gods, he appeals to a standard that is unattainable, according to the skeptic. Andrew Dyck attempted to explain the apparent inconsistency as follows: "Skepticism has two faces...: here Cotta is speaking as an agnostic, not a probabilist, and therefore raises the bar of proof for the dogmatist as high as possible."[32] Dyck neglected, however, that Cotta is an agnostic *because* he is a probabilist; the two cannot be so easily separated. A better reconciliation of Cotta's two remarks recognizes that he utters those sentences explicitly *as a priest*, as a person with religious duties who, from the standpoint of performing those duties, would like to believe that they have a solid foundation.

Despite his doubts, Cotta declares that he will not challenge the near-universal belief that the gods exist: "it is agreeable to almost all people and to me myself" for gods to exist (*Nat. D.* 1.62). The word *placet*, which I have translated "it is agreeable," can also mean "it pleases" or (with *mihi*) "I accept."[33] To say "it pleases me" is less than an affirmation that gods do exist, but to say "I accept" may be an affirmation. Cicero uses an ambiguous word when he could use a number of other expressions (e.g., *puto, arbitror, opinor, mihi persuasum est*) if he wanted Cotta to affirm clearly that gods exist.

Cotta then undercuts his politically sensitive remark by attacking Velleius's argument from consensus on the grounds that Velleius has no way to know the opinions of all nations and that history provides examples of well-known atheists (*Nat. D.* 1.62–64). The argument based on atomism is also unfounded, Cotta says; if the gods are made of atoms, they cannot be immortal (*Nat. D.* 1.65–68). Velleius has earlier anticipated that criticism by claiming that the gods' appearance is not that of body but "quasi-body" and that "it does not have blood, but quasi-blood" (*Nat. D.* 1.49). But Cotta rejects that description as incomprehensible (*Nat. D.* 1.68,71,74–75), declaring along the way his surprise that an Epicurean can keep a straight face when talking with another Epicurean (*Nat. D.* 1.71). That is Cotta's first hint that Epicurus did not really believe his own teaching about the gods.[34]

Yet that is not the only interpretation of Epicurus that Cotta entertains. He says that "the yawning Epicurus rambled" when delivering his teachings; after all, "he boasted that he had no teacher" (*Nat. D.* 1.72). Far from being a careful practitioner of esotericism, Epicurus may have been a mere fool.[35] Concerning Epicurus's saying that whatever being is happy neither has trouble nor gives it to anyone, Cotta offers that Epicurus pronounced that cloudy remark "in ignorance of speaking plainly" but that there are those who think he did so deliberately. Those people "think badly concerning the least cunning man.... He truly thinks that gods exist, nor have I seen anyone who feared more those things that he denied should be feared—I speak of death and gods" (*Nat. D.* 1.85–86).

The same interpretation could hold for Epicureans as for their leader. Cotta claims generally that wise men conceived the anthropomorphism of gods in order to encourage the ignorant masses to be religious; alternatively human vanity could have caused the belief that gods have human form. If the gods have the form of neither humans nor heavenly bodies, he asks Velleius, "Why do you hesitate to deny that gods exist? You do not dare. Indeed wisely, although in this matter you fear not the people, but the gods themselves" (*Nat. D.* 1.85). Epicureans claim to have liberated humans from fear of gods, but they have not liberated even themselves.[36]

Of course the statement, per se, that Epicureans do not dare to deny the gods' existence could also mean that Epicureans do not believe in the gods but are afraid to voice their atheism. Cotta gradually turns to that interpretation of both Epicurus himself and other philosophers who abolished any reason for religious observance among people when they denied that the gods were beneficent (*Nat. D.* 1.117,121). That charge is ambiguous because it does not specify whether that abolition was intentional or unintentional. Cotta removes the ambiguity as he continues his attack: concerning Epicurus's treatise on holiness, Cotta says that "he sports with us, although he is not so much a wit as a man unrestrained and licentious in writing. For how can holiness exist if the gods do not care for human affairs, but what is the meaning of an animate nature that cares for nothing? Therefore it is doubtless truer ... that Epicurus thinks that no gods exist, that he said whatever he said about immortal gods for the sake of warding off ill-will" (*Nat. D.* 1.123; cf. *Nat. D.* 3.3). The use of the comparative "truer" instead of the absolute "true" shows the appropriate uncertainty on the part of the Academic.

If Epicurus turns out to be a careless practitioner of esotericism according to Cotta, his followers fare no better, as we have already begun to see. Cotta accuses Velleius of having dogmatically chosen to follow Epicurus before he understood Epicurus's theological views (*Nat. D.* 1.66). More than once, Cotta distinguishes himself from Velleius by displaying respect for philosophers of different views (*Nat. D.* 1.94,120).

A final, remarkable sign of Cotta's openmindedness in Book 1 is his criticism of the Epicurean view—indeed of the view we tend to associate with ancient philosophy in general—that rest is superior to motion. Epicureans are wrong, he says, to maintain that a god, or any being, at rest is capable of greater happiness than a being in motion. Moreover, Cotta makes his case against that principle on mainly Aristotelian grounds: "It is fitting that he who is going to be happy will use and enjoy his good things" (*Nat. D.* 1.103); certainly happiness exists "in no way without virtue, but virtue is active" (*Nat. D.* 1.110). The idle gods of the teaching of Epicurus do nothing for humans, so why should humans do anything for them (*Nat. D.* 1.115–16)?

Cotta versus Stoicism

In Book 2, before Balbus presents the Stoic theology, he criticizes Cotta for what he sees as an inconsistency: as a priest Cotta is committed to upholding Roman religion, but as a philosopher he admits to doubts about the gods' existence. Balbus says, "It is right for a philosopher and a priest and Cotta to have not an errant and wandering sentiment about the immortal gods, as the Academics do, but a stable and definite one, as our school does" (*Nat. D.* 2.2). Cotta's reply comes at the beginning of Book 3: Balbus's criticism means that "I should defend the opinions about immortal gods that we have received from ancestors, and the sacred rites, ceremonies, and religious observances. Truly I will always defend them and always have defended them; nor will the speech of anyone, either educated or uneducated, ever move me from this opinion that I have received from ancestors about the worship of immortal gods" (*Nat. D.* 3.5). The Roman religion, he continues, consists of sacred rites, auspices, and prophetic warnings from interpreters and augurs; as established by the first two kings of Rome, it forms the foundation of the city. He concludes this part of his speech, "Balbus, you have what Cotta, what a priest, feels; now let me understand what you feel. For I ought to receive a reason for religious observance from you, a philosopher, but I ought to trust our ancestors even with no reason rendered" (*Nat. D.* 3.6). The word I have translated "feels" (*sentiat*) is often translated "thinks," but its primary meaning is "[t]o perceive by any one of the senses."[37] Less reasoning by Cotta is implied than if Cicero had used another word (e.g., *puto*, *arbitror*, *opinor*). Less reasoning by Balbus is implied too, as Cotta makes a request of Balbus using the same word.

Yet Cotta also refers there to Balbus as a philosopher. He thereby shifts the burden of philosophizing from himself to Balbus. It is appropriate that Cotta uses the word "feels" to Balbus because his reply at the beginning of Book 3 does not fully meet Balbus's demand of him at the beginning of Book 2. Balbus wanted a firm opinion on gods from "a philosopher and a priest and Cotta"; Cotta explicitly gives him the view of only the last two of those three.[38] What he thinks as a philosopher goes unsaid in that passage. Demanding that Balbus instead philosophize as best he can, Cotta reserves his reasoning for understanding Balbus.

Of course Cotta has already partly revealed his reasoning to Balbus in Book 1, when he admitted to having doubts about the gods' existence. Why does he not voice those doubts in the passage just examined? To do so would detract from the point he has begun to raise concerning the importance of trusting ancestral authority, even without any accompanying reason. Later Cotta will ask parenthetically, "What is less appropriate for a philosopher" than "to take away gods" (*Nat. D.* 3.44)? The same factor accounts for his remark to Balbus that "it cannot be shaken from my spirit that gods exist; nevertheless, as to why that very thing is so, of which I have been persuaded by the authority of ancestors, you teach me nothing" (*Nat. D.* 3.7).[39] When Balbus asks him what he wants to be taught, Cotta replies that he wants to know why, if almost all people believe in the gods, Balbus spent so much time arguing for the point. Balbus responds that for Cotta to ask that question is as if he were to ask why Balbus looked at him with two eyes instead of only one (*Nat. D.* 3.8). There Balbus analogizes from the senses, or what is felt, to reason, or what is thought. Cotta replies, "How far that resemblance exists, you may see [*videris*]" (*Nat. D.* 3.9). Again relying on the distinction between feeling and thinking, Cotta ironically uses a word for one of the senses to suggest that the inadequacy of Balbus's analogy is evident even without much thought.

Cotta continues with his criticism of Balbus's reliance on a number of arguments to prove a point that Balbus considers settled by consensus, when for Cotta ancestral authority would have been sufficient reason in itself. But according to Cotta, Balbus despises authority, preferring to fight with reason. "You adduce all these arguments why gods exist, and by arguing you make doubtful a matter that is, in my sentiment, least of all doubtful" (*Nat. D.* 3.10). The word I have translated "least of all" (*minime*) may also be translated "not at all." At a minimum Cotta says he finds little doubt that gods exist. That statement may seem surprising from someone who said in Book 1 that many disturbing things sometimes caused him to think that no gods exist. But again, how could he say otherwise and not undermine his argument that ancestral authority is sufficient reason for believing in gods?

Nevertheless, Cotta will not pretend that he understands what he does not understand. Concerning divination he says that it is not always an advantage to know in advance what will happen, because humans cannot avoid fate, and that knowledge would remove the prospect of consolation (*Nat. D.* 3.14). Divination relies on such signs as the shape of a creature's entrails or a raven's singing. "I trust in those things ... but I ought to learn from philosophers how those things are understood, especially since those diviners lie about many things." Balbus has said that physicians are also often wrong, but Cotta rejects that comparison: "What is the resemblance between medicine, the method [*rationem*] of which I see, and divination, which springs from a source I do not understand?" (*Nat. D.* 3.15). The soundness of medicine is evident to Cotta's reason and his senses, but he finds divination incomprehensible.

The picture of Cotta that emerges from these encounters with Velleius and Balbus is of a man who says that (1) he trusts, on ancestral authority, that gods exist; (2) belief in the gods' existence cannot be extirpated from his spirit; and (3) he even trusts in the signs of divination. But in addition (4) he claims not to understand those objects of his trust, and (5) sometimes it seems to him that no gods exist. How well do those claims square with one another?

Clearly there seems to be an inconsistency between (1) and (5). To see that Cotta could have spoken more carefully (even allowing for the dialogic character of this work), we will need to contrast his arguments with those of Cicero himself as a character in the sequel to this dialogue, *De Divinatione*.

First, we need to look further at some of Balbus's theological arguments and Cotta's replies to them. Balbus divides the subject into four parts: the gods' existence (*Nat. D.* 2.4–44), their characteristics (*Nat. D.* 2.45–72), their governance (*Nat. D.* 2.73–153), and their care for human affairs (*Nat. D.* 2.154–67). Regarding the gods' existence he maintains that (1) observation of the heavens makes it obvious that an intelligent power rules the universe; (2) gods often show themselves in epiphanies; (3) divination is a proven way of gauging the gods' will; (4) the consensus of mankind is that gods exist, with that consensus having been shaped by divination, human enjoyment of the earth's fruits, terror from natural disasters, and the ordered beauty of the heavens; (5) as argued by Chrysippus,[40] the existence of something that could not have been made by humans proves the existence of something greater than humans; (6) the source of something as marvelous as human reason must be divine; (7) the interconnection of the processes of the universe manifests a divine intelligence; and (8) the whole universe must be better than any of its elements, and humans are an element with reason, so the whole universe must be guided by reason. Regarding the gods' characteristics, Balbus describes them as spherical (thus enabling uniform motion and arrangement in the heavens), creative, artistic, providential, and supremely beautiful. Regarding the gods' governance of the universe, Balbus calls it providential because (1) nothing is more outstanding than governing the universe, so that is what one would expect gods to do; and (2) nature shows order and a resemblance to art. Regarding the gods' concern for human beings, Balbus notes that everything in the world has been made for human enjoyment (beasts for hunting and forests are two examples given), while divination teaches humans what to acquire and what to reject. The gods make sure that human virtue gains true rewards in the end, he concludes.

In Book 3 Cotta denies that observation of the heavens must lead to belief in the gods, because Epicureans and many others will not admit that heavenly objects are alive, much less that they are gods (*Nat. D.* 3.10–11). To let the consensus of mankind decide whether gods exist, he continues, would allow fools to judge (*Nat. D.* 3.11). Balbus's assertion of divine manifestations relies on the resurrection of the dead, which is incredible (*Nat. D.* 3.11–12). We have already noted Cotta's criticism of divination as useless, even if true (*Nat. D.* 3.14–15). According to Cotta, human reason is not divine—or if it is, it is a curse from the gods and not a blessing (*Nat. D.* 3.65–85). Reason has proven disastrous to most people, beneficial to only a few. Providence should have known that humans would abuse reason, so it should not have made that gift. The gods do not show care for humans, but Cotta praises the foresight of the god Dionysus for seeing clearly that crime pays, further evidence that the gods allow the good to suffer evils while the wicked often flourish. Humans must seek the virtues within themselves, not from gods. Cotta says he would regret giving comfort to evildoers with his speech, except that a guilty conscience will deter evil.

None of Cotta's objections mentioned in the previous paragraph is anything other than a refutation or a radical reflection by a skeptic. The nature of his argument changes, however, as he begins to confront the claim of Chrysippus (noted two paragraphs before). Cotta says he would agree with Chrysippus that the universe should be considered the home of gods, "if I thought it had been built and not, as I will teach, formed by nature" (*Nat. D.* 3.26).[41] Here we see the beginning of Cotta's dogmatic naturalism, as he rules out the possibility that gods ultimately created the universe.

Balbus has suggested that Socrates embraced the existence of a divine, rational spirit pervading the universe when Socrates spoke of the way humans acquired their intelligence (*Nat. D.* 2.18, referring to Xenophon, *Memorabilia* 1.4.8). Cotta accepts that depiction of Socrates when he broaches the subject. But whereas Balbus agreed with Socrates's alleged view, Cotta disagrees. Socrates was wrong, Cotta asserts, because reason and its effects "are from nature—not nature walking like a craftsman, as Zeno states,[42] ... but causing everything to go and driving everything onward by its own motions and changes" (*Nat. D.* 3.27). Nature "coheres and persists by the forces of nature, *not by those of the gods*" (*Nat. D.* 3.28; emphasis mine). Cotta seems to think that he has caught Socrates slipping into a dogmatic position here. In fact, however, there is good reason to suspect that Socrates did not definitely believe in a divine, rational, universal spirit. In Plato's *Apology of Socrates* he repeatedly denies knowledge of divine matters.[43] There is good reason to conclude that it is Cotta and not Socrates who is guilty of being dogmatic. For although we might be extraordinarily generous to Cotta and understand every statement of his with the caveat "This is only what seems probable to me," we must observe the way in which he speaks on an extremely difficult question. He speaks very definitely, without the hesitation characteristic of the Academic approach and found in the Socratic method of questioning.[44] In short, Cotta affirms a dogmatic naturalism: reason can be entirely explained in terms of matter in motion. Cicero is suggesting here how easily the naturalistic tendencies implied in the Academic approach may harden into fixed belief, especially when an Academic takes Socrates for his foe.

By the end of the dialogue, when Cotta claims of his role, "I have preferred discussing those points I debated to judging them" (*Nat. D.* 3.95), we may understand that he is deceiving himself, for he has made judgments and not merely engaged in discussion. To see how Cotta could have made more skeptical arguments, and hence why Cicero judges Balbus's speech superior, we need to examine Cicero's speeches in *De Divinatione*.

Cicero's Skepticism

The dialogue *De Divinatione* is set in 44 B.C., contemporary to its composition. The interlocutors are Cicero and his younger brother Quintus, who held a number of civil and military offices and was an avid reader and writer. The location is Cicero's villa in Tusculum, more specifically the gymnasium called Lyceum, a fitting place for this Aristotelian dialogue.[45] Aristotle's dialogues are lost, but we have a letter by Cicero to his friend Titus Pomponius Atticus of June 45 B.C. in which he describes his recent dialogues as following the "Aristotelian custom, in which others' conversation is introduced in such a way that the preeminence belongs to [the author] himself" (*Att.* 13.19.4).

In introducing the conversation between his brother and himself, Cicero refers to belief in divination as "an ancient opinion, drawn even from as long ago as heroic times, and strengthened by agreement of both the Roman people and all nations" (*Div.* 1.1). He calls divination "a magnificent and salutary kind of thing, provided that there is any." The ancients' approval of the practice was due more to their "having been admonished by the outcomes of affairs" than to their "having been taught by reason" (*Div.* 1.5). In other words, ancient thinkers and doers approved of divination because of its political utility, especially its promotion of respect for authority. But Cicero does not give a definite judgment about divination here, for he refers to himself as seeking what judgment to make and as "fearing that I might rashly assent to something either false or insufficiently ascertained.... For rashness in assenting and error are disgraceful in all matters" but especially in religion, where one must avoid the twin dangers of neglecting any existing gods and falling victim to superstition (*Div.* 1.7).

As the dialogue begins, Quintus says that he has just finished reading Book 3 of *De Natura Deorum* and that the Book has caused his judgment of religion to slip but has not "done away with it from the foundation" (*Div.* 1.8). His brother replies that he is glad, because "Cotta himself debates more for the purpose of refuting the Stoics' arguments than for the purpose of destroying human religion."[46] Note the comparative nature of that statement: Cicero does not claim that Cotta's entire purpose is refutation. Cotta's dogmatism may have not only the effect but also the purpose of overthrowing religion, because that dogmatism is accompanied by the attitude that everyone should believe as the dogmatist believes. If Cotta tries to convince Balbus of the truth of naturalism, what believer in gods might he not try to convince? But even if only Cotta's effect and not his purpose were involved, we could see in the harmful consequences for religion part of the reason why Cicero considers Cotta's arguments inferior.

The subtlety of Cicero's statement about Cotta's purpose escapes Quintus, who responds so as to imply that Cotta's sole purpose is refutation, that Cotta wants "not to seem to transgress common rites; but in his eagerness to argue against the Stoic gods, it seems to me that he does away with them from the foundation." Quintus does not suffer the personal overturning of religious belief that he fears many others are liable to because he thinks that "religion was sufficiently defended in the second book by Balbus, whose argument seemed to you yourself nearer the truth, as you write at the end of the third book" (*Div.* 1.9). Again, Quintus cannot quite fathom his brother's thinking: Cicero wrote that Balbus's argument seemed "nearer *the appearance of truth.*"

After Quintus presents the Stoic arguments for divination in Book 1, Cicero gives himself the rebuttal in Book 2.[47] He says that he must respond to Quintus in such a way that "I affirm nothing, I question everything, doubting for the most part and distrusting myself. For if I held as definite anything I said, I myself would be divining who deny that divination exists" (*Div.* 2.8). That implies that to speak definitively about divination—perhaps Cicero would add, about any other subject as well—would be to assert a claim to divine revelation. And Cicero does not speak too definitively here, because to deny that divination exists is not to deny that it is possible.

Cicero seems to adopt a dogmatic naturalism in some passages, but he does not actually do so. He says that mathematicians make calculations to predict eclipses of the sun and the moon, which then happen according to "the necessity of nature" (*Div.* 2.17). But he does not address there the question whether nature itself has an ultimate divine cause. Thus that passage differs significantly from Cotta's claim that nature operates by its own forces, not by those of the gods. Similar is the following remark of Cicero: "It is necessary that whatever arises, whatever sort of thing it is, has its cause in nature" (*Div.* 2.60). Also similar is Cicero's very definition of nature as "that because of which the spirit can never be stationary and free from activity and motion" (*Div.* 2.128). In neither of those two sentences does Cicero exclude the possibility that nature has a divine cause. Rather he warns that it is "great foolishness" to assume that gods caused things that may have happened by nature or chance, instead of investigating the causes of those things (*Div.* 2.55).

Cicero leaves the strongest impression of dogmatic naturalism in his treatment of dreams. Quintus has argued that gods are sometimes the cause of human dreams, and he has provided many famous traditional examples. Cicero responds, "First, it must be understood that no divine force is the producer of dreams. And indeed it is clear that nothing seen in dreams began in the will of the gods; for the gods, for our sakes, would do so in such a way that we could foresee the future" (*Div.* 2.124; cf. *Div.* 2.126–27). That response must be understood as saying, in effect, "On the Stoics' own terms it does not make sense to conclude that gods cause dreams." It must be so understood because one of its premises is that the gods show a benevolent care for human beings, and that is a key Stoic tenet. By contrast, Cicero cannot exclude the possibility of gods who do not care for human beings, and he gives the example of Epicureans as being among those who can also imagine indifferent gods (*Div.* 2.104). Thus Cicero's just-quoted response to Quintus cannot be taken to represent his own thought on the basis of that statement alone.

Cicero continues, "For all dreams, Quintus, there is one explanation" (*Div.* 2.136). Soon he gives that explanation: "Spirits have such a force and nature that, when they are awake, they are lively not on account of any foreign impulse, but on account of their own motion and a certain incredible swiftness" (*Div.* 2.139). In the passage between the two just quoted, Cicero ridicules the atomic theory of the Greek philosopher Democritus, whose approval of divination Quintus has appealed to in Book 1. Democritus asserted that all bodies emit images, the impact of which on human sense organs causes sensation. By extension, that theory could explain the source of dreams as the seizing of humans' spirits by those images, but Cicero will have none of it. It is in that context that he denies the causing of dreams by "any foreign impulse"; he does not mention gods there. He does attribute the spirit's liveliness to its own motion. But since each spirit originates from two parents, it cannot literally be the cause of its own motion. Cicero does not answer the question of what causes the spirit's own motion. Moreover, Cicero's use of the word "incredible" (*incredibili*) to describe the spirit's swiftness is an admission that he cannot give a complete account of the human spirit.

If Cicero were dogmatically excluding the possibility of the gods' serving as a force behind nature, he would be speaking contrary to his own character, for his openmindedness is evident at several other places. Regarding soothsaying he says, "And certainly, if there is any force in entrails to tell the future, it is necessary that it be either joined with the nature of things, or formed in a certain way by the will of the gods" (*Div.* 2.29). He does not believe that entrails can be used to prophesy, but he recognizes that either nature or gods would be the causative force if they could be used. He is even willing to refer to nature itself as "divine" for the purpose of contrasting it with the gall of a chicken or the liver of an ox. What relation, he asks, could those supposed signs have with the nature of things, even if nature is a harmonious whole? The view that nature is a coherent whole "was agreeable to the natural scientists" (*Div.* 2.33). Cicero's use of "was agreeable to" (*placuisse*) sagely captures, without endorsing, the faith in the harmony of the universe that influenced the work of many natural scientists in his day and still does in ours. For himself he will concede only that there is "some connection in the nature of things"—that is, some sort of natural connection among the distant things in the universe. That view stops well short of dogmatic naturalism. Cicero does not deny that gods could possibly influence humans' lives: "For my part I do not plainly despair that those things are true, but I do not know and I want to learn from you" (*Div.* 2.48).

To maintain that Cicero is illustrating Academic skepticism in *De Divinatione* is not to deny that he also has a political purpose, even a twofold one, in writing it. First, he clearly wants not to harm Roman religion. In fact he does not even want to abolish the practice of divination. He writes about soothsaying that "it ought to be cultivated for the sake of the republic and common religious observance" (*Div.* 2.28), despite the fact that Roman augurs no longer look for meaning in the signs (*Div.* 2.70–71). Divination promotes obedience to law and controls the excesses of both the masses and dangerously ambitious politicians (*Leg.* 2.31; cf. *Rep.* 2.16–17, 26–27). But because Cicero is alone with his brother, they may question the intellectual soundness of the practice. Separating the question of the gods' existence from that of divination, Cicero maintains that although the latter "is clearly done away with [as a practice that leads to trustworthy results], the gods' existence must be retained" (*Div.* 2.41). The context of that sentence makes it clear that he is not attempting to eliminate the rituals of divination. He will launch an assault on the trustworthiness of divination but not a rejection of its practice nor a rejection of the existence of gods.

The second part of Cicero's political purpose is what he sees as a duty to "throw out all the roots of superstition" (*Div.* 2.149). He says that if he can "do away with it from the foundation" (*Div.* 2.148) he will have performed a great public service, because it has "seized upon a weakness" in "the spirits of almost all people." Superstition is partly to blame for the rash assent that he is concerned to avoid at the beginning of their discussion. The power of superstition makes it crucial that he warn his intelligent readers—who may be included, to some extent, in "almost all people"—against falling victim to that foolishness. Cicero's attempt to eliminate as potent a force as superstition requires extraordinary rhetorical vigor, and he says that he has had to devote special effort to the subject of dreams because of the extreme cleverness of the Stoic philosophers who saw gods as the force behind dreams (*Div.* 2.150). That helps to account for the vehemence of parts of his speech and their coming as close as they do to dogmatic naturalism.

In short Cicero attacks superstition at its "roots," but he preserves its branches, that is, the practices of divination, for their political advantage. Educated augurs, he seems to think, should keep those practices from producing deleterious results.

Cicero's amazing ability to pull off this simultaneous defense of religion and attack on superstition, all the while remaining an Academic skeptic, is encapsulated in one brief passage toward the end of the dialogue: "Truly—for I want this to be carefully understood—by doing away with superstition, religion is not done away with. For it is the part of a wise man to protect the ancestors' institutions by retaining the sacred rites and ceremonies; and the beauty of the universe and the order in heavenly things compel a confession that there is some preeminent and eternal nature that the human race should respect and admire" (*Div.* 2.148). The end of that passage might also seem to lapse into dogma. But Cicero does not claim that the beauty and order in the universe compel *him* to confess the existence of an eternal nature, only that they compel *someone* or *some people* so to confess.

In distinguishing religion from superstition, Cicero suggests the proper way to approach the former when he observes that religion is "linked to the knowledge of nature" (*Div.* 2.149). That approach is what we would today call natural theology; any god is to be found through the use of one's natural powers, not through revelation, and skepticism that leads to inquiry is the natural starting point. Indeed, Cicero's last speech in *De Divinatione* is a restatement of that skeptical outlook: "Moreover, it is characteristic of the Academy not to interpose its own judgment, [but instead] to test those judgments that most appear to be true, to compare reasons, to express what can be said in behalf of each sentiment, and, without employing any authority of its own, to leave the listener's judgment untouched and free. I will hold to this habit, bequeathed by Socrates, and as often as possible I will use it between us, if it pleases you, brother Quintus" (*Div.* 2.150).

The first sentence of that passage would suggest not only that the entire discussion in *De Divinatione*, both Quintus's and Cicero's speeches, illustrates Academic method but also that Cicero's speech is no more indicative of skepticism than that of Quintus. The latter suggestion is untenable, however, because Quintus's speech illustrates Stoicism and Cicero's illustrates skepticism. Thus in the second sentence of the just-quoted passage, Cicero says that *he* does, and will, employ skepticism, as indeed he has told Quintus he will affirm nothing and question everything. Academic method, then, is to be found both in Cicero's overall presentation of the arguments for and against divination and in his own arguments in Book 2. He relies not on any authority of his own in Book 2 but on reason, and he leaves the reader's judgment free to weigh the respective merits of Quintus's and his own arguments.

Cotta's Inadequate Skepticism and Cicero's Verdict

We are now in a better position to see how Cotta's arguments in *De Natura Deorum* could be more skeptical. First, he could be more careful not to confess a strong belief in the gods' existence, as when he remarks that "it cannot be shaken from my spirit that gods exist" (*Nat. D.* 3.7). Cicero speaks more impersonally (*Div.* 2.148). Second and conversely, given his position as augur, Cotta should not admit to doubts about the gods' existence (*Nat. D.* 1.61). The Academic approach need not be so confessional. Third, Cotta does not need to say that he trusts in the signs of divination (*Nat. D.* 3.14). It would suffice to claim that the practices of divination should be retained (*Div.* 2.28,148). Fourth, he carelessly lapses into asserting, without proof, that nature persists without the gods' help (*Nat. D.* 3.26–28). In *De Divinatione*, Cicero manages not to do so.[48]

Thus we have sufficient reason to judge that Cicero's verdict in favor of Balbus and against Cotta is not an exercise in dissimulation; Cotta is deficient as an Academic spokesman. As an Academic himself, and therefore someone who reserves the right to change his mind, Cicero can hardly fault Cotta for not maintaining perfect intellectual consistency throughout his speeches. Any inconsistency must be reasonable, however, and we have seen Cotta fail in more than one way. He fails philosophically because he slips into dogmatic naturalism. He fails politically because his speeches have the effect, and maybe the purpose, of undermining support for religion.

Why does Cicero publish *De Natura Deorum* knowing that it may have that effect? For one reason, he can show his readers, likely to be highly educated, how easy it is to undermine public support for religion. Some of his readers will not fail to notice Cotta's emphasis on the maintenance of respect for ancestral authority. But Cicero knows that his audience also needs a thorough discussion of theological matters, and he provides the opportunity for each reader to judge the strengths and weaknesses of the arguments of the three schools. Moreover, it is quite possible, even likely, that before completing *De Natura Deorum*, Cicero has planned to write *De Divinatione*, in which he goes to great lengths to bolster public support for religion.

It may be that the inadequacy of Cotta's arguments is not the only factor behind Cicero's verdict. Perhaps Walter Nicgorski was correct to say that "Cicero regarded the Stoic teaching as the best even if wanting in many ways."[49] That could be true especially because the Academy had no teaching of its own. Could Cicero's approval of Balbus reflect a judgment that his fundamental claim about the existence of a divinity or divinities is more likely true than false? We have seen that Cicero announces such an opinion in the prologue of the work, not just at the end. If his approval does reflect that judgment, that would be despite his obvious objection to the Stoics' dogmatic method.[50]

In the end, Cicero has his way: we do not have access to his deepest thoughts on the question just posed. I conclude more safely that Cicero has something to say to both scientific and humanistic students of politics today. He deserves far more respect as a philosopher than he has received since the nineteenth century. Many scholars of Cicero have taken the view that he lacked an original mind, and they have been obsessed with the question of his sources for his accounts of the philosophical schools. In yielding to that obsession, those scholars have assiduously avoided fundamental questions themselves and wrongly assumed that Cicero did the same. It is all too easy to say, as Joseph B. Mayor did in his edition of the Latin text of *De Natura Deorum*, that Cicero's pro-Stoic verdict "may be considered to point the way, vaguely indeed and hesitatingly, to the mysticism of later times, when the human mind wearied out with its fruitless search after truth, abjured reason for faith, and surrendered itself blindly either to the traditions of priests or to the inward vision of the Neo-Platonists."[51] Close reading shows instead that Cicero treated theological matters with profound intellectual depth and marvelous care. Cicero never tired of searching for truth, even if he thought that an approximation was as near as he could come to it.

NOTES

I thank Allison Johnson for her assistance with research for this essay, Mark Lutz for his comments, and Stacey Stonum Fott for her editing. All translations in this essay are mine.

1. Sagan, *Cosmos*, 1.
2. My account of Epicurean and Stoic theology is indebted to Rackham (introduction to *De natura deorum, Academica*, viii–ix). I will use the term Academic to refer to the New Academy, as opposed to the Old Academy. The Old Academics ruled Plato's school after his death and systematized his teachings. The New Academics arose around 275 B.C. and, to one degree or another, took a skeptical approach toward philosophical questions, claiming to be more faithful to Socrates and Plato in doing so.
3. Another conceivable, but inadequate, translation of that passage would have Cicero claim that "Cotta's argument seemed truer [to me] than that of Velleius." For the reasons why that would be inadequate, see Taran, "Cicero's Attitude towards Stoicism and Skepticism," 6–7.
4. I omit what Hume has written about Cicero and theology in some editions of his essay "Of the Rise and Progress of the Arts and Sciences" because it was omitted from the final edition published in his lifetime (see

Hume, *Essays*, 623). Hume's *Dialogues concerning Natural Religion* was to some extent inspired by *De Natura Deorum*, but I do not think one may infer from Hume's work an interpretation of Cicero's verdict.

    5. Augustine, *On the City of God*, 5.9.
    6. Quoted in French in Pease, introduction to *De natura deorum*, 1:60.
    7. Montesquieu, "Discourse on Cicero," 94.
    8. Momigliano, "Theological Efforts of the Roman Upper Classes," 208.
    9. Ibid., 209.
    10. Glucker, "Cicero's Philosophical Affiliations" and "Cicero's Philosophical Affiliations Again."
    11. DeFilippo, "Cicero vs. Cotta," 169–70 n. 2.
    12. Görler explained the lack of evidence in detail ("Silencing the Troublemaker"). The lack of evidence also serves to refute Schofield's claims that Cicero turned to Academic skepticism late in his life for stylistic reasons, and that there is no trace of skepticism in the earlier dialogues *De Re Publica* and *De Legibus* ("Cicero For and Against Divination," 47). To give just one such trace—but a crucial one, concerning the foundation of natural law— Cicero says that "it has pleased highly educated men to commence with law—probably rightly, provided that, as the same men define it, law is highest reason, implanted in nature, which orders those things that ought to be done [and] prohibits the opposite" (*Leg.* 1.18). Skepticism is indicated by the words "probably" and "provided that" in that sentence, as well as by Cicero's appealing to the judgment of "highly educated men," not necessarily his own. Dyck claimed that the words *si modo*, "provided that," carry "no implication of doubt" (Dyck, *Commentary on Cicero, De Legibus*, 109). But Dyck gave no reason to think that the meaning was other than conditional—that is, implying the possibility of doubt. For further evidence of skepticism in *De Re Publica* and *De Legibus*, see Steinmetz, "Beobachtungen zu Ciceros philosophischem Standpunkt."
    13. DeFilippo, "Cicero vs. Cotta," 186.
    14. Walsh, introduction to *The Nature of the Gods*, xxxvi–xxxvii.
    15. Pease, "Conclusion of Cicero's *De Natura Deorum*," 29.
    16. Ibid., 31–32.
    17. Ibid., 33.
    18. Ibid., 35–37.
    19. Ibid., 36.
    20. Levine, "The Original Design and the Publication of the *De natura deorum*," 20.
    21. Ibid., 19.
    22. Ibid., 21.
    23. Levine, "Cicero and the Literary Dialogue," 150.
    24. Levine, "The Original Design and the Publication of the *De natura deorum*," 19.

25. Contrast part of another dialogue, where Cicero says he treats Stoic ethics with a view to its internal consistency, not with a view to the truth (*Fin.* 5.83).

26. Pease, "Conclusion of Cicero's *De Natura Deorum*," 36.

27. Price, "Sceptics in Cicero and Hume," 106.

28. Only two other dialogues—*De Legibus* (which was never listed by Cicero among his published works and probably unfinished) and the first edition of *Academica*—have such an unspecified dramatic date.

29. Only one other dialogue, *Laelius De Amicitia*, has such an unspecified location.

30. Only one other dialogue, *Tusculanae Disputationes*, has such unspecified discussants. For another mention of Velleius and Balbus, see *De Or.* 3.78.

31. Regarding the scholarly controversy over whether Cicero actually published this dialogue, I follow the affirmative argument of Dyck, *De natura deorum*, 2–3.

32. Ibid., 143.

33. *Oxford Latin Dictionary*, s.v. "*placeo.*"

34. Dyck, *De natura deorum*, 151.

35. Ibid., 152.

36. Ibid., 168.

37. *Oxford Latin Dictionary*, s.v. "*sentio.*"

38. DeFilippo, "Cicero vs. Cotta," 180.

39. The word I have translated "spirit" (*animo*) may also be translated "mind."

40. Chrysippus (c. 280–207 B.C.) was the third head of the Stoic school of philosophy.

41. The passage in which Cotta teaches naturalism may be *Nat. D.* 3.27–28 (examined below); or it may be in one of the lost parts of Book 3.

42. Zeno of Citium (335–263 B.C.) founded the Stoic school of philosophy.

43. Plato, *Apology of Socrates* 19c–d, 20d–e, 21b, 29b.

44. Mayor correctly assessed those statements by Cotta as "simple assertion on the part of the Academics" (introduction to *De natura deorum*, 3:xxii). But he did not link Cotta's dogmatism to Cicero's verdict.

45. MacKendrick, *Philosophical Books of Cicero*, 185.

46. The presence of the Latin *sic* in the sentence could indicate that it should read, "Cotta himself debates more with the result of refuting the Stoics' arguments than with the result of destroying human religion." But a purpose clause seems to make more sense here than a result clause. A number of scholars have agreed: e.g., Pease in his edition of the Latin text (67); Falconer, Poteat, and Yonge in their English translations; MacKendrick, *Philosophical Books of Cicero*, 185.

47. Controversy exists over whether Cicero's speech in Book 2 represents his view of divination. For the view that it does, see, e.g., Schofield, "Cicero For and Against Divination"; for the view that it does not, see, e.g., Beard, "Cicero and Divination." I side with the former because it is well established that Cicero takes a skeptical approach to philosophical questions, and what he says in Book 2 is a logical result of that skepticism. Of course, as Beard said, we must always remember Cicero's caveat against assuming his forthrightness on philosophical questions (ibid., 35).

Cicero's arguments in *De Divinatione* appear to contradict his view in *De Legibus*: "I feel that divination exists ... and that the part of it that concerns birds and other signs belongs to our discipline. For if we admit that gods exist, that the universe is ruled by their mind, and that the same beings take care of the human race and can show us signs of the future, I do not see why I should deny that divination exists.... But there is no doubt that this discipline and art of augurs has already passed away through old age and neglect. So I agree neither with him who denies that this skill ever existed in our college [of augurs] nor with him who thinks that it now exists" (*Leg.* 2.32–33). There are two reasons why the contradiction between the two works is only apparent: (1) Cicero's initial statement in the above passage uses the word for "feel" (*sentio*), not "think," which two words I have previously distinguished. At the dramatic date of *De Legibus*, Cicero was serving as an augur. It is reasonable to say that Cicero gives his impression as an augur, just as Cotta does (*Nat. D.* 3.5–6). Cicero's last statement in the above passage voices his *disagreement* with anyone who "thinks" (*putat*) that divination exists in his day. He will admit only that in prior centuries, when Romans were more observant of religious ceremonies, augurs knew how to conduct their business. (2) The above passage uses Stoic arguments for the gods' existence, as well as for divine providence and benevolence, but we have already seen Cicero's skepticism in *De Legibus* toward Stoic arguments (see note 12 above concerning Schofield). Dyck noted that each of Cicero's dialogues has "a different method and goal" (*Commentary on Cicero, De Legibus*, 348). *De Legibus* has a political purpose: the presentation of laws on religion and magistracies that Cicero hopes a Roman republic would adopt. The purposes of *De Natura Deorum* and *De Divinatione* differ from that.

48. Although DeFilippo was correct to judge Cicero's verdict in favor of Balbus to be sincere, it should now be apparent that one of DeFilippo's premises, that Cicero is more dogmatic than his character Cotta, is the opposite of what he should have held.

49. Nicgorski, "Cicero and the Rebirth of Political Philosophy," 94.

50. Cf. Nicgorski, "Cicero's Paradoxes and His Idea of Utility," 571: "The extensive and dogmatic claims of stoic natural philosophy also repel Cicero; he considers stoicism the worst example of a failing that characterized to some extent all the schools except the academic. The stoics abuse reason by

their forced attempt to explain with certainty and consistency all things; this is especially evident in the stoic explanation of origins, the heavens, and divinities. The stoics confidently, in fact arrogantly, assert explanations of matters shrouded in obscurity for most intelligent men." As I have shown, even an Academic can succumb to dogmatism in natural philosophy.

51. Mayor, introduction to *De natura deorum*, 1:xxxvii.

8

Between *Urbs* and *Orbis*

Cicero's Conception of the Political Community

XAVIER MÁRQUEZ

The articulation of models of political community in the Western philosophical tradition was, before Cicero's time, a distinctively Greek enterprise carried on by Plato, Aristotle, and their successors in the various schools of Hellenistic philosophy. The models available to Cicero in this tradition thus bear the imprint of Greek, not Roman, experiences: the experience of the Greek *polis* for Plato and Aristotle and the experience of its decline in Hellenistic times (first under Macedonian and finally under Roman dominion) for the successor schools of Hellenistic philosophy (Stoics, Peripatetics, Academics, and Epicureans). These experiences gave rise to two distinct and very general models of political community: an "urban" (*urbs*) one (found in Plato and Aristotle's work, as well as in various strands of the work of later thinkers) and a "cosmic" (*orbis*) one (found primarily but not exclusively in Stoic sources), both of which are, in turn, quite different from the model of the national state common in political thought today.

Cicero inherits these two models of political community (the "urban" and the "cosmic") at a point when it is becoming increasingly clear that Rome does not "fit" either of them.[1] Rome's imperial expansion had long made Rome much more than an urban center, and though the peculiar development of its legal institutions had already suggested to earlier thinkers that Rome represented an unparalleled, even universal, political order,[2] Rome was nevertheless not readily imaginable as a stoic *cosmopolis*.

Rome's political peculiarity, I submit, was that it was not simply a *polis* with an empire attached to it (like Athens or, in later times, Venice or Genoa); it was a full community of *citizens* over a large territory, integrating a vast number of people in the Italian peninsula within a *political* organization who in a "normal" empire would simply have been subjects of the metropolis. Thus, though the level of political integration in the Italian peninsula in Cicero's time was not yet as high as it would be in Augustus's time a generation later (when Augustus could speak of *tota Italia*), it was certainly comparable to the level of political integration of a proto-modern state (seventeenth-century France, for example). To put the point provocatively, the Roman commonwealth in Cicero's time, at least in the Italian peninsula, had more in common in important respects with a proto-modern state than with a small Greek *polis*, despite the superficial similarity in political institutions between Rome and the typical Greek *polis*.[3] This made it difficult for *existing* models of political community to make sense of Rome.

To be sure, it is and was possible to describe Rome by using the urban or the cosmic models of political community available to Cicero. The models would then have served as "standards" against which the reality of Rome could be measured.[4] Neither Cicero nor his contemporaries, moreover, ever abandon the traditional language of their inherited political theory: they were not in the business of "inventing" new models of political community. Yet if Rome was to be "saved" for political thought, the notion of political community had to be made large enough to accommodate the Romans, and precisely by expanding or modifying the existing models of political community, however unconscious and unintended this process might have been.

I argue in what follows that Cicero, despite his obvious and large debts to Greek political theory, develops a new model of political community that can make better sense of Roman reality than any Greek models available to him. Cicero's model of political community can thus be understood as an implicit response to the theoretical inadequacies of the available Platonic-Aristotelian (*urbs*, or "city") and Stoic (*orbis*, or "world") models of community in the face of Roman imperial expansion. Cicero attempts to synthesize elements of both of these models of political community in an attempt to sufficiently account for Roman political reality, both normatively and empirically.[5] The result of this synthesis is a model of political community that bears strong structural similarities to the model of community current today, namely the national state, and indeed is a direct ancestor of it via Augustine and later the "republican" tradition of political thought.[6] Moreover, Cicero's model of political community, and in particular his understanding of the community as a *patria*, provides Cicero with a certain "picture" of the adequate loyalties required of citizens and justifies a certain backward-looking, even "conservative," orientation to politics, though not one devoid of critical force.

I do not aim to resurrect the Ciceronian model of political community or defend it as normatively better than the current national model of political community. But the exercise may nevertheless suggest different ways of imagining political communities, in part by laying bare the structures of both models and the theoretical steps by which one of these came to be. All modern political communities, like Cicero's Rome, stand between *urbs* and *orbis*, between city and world. But we may still learn something about why the political community came to be placed there and about the tensions inherent in that position. More specifically, by looking at the problems confronted by Cicero at an important point in the history of political thought, we can be drawn to explore how the tension between particularism and universality inherent in being between *urbs* and *orbis* may be managed.

This chapter is divided into two main sections. In the first, I discuss the general idea of a model of political community and illustrate this discussion with a description of a common current model of political community, namely, the nation-state, or national state. In the second, I sketch briefly the urban and cosmic models of political community available to Cicero and then reconstruct Cicero's own model of the political community, emphasizing the ways in which it draws on both of these earlier models and yet goes beyond them. I draw primarily but not exclusively on evidence from his dialogue *De Re Publica*. A short conclusion summarizes the elements of this model and contrasts it with the model of the modern national state.

Models of Political Community

Models of political community are both descriptive representations of existing communities and normative standards for their evaluation. Such models commonly specify the actual or proper *active* part of a political community, its proper *passive* part (the object of the action of the active part), and the kind of relation (the specific action and instrument governing it) between the two. We might say that models of political community are analogies between the community and the structures of human action, though they are not merely that. To take an obvious example, Plato's *Republic* offers a model of political community that is based explicitly on an analogy between the city and the soul and whose normative import is premised on claims about how human souls normally act and should act (e.g., assumptions about the appetitive part of the soul and the need to restrain it). Its elements can thus be understood as defining the community in terms of appropriate and inappropriate agents (e.g., guardians or philosophers v. the many or the people), appropriate and inappropriate objects of care (the whole city v. only some classes of people), appropriate and inappropriate forms of care (education into virtue v. laissez-faire government), and appropriate and inappropriate instruments of care (specific laws, guardians, etc.), that is, in terms of the elements of human action generally.

But even when the analogy between city and soul is not explicit, models of political community often incorporate basic categories of human action. For example, the most common (and the most highly differentiated) model of political community today, the national state,[7] can hardly be said to be "anthropomorphic" in the way in which the Plato's *Republic* is anthropomorphic; and yet the various aspects of the nation-state can be analyzed in terms of the proper *agent* the model identifies (which we may call the people), the proper *instrument* used by this agent (which we may call the state), the proper *object* of intentional action by the agent (which we may call the nation), and the proper *relation of care* between agent and object (which we may call "government"). Let us briefly examine this model in greater detail, since it will provide a useful point of comparison with Cicero's model of political community later in this paper.

The Nation

The nation represents the political community in its unity on the basis of a *cultural* principle, the principle of nationality. Whether nationality is understood to depend ultimately on "natural" human features such as kinship or race, or on more narrowly cultural factors such as language, or even on will and consent (Renan's "the nation is a daily plebiscite"), it is conceived as a culture, that is, a way of life with unique and valuable features extending in time through a history and in space through association with a homeland[8] and worthy of preservation and care ("culture," from *cultus*).[9] From this point of view, the political community is a passive *object of care*.

The State

The state represents that element of the political community through which the community acts on itself. It appears as a uniform, hierarchically structured, and actively modified (hence positive and historically developed) legal order, effective over a clearly delimited territory, which (in theory) coincides with the national homeland, and culminating in a sovereign "apex," which we might call "the government."[10] The "state" of the community as a whole is thus determined through the modification of this legal order, which serves both as the instrumentality of the community (the "machinery of the state") in its active aspect and as the indicator of its condition (its "state")—that is, its norms (laws and constitution), membership, and general health or strength—in its passive aspect.[11] From this point of view, the community appears as the *instrument* of its own care, insofar as its being (or having) a "state" enables it to determine (in both senses of the word: to "set" and to "learn") its own condition (its own "state").

The People

The community is active as a *people*, and hence as potential citizens, that is, bearers of political rights in the legal order of the state. And it is also (*qua* people) the source of the legitimacy of the state and thus of its *political* power, as we can see, for example, in the long tradition of social-contract theory beginning with Hobbes. In theory, the people coincide with the cultural group defined by the nation, which lends its historical substance to it,[12] and in turn both coincide (again in theory, if not always in practice) with the legal status of citizenship determined by the state. This triple coincidence of nation, citizenry, and people leads to an understanding of the political community that is at least *potentially* (but not necessarily) democratic and of the state in the narrow sense as "representative," that is, representative of the people's interests (however much it may in fact diverge from standard conceptions of electoral democracy). From this point of view, therefore, the community appears as an *active subject*, responsible for its own care.

Government

These three elements or aspects of the community are held together by a specific understanding of common *care*: the citizens (the community in its active aspect) take care of the common affairs of the nation (the community in its passive aspect) by entrusting (via appropriate legal mechanisms) their management or government to their agents in the state (e.g., the government), who, in theory at least, "represent" their concerns (i.e., attempt to make them present once again in the legal order of the state, as they are already present in themselves) and "manage" (govern) the affairs of the community in light of these concerns. Because the community is understood as a "nation," such common care (in theory) involves the attempt to preserve the homeland and the way of life of the community; because it is also understood as an active subject, such common care (again in theory) involves the attempt to preserve the rights and liberties of the people; and because it is understood as a legal order, such common care involves the subordination of all social action under a single framework of rules. Government, then, appears as the form of care that a people exercises for itself as a nation through the intentional use and modification of a legal order.

These four elements define a model of a political community, though actual communities will, of course, vary in how far they can be said to "fit" the model (nations and peoples do not necessarily coincide, for example, and states as legal orders are not the only instruments they use for their care). Moreover, the model is not an exhaustive account of all the relevant aspects of a political community. We could complicate it with other relevant concepts and distinctions, such as the idea of a political regime, or the public-private distinction, which bring out dimensions of the political community not easily captured through the analogy with human action. But we should note that a model of a political community is *not* a description of its "constitution" or "form of government." For example, though the nation-state, insofar as it identifies the people as the potentially active part of the community, appears to imply a democratic set of institutions, this need not be the case so long as the state can persuasively (and how persuasively will depend on the historical context) claim to represent the people (through whatever institutional means).

What a model of political community gives us, in other words, is less a description of institutions than a frame for thinking about the limits and purpose of political institutions more generally. Thus the model of the nation-state tells us that in any given "national" community the *people* are the appropriate agent for the care of the community (not some other group); the *state* (in the sense indicated above) the appropriate instrument for such care (so we have talk of state-building and state failure); the nation (understood to have a cultural principle of unity) the appropriate *object* of this care (so we have talk of national interests); and the preservation and improvement of a people's distinct culture (including the legal rights and duties of its people) the appropriate form of this care.

Ancient models of political community differed from this common model of political community today along one or more of these dimensions: the appropriate agent was not always thought to be the people; the object of their care was not necessarily thought to be a "nation"; the instruments of this care were not understood to be a legal order that could be modified on demand; and the care of the political community for itself was not necessarily understood as the preservation and improvement of a certain way of life through the representation of the concerns of the people in this legal order. Yet as we shall see, Cicero's own model of political community comes very close to these modern ideas. How and why this was so is something that we will explore in the next section.

Cicero and the Available Models of Political Community in His Time

In the ancient world, as I have already indicated, two basic models of political community can be readily identified: the "urban" model (most clearly described in the texts of Plato and Aristotle) and the "cosmic" model (most clearly depicted in the writings of the Stoics). Cicero took elements from both of these models to create his own original conceptual synthesis, in the process breaking free of their limitations.[13] Let us examine each of them in turn.

The Urban Model of Political Community

In our extant texts, the "urban" model of community is chiefly articulated in Aristotle's *Politics* (a work that we cannot be sure that Cicero read), but it is also present in a number of Platonic works (e.g., Plato's *Republic* and *Laws*, which Cicero certainly knew), and aspects of it are present in many other works throughout antiquity. Though there are substantial differences in the way these two key thinkers (and their successors and near-contemporaries) articulate it, we can say that the hallmarks of this "urban" model are (1) an emphasis on the rootedness of the political community on human need, that is, on the natural interdependence of human beings for the purposes of production and reproduction (cf. *Republic* 2.369b–e);[14] (2) a distinctive understanding of the *citizenry* (as defined by a particular political regime, such as the *demos* in democracy or the wealthy in an oligarchy) as the active element of the community, and (3) an insistence that the purpose of political life is the promotion of the "good life," properly understood as a life of virtue, through human cooperation. A political community, in other words, is conceived on a first approximation as a network of cooperation that is to be nurtured or cared for rather than as a culture with a specific way of life; its care is presented as the promotion of the life of virtue among at least some part of this network of cooperation through the appropriate use of laws, education, and ritual; and this is thought to be the primary task of the citizenry, as defined by some particular political regime.

Thus the *polis* is understood by both Plato (*Laws* 676a–682b) and Aristotle (*Politics* 1280b29–35) to be constituted in the first place by *oikoi*, households, rather than by individuals, that is, by human communities or partnerships that are more or less self-sufficient for the satisfaction of basic material needs but which need each other for the purpose of defending themselves and enabling the exercise of the virtue.[15] In partial tension with this idea, we also find an emphasis on the idea that the key "economic" feature of the *polis* is the presence of a division of labor in which the needs of some are met by the labor of others and vice versa and which enables some to dedicate their activities toward the care of the city as a whole. The *polis* builds on the relative material self-sufficiency of the *oikos* for the purpose of a life that goes beyond mere material self-sufficiency and can therefore be called good as a whole (*Politics* 1252b29–30, 1280b39, 1326b7–9). Conversely, a relatively self-sufficient *oikos* makes citizenship possible.[16]

On this view, the limits of a proper community as both object of care and active subject are given not by cultural features of the community (e.g., kinship or language) but by the goals that cooperation, based initially on mutual need, is supposed to accomplish and the "technical" conditions that make the attainment of such goals possible. On this point, the "urban" model of the community is self-limiting. Given that the goal of the community is the promotion of virtue, the citizenry must necessarily be a small group (however democratic the constitution) that has the leisure and personal independence to learn and practice virtue,[17] the personal knowledge of each other to make reasonable character judgments about themselves, and sufficient opportunity to participate in ruling (itself an educative activity).[18]

In this model, the "citizen" thus appears in a double aspect (manifest in Aristotle's twofold discussion of citizenship in the *Politics*): both as a regime-determined coruler (the many in democracy, the rich in oligarchy, etc.), and as a member of an already materially self-sufficient household or community who ought to share in the decision-making process that affects this common life. As in the nation-state, the urban model of political community has "democratic" tendencies, but these are counterbalanced by the understanding of the proper care of the community as the promotion of virtue, lending classical Greek political theory its peculiar ambivalence toward democracy as both *the* paradigmatic case of political community and as the *wrong* sort of constitution.

The arrangement or order of these citizens—their *politeia*, that is, the "institutions" of the city, including both the "constitution" and the laws that determine the citizens' *paideia*—enables them to pursue their common good in better or worse ways, that is, to care for themselves in one way or another. The *politeia* is thus the community in its instrumental aspect (as the *polis* represents the community as an object of care and the *politai* the community in its active aspect). But given the understanding of the goals of political life and hence of citizenship embedded in this model, the *politeia* is not understood as a different *part* of the *polis*, a fully differentiated aspect of the community, unlike the modern state. It is not the separate instrument of the citizens (the organization that the citizens can manipulate via elections, votes, etc.) but simply the pattern constituted by the citizens in their attempts to take care of themselves, a pattern that may, of course, be consciously altered depending on circumstances. To be sure, some *politeiai* are more instrumental than others (for example, monarchy); but even in that case the *politeia* is not a mere instrument that can be manipulated by the citizens. There is no concept of representation in Greek thought.

The Cosmic Model of Political Community

In contrast to the "urban" model of political community, the "cosmic" model of political community is a creation of the Stoic school, in works mostly lost today but available to Cicero and preserved in later writings in quotation or paraphrase, often in Cicero's own works.[19] In this model, the only *true* political community is an *ethical* community of those who discern and live according to the natural law, understood as the order and regularity of nature insofar as it tends to the good.[20] This is a community of the virtuous, but while the urban model of community is also preoccupied with citizen virtue, and hence with the *paideia* of the citizens through political institutions in order to help them achieve it, the Stoic model rejects most conventional and institutional *paideia*.[21] Law is not primarily an instrument of education but the very expression of reason in the world and the first element of all political community.

The emphasis here is on the identity of community and law, and law and reason.[22] Thus in the true community the good citizen is identical with the good man and the good man identical with the wise man, who is in turn a fellow citizen with every other wise man, wherever he may live.[23] The community in its active aspect appears as an agglomeration of the wise, who are simply those whose reason is in tune with the universal reason and hence friends with each other. Since through their virtuous activity they sometimes care for others who are not wise, the community in its passive aspect appears as an agglomeration of all human beings, sometimes divided into particular communities on more or less arbitrary principles. Here the law is not a mere instrument of a people prior to it but constitutes the community in its active aspect (as the wise men who have internalized it). Moreover, the "naturalness" of the community is not tied to the satisfaction of human *need* and can contain any number of people. The universe then becomes the "habitation" of the true city, indeed *the* true city, an organization of gods and men for the benefit of both.

The distinctive contribution of the Stoics to ideas of political community, in brief, is the extreme dissociation of community from any particular set of institutions, whether in the form of a particular political regime (even if, as Erskine argues, they were originally sympathetic to democracy, a controversial contention) or in the form of the tightly linked institutions that guaranteed a Greek *paideia* (as Zeno's rejection of conventional education suggests).[24] This dissociation is in turn associated with an emphasis on the virtuous individual who realizes the harmony of the cosmos in himself and in the city as the only properly active part of the community. As we shall see below, Cicero made use of both ideas to reinterpret creatively the "urban" model of political community in his quest to make sense of Rome as a political community.

Cicero's Model

The problem of the conceptual inadequacy of Greek political categories for the analysis of Roman reality is not explicitly treated in Cicero's work; and even any discussion of the most obvious theoretical problems associated with Roman expansion and the integration of the Italian peninsula into Roman political institutions is generally lacking, though this may be due partly to the fragmentary state of the extant texts.[25] Moreover, Cicero does not understand his own conception of political community to be fundamentally different from the conceptions of political community from which he draws—those of the Stoics, the Academics, and the Peripatetics. His redefinition of the political community is for the most part unconscious.

A redefinition of the Greek conceptions of political community is nevertheless evident in the most explicit discussion of political community in his work. In *Rep.* 1.39–41, Scipio, the main speaker of the dialogue, provides a famous, if somewhat cryptic and incomplete, definition of a *res publica*, a term that I take to be the equivalent of "political community."[26] There he distinguishes a *res publica* from a *civitas* insofar as the *civitas* is the *constitutio* (the "organization," in Zetzel's translation) of a "people," whereas the *res publica* is their common concern, the *res populi*.[27] That is, the *res publica* is defined not in "organizational" or "legal" terms (as the *civitas* is) but in "affective" terms as whatever the people care about in common or can be understood as their common property (such as its laws and values). In turn, a people is defined by its common agreement on law and values (1.39; *consensu iuris et utilitate communione*), so that the *res publica* is simply the common space that emerges from the people's care for themselves through their laws and institutions. To the extent that the *res publica* is identical with the concern of the people for themselves, it does not have a clear "natural" size or extent, unlike the Platonic-Aristotelian political community, even if Cicero does not point this out.

To be sure, Cicero appears to be taking a standard Stoic-Aristotelian line on the origins of political association. Thus at

Rep. 1.39, the *people* is explicitly said to be a natural association; and the fact that the people come together in part through *utilitate communione*, common utility or interest, is a nod to the Platonic-Aristotelian notion of the city as rooted in the satisfaction of human needs through cooperation, while Scipio's subsequent comment about the independence of human sociality from economic interdependence (cf. also *Fin.* 3.62–64 and *Off.* 1.158) merely appears to echo Aristotelian and Stoic views of the natural sociality of human beings (cf. *Politics* 1278b15–30). Yet by suggesting that it is not the *res publica* itself but the *people* (merely a component of the *res publica*) that comes together through this natural sociality, Scipio partially severs the connection between natural interdependence, natural sociality, and the *polis* that is key to Aristotle's political thought.[28] The emphasis is on the *agreement* on law and common values and on the care of the people for these laws and values, which paves the way for Scipio to argue later that a genuine *res publica* exists if (and only if) there is the right sort of agreement in law and common values, independent of any "economic" or "organizational" facts. The *res publica* ceases to exist whenever such agreement is not present, even if the *civitas* (the "state") remains (*Rep.* 3.43ff.).

We must be careful here. Cicero is *not* suggesting, through Scipio, that *any* sort of agreement on *ius* constitutes a people (and hence that there could be a tension between *ius naturale* and the *consensus iuris* of a people). Scipio's definition is explicitly preliminary, as Zetzel has argued.[29] It is only after Laelius, the other main speaker of the dialogue and friend of Scipio, denies that *injuria*, the lack of *ius* (justice, right) can ever benefit the *res publica* (*Rep.* 3.32–42) that we finally arrive at the "purified" idea of the *res publica*, in which the *ius* in the *consensus iuris* that constitutes the people must be identical to the natural *ius* (3.43–45).[30] This "solution" to the problem of the tension between the *consensus iuris* and the genuinely just also obviates the need to consider any tensions between the just and the common utility: the common utility of the community must be congruent with genuine justice or fail to exist at all. These are all very standard Stoic ideas, and they clearly distinguish Cicero's conception of the political community from the "contractarian" alternative represented by the Epicureans (and some of the sophists portrayed by Plato), which derives the political community from human weakness and reduces *ius* to mere agreement.

But Cicero interprets these Stoic elements in the idea of political community in a way that we might call, for lack of a better term, "egalitarian." Instead of the older Stoic idea of a community of the wise whose individual reason is in conformity with the order of the cosmos, we find a community of non-wise people who merely acknowledge as valid an externally given (but reasonable) set of normative expectations.[31] In this sense, the people become a legal concept: what is, and what is not, a people has almost nothing to do with the common fate of a cultural community (as in modern states) or with the limited but necessary interdependence of families and individuals for the sake of production and reproduction (as in the urban model of community), but only with the indefinite agreement of a community on the proper rules of interaction (natural law).

Cicero does not, to be sure, abandon the idea that a political community is tied to the satisfaction of natural needs, and indeed of the natural needs and interdependence of both wise and non-wise. But he is permissive about what this might entail with respect to the limits of the community and its institutional forms, unlike, for example, Aristotle or Plato. Take the case of property. In the "urban" model of political community, property appears as a side-effect, as it were, of the process of production and reproduction from which the community emerges: it is because we eat and have families that there is property at all, and it is because different forms of property stimulate our desires in particular ways (potentially interfering with the possibility of living a virtuous life) that it must also be regulated. The question for Aristotle or Plato then is about what form of property (common vs. private vs. some mixture of the two; limited through legal regulation or not) will preserve the processes of production and reproduction of the community without endangering the possibility of a virtuous life.

But this link between property and production and reproduction on one hand, and the life of virtue on the other, is almost totally lost in Cicero due to his focus on *iuris consensus* as the fundamental principle of the community. Thus, for Cicero the *res publica* is instituted, at least in part, to *safeguard* private property (*Off*. 2.73, 2.78), which is assumed to preexist its establishment; but property is not itself justified with reference to the production and reproduction of life in the community, or with respect to its effects on virtue. Indeed, Cicero suggests that (private) property is not "natural" in the sense of being a natural side-effect of the natural processes of production and reproduction of the community, and hence should be justified not by reference to its effects on them (or on the processes that produce virtuous characters, for that matter) but on (what we might call) purely legalistic and positive grounds, that is, "long occupancy... conquest... due process of law... purchase, or allotment" (*Off.* 1.121). These "modalities of acquisition and transfer," to use non-Ciceronian terms, are capable of being regulated by fixed rules (and thus are appropriate to a conception of justice as natural law), but they are compatible with any kind and degree of property accumulation. Hence Cicero's rigid rejection of any redistributive schemes except when accompanied by adequate compensation (cf. *Off.* 2.81); like Locke, Cicero seems to think that once legal relations come into play, what justice requires is merely the regulation of the *process* of acquisition and transfer, not of the outcomes of such transfers, and the idea of the "common utility" does not seem to impose any meaningful constraints on these outcomes.

Indeed, by defining the community as the *res*, the property, of the people, Cicero introduces legalistic connotations into the earlier idea of a community as a network of cooperation, and opens the way to an account that no longer makes much reference to the natural interdependence of human beings. We may even say that the property of the people, like the property of an individual, may come to be established through "long occupancy... conquest... due process of law... purchase, or allotment" (*Off.* 1.121, referring to private property) rather than through any organic unity of cooperation in a particular area, and hence that it is now compatible with communities of any extent, including empires. To be sure, the political community in Cicero always remains tied to actual families and other natural associations, as in Aristotle (cf. *Off.* 1.53–57, where the *res publica* is said to encompass all our loves, both subordinate and superordinate). But these families and natural associations can be loosely articulated over a much larger area than Aristotle, for example, was prepared to countenance, and they play little further role in Cicero's conception of the community: the *res publica* mediates between all levels of community, from the human race to the nuclear family, but is not itself constituted by any of them.

More important for our purposes is Cicero's differentiation of a concept of *consilium* (*Rep.* 1.41), a part of the community (which could be a monarch, an assembly of aristocrats, or the people as a whole) to which the care of the community as a whole is entrusted, and which thus "represents" it. Here we find the seeds of an idea of the "state" as a specialized organ of the community whose function is to care for the whole through its legal activity, different from the superficially similar idea of the *politeia*, the constitution or regime type that we find in Aristotle and other Greek writers. While the *politeia* merely reflects the authority relations actually existing in a society (it is an *aspect*, not a *part* of it), Cicero understands the *consilium* as a functional part of the community that ensures its continuity and to which the care of the whole can be entrusted (it is a *part*, not an *aspect* of it).

The above considerations on Scipio's definition of *res publica* have three important implications. First, Cicero understands the *people* as the ultimate *agent* of its own care, though in a way that is regime-independent. That is, he does not assert that the fact that the *res publica* is the concern or property *of* the people means that they must be the ones directly responsible for its care, that is, that the political regime must be democratic, in contrast to the urban model of political community, in which the *citizenry* (defined in a regime-dependent way) is always the direct agent of the community's care. This means, second, that the people also becomes a passive object of care, a care that they "entrust" (as one entrusts the care of property to a steward) to those who have the right *consilium*. We thus find the glimmers of an idea of representation in Cicero's model of the political community, an idea that provides a better way of conceptualizing Rome than the Aristotelian idea of a citizenry that is *directly* responsible for the care of the community. Finally, as I have already indicated, "the people" appears as an essentially *legal* concept, despite its associations with the natural sociality of man: its extent delimited not by culture or the interdependence of individuals, but by itself in a reflexive manner through its *consensus iuris*.

Offsetting the abstractness of this idea of the people we find the introduction elsewhere in Cicero of the idea of the *patria*. If the people appears as a legal concept, only thinly related to the natural sociality of man, the *patria* appears as an "affective" concept, the community that "embraces all our loves" (*Off.* 1.57), mediating our particular loves for family, birthplace, ethnic group, and even the rest of the world.

The *patria* is not ethnically or culturally defined: Cicero distinguishes the *civitas* (*Off.* 1.53; here synonymous with the *patria*) from the *natio* and the *gens* in a fairly standard Stoic way (compare with Hierocles in Stobaeus, 4.671,7-673,11 = Long and Sedley, 57G), and nowhere clearly identifies the *patria* with any of these plausibly "natural" communities. At any rate Rome, as Cicero well knew, like other ancient empires, contained in its territory, and even in the Italian peninsula (the most integrated part of Rome), diverse *gentes* and *nationes* and peoples who spoke various languages, despite an advanced process of "latinization" in the core of the empire.[32] It would thus have been odd for Cicero to emphasize the cultural unity of his *patria*, though he does at times come close to doing just that.[33] Even the setting of the *De Re Publica* suggests that the *patria* cannot be understood in exclusionary ethnic or cultural terms. Scipio is, after all, the champion of the Italians, the proponent of a policy that Cicero also endorsed, the treatment of the allies as equals.[34]

Yet though the *patria* is not a cultural or ethnic community, it is also not simply, unlike the people, a creature of agreement and law alone, but the result of a historically concrete love for particular people, institutions, places, and stories. Thus in Book 2 of *De Legibus*, Marcus (Cicero himself, as a character in the dialogue), claims that "all those who came from the towns" (*municipia*) "have two fatherlands, one by nature [*naturae*], the other by citizenship," and goes on to give the example of Cato, who was "Tusculan by origin [*cum ortu*], Roman by citizenship," though his own example is just as pertinent: Marcus, as he notes, is from Arpinum (by origin or by nature) but a Roman citizen by law (*Leg.* 1.5–6). The point here is that Rome as a community is rooted in but transcends local loves to become the concrete love of the institutions of the republic, exemplified in Cato's attachment to the "ancestral" constitution.

Note that the contrast Cicero draws here between law and nature, and in particular between the *patria* by "nature" (Arpinum—the smaller, apparently less "perfect" community) and the *patria* by law (Rome—the larger, apparently more "perfect" community), is alien to the urban model of community. Unlike previous thinkers, Cicero seems to be suggesting that it is the community "by law"—which in the particular case of Rome comes into being through conquest, as he well knew, rather than as a natural outgrowth of human interdependence—that should be most worthy of our affection, rather than the community by nature. To be sure, the opposition between law and nature in this passage should not be pressed too far; "by nature" here means something close to "by birth," and at any rate Marcus argued at length in Book 1 of *De Legibus* that "law" properly speaking is rooted in nature. So to some extent to say that one has a fatherland "by law" and another "by nature" is not necessarily to fully oppose the first fatherland to the second, as the first may be rooted in "natural law." But it is to problematize, in ways alien to the urban model of the political community, the relationship between the political community and nature by the introduction of an idea of history: it is the historical community, not the natural community, that should be the object of our affection.

One might object that Cicero's point is that Rome, the larger community, makes possible not just "life" but "the good life" (cf. *Politics* 1252b30), and hence that Cicero's understanding of the political community is compatible with some version of the urban model. As Nicgorski puts it (with reference to our passage of Cicero), "a certain kind of community has the material as well as the qualitative aspects to provide for a proper and happy human life."[35] From this point of view, we might think that Arpinum or Tusculum are just too small to provide for a fully flourishing human life; they are only partial communities, presumably because their small size does not make possible a full political life—only Rome enables this possibility.

But this is not, I take it, what Cicero is suggesting. To begin with, it is not altogether clear that there is something about Rome that makes it a more perfect community than Arpinum or Tusculum. The distinction cannot be simply the one that Aristotle made between the *polis* properly speaking and the villages that constitute it (*Politics*

1252b15–35). Aristotle claims that the village came into being for the sake of "nondaily needs" though it is nevertheless not fully self-sufficient by itself. But as Cicero well knew, *municipia* such as Arpinum or Tusculum used to be self-governing communities.[36] These were *poleis* in their own right, who had been conquered by the Romans in the past or had themselves voluntarily submitted to incorporation into the Roman commonwealth. Indeed, within Cicero's lifetime, many of these *municipia* had struggled against the Romans to recover their independence during the "Social War" (91–89 B.C.).[37] These were not the villages of Aristotle, able to provide for life but not for the good life; they were true *poleis*.

Perhaps sensing this objection, Cicero *does* attempt to assimilate these cities to Aristotelian villages coming together to create a more self-sufficient community. He suggests that places like Arpinum or Tusculum were much like the Athenian demes, whose inhabitants were "compelled" by Theseus to move from the countryside to the town (*Leg.* 2.5), and hence indicates a possible way of assimilating Rome to the urban model of community. But of course the *demes*, the villages of Aristotle, were in fact quite different from the self-governing, independent communities of Italy that came to be part of the *ager Romanus* through conquest or voluntary incorporation, as I have already indicated. Moreover, the *demes* all occupied a fairly small area around Athens, whereas the cities that became part of Rome were dispersed throughout Italy (Arpinum, Cicero's birthplace, was sixty miles southwest of Rome's urban core, several days' journey from it). Finally, even assuming that places like Arpinum and the Attic *demes* were roughly comparable units, Theseus "compelled" (or rather commanded, *iussit*) the *demes* to join into one city as part of an act of foundation, whereas the Romans conquered Italy long after the city had been founded. Cicero's account of Athens' foundation thus obscures the imperial character of the Roman commonwealth, probably intentionally, as the facts of Roman conquest were certainly not unknown to him.

Yet Cicero's comparison between the foundation of Athens and the expansion of Rome does point out, perhaps inadvertently, that Roman expansion in Italy did result, by Cicero's time, in the coming into being of an "Italian" society directed from Rome.[38] Thus, in a sense, the expansion of Rome was the foundation of Italy, not in a single act, as in the mythical story of Theseus, but in a long, drawn-out process. Both the foundation of Athens and the foundation of Italy, furthermore, were coercive acts, according to Cicero. Italians were not even a single *natio* until the Romans *made* them so, just as the inhabitants of Attica did not form a single city until Theseus compelled them to do so. Thus by stressing the compulsion of the act of foundation and downplaying the differences between the Athenian *demes* and the Italian *municipia*, Cicero again (whether intentionally or not) suggests that the *patria* is created by will, not nature, and is the result of history, not natural sociality. To put the point more strongly than Cicero might have wanted to put it, the *patria* is not created for the sake of the good or self-sufficient life in the union of partial communities but emerges from the long-term assimilation of conquered subjects into citizens and thus lovers of its institutions.

This historical dimension in the idea of the *patria*, absent from the notion of the people, seems to be a completely new element in models of political community. And indeed we find a tension in Cicero between the abstract idea of the people as a community united through agreement in law and the idea of the *patria* as the historically developed object of the people's love. This is manifested in at least two ways. On the one hand, as Cornell has argued,[39] Cicero's historical survey of Rome in *De Re Publica* 2, by omitting any indication of the "Trojan" past of Rome, makes it hard to figure out how there could have been a *Roman* people for Romulus to rule: Cicero simply seems to assume that there existed a "people" who had the right kind of *consensus iuris et utilitate communione* before Romulus took over them. On the other hand, Scipio's retelling of this history of Rome, while "illustrative" of the argument about constitutions that precedes it, and hence not meant to be complete or perhaps even entirely accurate,[40] is obviously an *encomium* of Rome (*Rep.* 2.64), that is, an attempt to specify what is specifically lovable about Rome. But this account tries too obviously to omit and rationalize dubious aspects of Roman history that would tend to weaken the case for the Roman people as having the right kind of *consensus iuris et utilitate communione* that makes Rome into a *res publica*. Let us examine this last point in more detail.

The story Scipio tells is first of all a *rationalized* history of Rome. Scipio omits inconvenient or not very edifying details, such as the murder of Remus; tidies up and deemphasizes mythical stories, such as Romulus's ascent into heaven;[41] and overemphasizes the wisdom and foresight of those rulers who introduced new laws and institutions.[42] To be sure, Scipio stresses that Rome was not built by a single man; it is the accumulation of the insights of many men "over many generations" (*Rep*. 2.2) that accounts for its greatness. But Scipio constantly argues that the actions of various rulers and citizens were rational responses to circumstances, to the point where Laelius remarks at several points in the conversation that Scipio's version of Roman history leaves no room for chance and accident.[43] The emphasis is on virtuous leaders as builders of a "rational" Rome and hence as models for emulation by the younger generation: to love the *patria* is to love the deeds of the ancestors, of the *rectores rei publicae* that Scipio apparently described in some detail in the mostly lost Book 4.[44]

Moreover, Scipio goes out of his way to emphasize that at least some part of Rome's development is the result of *native* efforts rather than foreign wisdom. Thus, he energetically rejects the suggestion that Numa Pompilius's laws had been influenced by Pythagoras (2.28–30),[45] and though he does not deny that much Greek learning eventually contributed to Roman institutions (2.34), he suggests that it was a Greek learning that built on properly Roman foundations (those of Numa Pompilius, for example) and "romanized."[46] To love the *patria* is to recognize it as the work of *one's own* ancestors.

We can see here a conceptualization of the *patria*, the community as an object of care, as the historical *achievement* (never quite completed) of the rationality and justice promised in the definition of the people. By judiciously excising the more unsavory aspects of Rome's history and explaining the development of the city as the (almost) ineluctable march of reason in history, Scipio thus seems to want to redefine the love of country as a love of virtuous acts and good institutions that must be constantly renewed. Scipio "purifies" the historical tradition of Rome not merely because he is providing examples of the constitutional theory he described in Book 1 but because there is something important that the "myth" of Rome can teach young Romans (like Tubero: cf. *Rep* 2.64): Roman institutions and Roman deeds dimly reflect the natural order and genuine virtues, and to care for the *patria* is to renew them through action.

Yet Scipio is traversing a difficult middle way. His Rome, even as a well-mixed regime, is not the embodiment of the *kallipolis*. But it is also not the dispiriting reality of actual fact; the ragged edges of history have been excluded from this Rome's story. Scipio's Rome is the aspiration of the Romans. It is not a regime "alien to human life and customs" (*Rep.* 2.21) since it is still a recognizably Roman regime. It is not even, perhaps, the best regime under the circumstances. Rather, it points toward the best regime without abdicating responsibility for actual political life.

The significance of this point becomes clear if we contrast it with the Aristotelian idea (dominant in much Ancient political thought) that the *polis* is the *telos* (the completed form) of human social existence. As I have already indicated, for Aristotle, the *polis* exists not simply for the sake of living but for the sake of living well; it thus completes the other human partnerships by providing for the possibility of a "self-sufficient" human life (*Politics* 1252b28–1253a1). The achievement of this *telos*, however, is not a matter of historical development; rather, it is immanent in the constitution of the *polis*, even of those *poleis* that do not have the best regime but are nevertheless *potentially* capable of providing the possibility of "living well." By contrast, Cicero's understanding of Rome suggests that the political community achieves its *telos* historically rather than immanently, and moreover that the achievement of this *telos* can and must be presented as a historical myth rather than simply as an analytic description of the right institutions of the *polis*.[47]

This new understanding of the *telos* of political existence as located in history, however, is fraught with danger. For though people like Laelius know that Rome was never the best regime, young aristocrats (like Tubero, who is dissatisfied with Scipio's procedure, and wants a more abstract account of the best regime) do not. Cicero runs the risks of encouraging a sterile conservatism, blind to the real exigencies of present circumstances and wedded to outdated and useless institutions and practices. Thus, the respectful but critical relationship to tradition characteristic of a Laelius may degenerate into the politics of nostalgia, so dangerous to any political community and so alien to the spirit of Aristotelian and Platonic philosophy, with their relatively ahistorical rationalism.

The problem that Scipio's depiction of Roman history ultimately raises concerns the way in which love of country or patriotism should be grounded in "history." Too much skepticism about history, that is, too much awareness of history as shaped by accident rather than reason and human will, makes it "inert" as a source of patriotism. A skeptical history has no pedagogical value as a source of *civic* education (though it may in fact be true, as Laelius's remarks intimate). But too little skepticism about it may make for dangerously uncritical conservatives. Scipio tries (with mixed results in the dialogue) to straddle a middle way in his own history of Rome, attempting to transform the actual fact of Rome into an ideal aspiration: a Rome recognizable enough to be *his* Rome, created by the considered actions of the ancestors of the assembled company (and hence recognizable enough to engender love), yet pointing toward a higher reality, shimmering like a mirage in the "in between" of political action, mediating between the *kallipolis* and the realities of empire. This Rome is not offered as a mere reform program (since it embraces the past as well as the future of the republic) though it can be (sometimes) interpreted as that (e.g., in *Leg.*).[48] It is the intimation of nobility revealed in the actuality of the city's history and practice, an intimation that can inspire others to recover such nobility in the present. We might say that Cicero, unlike Plato, wants no noble lies as the source of the love of country, though he might settle for noble half-truths.

Conclusion: Cicero's Cosmopolitan and Constitutional Patriotism

The Ciceronian model of political community we have examined above—the *res publica*—looks strikingly similar to the model of the modern national state I discussed in the first section of this paper, even though it draws on Greek models of political community very different from it. In Cicero's model the *populus* corresponds to the people, actively caring for itself; the *civitas* and *consilium* correspond to the state, that is, the part of the community that is the instrument of this care; and the *patria*, the fatherland, corresponds to the nation, that is, the *object* of the care and affection of the people. Cicero understands the people in terms recognizable to modern thought as a group united in agreement about certain rights and values and acting through what we might call "representative" institutions for its own care, and he understands the community that is cared for (the *patria*) as a *historical*, if not quite a cultural, entity, embodying certain principles in its institutions that deserve to be renewed and recovered through the political action of individuals. All of this is in contrast to ancient models of political community in which the active part of the community was directly defined by the political regime (as the citizenry) and limited either by the natural interdependence of human beings or by internal characteristics of its members (such as wisdom).

The similarity between Cicero's model of political community and the model of the modern national state is not entirely surprising, as I have already intimated, since Rome shows important similarities to the modern state. There are, however, differences worth noticing. Cicero's notions of the *civitas* and the *consilium* do not yet have the full force of the modern notion of the state, even though Cicero's understanding of the constitution of the *civitas* as determining a *status rei publicae*, a condition of the republic (*Rep* 1.43), opens the way for a differentiated understanding of the state as the organization and legal order that jointly determine the political state of society. Cicero's patriotism, like Habermas's "constitutional patriotism,"[49] or like the American kind,[50] is attached to those principles of justice that it divines in the historical institutions of its country, though it still retains a link to Stoic ideas of natural law that avoid some of the apparent paradoxes of the national state in connection to "human rights."[51] By the same token, however, Cicero's political community is—in contrast to the modern national state but like Rome—potentially unlimited: it justifies an empire ruled by law that succeeded in integrating politically many of its conquered peoples, but an empire nonetheless.

NOTES

1. Cf. Millar, *The Roman Republic in Political Thought,* chaps. 2 and 7.
2. So, for example, Polybius (*Histories* 1.1) speaks of the achievement "without parallel in human history" of the Romans, which he attempts to explain in part by looking at the institutions that enabled Rome to raise

manpower for its armies and politically integrate a wide variety of communities in Italy.

3. Cf. Millar, *The Roman Republic in Political Thought*, chap. 7. Millar's claim that Rome in Cicero's time was very much like a quasi-national state (especially in the Italian peninsula) is controversial, and more than one historian is likely to balk at it. There are, of course, many important differences between the Rome of Cicero's time and European national states, not least the fact that European national states existed and exist in a *system* of competing states of a similar kind, whereas Rome did not. But I am *not* claiming that Rome can simply be understood in categories derived from modern national states, only that there are interesting similarities between the Rome of Cicero's time and modern states that are obscured if we think of Rome simply as a large *polis* or as an agrarian empire like other agrarian empires of the time.

4. See, for example, the imaginative attempt of Millar to describe what Aristotle might have made of Rome in *The Roman Republic in Political Thought*. Aristotle, according to Millar, would have thought Rome was too big to be a proper commonwealth.

5. Cf. Zetzel, *On the Commonwealth and On the Laws*, xvii-xviii.

6. Cf. Haakonsen, "Republicanism," 569; and Kempshall, "*De Re Publica* I.39 in Medieval and Renaissance Political Thought."

7. Cf. Canovan, *Nationhood and Political Theory*; and Giddens, *A Contemporary Critique of Historical Materialism*.

8. Smith, *Nationalism*, chaps. 1 and 2.

9. To be sure, it makes a great political and theoretical difference whether the unique and valuable features of the nation are understood to be pre-political values such as "blood and soil" or particular political institutions such as a written constitution, but for our purposes all that matters is that such features are seen to be integrated into an entire way of life that limits the possible extent of the community to those who share in and value that way of life.

10. For a quick survey of the forms that the idea of the state has taken in modern political thought, see Bobbio, *Democracy and Dictatorship*, chap. 3. I stress here the legal, rather than the purely organizational, aspects of the modern concept of the state: insofar as the state is an element of the modern model of political community, it appears primarily as a legal order that structures the possible forms that social organization can take, not just as an organization among other organizations. I do not mean to suggest, however, that the state should be simply *reduced* to the legal order, as Hans Kelsen argued. For the connection between the legal and the organizational aspects of the state, see Bourdieu, "Rethinking the State," and, of course, Max Weber, *Economy and Society*, I.i and I.iii.

11. The word "state" as used today in this latter sense thus still bears traces of its Latin antecedents in Cicero and other Latin writers as the *status*

of the community, the *status rei publicae*, embracing the fundamental facts about its legal order, constitution, and general health or strength (cf. *Rep.* 1.42: "*vocamus... regnum eius rei publicae statum*"; *Fin.* 5.11; *Leg.* 3.20; *Cat.* 1.1; *Leg. Agr.* 1.26, 3.4; *Red. Sen.* 7.16; etc.). Rousseau could still understand the word *état* in this sense: cf. *Du Contrat Social* 1.6: "*Cette personne publique qui se forme ainsi par l'union de toutes les autres prenait autrefois le nom de Cité, et prend maintenant celui de République ou de corps politique, lequel est appelé par ses membres État quand il est passif, Souverain quand il est actif, Puissance en le comparant à ses semblables.*"

12. Cf. Canovan, *The People*; and Yack, "Popular Sovereignty and Nationalism."

13. As Zetzel argues, "[i]n adapting Platonic and Aristotelian theories based on the small, self-contained, and relatively homogeneous society of the polis to the conditions of the Roman *imperium*, Cicero made use of Stoic ideas of the *cosmopolis* and of natural law to develop a complex and ambitious argument, linking the traditional values and institutions of Republican Rome on the one hand to Aristotelian ideas of civic virtue and on the other to the order of the universe itself." See Zetzel, *On the Commonwealth and On the Laws*, xvii. I focus here on a different aspect of Cicero's adaptation of these ideas.

14. The natural interdependence of human beings as the root of political community receives greater emphasis in some of the sophists (Protagoras, for example, if Plato's *Protagoras* can be taken as evidence of the position of the historical Protagoras; cf. *Protagoras* 321d–322d); and later in the Epicureans and Polybius. Such an emphasis leads naturally to "contractualist" models of community. See Schofield, "Epicurean and Stoic Political Thought," 437–43.

15. The Greek household was not merely a unit of consumption, as the modern family. Rather, it was a more or less self-sufficient enterprise for the purposes of material production and reproduction. By contrast, the modern family is a partnership of *jobholders*; the locus of production in modern society is outside the home (in the "workplace"), which means that the modern family cannot be self-sufficient in the Aristotelian sense. See Nagle, *The Household as the Foundation of Aristotle's Polis*, 1–10.

16. Ibid., 10 n. 25. There are subtle differences between Plato and Aristotle on this point, however. Plato, unlike Aristotle, sees the *oikos* as an obstacle to the perfect community, and hence (in the *Republic*) attempts to merge them by abolishing the distinction between them (cf. also *Statesman* 258e–259c, the upshot of which is to subordinate the *oikos* to the order of the city, a point that Aristotle is concerned to refute in *Politics* 1.1); but the point is that, like Aristotle, he understands the primary component of actual *poleis* to be the households that in fact provided for productive and reproductive needs, even if his distrust of the household leads him to emphasize the division of labor in society as a whole (see, e.g., *Republic* 2.369bff, though even there the *polis* is defined as a *sunoikia*, a gathering of *oikoi* or *oikiai*; and *Statesman* 287a–290e)

more than the economic independence of the household (which Aristotle stresses). At any rate in the *Laws* Plato is quite explicit in holding that actual communities are based on the household, not on the individualistic division of labor he described in the *Republic* or the *Statesman*. The Platonic vision of the *Republic* and the *Statesman* is in a sense realized in modern societies, in which the household no longer has any real productive role or economic independence due to the extensive division of labor; yet Plato's model still ties the political community to human need, not (as in the contemporary model discussed above) to culture or language or the like. For a different, though in some ways complementary, perspective on this point, see Schofield, "Plato on the Economy." Among modern thinkers, Rawls's view of political association as "scheme of cooperation" without which "no one could have a satisfactory life" comes closest to the Platonic idea. See Rawls, *Theory of Justice*, sects. 2–3, especially 8, 14 (the quotation is from 14).

17. Such leisure and personal independence are provided by the self-sufficient *oikos*, which by using slavery and preventing citizens from being personally dependent on other citizens for their livelihood makes them available for political and moral improvement. Thus the contempt for the *thēs*, the hired laborer, from Homer to Aristotle. The absence of personal dependence is the essence of freedom in this model, as the later "republican" tradition would also argue. See Pettit, *Republicanism*; and Viroli, *Republicanism*.

18. Hence Aristotle emphasizes that the city should be *eusunoptos*, able to be taken in at a glance; and he even criticizes Plato for suggesting that the city of the *Laws* should have 5040 households, which Aristotle considers excessive (*Politics* 1265a10–20). For Aristotle, the "Normalpolis" probably had only about five hundred households. See Nagle, *The Household as the Foundation of Aristotle's Polis*, 74–75. At any rate, both Plato and Aristotle suggest that the *polis* is necessarily smaller than the *ethnos* (cf. *Politics* 1276a27), which can provide citizens with no real opportunities for deliberation and political virtue due to its size; and they were certainly right that given Greek technical capacities an urban core with a relatively small countryside was able to achieve the kind of self-sufficiency they thought appropriate to human beings, even if such a city could not be materially entirely self sufficient (cf. *Laws* 12.949e–953e). But, to be sure, if one does not think that the political community exists for the sake of enabling people to pursue a virtuous life but merely for the sake of preservation or to enable people to pursue their own private goals, then a conception of society as a network of cooperation may lead to the conclusion that the political community can only be limited by available technical capacities for cooperation. Thus today a conception of society as a network of cooperation can easily support a conception of the political community as large as the entire world. See, for example, Singer, *One World*. In this respect modern cosmopolitanism is crucially different from ancient Stoic cosmopolitanism, on which it sometimes attempts to draw.

19. For a reconstruction of the evidence on the Stoic idea of the city, which I follow, see the admirable work of Schofield, *The Stoic Idea of the City*. A contrasting perspective in many ways is provided in Erskine, *The Hellenistic Stoa*.

20. For a contrary view, see Erskine, *The Hellenistic Stoa*, where he argues that at least in the case of Zeno, the community was supposed to be an actual political community, not a merely ethical one.

21. Diogenes Laertius, 7.32–34 = Long and Sedley, 67B, summarizing the views of Cassius who in turn is summarizing and arguing against Zeno's *Republic* (the foundational text of Stoic political thought, now lost). For source criticism, see Schofield, *The Stoic Idea of the City*, chap. 1.

22. Contrast with the Platonic-Aristotelian distinction between law (at least positive law) and reason: *Statesman* 294a–b, *Laws* 645a–c, 713e–714a, *Politics* 3.1285b35–1288a30. There is no doctrine of natural law in the "urban" model of political community.

23. Though there were perhaps some disagreements among later Stoics as to whether the wise needed to live "in the same place" in order to form a community; see Schofield, *The Stoic Idea of the City*, 73, citing Dio Chrysostom's *Logos Borysthenikos* (36.20 = Long and Sedley, 67J) as an exponent of those later Stoic views who thought that the wise needed to live in the same place to benefit each other.

24. Schofield, *The Stoic Idea of the City*, 52.

25. Thus, for example, there is only a very fragmentary discussion of the justice of empire in *De Re Publica* 3; see 3.21b (a fragment reported by Lactantius, on the injustice of imperial expansion), 24b (Philus begins the discussion of imperial expansion and its injustice); 3.36 (reported by Augustine, on the justice of empire if "done rightly"); 3.41 (Laelius defends the justice of Rome's empire but warns against the possibility of misrule by criticizing Roman behavior in one isolated instance). To be sure, there's a great deal of discussion of the *ius gentium* in *De Officiis*, much of which seems to suggest that Cicero regarded the imperialism of his time as unjustified or at least not sufficiently justified, but much of it accepts that Roman expansion in Italy before Cicero's time was justified. See Pangle, "Socratic Cosmopolitanism," and also Millar, *The Roman Republic in Political Thought*, chap. 7, for more on Cicero's "blind spots."

26. For more on the context of this passage, see Schofield, "Cicero's Definition of *Res Publica*," and Zetzel, *Cicero: De Re Publica, Selections*, 17–22, 127–30.

27. It is true that *civitas* is sometimes used as a synonym for *res publica* or even *populus*, but in *this* particular passage it is clearly distinguished from both. See Zetzel, *Cicero: De Re Publica, Selections*, 130, note to 41.3.

28. Pace Zetzel, *On the Commonwealth and On the Laws*, 18 n. 53.

29. Zetzel, *Cicero: De Re Publica, Selections*, 127.

30. Ibid., 26.

31. Cf. Pangle, "Socratic Cosmopolitanism."

32. As late as the Social War, "several languages other than Latin were still spoken in the peninsula, and this linguistic diversity was no doubt matched by a continuing sense that different Italian peoples in fact stemmed from different ethnic groups" (Beard and Crawford, *Rome in the Late Republic*, 79. For the "cosmopolitan" character of Rome since its foundation (and its uniqueness in this respect in the ancient world) see also Beard and Crawford, *Rome in the Late Republic*, 78–79; and Cornell, *Beginnings of Rome*, especially 60, as well as Livy's own presentation of the early Romans as a people of immigrants, open to new arrivals, a kind of New York City on the Tiber (Livy I).

33. Thus he will occasionally insist on the need to make Rome, as a Latin-speaking community, independent of Greek philosophy (*Div.* 2.2.5).

34. Zetzel, *Cicero: De Re Publica, Selections*, 8.

35. Nicgorski, "Nationalism and Transnationalism in Cicero," 790.

36. It may be argued that Arpinum and Tusculum were self-governing but not self-sufficient communities in the Aristotelian sense, i.e., able to provide for a fully flourishing human life. It is not clear to me, however, exactly what features of a flourishing human life would be unavailable in Arpinum or Tusculum but available in Rome, unless one were to argue that Rome was where the action was, so to speak: great ambition could not be fulfilled elsewhere.

37. Cicero saw service in the Social War, though on the Roman side (Arpinum did not rebel). Both Arpinum and Tusculum had been independent cities at one time, even though by the time of the Social War they had already been fully incorporated into Rome. Take the case of Tusculum. The city had an independent existence until 381 B.C., when it was captured by the Romans without a fight (but with an army—this was no voluntary incorporation), and its inhabitants were granted full Roman citizenship. Nevertheless, the Tusculans revolted during the Latin revolt of 341, and its citizenship was revoked, to be restored only in 338. See Cornell, *Beginnings*, 323, 347–49. Arpinum was annexed in 303 as a *civitas sine suffragio* (i.e., its free inhabitants had all the duties of citizens, including fighting in wars, but only a few of its rights, not including the right to vote in the Roman assemblies or to hold office; this situation eventually changed, and the Arpinates acquired full citizenship in 188 BCE). See Cornell, *Beginnings of Rome*, 357; and David, *The Roman Conquest of Italy*, 102, reporting a story told by Cicero about Arpinum that shows that the city was fairly self-governing even in 115.

38. See Beard and Crawford, *Rome in the Late Republic*, 82–84, on the "Romanisation" of Italy during the first century B.C.; see also Millar, *The Roman Republic in Political Thought*, chap. 7. The process of Romanization was not complete in Cicero's time, but it was certainly well advanced.

39. Cornell, "Cicero on the Origins of Rome," 50–52.

40. Powell, "Were Cicero's Laws the Laws of Cicero's Republic?"

41. He uses phrases like "people believed" and "Proculus Iulius was said" and avoids positively affirming that the legend is true. In fact, one could interpret the phrase "Romulus's intelligence and virtue were so great that people believed the story about him told by Proculus Iulius" as implying that Scipio himself did not believe the story, but could understand how it came to be believed. He rationalizes the legend without entirely undermining it (unlike Cicero himself in *Leg.* and *Off.*).

42. The version of Rome's foundation presented in *Rep.* 2.4–5 mentions Remus but not his murder at Romulus's hands. Cicero discusses the full story in *Off.* 3.41, where Romulus is condemned in the strongest possible terms for slaying his brother. Similarly, in *Rep.* 2.17–20, Scipio spends a great deal of time arguing that Romulus could have become a god after his death (Quirinus), whereas he expresses some skepticism about this, at least implicitly, in *Off.* 3.41 and more strongly in *Leg.* 1.3–4. Livy reports that Romulus was probably killed by the senate, and implies that the story of his ascent into heaven was invented later as a way to cover up the crime (Livy I.15–16). Cicero evidently had heard of this version, and he spends a lot of time trying to refute it (see *Rep.* 2.20: "the Fathers . . . wanted to dispel the suspicion that they had caused the death of Romulus"). Nevertheless, he sometimes stops short of *fully* rationalizing Rome's history, as his comments on the institution of the tribunate show (*Rep.* 2.57: "this development was perhaps not completely rational, but the nature of commonwealths often overcomes reason").

43. See *Rep.* 2.22, for example, contrasting Scipio's procedure with Plato's: "You have preferred to attribute your own discoveries to others rather than inventing it all yourself in the manner of Plato's Socrates; and you ascribe to Romulus's deliberate planning all the features of the site of the city which were actually the result of chance or necessity." See also *Rep.* 2.33 for more ironic commentary from Laelius.

44. Zetzel, "Citizen and Commonwealth."

45. See also Hathaway, "Cicero, *De Re Publica II*, and His Socratic View of History."

46. Lucius Tarquinius, the king who brought Greek learning into Rome, "changed his name from what it had been in Greek, so as to be seen to follow the customs of this people [the Romans] in all respects" (2.35). It is also significant that Lucius Tarquinius's Greek learning is introduced after Numa Pompilius's Greek learning had been energetically disclaimed; see Hathaway, "Cicero, *De Re Publica II*, and His Socratic View of History," 5.

47. This is true even though Scipio also justifies Rome as the embodiment of an abstractly defined "mixed regime." The point is not whether the mixed regime can be defined abstractly (it can) but whether the concrete

development of Roman institutions leads to it (it does). This does *not* mean that Cicero believes in any kind of teleological theory of historical "progress," only that the (contingent and reversible) achievement of the completeness of the *polis* is now located in history. As Hathaway rightly notes, neither Cicero nor any other major ancient thinker believed in "progress" in the modern sense.

48. The extent to which *De Legibus* should be seen as a "reform" program is debated. For "anti" views see Benardete, "Cicero's *De Legibus* I," 295; for the "pro" views, see Girardet, *Die Ordnung der Welt*; and Rawson, "The Interpretation of Cicero's *De Legibus*." At any rate, it is clear that Cicero thought fundamental change required changes in *mores* and character, not just in institutions (*Leg.* 3.29), as Zetzel, *Cicero: De Re Publica, Selections*, 27–29 rightly notes.

49. Habermas, "The European Nation-State." The idea of constitutional patriotism is introduced by Habermas as a bridge between exclusionary solidarity of the national state (the *urbs*) and the universal demands of human rights (the *orbis*).

50. See Walzer, *What It Means to Be an American*.

51. See the classic discussion of the incompatibility of universal human rights with the national principle in Arendt, *The Origins of Totalitarianism*.

9

Cicero on Property and the State

J. JACKSON BARLOW

Even a cursory reading of Cicero's letters reveals a man who took a keen interest in his properties and who devoted a great deal of attention to managing his wealth. We know, too, from his activities in the courts and in the Senate, that he made a career out of courting Rome's wealthy classes and working steadfastly on their behalf. Perhaps it would come as no surprise to find that a member of and advocate for the propertied classes had a firm commitment to the security of property rights. Yet in his philosophic works, Cicero's comments on property rights are few and do not seem so straightforward. For example, in spite of what he says in his rhetorical treatise *Topica*—that natural law guarantees to each the right to his own property—he seems drawn to the Stoic idea that private property is not by nature.[1] This Stoic view is summed up in *De Finibus* when Cato compares property to a seat in the theater: by nature the theater is common property and yet by convention the seat one occupies is for the moment one's own. No principle of natural justice, Cato concludes, argues against private property, but of course this is not to say that anything in nature argues *for* private property; it may be a matter of indifference what the legal regime of property rights is.[2] In *De Re Publica*, which perhaps more nearly reflects Cicero's own position, Scipio argues at 1.27 that by nature a thing belongs to the one "that knows how to employ and to use it." Yet this comment is merely suggestive; lacking as we do the full text of *De Re Publica*, we cannot be sure how Cicero might have developed this position.

In *De Officiis*, however, Cicero has much more to say about property, and indeed property rights seem to take center stage. Far from being a matter of indifference, property and its preservation seem to become the very basis of the polity. At *De Officiis* 2.73, Cicero says: "For the main reason for establishing political communities and citizenships was so that men could hold on to what was theirs." Here Cicero seems very much the advocate for those with property to defend. The clear implication is that a polity that does not protect property undermines its own reason for being. This seems very far from saying that property rights are matters of indifference. To make matters more complicated, however, there are indications in *De Officiis*, too, that Cicero accepts the Stoic position on property. Richard Schlatter may understate the matter when he says that in *De Officiis*, "Cicero has more to say about property [than he does in *De Re Publica*], but his statements here are also ambiguous."[3] This ambiguity is reflected in Cicero's own statement at 1.17 that greatness of soul reveals itself in simultaneously increasing one's property and resources and "also much more in disdaining the very same things."

But which of these is more important? Can one really do both at the same time? And if not, what are the principles for deciding between them? How can we understand Cicero's stance toward property? In Neal Wood's *Cicero's Social and Political Thought*, the balance is tipped decisively toward the principle of acquisition. Cicero appears primarily as the advocate of property rights.[4] Wood not only uses Cicero's comment at 2.73 to explain his attitude on property, but he goes further to make the preservation of property rights the central principle of Cicero's political philosophy as a whole. Although the argument is provocative, we may ask whether Cicero's ambiguities can be so firmly resolved. It is worthwhile to accept Wood's invitation to examine Cicero's understanding of property rights and polity.

Wood's Argument

Wood expresses his view of the place of property rights in Cicero's thought in bold terms: "Cicero ... is the first important social and political thinker to affirm unequivocally that the basic purpose of the state is the protection of private property."[5] This is a somewhat more compact restatement of his earlier claim that Cicero "is the first important social and political thinker to give a succinct formal definition of the state, and to conceive of its major purpose largely in non-ethical terms, as the protection and security of private property."[6] Wood's evidence for this claim comes from a number of sources in Cicero's writing but primarily from the formal definition of the polity in *De Re Publica* 1.39 and several passages in *De Officiis*. The most explicit support comes from *De Officiis* 2.73, where Cicero says: "For the main reason for establishing political communities and citizenships (*res publicae civitatesque*) was so that men could hold on to what was theirs. It may be true that nature first guided men to gather in groups; but it was in the hope of safeguarding their possessions that they sought protection in cities."[7]

In order to make sure that his audience has not misunderstood the point or taken it as mere rhetorical overstatement, Cicero reminds them at 2.78: "For, as I said above, it is the peculiar function of citizenship and the city (*civitatis atque urbis*) to guarantee to every man the free and undisturbed control of his own particular property (*ut sit libera et non sollicita suae rei cuiusque custodia*)." Because *De Officiis* offers the fullest statements about property rights in Cicero's surviving writings, it is appropriate to concentrate on that book, as Wood does.

The explicit statements on the purpose of the polity are extended and supported, Wood argues, by the general doctrine of *De Officiis* that there can never be a conflict between right or justice (*ius*) and expediency or utility (*utilitas*). In Wood's interpretation, this means that the test of justice for Cicero is whether the polity serves the private interest or utility of individuals. The argument is that because private property ownership is useful for the individual, securing that ownership is in the interest of the community as a whole and therefore becomes a defining characteristic of justice within the polity.[8] This view, Wood argues, sets Cicero apart:

More than any other ancient thinker he foreshadowed some of the views that were to be basic to the early modern conception of the state whose principal architects were Machiavelli, Bodin, Grotius, Hobbes, and Locke. Cicero was the first major social and political thinker of antiquity to offer a concise formal definition of the state. He was also the first to stress private property, its crucial role in society, and the importance of the state for its protection. In other words he gave to the state, with reservations, a central non-moral purpose. For Cicero the state exists primarily to safeguard private property and the accumulation of property, not to shape human souls according to some ethical ideal of the virtuous. He was the first major social and political thinker to distinguish clearly state from government.... Permeating his reflections on all these subjects was a marked moral, economic, and political individualism—possibly in part reflective of the social atomism of his age—that was so uncharacteristic of the thought of Plato and Aristotle and was to be such a pronounced trait of much of the early modern social and political outlook.[9]

According to Wood, Cicero's individualism is not in tension with the idea that the polity is natural. But it is not natural in the sense that Plato and Aristotle might recognize. Instead, Wood argues, Cicero holds the polity to be natural because the desire for possessions, and more generally the desire to secure one's interests, is basic to human nature. Polities are natural "insofar as they satisfy natural human wants." "Nor," Wood adds, "is Cicero's conception of the authentic state as the embodiment of justice at odds with the purpose of securing property. Any violation of private property is unjust. Hence, in order to be just, the state to be a true state must guarantee the security of each citizen in his possessions. This means, of course, that property differentials, which are characteristic of human society, must likewise be maintained and protected if the principles of natural justice are not to be violated."[10]

In other words, natural justice comes to view as the security of individual self-interests. This conception of justice is in keeping with what Wood calls Cicero's "economic individualism," which is grounded in a distinction between the common and the private that antedates human society. Wood notes that Cicero stops short of endorsing a natural right to property yet holds that each is entitled to appropriate from the common stock as much as is necessary for himself and his family.[11] Nature creates families, the first society, while the desire to protect property creates the second society, the "state." This state, then, exists to regulate the advantage-seeking to which men are prompted by nature, guaranteeing to each his own, no more and no less. Wood concludes that this allows Cicero to maintain that Rome embodies the principles of the best regime, because it authorizes but also moderates the "acquisitive individualism" of Roman society: "The acute competition and struggle of members of the ruling class for power and riches, the unbridled exploitation of the provinces, the resort to violence and the proscription of great families, and the rapid rise and fall of family fortunes are all manifestations of an increasing social atomism that brings to mind a Hobbesian state of nature.... [Cicero's] message to his contemporaries is to seek their own economic advantage, but always in a rational and enlightened way."[12] By putting the economic individualism characteristic of Roman society together with the descriptions of the formation of states in *De Officiis*, Wood is able to give property rights the same pivotal importance in Cicero's theory that it has for the early modern theorists.

Further, by tying Cicero's "economic individualism" to a defense of the class interests of the Roman aristocracy, Wood can use what we know of Cicero's personal interests and commitments to reinforce the point that he considers protecting property to be the end of the polity. Wood finds support for this interpretation of *De Officiis* in Cicero's correspondence and from his politics. As a *novus homo*, Cicero had worked to advance his political career by assiduous attention to the interests of the wealthy, and indeed he comments to Atticus at one point that the rich are "my army."[13] The centerpiece of his politics was the defense of the traditional role of the Senate and the senatorial class bolstered by an alliance with the wealthy *equites*. He clearly shared the acquisitive tendencies of his countrymen and believed that having the right properties was crucial for maintaining his own status in the community.[14] To the extent that the laws secured the Senators' property, the laws also guaranteed their power. Hence, in Wood's penultimate formulation, "the basic function of the state is the protection of private property *and the security of the dominant propertied classes.*"[15]

Wood's argument that protecting property is the "main" or "basic" function of the polity in Cicero's political thought, and that he drew upon this theoretical position to defend the interests of the Roman aristocracy against schemes of redistribution, must be taken seriously. Some of Cicero's explicit statements and his overall political program seem to support this view. But if Wood is correct, this conservative program engendered a reorientation of political philosophy, away from the Platonic-Aristotelian concern with the role of politics in forming human excellence and toward the modern focus on politics as a necessary restraint on human nature. Our task, then, if we are seriously to examine Wood's thesis, must be to proceed along several lines. First, we must make clear why, in spite of Wood's evidence, his thesis might deserve further exploration. We must then discuss Cicero's political program, as he conceived it at the time *De Officiis* was written in the latter part of 44 B.C. Next, we must look at the theoretical grounding Cicero gives to support that project. Part of this inquiry is necessarily negative: Can we, as it were, falsify Wood's hypothesis concerning Cicero's theory of property? If so, then in the final section of this essay an alternative can be proposed.

Preliminary Concerns

It would be foolish to deny that Cicero considers property rights important. But is the security of private property "*the* basic purpose of the state"? Is the defense of property supported by a "moral, economic, and political individualism" that looks very much like modern liberal individualism? There are some initial reasons for approaching Wood's thesis with skepticism. We might pause, for example, at the claim that Cicero conceives of "the state" and its purpose "largely in non-ethical terms." At least on the surface, the great majority of Cicero's specific comments and all of his conclusions place ethics in the foreground, and in *De Officiis* he explicitly condemns those who subordinate the just to the useful. We must therefore either find evidence that Cicero was selectively revealing his views or else assign reasons for giving some explicit statements priority over others.

Also at the threshold, we are confronted with what has long been held to be Cicero's more or less accurate reporting, and perhaps acceptance, of Stoicism in *De Officiis*.[16] The Stoic position, which Cicero also articulates elsewhere (notably in the *Tusculanae Disputationes* and

De Finibus), is that virtue alone is sufficient for happiness and that external circumstances such as wealth or poverty do not affect it one way or another. The wise man would be happy on the rack. Although it is written for the practical man of affairs and not the philosopher, *De Officiis* does not explicitly contradict this Stoic tenet.[17] What Cicero explicitly does say is that justice always controls utility and not the other way around, that is, that "the state's" basic purpose is ethical. If Wood is correct that for Cicero "the basic purpose of the state is the protection of private property," then Cicero must somewhere signal his disagreement with the Stoics. But in the first book especially, Cicero seems to make it clear that the purpose of the state is the promotion of just relations among human beings, that is, its purpose is ethical rather than economic, or perhaps better, public rather than private.[18] Further, Cicero's practical objective, to restrain the atomistic pursuit of wealth that is the root of Rome's political trouble, does not quite fit with a program of simply moderating the Hobbesian jungle. In common with the Stoics, Cicero seems to be aiming at something more than enlightened self-interest.

There is also a problem of terminology. Cicero's terms are not as readily translatable as they might seem; for example, in the passages from Book 2 cited earlier, the phrase "that one's own might be held (*ut sua tenerentur*)" does not use a noun at all, nor does the frequently used phrase *suum cuique*, "to each his own." To render Cicero's "one's own" as "private property" is not unreasonable, but the translation does bring with it some contemporary baggage that may exaggerate the parallel with modern thought.[19] *Res publica* is equally troublesome; we cannot simply translate it by "republic" as we would like, and "state" seems even more problematic, given the modern distinction between "state" and "society." In Roman law, *res publica* is the entire public sphere, including "public property" as distinguished from *res privata*. The public property is property that "could be owned by no individual and could be used by everyone," such as beaches or waterways.[20] This legal doctrine may make it less surprising to find, as Wood does, that "Roman notables sometimes even think of *res publica* as their possession, to be used as they would their own property."[21] To think of the public things in the modern way implies a detachment of possessors from things possessed that is foreign to Roman thinking. The distinction between *res publica* as "public property" (e.g., the beach) and *res publica* as "state" or "government" is much clearer to us than it would be to Romans. As Christian Meier says in discussing the crisis of the late Republic, "the citizen body could be said to *be* a political order rather than to *have* one, and ... there was no duality of society and state; rather the body politic had itself become a political unit."[22] We should not attribute to the Romans the concerns, and the politics, of a later age, and we must beware likewise of introducing our own priorities and assumptions into Cicero's defense of private property. With this admonition to skepticism, we begin our investigation of Wood's thesis.

Testing Wood's Claim

We may begin by considering the place of property rights in Cicero's political agenda in 44. The program he develops in *De Officiis* is twofold. First, he intends to teach Marcus how to be a gentleman who can also succeed in Roman politics. Second, through Marcus, Cicero wants to address the general crisis of the Roman Republic. The two objectives quickly collapse into one. A gentleman needs to understand how to manage his property, but more importantly he needs to understand how to put it into perspective, and this perspective is missing in Marcus's generation. Accumulating wealth or property is necessary and also honorable, at least up to a point, because it contributes to one's reputation and power. Yet thanks to Cicero's generation in general, and Julius Caesar in particular, the competition for reputation, power, or *gloria* among the Roman elite had exceeded all bounds by 44.[23] This competition is at the root of the "social atomism" Wood describes, which Cicero sees as causing the destruction of the Roman republic. He must persuade Marcus and his contemporaries to put aside their private ambitions and become public-spirited men, like the great heroes of the Roman past. In effect, in this book Cicero is attempting the awkward task of putting the genie back in the bottle.

The central questions of *De Officiis* concern the conditions of success in Roman politics. Cicero proposes to redefine "success."[24] This is an important element of Books 2 and 3, for it is with respect to the useful things—wealth, military success, friends, influence, position—that Marcus is likely to be misled by examples from contemporary Roman politics. The bad examples Cicero has in mind, of course, come from the series of politicians from the Gracchi onward who have taken property from some and given it to others, and especially Sulla and Caesar. Sulla followed up his "honorable cause (*honestam causam*)" with a dishonorable victory, by auctioning off the confiscated goods of his political enemies and claiming that he was selling "his spoils." The hope of seeing another such division of the spoils is a constant incentive to civil war.[25] The disrespect for property rights shown by Sulla is not only a precedent for future redistributions but an incentive to them, as Cicero says at 2.29: "The seed and occasion of civil wars will be present for as long as desperate men remember and hope for that bloody spear [indicating an auction of "spoils"]." By introducing this incentive, Sulla and Caesar have broken the harmony, or *Concordia*, of the society in such a way that repair is extremely difficult.

The primary example, however, is Caesar, who embodies the argument for expediency.[26] His pursuit of *gloria* was a spectacularly successful instance of what, to Cicero, is a misunderstanding of true glory. But Caesar is not alone. He may be the most successful, but he is not the only one who has used his wealth and military renown as a path to power. Cicero quotes Marcus Crassus as saying that "no amount of wealth is enough for someone who wishes to be the leading man in the republic unless he can support an army from its income" (1.25). Cicero does not take issue with Crassus on whether one should have a private army; he merely notes that one ought to avoid acquiring property unjustly. The practical problem is that justly acquired resources may not be enough, as the examples of Sulla and Caesar show. Most men will respond to those who promise the greatest rewards; they do not behave like Stoics, for whom wealth is a matter of indifference.[27] A philosopher may be privately disdainful of cupidity, but in politics one cannot ignore it as a human incentive. Sulla and Caesar had succeeded by drawing followers who expected to profit and were indifferent only to whether their profit came at another's expense. But rewarding political loyalty with the confiscated estates of fellow citizens undermined the trust (*fides*) that is fundamental to the polity.²⁸ This is the political reason why Cicero is so emphatic about respect for property rights in *De Officiis*. The disrespect for property rights shown in Sulla's day and afterward was expedient but hastened the day when Roman politics would be dominated by those seeking power for private rather than public ends.²⁹

That Cicero's defense of property is an argument for allowing those who have property to keep it hardly seems remarkable. For one thing, throughout *De Officiis* Cicero tends to blur the distinction between the just and the legal, consistent with his objective of staying inside the politician's conventional horizon. For another, he had little sympathy, theoretical or practical, for the propertyless and never advocated giving them more than a token share of political power. But to view his defense of private property as an aspect of the class struggle seems to miss the point.³⁰ Generally speaking, the Caesarian revolution merely redistributed wealth and power within the propertied classes. Further, we cannot overlook the significance of Cicero's condemnation of Sulla, who can hardly be called a leader of the masses. Sulla's proscriptions had sowed the seeds of the next and of all future rounds of civil unrest. The point is that legal justice demands that each keep his own, or else the laws become ineffective and irrelevant. And although obeying the law is not justice, respect for the laws is an element of a just polity. Cicero is unequivocal that proscription and confiscation—"robbing some to enrich others"—are unjust, not only because they violate legal rights but also, and perhaps more importantly, because they introduce a destabilizing precedent. Any redistribution by political action creates a misunderstanding of the purposes of the polity and with it of the conditions of glory. The polity is no longer a "partnership in justice," supported by trust, but a tool for seeking one's own private ends; glory no longer comes from advancing the common good, as it did in the republic's best days. For Cicero, Caesar is the culmination of the process by which the public is subordinated to the private.³¹

If Marcus is to be successful in politics, he must know one more thing: rewarding one's followers with the property of one's enemies is not only unjust but inexpedient. It does not win permanent friends, and it both creates new enemies and confirms the old ones in their enmity. The passage could have come straight from Machiavelli: "And yet, when it comes to measures so ruinous to public welfare, they do not gain even that popularity which they anticipate. For he who has been robbed of his property is their enemy; he to whom it has been turned over actually pretends that he had no wish to take it; and most of all, when his debts are cancelled, the debtor conceals his joy, for fear that he may be thought to have been insolvent; whereas the victim of the wrong both remembers it and shows his resentment openly."[32] Disturbing property rights will not have the effect one desires. That people will live peaceably within the laws so long as their property is not taken away by arbitrary government action is an observation requiring neither deep theoretical insight nor a special commitment to property rights. Even those who are committed to their own selfish interests should be able to see it.

Cicero's political program in *De Officiis* is to dissuade Marcus's generation of Roman politicians from trying to become the next Caesar. This is not an easy assignment. As A. A. Long notes, the Romans were always at risk of confusing what was worthy of being praised with what was praised. To be persuasive, Cicero must show that the things praised, such as wealth and political power, are not truly praiseworthy in the absence of justice and that justice, in turn, does not exist in the absence of public-spiritedness. Stealing "from one to enrich another," however much it may be praised, is not truly worthy of praise.[33] To the extent that such theft had become, or was becoming, the norm in Roman politics, it threatened an endless chain of proscription and civil war. Such an unqualified disaster deserves unqualified condemnation, and the rights that are threatened deserve unqualified support.

Property Rights as the End of the Polity

Cicero's immediate political project, then, calls for the defense of property rights less to defend class interests than to reduce the stakes of factional strife. This project is supported by theoretical premises regarding the protection of property as such. We must examine Cicero's theory with respect to two issues raised by Wood. The first is whether he embraces "economic individualism" and more generally how he approaches the distinction between public and private. We must then turn to Cicero's account of "the basic purpose of the state" and consider how and why justice demands that private property be respected by the political community.

Because Cicero's alleged individualism is central to Wood's account, we must look with some care at Cicero's discussion of the growth of the polity out of the household. At 1.12, Cicero says that nature encourages each head of household privately to acquire from the common stock. But what follows from this? Is it the naturally prompted tendency to acquire that makes things private property? Cicero is unclear about exactly how what was once common to all mankind becomes private. Clearly, heads of households have a responsibility to provide for those within the household, and that responsibility is somehow natural.[34] Thus far, it makes sense to say, as Wood does, "each person is expected to appropriate from the commonness of nature the things needed by himself and his family. At the very beginning of time and before the institution of the state, therefore, a distinction was made *by men* between common property and private property."[35] Yet on closer examination Wood's "therefore" seems premature. Do the things that are appropriated from the common stock become either "private" or "property"? To be sure, the common/private distinction seems to be conventional even before a polity is created. But what, exactly, is this pre-political condition, and why does Cicero bring it up? It is generally thought that in this passage Cicero is following Panaetius's Stoic doctrine, but it is not clear that either of them means to go further here than to suggest a natural *disposition* to acquire property that precedes the founding of the polity.[36] This disposition is connected with the two fundamental human characteristics of sociability and rationality, manifesting themselves as love of one's offspring, on one hand, and foresight, on the other. That is, the disposition to acquire property stands on the same foundation, by nature, as the disposition to associate with others in the polity. Yet some universal dispositions are more important than others. Cicero seems to intend to sketch out a hierarchy in 1.11–12. Cicero places the desire to acquire "the things necessary for life" together with self-preservation and procreation as dispositions humans share with animals. But humans, he says, are set apart because of their faculty of reason. The quality they share with each other is of higher rank than those they share with the beasts. In Cicero's account, reason, not survival, brings humans together, and it gives them a rational commitment to provide for their families, in addition to and distinct from the mere natural disposition. Because it is rational, this commitment is specifically natural to humans and thus properly subject to the rules of natural justice. But this is not yet to say that property itself is natural.

We may approach this issue in another way. For Locke, for example, labor is the title to individual property because each individual owns himself by nature.[37] The Stoics agree with Locke that each person is the proper owner of himself. But it is not similarly clear from Cicero's account in Book 1 that this self-ownership is the key to property rights or is even economic in our sense of the term. Instead, one's ownership of oneself seems a moral more than an economic starting point.[38] Self-ownership stands at the center of an expanding circle of human relationships, extending through family, friends, and fellow-citizens to mankind as a whole.[39] For Cicero, however, if not for the Stoics, one of these circles stands out as clearly most important, that of the polity (1.57). Indeed, it is the one that gives the others their significance. The emphatic endorsement of the centrality of politics in *De Officiis* contrasts with the otherwise similar account of the kinds of human relationships in *De Finibus* 5.65–68, where Cicero is discussing the wise man who is able to rise above all such considerations. In *De Officiis*, all of the things that might count as "one's own," such as the wise man's wisdom, must be understood in light of the justice that holds the political community together.[40] Cicero's purpose in Book 1 is not to explain how common property becomes private but to emphasize that justice is the common thread in all human relationships. Property, in this regard, is to be understood not as a relationship between a human being and a material object but as a consequence of the relationships among human beings. If private property is natural, then, it is because it has some role in human society.

So far, it appears that Cicero's discussion of what is common by nature leads in the end to the observation that even what seems most private, one's own reason, is to be understood in light of the justice that binds the community and is thus a kind of common property.[41] One cannot separate one's private good from the public good. The discussion has thus led us to the conclusion that *political individualism* seems to be foreign to Cicero. There is no evidence to support the idea that the common good is simply the sum of the private goods of individuals, cemented by an agreement to leave each other alone.[42] Perhaps, however, the idea that Cicero promotes economic individualism receives greater support from the discussion of wealth creation in Book 2. Cicero's discussion, a shortened version of Panaetius's he says, occurs at 2.12–16. He divides the things useful for life into animate beings and inanimate things and then proposes a distinction among animate beings between rational and irrational ones. Cicero notes, however, that even many inanimate things are not simply given by nature but are provided by human effort, just as human effort makes domestic animals useful. In general, Cicero approaches economic life in 2.12–13 as a social phenomenon, an example of the principle that human beings are born to help each other.[43] Because it is a social creation through the cooperation of many, economic life is governed by principles of justice, which is concerned with the way people act toward one another. As he says at 2.15, property, in the form of things useful for life, stems from the same impulse of human sociability that is also the foundation of the political community.[44] Any human artifact stands at the end of a social chain: ideas must be communicated, animals trained, metals forged, and so forth. It would be absurd to expect any human being to survive alone, without the cooperation of others. Without society there would be no producing, no selling, and no property. That is, for Cicero human cooperation precedes economics and politics in the natural order of things and provides them with their purposes. The rules governing that cooperation look to the improvement of the cooperation and not to securing the interests of the individual participants.

Property, then, like the *res publica* itself, is a realized form of human cooperation and is subject to the rules that govern that cooperation, that is, the rules of justice. To the extent that property is "by nature," then, it is so because human cooperation is a natural phenomenon as well as a natural obligation. Indeed, Cicero says bluntly that "there is no such thing as private property by nature (*sunt autem privata nulla natura*)" (1.21, 1.51; cf. *Fin.* 3.67–68). One may even say that for Cicero labor itself is not private, as it is for Locke, but public or at least quasi-public. Like virtue and wealth, labor is, in its most important sense, in the service of the community.[45] Moreover, economic activity is not the defining human characteristic, reason is.[46] Cicero never deviates from this position. Thus property as something to be acquired and desired is always on the list of "things preferred" but not among the things required for happiness, as Cicero follows Panaetius's Stoic usage. Reason and the society that reason produces, however, are among those requirements. Property itself, as a creature of law and of cooperative activity, is a social phenomenon. When he lists the ways in which property becomes private in 1.21, Cicero's list presumes a prior organization of society. He does not connect it with the natural disposition to acquire. Individualism, economic or otherwise, does not seem to describe Cicero's position.

We turn, then, to the purpose of the polity, beginning with the issue of how we get from the pre-political to the political condition. In 2.73, Cicero gives a two-part account of the growth of human association that seems familiar from social contract theory. The question is whether Cicero intends this to be a full statement of his position on the issue, as Wood suggests it is. The passage at 2.73 is the third time in *De Officiis* that Cicero has discussed the process of founding the polity, and each time (1.11–12, 1.53–55, 2.73) he varies the account slightly. There is no intrinsic reason for giving the statement at 2.73 priority over the statements in Book 1, which are less emphatic about property rights. Indeed, since Cicero is discussing merely useful things rather than ultimate ends in Book 2, perhaps we should expect a difference in emphasis. Perhaps it can be explained without reference to political or economic individualism. It may not even be original.

Seen against the background of his emphasis on the centrality of justice, the account Cicero gives in *De Officiis* 2.73 seems to have more in common with the two-step founding of the *polis* in Aristotle's *Politics* than with modern social contract theory. Aristotle concludes his account by saying that "there is in everyone by nature an impulse toward this sort of [civic] partnership. And yet the one who first constituted [a city] is responsible for the greatest of goods."[47] For Aristotle, the household, which is not self-sufficient, needs to be completed by the founding of the city. Cicero signals his agreement with this position by arguing in 1.57 that the most important of social links is the one between the individual and the polity and in 1.158 that humans did not create political communities for the sake of supplying necessities. Nature's intentions are not identical with the process of formation of the various institutions; the last in time is first by nature. Furthermore, Cicero distinguishes between the purpose of an institution (by nature) and the motives of those who form it.[48] The end of the polity, in particular, is more than the sum of the purposes of those who framed it. The men who first created the polity were unformed by the moral and civic education that the household alone cannot provide. It is nature's intention that men should form cities so that that education can take place. The ends or purposes of the institution are not fully revealed in or determined by its beginnings.[49] The existence of the household prior to the state does not, in itself, support the idea that protecting individual property is the state's end or purpose for Cicero, any more than it does for Aristotle.

It is revealing that in discussing Cicero's concept of "the state," Wood omits half of Cicero's definition. In Book 1 of *De Re Publica*, Cicero defines a *res publica* in this way:

> [*Scipio*] Well, then, a commonwealth (*res publica*) is the property of a people (*res populi*). But a people is not any collection of human beings brought together in any sort of way, but an assemblage of people associated in an agreement with respect to justice (*iuris consensu*) and a partnership for the common good (*et utilitatis communione*). The first cause of such an association is not so much the weakness of the individual as a certain social spirit which nature has implanted in man. For man is not a solitary or unsocial creature, but born with such a nature that even in a condition of abundance ... [he would not wish to be isolated from other human beings].[50]

Wood summarizes this definition as: "The purpose of the state as given by Cicero in his formal definition is the common interest, utility, or advantage (*utilitas*)."[51] In other words, Cicero's two-part definition of a polity is collapsed into a single one and then applied to "the state," which is the people's property. Yet as his definition suggests, for Cicero, the common interest is linked with the existence of a social consensus concerning justice. By reading out the consensus about justice, Wood can argue that the social instinct reveals itself as the urge to associate with one's family, the "basic natural human association in which all things are held in common." The social instinct is limited to this small circle, while the state preserves "the property of citizen heads of households regardless of class or status." Wood thus reads the definition of a people in the light of the social contract process of state formation he attributes to Cicero. By reading out half of Cicero's definition of the *res publica*, Wood can read into Cicero the public-private dichotomy that is characteristic of modern liberal political thought.

Cicero's context suggests a different result. In the passage that follows his definition (*Rep.* 1.41), Cicero makes clear that the "deliberative body" in the polity "must always owe its beginning to the same cause that produced the state itself." The first, fragmentary sentence in that section indicates a common origin for the state and for the virtues, which presumably is the naturally implanted "social spirit" coupled with reason, as we also saw in *De Officiis*. Thus a fuller examination of the passage suggests that a concern for the common interests of the society is not the founders' only motivation but that the consensus about justice is equally fundamental. Wood later notes, correctly, "that for Cicero no contradiction existed between the two key elements of his definition of the state: *ius* and *utilitas*, right or justice and interest."[52] Yet by his insistence that the purpose of "the state" is "the common interest of those concerned, interest defined in terms of security, protection, and well-being," Wood appears to make *utilitas* the prior principle, indeed the test of whether justice is being served. This does not appear to be supported by Cicero's explicit statement. For Cicero the *iuris consensus* is the prior principle by nature, for it is the principle most in keeping with the nature of man as a rational and social being.

As Wood admits, for Cicero the fundamental cause of the political community is human nature understood as rational and social. Cicero's position on this issue is consistent throughout his political writings, from *De Re Publica* to *De Officiis*, and there is no need to multiply examples here.[53] But Cicero does say, both in *De Re Publica* and in *De Officiis*, that "common interests" are also important. We may observe that the two parts of Cicero's definition of *res publica* in *De Re Publica* match up with the division of subjects in *De Officiis*. The first book of *De Officiis* is concerned with a gentleman's activity with regard to the society's agreements about justice. Book 2 then concerns his activity with respect to the common interests, and the third book deals with the potential conflicts between them. The ambiguities and ambivalences in *De Officiis* may be in part attributed to Cicero's efforts to harmonize the gentleman's conventional horizon with that of nature, that is, the social consensus about justice with justice by nature. Wood wants to see Cicero's project as borrowing Greek philosophy to shore up the position of the ruling class; it becomes simply an ideology. But this may too quickly pass over Cicero's conviction that the values of the senatorial oligarchy needed to change, lest it produce more Caesars.[54]

In testing Wood's hypothesis, we must also consider the context of Cicero's strong declaration of the value of property rights. Cicero follows his explicit defense of property rights in 2.78 with an almost Machiavellian explanation of why this principle is one the politician violates at his peril, as we have seen. But it seems clear that Cicero's emphatic endorsement of property rights gives them no special or foundational standing in the polity. Such rights remain firmly within the horizon of the expedient or convenient or useful things. Only in Book 2, that is, only in the context of his discussion of useful things do property rights assume this kind of importance for Cicero. A just polity will protect property rights. But the polity must also do many other things (control its territory, raise revenues, and so forth) that cannot be said to constitute its purpose. In Book 2, Cicero puts the protection of private property in the category of things that any polity must do to survive in the long term. It does not affect the conception of the polity as fundamentally in pursuit of other ends, specifically in *De Officiis* of a justice that is grounded in human rationality and sociability. Preserving vested property rights promotes the social trust that permits justice to flourish.[55] It is useful to justice, but it is not justice.

We are now in a position to make a conclusion about the hypothesis of Cumming and Wood, that Cicero "was the first important political thinker to affirm unequivocally that the basic purpose of the state was the protection of private property."[56] We have noted above that this is indeed what Cicero says in 2.73 and 2.78 and that this claim is made in the context of a condemnation of any type of forced redistribution of goods or wealth. Yet it seems clear, on a review of the evidence, that Cicero, first, does not endorse individualism, economic or political. Second, he does not say that the protection of property is *the* basic purpose of the state. As emphatic as he is in 2.73 and 2.78, Cicero's endorsement of property rights is in fact equivocal. Protecting property is just, but it is not justice. The purpose of the political community is to establish justice, which depends on observing good faith. Good faith engenders trust, which supports the natural human tendency to be social. For Cicero, property is an expression of a natural social trust and of cooperative activity that are extended and completed by political institutions. We must seek elsewhere for "the basic purpose of the state."

Cicero's Teaching on Property and the Polity

If securing property rights is not the basic purpose of the polity, what is? What is the point of Cicero's defense of property rights? In the course of reviewing Wood's hypothesis, some of the features of an alternative have emerged, but we must now try to bring them together. It is clear that Cicero understands property to be a good thing, and not simply a matter of indifference, as it is for the Stoics. Property matters politically, but it is an instrumental good, not one to be sought for its own sake. That there is no private property by nature means that it has no independent standing as a good but that its goodness is derived from its role in the polity and is therefore to be understood in that light. This is why Cicero's most emphatic endorsement of property rights occurs in his argument about the useful things and not about ultimate goods.

In the Roman politics of his time, property has become important because abuses of property rights have undermined trust among citizens. Restoring this trust in both institutions and fellow citizens is the political program of *De Officiis*, theoretical and practical. Beneath all of Cicero's admonitions to Marcus about his reputation lies the concern that he become someone worthy of others' trust. The foundation of trustworthiness is the virtue of justice. It seems there is a vicious cycle at work in Roman politics, where injustice breeds distrust, which then produces further injustice. It is, as Wood says, rapidly becoming a kind of Hobbesian jungle. Cicero believes that the terms of political success need to be redefined in such a way that striving for success no longer breeds distrust, and so he must establish, as he says at 1.23, that "keeping faith is fundamental to justice, that is constancy and truth in what is said and agreed." As we have seen, trust in one's fellow citizens is, for Cicero, the foundation of the political community, because it provides the social grounding for the exercise of the capacity to reason. Cicero emphasizes the importance of this point because, to the extent that trust or good faith has disappeared in Rome, the city threatens to cease being a political community altogether. Within this context, protection of everyone's property rights is a critical step in restoring and maintaining social trust.

Cicero's program in *De Officiis* requires him to use examples of conventional Roman attitudes and values in order to establish the principles of natural justice. Those conventional attitudes and institutions are, in their own way, facts with moral implications.[57] Cicero wants Marcus to think not only about what his natural duties are but about what people will think. Of course, these two requirements are not always harmonious. The uneasy relationship between conventional attitudes and natural justice can be seen in the "debate" Cicero stages between the Stoic philosophers Diogenes and Antipater in Book 3. The debate concerns whether a seller ought to disclose everything that he knows about the property or goods he is selling. Diogenes takes the position that one should not misrepresent goods for sale but need not disclose everything. There is no ethical reason, he argues, that one should not seek to sell his goods for as high a price as possible. Antipater, on the other hand, holds that a seller is morally bound to "consider the interests of your fellow-men and to serve society," hence one ought to disclose everything, even if it means accepting a lower price.[58] In their very thoughtful treatments of this debate, Malcolm Schofield and Julia Annas are both concerned about Diogenes: Does Cicero represent him fairly or accurately? Does he misunderstand Diogenes' argument? Could a Stoic really say these things? These are good questions, and both authors give thoughtful, if contradictory, answers.[59] But I suggest that in looking for Cicero's teaching about private property we also need to ask why Cicero introduces this debate and what benefit he expects Marcus and Marcus's generation to get from it.

Cicero ends up siding with Antipater, he says, because:

> The fact is that merely holding one's peace about a thing does not constitute concealment, but concealment consists in trying for your own profit to keep others from finding out what you know, when it is for their interest to know it. And who fails to discern what manner of concealment that is *and what sort of person would be guilty of it*? At all events he would be no candid or sincere or straightforward or upright or honest man, but rather one who is shifty, sly, artful, shrewd, underhand, cunning, one grown old in fraud and subtlety. Is it not inexpedient to subject oneself to all these terms of reproach and many more besides?[60]

In other words, Cicero urges Marcus to be honest in his business dealings not because (or not only because) it is good in itself but because it will contribute to a good reputation. This is the basic principle of Cicero's business ethics. Of course the best reputation would combine honesty with a certain shrewdness: one wishes to be considered honest without being taken as simply innocent. Thus although "an honest man will not be guilty of either pretense or concealment," Cicero does not fully commit him to Antipater's style of bargaining.[61] The point is not so much the transactions themselves as that people measure their fellow citizens by the trust they have in them. No one wants to do business with a habitual cheat. Trust is the foundation of a good reputation, as it is of the polity itself. In this regard, private property therefore seems to be a kind of link between the individual and the polity as a test of character for both.

This may become clearer if we consider more fully the issue of self-ownership. In his discussion of "seemliness" in Book 1, Cicero indicates that this is also a kind of property: "Each person must hold on to what is his as far as it is not vicious, but is proper to him, so that the seemliness we are seeking might more easily be maintained (*Admodum autem tenenda sunt sua cuique non vitiosa, sed tamen propria . . . .*)" (*Off.*

1.110). Unlike the discussion of material things in Book 2, here Cicero intensifies the "one's own" by adding the adjective "proper" and the qualification "as far as it is not vicious." One's character, we may say, is more emphatically one's own than one's goods.[62] Each person must understand his own capacities and role in order to understand what his particular duties might be or what is "seemly" for him. This seemliness is an aspect of justice (1.103). Once again, this is meant partly for Marcus's immediate edification: he should avoid trying to be something he is not. Seemliness is strongly connected with reputation and with the preservation of social harmony (1.99, 1.126). The existence of the polity advances justice in this regard because it allows one to realize and express fully that which is "one's own" in the most important sense. It is "property" in the sense that it is "proper" to the individual, and unlike material property this seems clearly to be "one's own" by nature. But of course one is not simply free to express any difference, only those that are consistent with virtue and do not disturb the peace. Still, we may say that in the limited sense of providing the conditions for each person's ability to develop a character in keeping with virtue, his own nature, and the harmony of the society—the protection of "one's own"—is indeed a "basic purpose" of the polity.

Does nature ever dictate a distribution of material property or indicate a property right? In *De Officiis* 1.21, as we have seen, Cicero is emphatic: "there is no such thing as private property by nature (*sunt autem privata nulla natura*)." All titles appear conventional in this formulation: long occupation, conquest, "or by law, by settlement, by agreement, or by lot" (1.21). There are no human ends associated with property ownership as such that would allow one to say that one title is superior to another, although the human beings who use the property are subject to the ends nature determines for human beings. In *De Re Publica* 1.27, however, Cicero suggests that sometimes nature does indicate rightful ownership. In recommending indifference to possessions, Scipio says that by the "common law of nature" things belong to the man who knows how to use them. Knowledge, then, may offer a title by nature, although the argument goes no further and the comment is something of a digression in its context.[63] A similar point is made more directly in *De Officiis* 3.28–32. There, Cicero is responding to the argument that one ought to treat family members differently from other fellow citizens and citizens differently from foreigners.[64] He goes on to observe that by the "tightest bond" of human fellowship it is against nature (or natural law) to deprive another of his goods unjustly. But then he continues that sometimes it is just to expropriate the goods of one who is worthless as long as the common good is the purpose of the expropriation. It is in this context that Cicero gives his explicit (and influential) endorsement of tyrannicide at 3.32: "it is not contrary to nature to rob a man, if you are able, whom it is honorable to kill." The essential natural principle is the fellowship of humanity, which governs not only property rights but the value of one's life itself.

But if property is merely an instrumental good and by nature subject to the requirements of the common good, how can Cicero imply that property rights are absolute, much less the basic reason for the existence of the polity? We may recur to the distinction between the motives of those who found the city and the purpose of the city itself, but here Cicero seems to have in mind the motives and perceptions of those who presently inhabit a city. Cicero understands very clearly that a polity that does not protect property will not be seen as just by those whose property is taken. The discussion from 2.73 to 2.79 centers on schemes of redistribution and, critically, connects them with the vice of avarice. Both threaten property rights for purely selfish reasons, either to enrich a politician or to enrich his supporters. Both redistribution and confiscation undermine, or else simply violate, the public consensus about justice, destroying both harmony and equity (2.78). Cicero goes further and suggests that even taxation is something to be avoided, although he stops short of saying it is unjust. It should, however, be a last resort and only when the polity faces a crisis. No doubt it would be preferable simply to tax the empire: if we refer to Cicero's formula of 1.21, non-Romans, as conquered peoples, are fair game.[65] The point seems to be that taxation, confiscation, and redistribution are unjust less by nature than because they are bad public policy, and thus they undermine public confidence in the government. The key is persuasion: if the people can be convinced that the situation is grave enough to require a tax, then it is not unjust. But simply to take from some and give to others because one has the power to do so is both unjust and imprudent.

It is striking that Cicero's Roman examples concerning property rights are uniformly negative, designed to support his thesis that invasion of property rights creates social disharmony. But does upholding property rights create harmony? The answer seems to be "that depends," if we look at the example of Aratus of Sicyon. Aratus was confronted with a situation in which an unjust expropriation of property had been made some fifty years previously. In trying to right the situation, Aratus faced a dilemma. The initial expropriation was unjust, but fifty years' occupancy also gives rise to certain just expectations. From Cicero's point of view, both titles are just and neither title is just. This opens the way for what Julia Annas calls Aratus's "wholly pragmatic" solution.[66] By securing a loan from the king of Egypt, Aratus bought out some of the current property holders—returning the property to the original owners—and compensated some whose property had been confiscated—negotiating each situation individually. A dedication to "property rights" in the abstract does not help to solve Aratus's problem, and indeed as Cicero's list of legal entitlements at 1.21 shows, there are always possibilities for conflict among competing claims. If Cicero were to give property rights a fixed meaning—for example, to preserve the property of *present* holders (which Wood suggests is Cicero's definition)—the actions of Aratus would not be worthy of praise. Cicero admires not Aratus's adherence to a specific definition of legal rights but his preservation of social harmony:

> As a result [of Aratus's actions], harmony was preserved, and all parties went their way without a word of complaint. A great statesman, and worthy to have been born in our republic! For that is the appropriate way to deal with citizens; and not, as we have twice seen, to plant the spear in the forum and submit a citizen's goods to the cry of the auctioneer. The Greek, as a wise and outstanding man, thought that he should consult the interests of all; and it showed the wisdom and extreme reasonableness that befits a good citizen that he did not tear apart the interests of the citizens, but held everyone together under a single standard of equity [*aequitas*].[67]

Preserving social harmony (*concordia*) is the ultimate principle of the polity as Cicero understands it, because the polity is an expression of the natural human impulse of sociability as improved and extended by a rational agreement on the principles of justice. Thus the practical value of respecting property rights supports the theoretical goal of establishing justice. To say that the polity's "basic purpose" or "main purpose" is the preservation of property rights confuses the means to an end with the end itself. Preserving property is of course necessary for survival. In practice, their property is also something that most people care about more than they care about virtue—political philosophy after all begins with Socrates's attempt to get the Athenians to care about their souls more than their property.[68] Property is something that people become especially passionate about when it is taken away by government to be given to someone else for political reasons. Both the passion to acquire and the passion to regain that which has been stolen are passions that create civil discord, as Cicero had seen very clearly in Rome.[69]

The basic purpose of the polity is to enable human beings to live happily, that is, virtuously, in keeping with their own talents and characters. Another way of saying this is that the polity exists to achieve the common good. Conventional institutions, such as private property, can be instrumental to achieving that purpose but are not ends in themselves. These conventions deserve respect not because they exist by nature but because they are products of the social and deliberative processes that both form the virtues and provide opportunities for their exercise. Nature establishes no plan for property rights. But once society has achieved a consensus on what those rights are, that consensus has moral and political consequences. Unlike the Stoics, Cicero recognizes that property and property rights are not matters of indifference to most people most of the time. Property is status, and wealth is power, and anyone who does not understand that will not understand politics. But not all conventions are correct by nature, or else Cicero would not have to correct the Romans' definition of success. No one is justified in violating legal rights for reasons of personal glory-seeking, as Romans have done. As Aratus's example shows, the common good, not personal self-interest or property rights, is the touchstone of justice.

Cicero's defense of property rights is not fully spelled out, but it does seem possible to present its main outlines. Property rights are important because political harmony is important if a just polity is to survive. Cicero does not question that the Roman Republic, at least in his idealized version, is such a just polity. He condemns redistribution of property as unjust in general, because he cannot conceive of Romans doing it differently than Sulla and Caesar have done. But he can imagine a non-Roman alternative in the example of Aratus. Rome's problem is that its citizens have come to regard the polity as serving their private purposes, and Cicero wants to stop this. If the Romans are to stop thinking of political action as a way of advancing their private ends, they need to regain the sense of perspective that characterized the great Romans of the past like Africanus:

> But as far as our lands, houses, herds, and immense stores of silver and gold are concerned, the man who never thinks of these things or speaks of them as "goods," because he sees that the enjoyment of them is slight, their usefulness scanty, their ownership uncertain (*incertus dominatus*), ... how fortunate is he to be esteemed. For only such a man can really claim all things as his own, by virtue of the decision, not of the Roman People, but of the wise, not by any obligation of the civil law but by the common law of nature, which forbids that anything shall belong to any man save to him that knows how to employ and use it; only such a man will consider that our military commands and consulships are to be classed among things necessary rather than things desirable, and that they are to be undertaken from a sense of duty and not sought for profit or glory. (*Rep.* 1.27)

NOTES

A draft of this essay was presented at the American Political Science Association annual meeting in 2002, and I am grateful to the many people who have made comments on successive versions, particularly Walter Nicgorski, Michael Zuckert, and the Juniata College Writers' Group.

1. *Top.* 90. For the texts and translations of Cicero's works, I have used the Loeb Classical Library editions except where noted.
2. *Fin.* 3.67. In *De Finibus* Book 4, where Cicero rebuts the Stoic position on ultimate goods, he does not comment on Cato's doctrine of property rights.

3. Schlatter, *Private Property*, 24–25.

4. Wood, *Cicero's Social and Political Thought*.

5. Ibid., 132. The thesis had earlier been presented in Wood's "The Economic Dimension of Cicero's Political Thought." I concentrate on Wood's argument here because he presents it compactly and clearly. Wood acknowledges his reliance on Cumming, *Human Nature and History*; and Ste. Croix, *The Class Struggle in the Ancient Greek World*. Cumming's argument about Cicero and property rights is scattered throughout his two-volume work. Although Wood's account of Cicero draws on Cumming, his position on Cicero's "economic individualism" seems a departure from Cumming's arguments. Ste. Croix mentions the issue of property only in passing and also relies on Cumming.

6. Wood, *Cicero's Social and Political Thought*, 120; cf. this passage at 105: "reason enables humans to create the state for the chief purpose of securing private property."

7. *Off.* 2.73. For the Latin text I have used the version in the Loeb Classical Library edition. For translations I have sometimes used Walter Miller's Loeb translation, sometimes used the Griffin/Atkins translation, and sometimes used my own. Miller's translation of the first sentence reads: "For the chief purpose in the establishment of constitutional state and municipal governments was that individual property rights might be secured." Wood appears to rely on Miller's translation, which may have misled him here and elsewhere. See, e.g., Wood, *Cicero's Social and Political Thought*, 84, and compare the Miller with the Griffin/Atkins translation of *Off.* 1.12.

8. Wood, *Cicero's Social and Political Thought*, 129–32.

9. Ibid., 11–12. More recently, Gloria Vivenza ("Renaissance Cicero") has discussed Cicero's influence on economic thought among Renaissance humanists.

10. Wood, *Cicero's Social and Political Thought*, 132.

11. Wood, "The Economic Dimension of Cicero's Political Thought," 742–43; *Off.* 1.11–12, 1.21–22. But see below: it is not clear that Cicero says more than that men by nature *want* to do this.

12. Wood, *Cicero's Social and Political Thought*, 115.

13. Ibid., 106–7; Shackleton Bailey, *Cicero's Letters to Atticus* (1978), 1.19. The context of this letter suggests that Cicero is thinking of the *equites* rather than the senators. Although there is not enough space to explore the issue here, it is possible that Wood's argument oversimplifies serious political divisions between and within these classes in the late Republic.

14. Walcot, "Cicero on Private Property."

15. Wood, *Cicero's Social and Political Thought*, 129, emphasis added.

16. Cf. Sabine and Thorson, *A History of Political Theory*, 159: Cicero's "philosophy was the form of Stoicism which Panaetius had ... transmitted to the Scipionic Circle." More recently, see Long, "Stoic Philosophers on

Persons, Property-Ownership, and Community," and Mitsis, "Stoics on Property and Politics."

17. Cf. 1.13, 61, 66, where "indifference" to material circumstances is encouraged.

18. Carter, "Cicero: Politics and Philosophy," 35–36, makes the point that the Stoic writers gave Cicero little in the way of systematic doctrine on the issue of property rights, owing to their indifference to the subject.

19. The legal tenet *suum cuique tribuere*—"to render each his own"—appears in Ulpian and later as a foundational principle of justice in Roman law. The evidence suggests, however, that it is not of native growth but a philosophic idea imported from the Greeks. See Raphael, *Concepts of Justice*, 57; and Schulz, *History of Roman Legal Science*, 135–36. Cicero uses many variants of the phrase throughout his works, but seems to want to extend the principle beyond the narrow application to property—see *Fin.* 5.65 and the discussion below in the final section of this chapter.

20. Watson, *Roman Private Law*, 59–60.

21. Wood, *Cicero's Social and Political Thought*, 126.

22. Meier, *Caesar*, 12; Geuss, *Public Goods, Private Goods*, 41.

23. Taylor, *Party Politics in the Age of Caesar*.

24. "Cicero preserves the traditional connotations of the buzz words *laus, decus*, etc., but thanks to his use of Greek philosophy he has shifted their denotations" (Long, "Cicero's Politics in *De Officiis*," 217).

25. 2.27–29; also see 1.85 on factionalism in Roman politics; cf. also the letters to Atticus, 9.7, 9.10, and 10.7. At the outset of the civil war in 49 B.C., Cicero was under no illusion that Pompey would be less of a threat to property than Caesar.

26. See, e.g., 1.26.

27. In 2.21–22, Cicero twice lists the reasons why men would support another's ambitions. In both lists the self-interest of would-be supporters figures prominently.

28. On *fides*, see Atkins, "Domina et Regina Virtutum," 268, 279.

29. Cicero discusses Caesar and *gloria* in 3.83–85; Long, "Cicero's Politics in *De Officiis*," 213–40, discusses ways in which seeking after *gloria* emerged as a problem, in Cicero's view.

30. Although there is not enough space to argue the point here, part of Cicero's reason for not granting full political participation to the lower classes seems to be the familiar issue that leisure is necessary to the full development of civic capacities and that the necessary leisure cannot be obtained by those who must work with their hands. This concern is not unique to Cicero nor in itself undemocratic, as the examples of Thomas Jefferson and John Dewey suggest. Meier, *Caesar*, esp. at 152–53, argues that it is wrong to view Caesar's transformation of Roman politics in terms of the class struggle. See also Taylor, *Party Politics in the Age of Caesar*, 21 and *passim*.

31. The view of the polity as a partnership is expressed in *Rep.* 1.39. On Caesar as seeking private glory, see *Rep.* 1.68; *Off.* 3.83–85; and Long, "Cicero's Politics in *De Officiis*," 215, 223–25.

32. *Off.* 2.79; cf. Machiavelli, *The Prince*: "Above all, he must abstain from the property of others, because men forget the death of a father more quickly than the loss of a patrimony" (67).

33. Long, "Cicero's Politics in *De Officiis*," 225; see also 215, 217, 225–28.

34. The discussions of common property are at 1.11–12, 21–22, and 51–55; cf. 3.21–22 and *Fin.* 3.67–68.

35. Wood, *Cicero's Social and Political Thought*, 111, emphasis added. Wood here conflates the discussions at 1.11–12 and 1.21–22.

36. Long, "Stoic Philosophers on Persons, Property-Ownership, and Community," 18–19, 28–29.

37. Locke, *Two Treatises of Government*, Second Treatise §27. The Renaissance commentators on *Officiis* seem to agree with Locke on the principle that private property is by nature, Vivenza, "Renaissance Cicero," 517 and 521 n. 44.

38. Mitsis, "Stoics on Property and Politics," 239–40.

39. Algra, "The Mechanism of Social Appropriation," 284–89; cf. *Fin.* 3.63–68; 5.65.

40. 1.155; Atkins, "Domina et Regina Virtutum," 258–59.

41. Ibid., 259–60, 217; and *Off.* 1.155.

42. Here I also disagree with Long, "Cicero's Politics in *De Officiis*," 234; cf. *Off.* 1.22; 3.63.

43. Cf. Vivenza, "Renaissance Cicero," 508, 513, who notes that the Renaissance humanists read Cicero in light of Aristotle's dictum that human beings are not self-sufficient.

44. See 1.12–15; and Nederman, "Nature, Sin, and the Origins of Society," 8; and also Cumming, *Human Nature*, vol. 2, 136.

45. On this, see Mitsis, "Stoics on Property," 239, and Cumming, *Human Nature and History*, 2:136, and the surrounding discussion. Although they appear to be in agreement about the purpose of the state, it is not clear that Cumming would agree with Wood's emphasis on Cicero's "economic individualism."

46. See 1.158, where Cicero says that people do not live together for the purpose of production.

47. Lord, *Politics*, 1253a. The second bracketed phrase is Lord's.

48. *Off.* 1.50ff.,158; *Rep.* 1.39.

49. Nichols, *Citizens and Statesmen*, 17–19; cf. Dyck, *A Commentary on Cicero, De Officiis*, 91–92.

50. *Rep.* 1.39. The ending of the last sentence of this fragment is missing, but the point is generally agreed to be identical with the point Cicero makes in *Off.* 1.158.

51. Wood, "The Economic Dimension of Cicero's Political Thought," 747–48, and *Cicero's Social and Political Thought*, 128–29.
52. Wood, "The Economic Dimension of Cicero's Political Thought," 749.
53. Schofield, "Cicero's Definition of Res Publica," 185.
54. Long, "Cicero's Politics in *De Officiis*," 217.
55. Atkins, "Domina et Regina Virtutum," 268ff.
56. Wood, "The Economic Dimension of Cicero's Political Thought," 750. See also Wood, *Cicero's Social and Political Thought*, 120; Cumming, *Human Nature and History*, vol. 2, part 4; and Ste. Croix, *The Class Struggle in the Ancient Greek World*, 286.
57. 1.148; see Schofield, "Morality and the Law," 173.
58. *Off.* 3.52. At 3.53, however, Cicero draws our attention to the fact that a strict interpretation of Antipater's position would mean the end of buying and selling altogether.
59. Schofield, "Morality and the Law"; Annas, "Cicero on Stoic Moral Philosophy and Private Property."
60. *Off.* 3.57, emphasis added.
61. *Off.* 3.61.
62. 1.113; cf. Schofield, "The Fourth Virtue," chap. 2 of this volume, 49–50.
63. Mitsis, "Stoics on Property and Politics," 243.
64. Martha Nussbaum, "Duties of Justice, Duties of Material Aid," has recently criticized Cicero for making a distinction between duties to mankind generally and the duties to those more closely related to oneself.
65. *Off.* 2.74. At 2.84, Cicero specifically recommends an expansionist policy.
66. Annas, "Cicero on Stoic Moral Philosophy and Private Property," 170.
67. *Off.* 2.83–84.
68. Plato, *Apology*, 29d–e.
69. See generally Long, "Cicero's Politics in *De Officiis*" on this issue; cf. *Dom.* 46–47 for Cicero's own case.

Appendix

Cicero and the Rebirth of Political Philosophy

WALTER NICGORSKI

Judged by the conventional standard of the number of monographs, scholarly articles, and dissertations on Cicero's philosophy, regard for Cicero as a serious thinker or even a serious political thinker is indeed low. The number of such items appearing in America in the last generation can be tallied on one hand, or perhaps two, depending on how one would classify several marginal entries.[1] A measure of Cicero's neglect can be found by simply comparing these items with the amount of public work being done, for example, on the political and moral thought of Plato, Aristotle, Hobbes, Rousseau, or Nietzsche. Are we simply witnessing a desirable winnowing, a sort of natural selection process, or are we being deprived in some ways by this neglect of Cicero?

This essay appears here as initially published in *The Political Science Reviewer* in 1978. Some necessary corrections are made in this version, and the notes appear here as endnotes in the format used throughout this book.

Although one hears an occasional lament for the neglect of Cicero and the Romans in college curricula, humanities' programs, and political theory courses, this is not a sufficient basis on which to conclude that this curricular gap or the corresponding lacuna in scholarship is inadvertent and deeply or widely regretted. If anything, one suspects that some American scholars share the view that the case is closed on Cicero as a serious thinker and in fact has been for some time; the verdict against Cicero is in, and it appears to have the imposing quality of being the cumulative judgment of generations. Even in the eighteenth century David Hume could write, as if it were a commonplace, that "the abstract philosophy of Cicero has lost its credit," but "the vehemence of his oratory is still the object of our admiration."[2] A form of that opinion expressed by Hume often held sway even when Cicero was more widely studied, for then as still today he was solely or primarily appreciated as the great orator and rhetorician of Rome and the master prose writer of the Latin language. Cicero the stylist is valued; Cicero the statesman and political thinker is set aside, if not actively eschewed. In any judgment of his own, Cicero would not permit such a severance of form from substance. If he could perceive his own positions as empty and opportunistic as some have regarded them, he would then see his rhetoric, as a few critics have, as but shallow bombast.

The tradition of controversy surrounding Cicero and opposition to him is substantial and extraordinary. In its persistence and extent it seems to overshadow such traditions which one finds in the wake of every great thinker and historical figure. Martin Luther for one, himself a center of considerable controversy, thought that Aristotle was a "blind" and "wretched" man, most of whose books but especially the *Nicomachean Ethics* should be discarded.[3] Every age and place appears to have its detractors of Plato. Their opinions are often as outrageous as that of Luther on Aristotle, but such views have not generally commanded the authority and support that mark the criticisms of Cicero. Although the extent of the controversy around the person and work of more recent figures like Rousseau, Hegel, and Nietzsche may be comparable to that swirling around Cicero, they have not, because of their alleged impact on the modern world, lost access to the philosophers' forum as Cicero has.

It is incumbent on one who proposes to reintroduce Cicero for serious consideration as a political thinker to note the extent and nature of the criticisms directed at him. Even if the comparative neglect of Cicero during the rebirth of political philosophy in America over the last generation is not to be accounted for primarily by the long-standing hostility to Cicero, this opposition as a historical fact is likely again and again to present itself in one form or another as an obstacle to renewed interest in him. Furthermore the opposition can be instructive at times in calling attention to certain problematic aspects of Cicero's life and thought. But such is the state of the study of Cicero that it first seems appropriate to say something, elemental and brief though it be, about the life and works that generated such a hearty tradition of hostility and, it should be added, a like tradition of acclaim, although the latter presently seems dormant or dead, at least in the United States. Furthermore, so implicated with his active public life are his writings and, in turn, criticisms of those writings that the sensible convention of treating philosophical texts independent of biographical and psychological studies of the author must be relaxed in re-approaching Cicero.

I

Cicero (106–43 B.C.) lived and suffered through most of the century of factional strife and violence preceding the death of the Roman Republic.[4] He was no mere citizen caught up in deteriorating political order; for much of that time, he was in the public eye and at key moments at the center stage of Roman politics. He saw himself, as have most observers then and now, as a great but ultimately frustrated defender of the Republic; some have charged, however, that his vanity and political ineptness contributed to the Republic's demise. Except for such personal deficiencies that may have compounded his problems, the dispute over Cicero that has continued down through the ages seems to spring from certain polarities that Cicero tried to bring together. One was the old Republic and the Rome of his time, Cicero's version of the ancients-moderns tension; the other was Greece and Rome, especially in the form of philosophy and politics.

Cicero was reared at Arpinum, a small town about seventy miles southeast of Rome. There his early education was conducted by his invalid father. His family did not belong to the patrician ruling circles of Rome, yet it was a family of some means and some ties to those circles. Marius, the hero of the popular party and its most notable leader before Julius Caesar, had also come from Arpinum. He had been the "savior" of Rome and its foremost leader during Cicero's youth, and he had reached this great distinction without a patrician background. This example was not lost on Cicero as he set his ambitions. At Arpinum as well as at Rome where his family moved after he was ten, Cicero was apparently nourished on the religious practices and customs of the Romans; he grew to love the greatness of Rome and the leading figures of her history. In the difficult times in which he found himself, Cicero aspired to political leadership, to statesmanship, and he sought these objectives through the power of oratory above all. The ebbing effectiveness of the old patrician-dominated order aided in opening to all Romans access to political power through oratorical ability. Cicero could rise as one of a "new breed," a "novus homo" as he was known, but he had to do it without the natural support of a ruling class that saw him as one of his own. Furthermore, winning support through oratory meant that one had to come to public attention through the contentions of civil and criminal trials. Cicero's path to office and leadership would not have been an easy one even in less troubled times; it was one wherein the making of enemies could hardly be avoided. Cicero must have been more than ordinarily ambitious to set such a goal and take such a path, but whether that ambition was "inordinate" in any way is not at all clear.

In his dialogue *Brutus*, Cicero described the various studies he undertook and the tireless efforts he made to attain the oratorical prominence which opened to him the door to political leadership.[5] From the age of sixteen, he constantly watched and listened to the oratorical matches reaching then, at the very eve and throughout the Social War, generally unparalleled levels of intensity and excellence. He assiduously practiced at oratory and sought the guidance of prominent teachers of rhetoric before and after his first known public oratorical appearances on behalf of Quinctius in 81 B.C. (*Pro Publio Quinctio*), and, about a year later in the case that brought him wide public attention, on behalf of Roscius (*Pro Sexto Roscio Amerino*). Near the end of his life, when all his philosophical works, except *De Legibus*, were already completed and in the hands of the public, Cicero acknowledged in his major work on ethics, *De Officiis*, that the title "orator" is more justly his than that of "philosopher."[6] This self-evaluation should not be grounds for dismissing him as a philosopher, for the major part of his studies and public efforts had gone toward oratorical achievement in the public service, and he had already received widespread acclaim and public success through these efforts. Furthermore, following Plato, Cicero thought that wisdom, the fruit of philosophy, was a necessary ingredient of true oratorical achievement; never losing sight of the noble goal of uniting rhetoric and philosophy (power and philosophy), Cicero had, however, to struggle with the temporal and psychological tensions of not merely discussing such a goal but reaching for it in a tottering republic.

Next to his pursuit of rhetorical skill, the study of philosophy received the most attention in Cicero's years of immediate preparation for public life. Philosophy was a Greek pursuit in the eyes of the Romans, and it was held suspect just as earlier the art of rhetoric had been. The Romans had since captured rhetoric for their own as a manifestly useful endeavor. Yet Cicero was apparently seen by many as a strange Graecophile; he did not fit the Roman mold. He developed an early love for philosophy and a respect for what it could do for human life. This, he later claimed, never left him even as he was compelled by necessity and duty to turn ever more of his attention and energy to public life. During the early part of his public life, he submitted wholly and enthusiastically to the instruction of Philo, who had been driven from Athens to Rome in 88 B.C. during the First Mithridatic War and was leader of a philosophical movement known as the Academics. Cicero also invited Diodotus, the Stoic teacher, into his own home and received instruction from him.

When, in 79 B.C. with his place in the public eye well-established, Cicero left Rome for two years primarily to strengthen his health and to temper his tense, vehement rhetorical style, his first six months were spent at Athens under Antiochus. Cicero speaks of him as a most famous and very wise philosopher of the Old Academy and the best of teachers and guides. Antiochus is known for having founded a movement known as the "Old Academy." This was an attempt to move away from the skepticism associated with other Academics known as the New Academy and yet to retain the Socratic method of questioning all opinions and doctrines. The Old Academy sought to emphasize the positive elements of the Socratic teaching, elements shared by the Stoics, Peripatetics, and followers of Plato. Under Antiochus, Cicero tells us, he renewed the study of philosophy which, without complete interruption, he had continued since his youth. Later in this same period, he studied under the Stoic Posidonius at Rhodes. In his later writings Cicero clearly associated himself with the Academics, but he made clear that this was not a commitment to the skepticism of debilitating indifference or indecision on important human questions. It was, rather, a commitment to a method of inquiry, dialectical and disputational exchange, which Cicero traced to Socrates himself and which, he believed, promised as much success as a human being could hope for in determining the probable or most likely answers to the important questions philosophy considers.

Shortly after his two years abroad, Cicero sought and won his first public office, a quaestorship in Sicily. He served with a distinction and honesty uncharacteristic of the Roman provincial officers of that time; his immediate reward was the manifest high regard and affection of the Sicilian people when he ended his tenure in that office. A few years later (70 B.C.) at the request of Sicilians, Cicero took the courageous step of accepting the prosecution of Verres, who was completing a term as governor of Sicily and was an unparalleled practitioner of the extortion and corruption then infesting the Roman, provincial public service. In prosecuting Verres, he accepted, against his own general advice, the unpopular role as prosecutor, and he spoke against a man and a set of practices that were associated with the traditionally powerful patrician families of the Senate. Cicero triumphed in this case and did so over Hortensius, the defense counsel and the acknowledged champion of Roman oratory. Primarily through this victory he came to be generally recognized as one of the very best speakers in Rome.

He continued in the next few years to ascend the ladder of offices (*cursus honorum*) which were formal requisites for the highest office in much the same way that an American politician is informally bound to serve in such offices as governor, mayor, or senator before being considered qualified to aspire to the highest office. In 63 B.C. Cicero became one of the Roman consuls, and from this highest office in the then mightiest nation in the world, he exposed and denounced what he regarded as the Catilinarian conspiracy against the state. The exposé brought him prominence as a statesman that matched his renown as a speaker. Cicero believed he had saved the state in the struggle with Catiline and his circle; whether that is true or not, one thing is sure—Cicero's action drew him decisively into the swirl of political intrigue and enmity that dominated the ensuing years of precipitous decline for the Roman Republic.

When Pompey clashed with Caesar, Cicero favored Pompey but he favored the Republic and peaceful unity above them both. After Caesar triumphed in 49 B.C., Cicero remained his cautious opponent. In the end, Cicero lost his life in the Roman political struggles in which he engaged so passionately; his opposition to Mark Antony, eloquently expressed in the *Phillipics,* became a political liability when Antony closed for a time the breach between himself and the young Octavius. Cicero's name finally appeared on one of the infamous Roman proscription lists. Plutarch reports that Cicero's severed head and hands were "fastened up over the Rostra, where orators spoke...."

Compelled to live his adult years as the Republic tottered under the force of challenge upon serious challenge and then at last fell to the forceful Caesar, Cicero remarked how these events were denying him the leisure to pursue learning, especially philosophy. Such learning was his first love but was not, given the circumstances of his lifetime, perceived as his first duty. Only in the usually very brief interstices of an active public life did Cicero succumb to the attraction of literature and philosophy. In the last years of the Republic, however, and in those six years Cicero lived after its fall, the persuasive power of the orator in Roman life gave way to physical intimidation and violence. Cicero proclaimed himself silenced by the death of the Republic. In this time, he eagerly turned to philosophy, and in the last three years of his life, he wrote all but three of his philosophical writings.

Cicero's written legacy consists of speeches, letters, and philosophical writings. The speeches which he usually polished for publication after delivery and the letters which have been sometimes used to damage his reputation as statesman and philosopher span the period of his public life. The philosophical writings, here taken to include his works on rhetoric (*De Inventione, De Oratore, Brutus, Orator, De Optimo Genere Oratorum, De Partitione Oratoria,* and *Topica*), were all written, save for the *De Inventione*,[7] after Cicero's politically active life was on the decline, within the last twelve or thirteen years of his death. His important dialogues *De Oratore* and *De Re Publica,* completed close to the period of his own public activity as orator and statesman, are the other two works done before a seeming flurry of philosophical writing in the last three years of his life.

Most of Cicero's philosophical writing is in the dialogue form. His dialogues, however, tend to be disputations rather than conversations, following more the form of the lost dialogues of Aristotle than those of Plato. Cicero turned to the dialogue under the immediate inspiration of Carneades (214–129 B.C.), a former leader of the Academics. Carneades and Cicero believed themselves to be following Socrates in seeking through dialogue to conceal their own opinions, to relieve others from error, and to seek always what appears most likely to be the truth. In accord with this understanding and the Academic method, a participant in a dialogue might uphold a position with which he did not ultimately agree in order to stimulate the truth-discovering process of exchange. This is the approach of Philus in Cicero's *De Re Publica* and apparently of Cicero himself on occasion. Despite his professed interest in concealing his opinion within the dialogue, Cicero's own opinion on many of the important questions taken up in his dialogues is revealed, as in the *De Oratore,* in the introductions that accompany these works. We are further able (though perhaps, in another way, put at a disadvantage) to know Cicero's own opinions, and to find the person in a dialogue who appears to speak for him, by our capacity today to read much of his correspondence and to take a synoptic view of most of his written work. Yet one of the characteristics of the Ciceronian dialogue is that contending positions are represented at their best. The "straw man" is not a feature of the Ciceronian dialogue, and Cicero seems in several of them, as in the *De Oratore,* to present an encounter over an issue that genuinely troubles him. Like those of Plato, Cicero's dialogues require attention to their dramatic details if a reader is to have access to the full richness of their teachings. It is especially to be noted that many of the participants in Cicero's dialogues are distinguished Roman public figures; they are usually found on a holiday from the business of the forum and are inclined or led, during their relaxing conversation, to discuss a matter not without utility to their active lives, such as the inquiry into the best regime in the *De Re Publica*.

It is noteworthy that the *De Re Publica*, rightly acknowledged as Cicero's chief work on political theory, is complemented at least in one obvious way by the *De Oratore*, Cicero's major rhetorical work. The *De Oratore* treats as a fundamental theme the education of the perfect or finished orator (*perfectus orator*) or the true statesman; it happens that the *De Re Publica* points to a consideration of the true statesman in that the best regime *ever realized*, the Roman Republic, has been attained and is maintained through the successive and cumulative efforts of great statesmen. But what the *De Re Publica* says about the true statesman and his education is lost to us with the missing portions of Books II and V of this dialogue.[8]

Traditionally among students of the history of political theory, Cicero's *De Re Publica* has been looked to along with his *De Legibus*, both dialogues which he explicitly paralleled with the *Republic* and *Laws* of Plato and which indicate that Plato was, with Socrates, Aristotle, and Carneades, one of his important and beloved philosophical resources. Book I of the *De Legibus* supplements and amplifies the brief sketch of a universal and natural law in Book III of the *De Re Publica*. Besides the famed statement on the natural law, several other topics are usually addressed when Cicero is examined in the often-sweeping views taken of the history of political thought. The most familiar of these are his defense of the active life of the statesman over that of the philosopher, his restatement of the Polybian analysis of the mixed regime as the best regime, and his location of the fullest actualization of that regime in the Roman Republic at its peak. It seems appropriate here to observe that a fuller and more coherent understanding of Cicero's political philosophy requires more development than has been evident of his defense of philosophy before practical men and would-be statesmen, of his conception of the model or true statesman, and especially of the foundation of his philosophical position. The latter implies there is such a basis from which Cicero sorts his way through the philosophical schools and movements of his time and on which he grounds his political philosophy.

Greater recovery of Cicero's political philosophy requires the kind of careful reading of the established political works which has become the standard of good work on primary sources. That warrants mention here only because the reputation of Cicero and specifically of his philosophical works seems at times to be an obstacle to giving him such careful attention. Beyond this, the recovery of a coherent Ciceronian understanding of politics is facilitated by and, in some instances, requires attention to his other major philosophical works. Cicero's approach to philosophy and his qualified embrace of the Academic school is explored in the *Academica*; that approach is further discussed in the *Tusculanae Disputationes*, and there it is exemplified on a question ("What constitutes happiness?") which separates the schools of his time.[9] Cicero applied his philosophical method and tested the schools' positions on the highest concerns in *De Natura Deorum, De Divinatione*, and *De Fato*.[10] Throughout his philosophical examination of the teachings of the schools, the moral or ethical implications of those teachings seem clearly to constitute the chief standard by which Cicero assessed them. In the two remaining major philosophical works of Cicero, *De Finibus* and *De Officiis*, he directly engaged the moral teachings of the schools and presented his own position. The *De Finibus*, which Cicero said at one time was his philosophical writing most worth reading, concerns that central question of moral philosophy which Cicero also came to consider in the *Tusculanae Disputationes*.[11] The *De Officiis*, in the form of an extended letter to his son, treats what might ordinarily be called ethics—namely, precepts or specifications on how to live in accord with the true end of a human being. Cicero's claim that the foundation of philosophy rests on the distinction between good and evil is one important reason for believing that his works in moral philosophy contain the basis for whatever coherent understanding can be found of his philosophical and political teaching.[12]

II

One of the charges against Cicero, and one that would indeed be damning if true, gives a special meaning to the search for the foundation or ground of Cicero's thought. This is the charge that Cicero is but a compiler and not a thinker, with which a generation or more of political scientists were introduced to Cicero in Sabine's text.[13] It makes Cicero's thought out to be entirely derivative and extensively eclectic. Sabine asserted, as he made the charge, that Cicero himself confessed to it, and here he no doubt has in mind a letter (May, 45) of Cicero to his friend Atticus wherein Cicero referred to his writings or *something he* has done as essentially a copy for which Cicero supplied the words.[14] May it now suffice to say that that single ambiguous reference runs against a multitude of others in which Cicero took most seriously his own engagement in philosophy, his appropriation of the method of Socrates, and the writings through which he hoped to introduce philosophy to Rome. It must further be said that as a lifelong student of philosophy in a period (like most periods thereafter) in which philosophy was presented in an atmosphere of contention among schools, Cicero's approach to philosophy was through the teachings of the schools. In being dependent on them and yet independent as he sorted through their teachings from his Academic perspective, Cicero appears eclectic. In fact, he was a self-confessed eclectic for he was not captured by a single school and was explicit about his sources and dependencies.[15] What there is no warrant to accept, however, is the frequent implication of the charge of eclecticism, namely, that it is mindless or without principle and form. That would leave Cicero as wholly derivative and not worthy of attention except as a reporter on philosophical positions the original materials on which are largely lost. It is precisely in that capacity as reporter, especially on earlier Stoicism, that Cicero as "philosopher" has often been valued and read.

Sabine considered Cicero as a reporter and transmitter. Despite evidence of much more extensive personal study of Cicero, Sabine's treatment of Cicero in *A History of Political Theory* is proportionate in space to the little regard he has for Cicero as a political thinker.[16] It is not unreasonable to see Cicero as presented by Sabine and so many others in this century as under the cloud of the severe attack on him in late nineteenth-century German scholarship and specifically in the histories of Rome by Drumann and Mommsen.[17] That was a wholesale attack on the person and achievement of Cicero which shortly requires attention here. What must, however, be noted is a recurring objection in recent scholarship to undervaluing Cicero as a thinker by stressing solely or primarily his function as reporter and transmitter. Richard

McKeon, already in 1950, was ill at ease with the tradition of reducing Cicero's contribution to that of an eclectic compiler; he concluded a substantial essay with the modest observation that "in those portions of his [Cicero's] writings in which we are able to compare his formulation of doctrines with existing sources . . . the modifications which he introduces are considerable, both in the orientation and use of the argument and in the manner of expressing it."[18] James Holton began his essay on Cicero in Strauss and Cropsey's *History of Political Philosophy* by, in effect, wanting to open the issue that seemed closed for Sabine as he began. Addressing that tradition which regards Cicero as primarily reporter and transmitter, Holton wrote:

> Such an assessment contains a measure of truth. It fails, however, to give serious consideration to Cicero's method or to his purpose in treating philosophical materials in the manner in which he did, to say nothing of the substance of his thought. It falls short, therefore, of that understanding essential to an adequate analysis.[19]

Then in 1968 the English scholar A. E. Douglas, in a worldwide survey of scholarship on Cicero, not only reported a general movement away from the "exaggerated" nineteenth-century criticisms of Cicero but also summed up the emerging view of Cicero's philosophical writings, ". . . not as a pale shadow of the great Greek forerunners, but as presenting a synthesis of the Greek and Roman experiences which is something in its own right."[20] And finally, the close study of Cicero in Cumming's *Human Nature and History* led him to similar reservations about the charge of eclecticism in Cicero. At one point he wrote,

> But Cicero's procedure (in political philosophy, at any rate) is not random eclecticism or even *bricolage*. His arrivals at solutions to political problems regularly take the philosophical form of reconciling other oppositions between philosophical positions by anchoring them all to their common opposition to Epicureanism.[21]

What has been reported here from McKeon, Holton, Douglas, and Cumming indicates a common resistance to the charge of mindless eclecticism in Cicero, but it hardly makes visible the real problems to be worked out in finding Cicero's distinctive political philosophy (namely, the ground and argument of his political thought). This must, of course, be the central task for students of political philosophy once they become convinced that Cicero is saying something that can be sought out. If Cicero sorted through and chose among the teachings of the philosophical schools, what standards or principles of choice has he employed? If Cicero developed the thought of his acknowledged greatest teachers, Plato and Aristotle, what were the additions and subtractions and the principles governing them? Similarly, if Cicero bends Stoicism back in the direction of Plato, what governed the degree of the curvature? If Cicero fused Greek and Roman things, what has determined the nature of the synthesis? Total consistency and internal coherence which can suggest more of ideology than philosophy are, no doubt, not to be expected, but the ground and case for Cicero's reconciliation must be found and articulated if the expectation that he transcended mindless eclecticism is to be established as fact.

Although mindless eclecticism is, perhaps, the most damaging charge to Cicero's possible stature as a political philosopher, it is not the only such charge. There is need to take a more complete view of the tradition of hostile criticism of Cicero, for it is, as already said, appropriate to do so on this occasion. Furthermore it will be discovered that much of the tradition of hostility to Cicero constitutes a kind of fabric of criticism in which is woven together an assessment of Cicero the man, the political leader, and the philosopher. What makes this fabric especially noteworthy is that it appears to address the ground toward which most efforts to comprehend the political philosophy of Cicero move, that being the centrality of political practice or statesmanship to Cicero's thought about politics. From the recognition of this informing center to his political philosophy and even, perhaps, his philosophy, it is a short (though, not necessary) step to interpret Cicero's thought as a simple projection of his life and commitments.

Never, it seems, has the criticism of Cicero been as total and rarely has it been as severe as that found in Mommsen. There Cicero was opposed because he stood as an apparent reactionary for the old Republic against the progressive, popular, and centralized rule that Caesar brought. In the light of this fundamental error, Cicero's character, political skills, rhetoric, and philosophical writings take on a yellowed hue that minimally betokens incompetence and maximally decadence. One scholar-friend of Cicero, even at the peak of Mommsen's influence on the Western perception of Rome, protested,

> Have we not the right to demand of the German historians that they set a less biased man to the task of rewriting the story of the Roman Republic, one who knows neither *ira* nor *studio*, and may we not expect at his hands a fairer treatment of the man whose unpardonable sin was a belief in free institutions?[22]

However extreme and exaggerated was the nineteenth-century German school's treatment of Cicero, it is a mistake to trace to it or even to Petrarch's rediscovery of the letters to Atticus the troubled reputation of Cicero.

Rather the problem of Cicero must be traced to his own time. Plutarch's account of Cicero's life and his comparison of Cicero and Demosthenes provide support for this claim. Even then it is support supplementary to what can be detected of Cicero's troubles in his own writings. Throughout his account Plutarch called attention to Cicero's vanity and excessive love of glory; from this flaw, above all, came whatever misjudgments Cicero made in politics and rhetoric.[23] One effect of this flaw that Plutarch especially singled out was Cicero's turning his natural wit into harsh sarcasm directed at opponents and even, at times, at friends. By this habit, Plutarch reported, Cicero, that "Greek scholar" as he was disrespectfully known in some quarters, "made himself odious with many people."[24] Then at one point Plutarch drew out the implications of Cicero's flaw for his efforts in philosophy, and there is found, perhaps, the first instance of what is here called the fabric of criticism of Cicero. Immediately after having noted Cicero's aspirations as a philosopher, Plutarch wrote:

> But the desire of glory has great power in washing the tinctures of philosophy out of the souls of men, and in imprinting the passions of the common people, by custom and conversation, in the minds of those that take a part in governing them, unless the politician be very

careful so to engage in public affairs as to interest himself only in the affairs themselves, but not participate in the passions that are consequent to them.[25]

What then was known of the personal and political life of Cicero became in a number of different forms the basis for evaluation and explanation of his philosophical writings. What was one to expect from a vainglorious politician who attempted a side or second career in philosophy but philosophical writings that were dashed off and, if not simply derivative and mindlessly so, then surely superficial and likely to be honey-coated (Cicero was, after all, a skilled orator) flatteries for his way of life and the regime under which he had risen to power? Even when Cicero's character and political actions were not adversely judged, there was the suspicion that his philosophical work must have suffered from its secondary place in his life or that his philosophy was too informed by his way of life and commitments and even that it is, simply a rationalization for them. Montaigne thought Cicero was deficient in not recognizing that ambition is the humor most contrary to solitude; without solitude there is little hope for substance. Cicero's eloquence was great but empty to Montaigne's ears. He concurred in the common opinion that Cicero had no great natural excellence.[26] So too Pascal wrote as if all discerning minds had seen the true nature of Cicero: "All the false beauties which we blame in Cicero have their admirers, and in great number."[27] A significant critique of Cicero that is still vigorously articulated concedes that his impact on subsequent philosophy has been powerful but regards that impact on the whole as harmful. It is charged that, in contrast to the Greeks, the Romans neglected speculative philosophy, theoretical science and mathematics, and that this neglect was encouraged by Cicero's defense of philosophy and all the arts in terms of the needs of the statesman-orator. Practically centered and vast in its aspirations (Cicero did present the true orator as an expert in all fields of knowledge.), Roman learning was bound to be superficial and reliant on handbook collections of earlier work. Neither original nor rigorous thinking were continued or developed in the Roman or Ciceronian tradition. Cicero, it is charged, played a key part in the birth of the "Dark Ages."

When respectable scientific subjects, together with the occult arts, were consigned by neglect to *viri doctissimi*, the doom of science in the West was sealed for a thousand years.

The turning of the way occurred in Republican Rome, and Cicero called the turn in Book I of his *De Oratore*. He points out that the Greeks placed the philosopher and the specialist on the pedestals of their intellectual world, while the Romans more sensibly reserved the place of honor for the orator.[28]

Even when Cicero's philosophical works were greatly appreciated and hence there was no temptation to explain perceived anomalies and deficiencies of those works by aspects of his life and political commitment, there has sometimes been a concern with lack of consistency in Cicero's life. So Petrarch could not understand Cicero's turning from the noble work of philosophy to the entanglements of politics, and John of Salisbury in his perplexity over certain actions of Cicero gave perhaps initial expression to what has later been called the problem of "the two Ciceros"—Cicero the politician and Cicero the teacher of a beautiful way of life.[29]

In this examination of the fabric of criticism directed at Cicero, coherent lines of argument explicit or implicit in criticism have been stressed and brought to the fore; and because the concern here is with the tradition of hostile criticism or underestimation of Cicero, much in the larger Western tradition that is appreciative and laudatory of Cicero's life and thought has been here set aside. Two observations seem to follow from the preceding exhibition of the fabric of criticism. The first is to acknowledge the simple good sense in the fabric of criticism which is an understandable response to the fabric or oneness of life. In other words, it is reasonable to stand perplexed and distressed before apparent inconsistencies between a man's life and his writings and to seek to find consistency by interpreting the latter in terms of the former. But Cicero would have to be much more manifestly a rogue or political opportunist than he can possibly be construed to be even from reports like that of Plutarch in order for there to arise a serious problem of consistency with his moral and political teaching. Allowing some space for the weakness of the human condition and for the realm of prudence or the contingencies of various situations, this reader does not find in the most direct sources available, Cicero's letters and speeches, evidence of such inconsistency.

What is more interesting is the other major aspect of the fabric of criticism, that is, the tie that is drawn between Cicero's major political involvement and his philosophical writings. The basic line of argument in this part of the fabric is that Cicero's political life has skewed his philosophic life and writings. This has happened either by necessary distraction from philosophy resulting in shallow or less than commendable thought or by a philosophic achievement that is distorted at critical points by the perspective of the active and committed statesman. Among those who have respected Cicero, it has been said that he wrote much that he did in order to justify his active life before the court of Plato. And in the most detailed interpretation of Cicero's key philosophic texts in the last generation in the English-speaking world, Cumming came around at a critical point to find Cicero's "philosophical highmindedness ... encumbered" with issues of Cicero's own "career."[30] It appears that the very problem Cicero struggled with, both personally and in his hopes for Rome, is imbedded in the tradition of criticism, and in this case not outrightly hostile criticism. Public life and philosophic life, the tradition of criticism seems to be saying, cannot be reconciled without damage to one or the other. Cicero's commitments and even excellences as a public man (rhetoric, for example) must inevitably, it seems, take their toll on Cicero the philosopher. Unwittingly perhaps, the tradition of criticism is saying that the unattenuated union of philosophy and power is impossible; Cicero is a case in point. At his best, Cicero offers attenuated philosophy, the political thought of a statesman; at his worst, he is a warning to those who would seek to bridge unbridgeable chasms.

That may well be at least partly correct. But a relevant question that captures another view must be raised. Can Cicero's public life have been on balance, an asset rather than a liability to Cicero the philosopher? Cicero himself thought so, and he has at times been appreciated as a philosopher precisely because of the practical, common sense perspective that informs his teaching and that was seen as rooted in his active life. Such was the view among some early Christians, during the Renaissance, in the republican tradition in England, and among American Founders as different as Jefferson and Adams. The perspective of practice is not, of course, the preserve of the actual political participant or, to be sure, leader. Yet is such participation not likely to make this perspective more accessible and more steady? In the case of the reflective political leader, is there not forced upon him a regular encounter with the larger practical questions and the constraints of human existence? It would seem as hard for the archetypal philosopher to keep in consideration the perspective of practice as it is for the archetypal statesman to attain the distance and isolation that are customarily associated with sound reflection and contemplation. Though Cicero apparently hoped for more isolation than life allowed him, he asserted, in effect, that the perspective of practice and of the greatest practice, statesmanship, is an advantaged perspective. It was advantaged in the sense of being the true perspective, the basis for a true philosophy of life insofar as man can attain that. The central role of the statesman in Cicero's political philosophy, the common sense foundation of his entire philosophy as well as other facets of his thought, may be read autobiographically as a projection of Cicero's "career" upon his philosophy; but that does not remove the applicability of the question of the truth of what he teaches. The principle involved here was made clear by Leo Strauss in one of his essays on historicism. Strauss cautioned that in observing that doctrines are related to their times, one must not overlook "that the situation to which one particular doctrine is related, is particularly favorable to the discovery of the truth, whereas all other situations may be more or less unfavorable."[31]

III

Cicero sought to encourage the birth and development of moral and political philosophy in Rome. He had only partial success within his lifetime and the immediately following years. More substantial success came through his writings among early Christians. Later he played an important part in the renewed vigor of moral and political philosophy during the Renaissance. In general there is no basis for suggesting that American universities and intellectual life are experiencing a renaissance of interest in classic authors or in the fundamental questions to which such authors direct their readers. Yet in the more limited quarters of political science, it is reasonable to speak of a renaissance of political philosophy in the last generation; at the very least there is a rebirth of interest in the study of political philosophy, and it manifests itself in the intensity, depth, and number of studies on political thinkers of classic stature. The scope of these studies and the concerns they reflect call for special notice, for they suggest Renaissance-like characteristics even if relatively small numbers of political scientists and others are involved. What is witnessed are scholarly interests in philosophical, theological, literary, and historical studies that are rooted in a concern with moral and political disorders of the present and recent past; also in evidence is an atmosphere of encouragement of language studies, especially the classical languages, so that primary texts can be studied. Thus in conception at least, the rebirth of political philosophy encourages such interests and scholarship without losing the focus implied in its association with American political science, namely, a concern with the American regime and the present and future of political order in the world.

Leo Strauss and Eric Voegelin have been the leaders and primary agents of this renaissance within American political science, and it is here proposed to examine how Cicero fares in their hands. What can be hoped for from such an endeavor is some help, from those to whom many are accustomed to go, in understanding this controversial figure Cicero. But it happens that some mutual illumination can result and that Cicero, himself a mediator of the tradition of political philosophy to Rome, brings to light some key issues in and some interesting differences between the primary mediators of the tradition of political philosophy to contemporary America.

Such a bold endeavor should imply the right of certain preliminary qualifications. The first and most extensive is to acknowledge that other currents besides those emanating from the work of Strauss and Voegelin are, of course, present in the contemporary study of political thought and political philosophy. Two in which Cicero plays a very important or even pivotal role seem deserving of special note here: the revived interest and scholarship in classical republicanism, the seeds for which appear to have been sown in Zera Fink's 1945 book, *The Classical Republicans*,[32] and the study of the history and crisis of liberalism as presented in Robert Cumming's *Human Nature and History*.

Fink's study focuses on the ideas of the English republican-reformers of the seventeenth and early eighteenth centuries. They include Harrington, Milton, and Sydney, whose ideas of republicanism were based on the Roman model and the concept of mixed government which, they learned through Polybius and Cicero, had been gradually infused in the Roman state. They sought to do the same in England though not in every respect as "gradualists," for there were other models of "how to do it" in the classical tradition (Lycurgus above all). The working definition of a "republican" in Fink's study is a supporter of "a state which was not headed by a king and in which the hereditary principle did not prevail in whole or in part in determining headship."[33] Reminiscent of Hobbes's finding Cicero and Aristotle responsible for unsettling democratic ideas in his time, Fink found the royalists in general holding the chief "declaimer" Cicero responsible for the republican thinking of the time. The seventeenth-century reformers had "the Ciceronian dialogues ... lurking in the background in their minds."[34] Not only was the teaching of Polybius on mixed government and the slightly moderated version of Cicero dear to the classical republicans, but Cicero's very view of the greatness of the Republic and the treachery of Caesar seems to have informed the republicans' view of Roman history. Sydney affirmed that "all that was ever desirable, or worthy of praise and imitation in Rome, proceeded from its liberty, grew up, and perished with it." That liberty was tied to virtue which Sydney thought honored in the days of the Roman Republic "to such an extent that it had never elsewhere been excelled."[35] The classical republicans' goal to build Rome anew in the West (England) passed yet further west to American shores where it became, among so many dissenters to the English Establishment, one important polestar in the politics and political thought of Colonial and Revolutionary America.

Near the end of *The Classical Republicans*, Fink began to trace the concerns and leading ideas of the classical republicans into the Whig political theory of the eighteenth century, a process continued and developed in Caroline Robbins's *The English Commonwealthman*.[36]

The impact on America of this tradition has been elaborated in the work of W. Trevor Colburn, Bernard Bailyn, and others, and J. G. A. Pocock has taken up the challenge of moving backward (as well as forward) from the republicans to a study, as clearly suggested by Fink, of the political thinking of Machiavelli and the Italian Renaissance as the primary source for the classical dimension of the English Republicans and what follows from them into America.[37] History of ideas should be no end in itself, and it is therefore important to recognize that significant discussions in American political theory can be illuminated not simply through a better understanding of the classical republican tradition but also by understanding better that alleged seminal thinker in that tradition, Cicero. Recent inquiries and disputes concerning the meaning of republican government, the bearing of the model of mixed government on the creation of the American Founders, the nature and relevance of republican virtue, the relationship of religion and the republic, and even the role of "common sense" and other non-Lockean elements in Founding political thought at least point the student of the American regime to the classical republican tradition. The classical republican ferment in the study of American political thought in turn points to Cicero as a key figure and thinker, but as yet there is no evidence in these circles of reexamination and renewed interest in Cicero's own writings.

In contrast to this classical republican ferment, Cumming's two-volume work seems to have been little noticed by students of political philosophy and is not symptomatic of an intellectual movement. In fact, Cumming's effort might well be understood as within the scope of the classical republican tradition, although there is no noticeable evidence of any mutual reliance between Cumming and the other body of scholarship. Cumming is concerned with the tradition of liberty and how its sources might help us better understand its modern problems. John Stuart Mill is taken as the prototypical liberal, and it is with analysis of his thought and the manifestation of the crisis of the liberal tradition in him that Cumming's *Human Nature and History* begins and ends.

The crisis of the liberal tradition is rooted in the tension in that tradition's dual attachment to specific historical achievements and a philosophy of human nature. Without the latter, political philosophy is dead; yet it is in the former that political philosophy finds realizations. Insofar as specific historical achievements become the liberal tradition, historicism swamps political philosophy. The historicist strain in the liberal tradition is traced by Cumming through Machiavelli to Polybius's rejection of Plato's model regime in favor of one realized in the Spartan or Roman state. Though he observed that Cicero like Polybius had his intellectual roots in Plato, Cumming set him off against Polybius as the philosopher of human nature, the "second founder" of political theory, the founder being Plato. Cicero's effort to reconcile history and human nature, or politics and philosophy, is the classical paradigm for the problem of the liberal tradition. So it is that Cumming wrote that "the outcome of this complex process of reconciliation will be the classical tradition in the guise in which it will exercise the most influence on the development of modern liberal thought."[38] At another point he added that "... Cicero contributed more decisively than any other classical thinker to the development of modern political thought, and in particular to the development of what Mill identifies as the principle of individuality...."[39]

In further contrast with the classical republican strain in recent and current scholarship, Cumming himself engaged in an extended and close study of the thought of Cicero; he compared aspects of Cicero's political thought with that of Polybius and that of Plato, and in explicating Cicero he fixed his attention specifically on the *De Re Publica* and the *De Officiis*. Those two works provide focal points for the dialectic that Cumming believed Cicero struggled with more explicitly than any classical thinker; in the *De Re Publica* Cicero is said to come forth as the champion of authority, and in the *De Officiis* as the champion of liberty. In Cicero's attachment to philosophy, Cumming found the champion of individualism and liberty; in his practical political life, the champion of authority.

Cumming's volumes are clearly thoughtful, ranging, and scholarly, and they are deserving of much more consideration than they have received. However at this stage of the study of his thesis and argument one has the sense that he has made more of individualism in Cicero than can be made. Supporting Cicero's role as the predominant classical figure for modern liberal thought is Cumming's distinction of Cicero from Plato and Aristotle on the ground that the individual plays a more important role for Cicero. This distinction merits further consideration as does Cumming's turning the tension in Cicero's life between the vocations of politics and philosophy into a form of the tension between authority and liberty and his presenting the *De Re Publica* and the *De Officiis* as a manifestation of the latter tension. These are, of course, key reservations given the thesis of Cumming, but it should be noted that he not only has taken Cicero seriously and sought to understand him as a philosopher but also has directed his attention to those three topics noted earlier as most requiring attention in Cicero: his defense of philosophy, the pivotal role of the orator-statesman in his thought, and the ground or fundamental principles of Cicero's philosophy.

Both Fink and Cumming, then, have stressed Cicero's seminal and positive contribution to modern liberal and republican thought. Neither Strauss nor Voegelin have denied the many continuities that run through Western political thought, but each found it more significant, in exploring who we are and where we are, to bring fundamental discontinuities to the forefront. Cicero is without qualification on the ancient side of the divide between the ancients and moderns which is central to Strauss's analysis. In a review of Fink's book, Strauss hesitated at the suggestion that the classical republicans were really classical, finding them more democratic than "their classical teachers" and more disposed to the modern belief in political perfection independent of the moral qualities of the citizens.[40] Cumming, apparently independently and despite his overall emphasis on the modern aspects of Cicero's thought, has joined Strauss in his denial of the frequent assertion that modern egalitarianism can be traced to Cicero.[41] Voegelin sees Cicero as both personally and culturally (for he lived in the "Ecumenic Age") distracted from the fundamental experiences and thus the high calling of the philosophical life; Cicero is then more implicated in the development of Gnosticism and disorder than he is successful at the passing on of the Platonic experience.

But two briefer preliminary qualifications are in order before turning to a more complete examination of Strauss and Voegelin on Cicero. It is necessary to be clear that the contemporary renaissance in political philosophy associated with Strauss and Voegelin has not been a particular boon for the study of Cicero. It is not, however, the strong forms of the tradition of hostile criticism of Cicero discussed in Part II that appear to be operating in these circles. Strauss has been clearly more respectful of and more dependent on Cicero than Voegelin. For each, nonetheless, and for the scholarship which their work has encouraged, Cicero has been of secondary interest; the reason for this is different for each and is entailed in the overall thesis on which each built his case for the renewal of political philosophy.

Finally there is need for some confession of concern in taking such an apparently oblique and surely unusual entree to the political thought and interpretation of two such formidable thinkers of this generation. There is no removing the concern that the consideration here of a part of their work may suffer from the fact that the effort to understand the whole of it is continuing. An examination of their consideration of Cicero proves, however, to be only *apparently* oblique, for Cicero's primary interest in bridging across the life of politics to the life of philosophy seems to have given him the power to bring to the forefront the understandings of Strauss and Voegelin on the relation between politics and philosophy and thus on the very nature of political philosophy. This is not to deny that other points of entree to their thought could lead as directly or even more directly to this central question.

IV

It is proper to begin by noting the obvious. Neither Strauss nor Voegelin has chosen to write a monograph or to make a major statement on Cicero. In the case of Strauss, Holton's positive and probing essay on Cicero's political philosophy has appeared under his cosponsorship in the volume on the *History of Political Philosophy*. In *Natural Right and History*, normally taken as the basic statement of Strauss's overall position in political philosophy, there are nearly as many references to Cicero as there are to Plato (the most) and to Aristotle (the second most). No other thinker is there cited nearly as frequently as these three: Plato, Aristotle, and Cicero. More restricted in scope than *Natural Right and History* is Strauss's *The City and Man* which, being constituted by studies on Plato, Aristotle, and Thucydides, is limited to the Greeks;[42] here too Cicero is cited with frequency but surrenders the third place to another Greek, Xenophon. In these books and in other writings, Strauss has cited almost exclusively the philosophical works of Cicero, and among those he has rarely referred to the rhetorical works. He has then ignored the speeches and letters, and it appears to be his intent to abstract from the controversies concerning the personal character and the more obvious political actions of Cicero. He gave one clear indication of this when he wrote that Cicero's "... political action on behalf of philosophy has nothing in common with his actions against Catiline and for Pompey...."[43]

Not only has Strauss held back from most of the swirl of controversy around Cicero's personal and public life and focused on "the political philosopher Cicero," he has also avoided any observation that could be seen as diminishing Cicero's political philosophy.[44] He did not write about or mention considerations like the eclectic, superficial, or even the derivative quality of Cicero's political philosophy. Why then did Strauss turn to Cicero with the frequency that he did? How, in other words, does Cicero enter the fabric of Strauss's thought as reflected in his writings? There appear to be two evident ways: Cicero's writings serve as a source for materials on the division and debate over natural right in ancient times, and Cicero's own position is an exemplification of the nature of classical political philosophy.

Like many others, Strauss valued Cicero as a source through which one could understand the course of philosophy and political philosophy as it passed from Plato and Aristotle to Christian times. Thus Cicero's dedicated and often dispassionate presentation of the teachings of the schools of his time has benefited Strauss as it has aided students of philosophy through the ages. Footnote references to texts of Cicero often indicate that Cicero has been the source or is to serve as the illustration of what understanding Strauss has of the Stoic and Epicurean teachings. More must shortly be said of Strauss's view of Cicero's relationship to the Stoics. It is through Cicero and Lucretius that Strauss most directly encountered ancient Epicureanism. Already in *Natural Right and History* he referred to the poem of Lucretius as "the greatest document of philosophic conventionalism and, in fact, its only document available to us that is both authentic and comprehensive...."[45] At the same time he argued that

Rousseau's *Second Discourse* was modeled on Lucretius and suggested the same of Hobbes's *Leviathan*.[46]

As one might expect, a much closer public study of Lucretius followed, and therein Strauss can be found using Cicero's Epicureans from the dialogues to support his interpretation of Lucretius and to illustrate the general character of Epicureanism. In this study, "Notes on Lucretius," Strauss drew attention to Lucretius's explicit claim that he was the first to be rendering into his "native speech" that truth of nature which was discovered not very long ago.[47] The intent of Lucretius, according to Strauss, was "to propagate Epicurean philosophy in Rome."[48]

This analysis of Lucretius invites a limited comparison with Cicero which is not explicitly in evidence in Strauss's writings. Whatever his own stature as a philosopher, Cicero clearly claimed to be putting Greek philosophy in his native speech.[49] Cicero's approach is apparently more pluralistic than that of Lucretius, although, as Cumming has already suggested, there is clear and unquestionable opposition to one school, the Epicureans, in Cicero's philosophical writings. Strange it is that although Cicero and Lucretius were contemporaries, in fact nearly coterminous, there is no evidence of interaction between them and apparently only a single brief reference in all of Cicero, and that in a letter, to Lucretius's *De Rerum Natura* which appeared in 55 B.C.[50] Cicero's silence concerning Lucretius may have a number of explanations; two of these, not exclusive of one another, are a strong sense of rivalry with Lucretius for the direction of philosophy in Rome and a preference, despite the seeming character of *De Natura Deorum*, to meet the threat of Epicureanism from a practical perspective rather than on the terms of Lucretius.

There is, perhaps, a more important matter to be noted concerning Strauss's encounter with the Epicureans through Cicero and Lucretius. As already implied in his linking Rousseau and Hobbes to Lucretius, the Epicureans indicated for Strauss the presence in premodern times of the modern alternative. In Lucretius and the Epicureans, wrote Strauss, "... premodern thought seems to come closer to modern thought than anywhere else."[51] The pivotal ancients-moderns distinction for Strauss was not, of course, a rigid periodization but a characterization of the predominant understanding of the end and nature of political life before and after Machiavelli. On each side of the divide between the ancients and moderns, there are present representatives, at least, of the other side. And then too, the divide is one between the predominant understandings of *political thinkers,* and if only in the light of Athens's treatment of Socrates, it can be said that societies only more or less incorporate such understandings. As the "modern" Epicureans were present in ancient times, so, Strauss has suggested, there is in modern times an "ancient" way of thinking as well as reservoirs of common sense which can provide support for a *healthy* liberal democracy.[52]

Even more noteworthy than Strauss's use of Cicero as reporter on Epicureanism and other ancient teachings was his regular reliance on Cicero to exemplify classical political philosophy. Strauss has chosen again and again to cite Cicero as he illustrated and documented the classical alternative with which Strauss sought above all to reacquaint the world. For Strauss, Cicero was one of three major spokesmen for the classical or ancient understanding of politics. Strauss has looked away from possible *ultimate* differences in the thought of Cicero, Aristotle, and Plato in order to point up the common defining core of classical political philosophy.[53] For Strauss one of these defining characteristics was that classical political philosophy takes its bearing from an inquiry into the "human things"; it is Cicero who above all or most explicitly seemed to draw Strauss's attention to this characteristic or, what might be called, the Socratic focus for inquiry.[54] The "human things" are the "things good or bad," not "the nature of man."

> Cicero draws our attention to the special effort which was required to turn philosophy toward the human things: philosophy turns primarily away from the human things toward the divine or natural things; no compulsion is needed or possible to establish philosophy in the cities or to introduce it into the households; but philosophy must be compelled to turn back toward the human things from which it originally departed.[55]

In taking its bearings from "the human things," political philosophy is the branch of philosophy closest "to non-philosophic life, to human life." It is related directly "to political life" which is charged with the questions of the good and the bad as they "are raised in assemblies, councils, clubs and cabinets" and raised "in terms intelligible and familiar, at least to all sane adults," terms drawn "from everyday experience and everyday usage."[56] Another characteristic of classical political philosophy, related to its focus on "human things," concerns the addressees of the ancient teaching. Strauss wrote that "the political teaching of the classical philosophers, as distinguished from their theoretical teaching, was primarily addressed not to all intelligent men, but to all decent men."[57]

These defining characteristics of classical political philosophy seem to point to a disproportion and a tension between political philosophy and philosophy, the search for the truth of the whole, the divine and the natural including the nature of man. Classical political philosophy was and understood itself as at least somewhat independent of philosophy or science.

> And Socrates was so far from being committed to a specific cosmology that his knowledge was knowledge of ignorance. Knowledge of ignorance is not ignorance. It is knowledge of the elusive character of the truth, of the whole. Socrates, then, viewed man in the light of the mysterious character of the whole. He held therefore that we are more familiar with the situation of man as man than with the ultimate causes of that situation. We may also say he viewed man in the light of the unchangeable ideas, i.e., of the fundamental and permanent problems. For to articulate the situation of man means to articulate man's openness to the whole. This understanding of the situation of man which includes, then, the quest for cosmology rather than a solution to the cosmological problem, was the foundation of classical political philosophy.[58]

Later in a discussion of Aristotle, Strauss spoke of ancient prudence or practical wisdom as "in principle self-sufficient or closed" to the impact of theoretical science (physics and metaphysics); then he added that it is but a qualified self-sufficiency for "prudence is always endangered by false doctrines about the whole of which man is a part...." Against such doctrines prudence is in need of defense and that "defense is necessarily theoretical." Prudence is "only *de jure* but not *de facto* wholly independent of theoretical science...."

Theoretical opinions defending prudence are not, however, "the basis of prudence."[59]

These considerations and others make "political philosophy... more questionable than philosophy as such," at least to philosophers.[60] It appears that the disproportion or tension between political philosophy and philosophy is a special case of the disproportion or tension between political life and philosophy. Classical political philosophy is seen in Strauss's writings as a mediation between politics (or the city) and philosophy; it defends philosophy before the city, and it defends political concerns before those inclined to philosophy, if not actual philosophers.[61] Like all mediators, the political philosopher (consider Cicero as well as Socrates) will find himself in tension with each pole between which he stands, between, in other words the city and philosophy as such. In the light of this understanding of classical political philosophy, Cicero must have been seen by Strauss not merely as an exemplification of the classical way but also as a superbly explicit one, for just as Cicero drew attention to the Socratic focus on the "human things," so too he recurrently and unambiguously commends philosophy to the city and the city to philosophy. In fact, it would be speculation but not unreasonable speculation to assert that Cicero played an important part in Strauss's recovery of the distinctive characteristics of classical political philosophy and in his seemingly related decision to concentrate his later studies on the founding father Socrates.

Strauss drew upon Cicero in two significant ways which have not thus far been considered here. Each when examined opens to important and difficult issues in Strauss's and Cicero's understandings of the relationship between politics and philosophy. Strauss found in Cicero, as have so many, a version of the Stoic natural law teaching. Although at times he simply stated the conventional view that Cicero transmitted the Stoic teaching, on other occasions he elaborated so as to make clear that the version of that teaching which Cicero presented, *but did not himself embrace,* is an already rigidified or corrupted version of an original Stoic teaching that was much more Socratic.[62] Cicero's own position on "natural law" was that of Socrates and Plato on natural right including the "hesitations and ambiguities" of that earlier view.[63] Those hesitations and ambiguities seem, above all, to be doubts about or qualifications of the view that natural law or natural right is in "natural harmony with civil society." This is the view without mitigation or qualification that Strauss found represented in Cicero's *De Re Publica* and *De Legibus* but thought not approved by Cicero.

Strauss's disengagement of Cicero from the version of Stoic natural law teaching presented in his most political dialogues is based on an interpretation of those dialogues, especially of their dramatic detail; the interpretation is followed and developed in Holton's essay. It is only possible here to cite some of the grounds for questioning this interpretation. In the *De Re Publica* it is Laelius who is spokesman for the natural law teaching (Cicero himself being spokesman in *De Legibus*). Strauss endeavored to sever Cicero's association with the natural law statement by Laelius by portraying the latter as "distrustful of philosophy in the full and strict sense of the term," as "absolutely at home on earth, in Rome," and as one who finds "no difficulty in reconciling natural law with the claims of the Roman Empire." The chief character of the dialogue, Scipio, is suggested as the representative of Cicero, and he "longs for the contemplative life" and understands that the Roman regime is not simply just, that it can be seen as the best regime only by a standard of "diluted" natural law. At the same time Strauss noted Cicero's identification with the Academic school and pointed out that another character in the *De Re Publica*, Philus, is an Academic skeptic and is called upon to attack the natural basis of right which Laelius above all defended.[64] This interpretation failed to address directly three considerations: the friendship and respect between those equals or near equals, Scipio and Laelius; that Cicero in his own name in an attack on Epicurean thought in *De Finibus* explicitly called upon the statement Laelius makes here; and the fact that Philus expresses his disgust and disagreement with the position he is here called upon to take.[65] Nor has a persuasive case been made that Laelius is any less aware than Scipio of the imperfections of the Roman past and the model Roman regime. But perhaps most important is the fact that although Scipio is the Roman spokesman in this dialogue for the merits and uses of speculative philosophy, the emphasis on the priority of moral and political philosophy which is put in the mouth of Laelius is consistent with Cicero's position throughout his writings.[66]

Much is made by Strauss and Holton of the "severe criticism" to which Cicero exposed Stoic metaphysics and theology in other writings, especially the *De Natura Deorum*. Even that work, however, provides especially in its closing lines ground for arguing that Cicero regarded the Stoic teaching as the best even if wanting in many ways. Cicero clearly wanted to distinguish the Stoic moral and political teaching from the metaphysics and theology. And what do Cicero's objections and doubts concerning the latter have to do with establishing his embrace of an earlier rather than later version of Stoic teaching? Would not either version be dependent on a first or fundamental philosophy, a satisfactory version of which Cicero has failed to find? And in fact those parts of the Stoic teaching, which Cicero has found more acceptable than others, were determined so not from a first philosophy but from the practical perspective, the fundamental concern with "human things" that Cicero shared with Socrates. It must be asked why for Strauss a Stoic teaching that asserts the harmony or congruence of natural law with the essence of civil society was regarded as inaccessible from the perspective of prudence.

Related to this problem is Strauss's remaining major reliance on Cicero. At least four times in Strauss's writings he credited Cicero with helping to expose a single important dimension of Plato's *Republic*. Strauss wrote that "... as Cicero has observed, the *Republic* does not bring to light the best possible regime but rather the nature of political things—the nature of the city."[67] Whether Cicero intended in the passage in question to point up the inherent impossibility of the regime portrayed in the *Republic* is a matter deserving further consideration. Here it is possible, however, only to comment on some apparent inconsistency in Strauss in holding to this interpretation of the *Republic* and on the general significance of such an interpretation. Strauss seemed to hesitate at times about the view that the best regime was impossible; that is reflected in his having written, for instance, that "the actualization of the best regime proves indeed to be impossible or at least extremely improbable ..."[68] This reader believes that the text of the *Republic* gives ample reason for such hesitation; then too, what is one to say of the logic in a presentation of a best regime that is in the nature of things impossible. The hesitation of Strauss was probably related to his recognition of this logical problem, for already in *Natural Right and History*, in commenting upon the contentions of Cicero and Burke that the best regime has been realized within their respective national experiences, Strauss wrote, "These contentions of Burke and of Cicero are, if taken by themselves, in perfect agreement with the classical principles: the best polity being essentially 'possible,' it could have become actual at some place and at some time."[69]

The attachment in Strauss to the notion that the best regime, that in thought or word, is impossible is akin to his reluctance to associate a Socratic-like Cicero with a natural law teaching that professes to be in harmony with the requisites of civil society. In each of these cases what is coming to the forefront is Strauss's finding in classical philosophy and his own conviction of a radical gap between the philosophic life and the civil or moral life, between philosophy and the city. "Justice and moral virtue," the very realm of prudence in which classical political philosophy is rooted, are "legitimated" only insofar as they are necessary conditions of the philosophic life. The sphere of prudence or morality is transcended by the philosopher who can look back upon it as a datum among others in the vast array of things to be understood.[70] Man is not set in a potentially harmonious ambience; the practical perspective does not blend with or flow into the speculative; it is only useful to, though incongruous with, the speculative. Here it is not appropriate to do more than say that this does not seem to fit Cicero, that Cicero was convinced of the overall harmony of man's setting, that he took his bearings from the practical perspective and made his judgments in the speculative realm in accord with that perspective. Cicero was capable of accepting the constraints of a given political situation, of working for a second-best when circumstances made it the best that could be had, of encouraging amelioration in Rome by portraying ancestors and ancestral ways as better than they actually were. He was as capable of this as he incontestably was of flattering an audience to win his case. These capacities need not entail, and do not seem to, an inherent incongruity between the peak of human thought about the right or the just and the potential of human nature.

Compared to Strauss's dependence on Cicero, Voegelin in his major works rarely turns to Cicero. There are relatively few citations of Cicero, but on several occasions Cicero or passages from his writings receive extended consideration. Voegelin looks to Cicero, the philosophical writer, giving no consideration to his speeches and letters. Although he finds Cicero seriously deficient as a philosopher, there is no evidence that the tradition of hostile criticism of Cicero is directly responsible for Voegelin's judgment; it appears, rather, that the grounding-points of his own thought, his understanding of the nature of philosophy and his historical elaboration of its life, set the standard for his judgment of Cicero. For Voegelin, Cicero is implicated with his judgment of Rome, and Rome is, in turn, implicated with the "Ecumenic Age," but this is, of course, a statement from the perspective of one looking at the substance of Voegelin's work as we now have it. Whatever encounter Voegelin had directly with the thought of Cicero no doubt helped him work out his view of Rome and the "Ecumenic Age."

As Strauss and many others, Voegelin employs Cicero as a source for information on philosophy at that time. This is in evidence in a significant discussion in his recently republished essay, "Reason: The Classic Experience"; there Voegelin draws on Cicero's *Tusculanae Disputationes* to reveal a Stoic understanding of "mental disease as a disturbance of noetically ordered existence."[71] What is noteworthy about Voegelin's use of Cicero as a source is that he draws information only on the Stoics from Cicero and that generally, though not explicitly in the instance just cited, he associates Cicero without qualification with the Stoic teaching. Voegelin takes, for example, the statement on natural law by Laelius in the *De Re Publica* as Cicero's "confession," and on another occasion he treats the critique of Stoicism in the *De Natura Deorum* simply as the statement of an Epicurean and in a manner that suggests that Cicero was not at all sympathetic with this attack.[72] Since "Ciceronian Stoicism" plays an important role in Voegelin's overall explanation of the life and "deformation of philosophy," it may seem understandable that Voegelin is only or primarily interested in the Stoicism in Cicero. It is remarkable, nonetheless, that he gives no evident attention to Cicero's claims to be an Academic and a follower of Socrates. Accordingly there is, in Voegelin's writings, no attention to Cicero's effort to sort out the claims of the schools of his time and a tendency to underestimate the complexity of Cicero's dialogues as vehicles of his teaching. Without attention to these matters Cicero has little chance to make any claim as a philosopher.

Voegelin's most direct attack on Cicero as philosopher occurs in *The New Science of Politics* wherein Augustine's dissatisfaction with

Varro giving priority to the "human things" over the "divine things" in Rome provides the occasion to take up Cicero.[73] "The more supple Cicero," wrote Voegelin, was in basic agreement with "his friend" Varro and that is best expressed in the *De Natura Deorum*. Cicero is then presented as a kind of Roman who represented "the compactness of Roman experience, the inseparable community of gods and men in the historically concrete *civitas*, the simultaneousness of human and divine institution of a social order." Roman compactness is for Voegelin an "archaic survival"; it is an anachronism in the process of historical "differentiation" and a somewhat innocent anticipation of "Gnostic immanentization."[74] Cicero's *De Re Publica* is interpreted by Voegelin as a document of this archaic compactness. It stands against the Greek way in its rejection of the "fictitious" city of the Platonic Socrates in favor of the superiority of the Roman political order. It will not range as Greek learning did but turns instead to problems useful to the Roman order, and it prefers "the *vita civilis* of the statesman ... to the *vita quieta* of the sage."[75] Later in *The Ecumenic Age*, Voegelin shows an additional perspective on Cicero's constricted view. There in the context of a detailed discussion of Polybius as "pragmatic historian," Voegelin sees in the work of that Romanized Greek the "appalling decline of philosophy" to the "common understanding," and a pragmatic outlook which holds that "what did not count in the game of power did not count at all." Then Voegelin turns aside to Cicero and adds:

> There was already in the making the attitude of Cicero who with a sneer dismissed the best polities of the Hellenic philosophers as fancies of no importance by the side of the best polity that was created on the battlefields by the imperatores of Rome. The intellectual and spiritual atmosphere forcefully reminds one of Stalin's dictum: How many divisions has the Pope?[76]

The "atmosphere" was that of the "Ecumenic Age" at its peak; that age was "an epoch ... when the societies which had differentiated the truth of existence through revelation and philosophy succumbed, in pragmatic history, to new societies of the imperial type."[77] The old societies are dissolved by "the blows of pragmatic history" into an ecumene which "had not yet sufficient life of its own to react against the orgy of obscene destruction...."[78] Cicero as a Roman is seen as infected with the virus of pragmatic success. Thus Voegelin appears to reach a fuller understanding of what first appeared to be almost a mystery of archaic Roman compactness.[79] His judgment of Cicero the philosopher remains, however, constant.

There seems at times to be almost an anger on Voegelin's part with what he clearly considers to be Cicero's betrayal of philosophy.

> The thinker who can speak of philosophy as a "foreign learning," to be respected but nevertheless to be considered as a spice that will add perfection to superiority, has, one may safely say, understood neither the nature of the spiritual revolution that found its expression in philosophy nor the nature of its universal claim upon man. The peculiar way in which Cicero mixes his respect for Greek philosophy with amused contempt indicates that the truth of theory, while sensed as an enlargement of the intellectual and moral horizon, could have no existential meaning for a Roman.[80]

Thus Voegelin reveals surely the most important basis for his judgment of Cicero. Cicero's teaching is ultimately without intelligibility for his psyche has not "become luminous for the order of reality through the revelation of the one, divine ground of all being as the Nous."[81] Cicero's outlook or "philosophy" is a form of what Voegelin calls a "secondary ideology"; it is "richly supplied with *ordo*, but lacking ... the noetic clarification that renders conscious the origin of the *ordo* in the existential tension toward the ground."[82]

Here it is appropriate to mention that the monograph *Cicero and the Politics of the Public Orthodoxy*, by Wilhelmsen and Kendall, appears to be a friendly attempt to refine Voegelin's assessment of Cicero as a philosopher. This essay draws on a Voegelinian framework of analysis and takes some direction from Voegelin's brief consideration of the *De Natura Deorum* in *The New Science of Politics*. Wilhelmsen and Kendall perform a more extensive analysis of the *De Natura Deorum* and draw out into the open a utilitarian strain in Cicero's thought which merits the closest attention. Overall the essay appreciates Cicero the philosopher; he is described as "deeply grounded in Plato, and by no means the popularizer and rhetorician of Stoic doctrine that some commentators have made him out to be." But Cicero as Roman statesman is not seen in harmony with Cicero the philosopher. Wilhelmsen and Kendall do not find the philosopher defeated by the patriot and statesman as Voegelin does, but they leave the reader with another version of "two Ciceros." Cicero is seen as unable to bring together two truths, "two orders of meaning," that of theoretical truth and that of society.[83]

There is, it should be noted, a bit of ambiguity, only that, in Voegelin's assessment of Cicero the philosopher. He acknowledges that Cicero through his *Hortensius* was a mediator to Augustine of the tradition of philosophy as a way of life.[84] But more importantly and as already noted, he treats Cicero as a Stoic as well as a Roman. Although on at least one occasion Voegelin was puzzled over the *coexistence* of civil and philosophic theologies in Rome, in the case of Cicero he has always seen the Stoic as subservient to the Roman.[85] And although in both capacities, as Stoic and Roman, Cicero is implicated with the loss of the ground of philosophic experience, in his very discussion of the "Stoic deformation of symbols" Voegelin observes that the Stoic symbolization "has the civilizational purpose and effect of protecting an historically achieved state of insight against the disintegrative pressures to which the differentiated truth of existence is exposed in the spiritual and intellectual turmoil of the ecumenic situation." Voegelin then singles out Cicero as having discerned "the forces of disintegration as well as the necessity of protecting the truth through language symbols..."[86] Earlier Voegelin suggested that the task of symbolization, necessary and important as it is, falls generally to lesser men.[87] On balance then, perhaps the thrust of Voegelin's critique of Cicero is to measure him against Plato.

The Roman Cicero might be said to have a "civilizational purpose" comparable to that of the Stoic Cicero. It is to protect truth through institutions. Voegelin wrote of this effort when he reflected upon Plato's recognition that "... institutions will be required for continuing and transmitting spiritual insights, as well as the intellectual culture that is necessary for their exposition and communication through the generations...."[88] In the light of this and other parts of Voegelin's consideration of Plato and Aristotle as well as his appreciation for the noetically informed common sense tradition of Anglo American institutions, one might expect some appreciation for Cicero, especially for Cicero the moral and political philosopher. But Rome-centered Cicero apparently exemplifies too much the stable, tradition-centered societies that for Voegelin are so infertile a ground for the development of a true science of politics. As he brought out clearly in his important article on "The Oxford Political Philosophers," Voegelin is wary of "philosophers" who are in too great a harmony with their environment.[89] But is Cicero so content with the Rome of his time? To embrace a tradition is not, of course, necessarily to abandon a critical posture, and that is especially so when the tradition does not authoritatively inform the immediate environment. Yet even if Cicero's prudent discontent is acknowledged, there is still a great gap between the "theophanic" peak that defines the philosopher for Voegelin and the practical perspective, the concern with "human things," from which Cicero takes his bearings. Whether that gap is unbridgeable, and it must be concluded that there is a fundamental incompatibility between these outlooks, should at least await a better attempt to understand Cicero the philosopher as he understood himself.

This essay has sought to recall the life and works of Cicero, to review the tradition of opposition to him and to point out and assess recent considerations of Cicero as a political philosopher, with particular attention to those by Strauss and Voegelin. It seems clear that whatever new attempts are made to understand Cicero the political philosopher must reach for an understanding of Cicero the philosopher and that such attempts will find themselves confronting the tension between philosophy and practice. That tension, which manifested itself in Cicero's life and in much of the tradition of hostile criticism of him, is deeply involved in the consideration of Cicero by Strauss and Voegelin. To take up Cicero anew is not at all to remove oneself from some of the most interesting and central questions in current political philosophy.

NOTES

1. The following have come to our attention: Hathaway, "Cicero, *De Re Publica II*, and his Socratic View of History"; Holton, "Marcus Tullius Cicero"; Kendall and Wilhelmsen, *Cicero and the Politics of the Public Orthodoxy*. This monograph was later republished in the United States in *The Intercollegiate Review* 5:2 (1968–69). There is an extensive discussion

of Cicero in Cumming, *Human Nature and History*. Finally, note Douglas, *Cicero*, which contains a survey that includes European studies of Cicero.

2. Hume, "Of the Standard of Taste," in *Of the Standard of Taste*, 18–19.

3. Martin Luther, "An Open Letter to the Christian Nobility," 93–94.

4. Much of what follows on Cicero's life is drawn from his own writings. In fact, Cicero's writings not only supply substantial materials toward an autobiography but also offer much toward a modest history of his times. See, for example, Lacey and Wilson, *Res Publica*, which is an account of Roman politics and society drawn almost entirely from Cicero's writings. The most recent of a continuing stream of English biographies of Cicero are Lacey, *Cicero and the End of the Roman Republic*, and Rawson, *Cicero*. They each contain helpful and current bibliographical essays on Cicero. An older work that should be noted is Petersson, *Cicero*. Plutarch's account of Cicero is a sensible starting place for a secondhand account of Cicero's life.

5. *Brut.*, 304–24.

6. *Off.* 1.2.

7. *De Inventione* is generally thought to have been composed around 90 B.C. Cicero apologized in the *De Oratore* (1.5) for this unfinished and rough work on rhetoric, which he produced as a very young man. In the *De Inventione* (1.4–5), however, he already hit upon a lifelong concern, the danger to a public man in an attraction to philosophy.

8. *Rep.* 2.51, 66–67. The text here indicates that missing passages considered the true statesman; Book 5 indicates in its remaining fragments that the true statesman was also considered here.

9. For a good and brief account of the various philosophical schools which developed between Socrates and Cicero and their sometimes subtle differentiations, see McKeon, "Introduction to the Philosophy of Cicero."

10. At *De Divinatione* 2.1–4 is found Cicero's own summary and characterization of all his major philosophical works except his *De Officiis*, apparently not completed at that time, and *De Legibus*, never completed and/or released in Cicero's lifetime. The text of *De Fato* which we have is badly fragmented.

11. *Fin.* 1.11.

12. See *De Divinatione* 2.2 for Cicero's statement on the foundation of his philosophy. The extant philosophical writings of Cicero not specifically mentioned in this and preceding paragraphs are the still frequently read dialogue-essays on old age and on friendship (*De Senectute* and *De Amicitia*) and the *Paradoxa Stoicorum*, consisting in spirited defenses of unusual aspects of Stoic ethics. This should be read in the context of Cicero's other writings on moral philosophy. There is evidence that at least three major works of Cicero are lost to us: *De Gloria*, *De Consolatione*, and *Hortensius*. The last is the dialogue that Augustine claimed in *The Confessions* had turned him to philosophy from a self-satisfied life as a teacher of rhetoric. Michel Ruch,

a French scholar, has attempted to reconstruct the *Hortensius* from extant fragments and other sources (Ruch, *L'Hortensius de Cicéron*).

13. Sabine and Thorson, *A History of Political Theory*, 161–62.

14. The original of this disputed passage and a discussion of it can be found in Shackleton Bailey, *Cicero's Letters to Atticus*, 5:161, 341–42. See also Douglas, *Cicero*, 29.

15. McKeon, "Introduction to the Philosophy of Cicero," 56ff.

16. Cicero is considered within six pages of Sabine's more than nine-hundred-page text. Sabine collaborated with Stanley Barney Smith on what is still the standard American edition of Cicero's *De Re Publica* (Sabine and Smith, *On the Commonwealth*).

17. See for example the impact of Mommsen in Haskell, *This Was Cicero*. Within Mommsen, see especially volume 5, Mommsen, *History of Rome*. Drumann's significance in the nineteenth-century interpretation of Cicero has been drawn to my attention by Douglas, *Cicero*, 4, and in Slaughter, "Cicero and His Critics," 123. Slaughter described Drumann as Cicero's "most diabolical detractor."

18. McKeon, "Introduction to the Philosophy of Cicero," 64.

19. Holton, "Marcus Tullius Cicero," 130.

20. Douglas, *Cicero*, 2, 31–32.

21. Cumming, *Human Nature and History*, 1:236.

22. Slaughter, "Cicero and His Critics," 130.

23. Robinson, *Eight Great Lives*, 146, 159, 181.

24. Ibid., 145, 160–63, 171.

25. Ibid., 167.

26. See his essays "On Solitariness," "A Consideration upon Cicero," and "Of Books" (Montaigne, *Complete Essays of Montaigne*).

27. Pascal, *Pensées*, i.31. The force of what is quoted here is even greater in the light of i.30.

28. Stahl, Johnson, and Burge, *Martianus Capella and the Seven Liberal Arts*, 232. There is a greater elaboration of this charge against Cicero in Stahl's earlier book *Roman Science*, wherein there is evidence of Mommsen's influence. Basic support for this charge but an overall much greater appreciation for Cicero is in evidence in Bird, *Cultures in Conflict*, especially 169–70.

29. Haskell's view, especially as captured in his last chapter, is one of the latest statements of "the two Ciceros" thesis (Haskell, *This Was Cicero*).

30. Cumming, *Human Nature and History*, 2:42ff.

31. Strauss, "Political Philosophy and History," 64.

32. Fink, *Classical Republicans*.

33. Ibid., x.

34. Ibid., 5.

35. Ibid., 157. The quotation in the previous sentence is Sydney as quoted by Fink.

36. Robbins, *The English Commonwealthman*.

37. Colburn, *Lamp of Experience*; Bailyn, *Pamphlets of the American Revolution* and *Ideological Origins of the American Revolution*; Pocock, *Machiavellian Moment*.

38. Cumming, *Human Nature and History*, 1:174.

39. Ibid., 227.

40. Strauss, "Criticism: Sixteen Appraisals," 291. It does not seem characteristic of the classical republicans to underestimate the importance to the political good of the moral qualities of the citizens.

41. Cumming, *Human Nature and History*, 1:234; Strauss, *Natural Right and History*, 135.

42. Strauss, *The City and Man*.

43. Strauss, "Restatement on Xenophon's *Hiero*," 127.

44. Strauss used this phrase in stating that Machiavelli was almost completely silent about Plato, Aristotle, "the political philosopher Cicero," and scholasticism. Strauss, *Thoughts on Machiavelli*, 290–91.

45. Strauss, *Natural Right and History*, 111.

46. Ibid., 168, 264, 271.

47. Strauss, *Liberalism Ancient and Modern*, 104. The phrase "native speech" is used in the translation of the relevant passage found in Latham, *On the Nature of the Universe*, 181.

48. Strauss, *Natural Right and History*, 107.

49. See, for example, the opening of the *De Officiis*.

50. In a letter to Quintus about a year after Lucretius's poem appeared, Cicero seems to have praised the poem as sparkling with genius and at the same time skillfully executed. The original (*multis luminibus ingenii, multae tamen artes*) has been differently interpreted as in E. S. Shuckburgh's translation: "The poems of Lucretius are as you say—with many flashes of genius, yet very technical." Shuckburgh, *Letters of Cicero*, 266.

51. Strauss, *Liberalism Ancient and Modern*, viii.

52. Strauss, *Political Philosophy: Six Essays*, 98. Regarding common sense, see "An Epilogue," which follows in this volume. See also Strauss, "Natural Law," 84.

53. Gildin has noted this in Strauss, *Political Philosophy: Six Essays*, xx.

54. Strauss, *The City and Man*, 13–14; *Natural Right and History*, 120.

55. Strauss, *The City and Man*, 13–14.

56. Strauss, *What Is Political Philosophy?*, 10, 27–28, 78, 80.

57. Ibid., 89.

58. Ibid., 38–39.

59. Strauss, *Political Philosophy: Six Essays*, 103.

60. Strauss, *The City and Man*, 18.

61. Strauss, *What Is Political Philosophy?*, 92–94; *Natural Right and History*, 152.

62. Strauss, *Persecution and the Art of Writing*, 11; see also "Natural Law," 82, and *Natural Right and History*, 146, 152ff.

63. Strauss, *Natural Right and History*, 163.
64. Ibid., 155–56.
65. See *Rep.* 1.18, 3.8–9, and *Fin.* 2.59, all of which are noted by Strauss after he made the interpretation under question here. So clearly, he considered these passages.
66. See especially *Rep.* 1.30, 33.
67. Strauss, "Plato," 41; *The City and Man*, 138; *Natural Right and History*, 122; and in *The Argument and the Action*, 1. In the last reference Strauss wrote that the *Republic* does not present "the best political order," suggesting that in fact no regime is presented in the *Republic* when it is properly understood. This line of interpretation would avoid the inconsistency pointed out in the remainder of this paragraph. *De Re Publica* 2.52 is the text of Cicero that Strauss has called upon in the four instances.
68. Strauss, "Natural Law," 81; see also Strauss, "Jerusalem and Athens," 57.
69. Strauss, *Natural Right and History*, 321.
70. Ibid., 151–52; *What Is Political Philosophy?*, 94. See especially Strauss's view of the "status of morality" in Strauss and Klein, "A Giving of Accounts."
71. Voegelin, *Anamnesis*, 99–101.
72. Voegelin, *Ecumenic Age*, 46, 40.
73. Voegelin, *New Science of Politics*, 87ff.
74. Ibid., passim, especially 168.
75. Ibid., 90.
76. Voegelin, *Ecumenic Age*, 128.
77. Ibid., 114.
78. Ibid., 128.
79. Rome never seems to get from Voegelin the measured respect he has for tradition-oriented later regimes as that in England and for regimes like the United States with a common-sense foundation.
80. Voegelin, *New Science of Politics*, 90–91.
81. Voegelin, *Ecumenic Age*, 237.
82. Voegelin, *Anamnesis*, 189.
83. Kendall and Wilhelmsen, *Cicero and the Politics of the Public Orthodoxy*, 97, 99.
84. Voegelin, *Plato and Aristotle*, 272.
85. Voegelin, *World of the Polis*, 13–14; *New Science of Politics*, 89, 91; *Ecumenic Age*, 44–47.
86 *Ecumenic Age*, 43–44.
87. Ibid., 39.
88. Voegelin, *World of the Polis*, 240.
89. Voegelin, "Oxford Political Philosophers," 101.

Bibliography

Achard, G., ed. *Cicéron: De l'Invention.* Paris: Les Belles Lettres, 1994.
———. "Langage et société: A Propos des *optimates* et des *populares.*" *Latomus* 41 (1982): 794–800.
von Albrecht, M. "Cicéron: Théorie rhétorique et pratique oratoire." *Les études classiques* 52 (1984): 19–24.
Alfonsi, L. "Dal proemio del *De inventione* alle virtutes del *De officiis.*" *Ciceroniana* 2 N.S. (1975): 111–20.
Algra, K. "The Mechanism of Social Appropriation and Its Role in Hellenistic Ethics." *Oxford Studies in Ancient Philosophy* 25 (Winter 2003): 265–96.
Allen, J. "Academic Probabilism and Stoic Epistemology." *Classical Quarterly* 44, no. 1 (1994): 85–113.
André, J.-M. *L'otium dans la vie morale et intellectuelle romaine.* Paris: P.U.F., 1966.
Annas, J. "Cicero on Stoic Moral Philosophy and Private Property." In *Philosophia Togata: Essays on Philosophy and Roman Society.* Edited by Miriam Griffin and Jonathan Barnes, 151–73. Oxford: Oxford University Press, 1989.
Annas, J., and J. Barnes, eds. *Outlines of Scepticism* by Sextus Empiricus. Cambridge: Cambridge University Press, 1994.
Appiah, K.A. *Cosmopolitanism: Ethics in a World of Strangers.* London: Allen Lane, 2006.
Arendt, H. *The Origins of Totalitarianism.* New ed. New York: Harcourt Brace Jovanovich, 1973.
Atkins, E.M. "Domina et Regina Virtutum: Justice and Societas in *De Officiis.*" *Phronesis* 35, no. 3 (1990): 258–89.
Bailyn, B. *The Ideological Origins of the American Revolution.* Cambridge, Mass.: Harvard University Press, 1967.
———. *Pamphlets of the American Revolution, 1750–1756.* Cambridge, Mass.: Harvard University Press, 1965.
Badian, E. "*Optimates, Populares.*" In *Oxford Classical Dictionary: The Ultimate Reference Work on the Classical World.* Rev. 3rd ed. Edited by Simon

Hornblower and Anthony Spawforth, 1070–71. Oxford: Oxford University Press, 2003.
Barlow, J. J. "The Education of Statesmen in Cicero's *De Republica*." *Polity* 19 (Spring 1987): 353–74.
Barwick, K. *Das rednerische Bildungsideal Ciceros*. Berlin: Akademia, 1963.
———. "Die Vorrede zum zweiten Buch der rhetorischen Jugendschrift Ciceros und zum vierten Buch des *Auctor ad Herennium*." *Philologus* 105 (1961): 307–14.
Beard, M., and M. Crawford. *Rome in the Late Republic*. Ithaca: Cornell University Press, 1985.
Beard, M. "Cicero and Divination: The Formation of a Latin Discourse." *Journal of Roman Studies* 76 (1986): 33–46.
Benardete, S. "Cicero's *De Legibus I*: Its Plan and Intention." *American Journal of Philology* 108, no. 2 (1987): 295–309.
Bénatouïl, T. "Le débat entre stoïcisme et platonisme à propos de la vie scolastique: Chrysippe, l'Ancienne Académie, Antiochus," in *Stoic Platonism and Platonic Stoicism*. Edited by M. Bonazzi and C. Helmig, 1–20. Leuven: Leuven University Press, 2007.
Béranger, J. "Les jugements de Cicéron sur les Gracques." In *Aufstieg und Niedergang der römischen Welt: Geschichte und Kultur im Spiegel der neueren Forschung*. Vol. 1. Edited by Hildegard Temporini, 732–63. Berlin: de Gruyter, 1972.
Bett, R. "Carneades' Distinction between Assent and Approval." *Monist* 73, no. 1 (1990): 3–20.
———. "Carneades' *Pithanon*: A Reappraisal of Its Role and Status." *Oxford Studies in Ancient Philosophy* 7 (1989): 59–94.
Bird, O. *Cultures in Conflict*. Notre Dame: University of Notre Dame Press, 1976.
Bobbio, N. *Democracy and Dictatorship: The Nature and Limits of State Power*. Minneapolis: University of Minnesota Press, 1989.
Bourdieu, P. "Rethinking the State: Genesis and Structure of the Bureaucratic Field." In *State/Culture: State Formation after the Cultural Turn*. Edited by G. Steinmetz, 53–75. Ithaca: Cornell University Press, 1999.
Boyancé, P. "Cicéron et la vie contemplative." *Latomus* 26 (1967): 3–26.
———. "*Cum Dignitate Otium*." *Revue des Études Antiques* 43 (1948): 172–91.
Brittain, C. *Philo of Larissa: The Last of the Academic Sceptics*. Oxford: Oxford University Press, 2001.
———, trans. *On Academic Scepticism*, by Cicero. Indianapolis: Hackett, 2006.
Brouwer, R. "Sagehood and the Stoics." *Oxford Studies in Ancient Philosophy* 23 (2002): 181–224.
Brunschwig, J. "The Cradle Argument in Epicureanism and Stoicism." In *The Norms of Nature: Studies in Hellenistic Ethics*. Edited by M. Schofield and G. Striker, 113–44. Cambridge: Cambridge University Press, 1986.

Brunt, P.A. "Aspects of the Social Thought of Dio Chrysostom and of the Stoics." *Proceedings of the Cambridge Philological Society* 19 (1973): 9–34.
———. "Cicero's *Officium* in the Civil War." *Journal of Roman Studies* 76 (1986): 12–32.
Büchner, K. *Cicero, De Re Publica: Kommentar*. Heidelberg: Winter, 1984.
Burckhardt, L.A. "Optimates." In *Der Neue Pauly Enzyklopädie der Antike*. Vol. 8. Edited by H. Cancik and H. Schneider, 1270–73. Weimar: Metzler, 2000.
Burnyeat, M. "Antipater and Self-Refutation: Elusive Arguments in Cicero's *Academica*." In *Assent and Argument: Studies in Cicero's Academic Books*. Edited by B. Inwood and J. Mansfeld, 277–310. Leiden: Brill, 1997.
Butler, S. *The Hand of Cicero*. London and New York: Routledge, 2002.
Canovan, M. *Nationhood and Political Theory*. Cheltenham and Brookfield, Vt.: Edward Elgar, 1996.
———. *The People*. Cambridge: Polity, 2005.
Carcopino, J. *La République romaine de 133 à 44 avant J.C. II: César*. Paris: Les Presses Universitaires de France, 1936.
Carter, J.M. "Cicero: Politics and Philosophy." In *Cicero and Virgil: Studies in Honour of Harold Hunt*. Edited by J.R.C. Martyn, 15–36. Amsterdam: Adolf M. Hakkert, 1972.
Colburn, W.T. *The Lamp of Experience*. Chapel Hill: University of North Carolina Press, 1965.
Cornell, T.J. *The Beginnings of Rome*. London and New York: Routledge, 1995.
———. "Cicero on the Origins of Rome." In *Cicero's Republic: Bulletin of the Institute of Classical Studies Supplement 76*. Edited by J.G.F. Powell and J.A. North, 41–56. London: Institute of Classical Studies, University of London, 2001.
Cumming, R.D. *Human Nature and History: A Study of the Development of Liberal Political Thought*. 2 vols. Chicago: University of Chicago Press, 1969.
David, J.-M.. "Eloquentia *popularis* et conduites symboliques des orateurs de la fin de la république: Problemes de l'efficacité." *Quaderni di storia* 6, no. 12 (1980): 171–211.
———. *The Roman Conquest of Italy*. Cambridge, Mass.: Harvard University Press, 1997.
DeFilippo, J.G. "Cicero vs. Cotta in *De natura deorum*." *Ancient Philosophy* 20 (2000): 169–87.
Douglas, A.E. "Cicero the Philosopher." In *Cicero*. Edited by T.A. Dorey, 135–70. London: Routledge and Kegan Paul, 1965.
———. *Cicero*. Oxford: Clarendon, 1968.
Dugan, J. *Making a New Man: Ciceronian Self-Fashioning in the Rhetorical Works*. Oxford: Oxford University Press, 2005.

Dyck, A. R. *A Commentary on Cicero, De Legibus.* Ann Arbor: University of Michigan Press, 2004.

———. *A Commentary on Cicero, De Officiis.* Ann Arbor: University of Michigan Press, 1996.

———, ed. *De natura deorum, liber I.* Cambridge: Cambridge University Press, 2003.

Engberg-Pedersen, T. *The Stoic Theory of Oikeiosis: Moral Development and Social Interaction in Early Stoic Philosophy.* Aarhus: Aarhus University Press, 1990.

Erskine, A. *The Hellenistic Stoa.* Ithaca: Cornell University Press, 1990.

Falconer, W. A., trans. *De senectute, De amicitia, De divinatione,* by Cicero. Cambridge, Mass.: Harvard University Press, 1996.

Ferrary, J.-L. "Le discours de Philus (Cicéron, *de re publica* III, 8–31) et la philosophie de Carnéade." *Revue des etudes latines* 55 (1977): 128–56.

———. "*Optimates* et *Populares*: Le problèm du rôle de l'idéologie dans la politique." In *Die späte römische Republik / La fin de le république romaine: Un débat Franco-Allemand d'histoire et d'historiographie.* Edited by H. Bruhns, J.-M. David, and W. Nippel, 221–35. Rome: École Française de Rome, 1997.

———. "Statesman and Law in Cicero's Political Philosophy." In *Justice and Generosity: Studies in Hellenistic Social and Political Philosophy.* Edited by A. Laks and M. Schofield, 48–73. Cambridge: Cambridge University Press, 1995.

Fetter, J., and W. Nicgorski. "Magnanimity and Statesmanship: The Ciceronian Difference." In *Magnanimity and Statesmanship.* Edited by Carson Holloway, 29–47. Lanham, MD: Rowman & Littlefield, 2008.

Fink, Z. *The Classical Republicans.* Evanston: Northwestern University Press, 1945.

Frede, M. "The Skeptic's Two Kinds of Assent and the Question of the Possibility of Knowledge." In *Philosophy in History: Essays on the Historiography of Philosophy.* Edited by R. Rorty, J. B. Schneewind, and Q. Skinner, 255–78. Cambridge: Cambridge University Press, 1984.

———. "On the Stoic Conception of the Good." In *Topics in Stoic Philosophy.* Edited by K. Ierodiakonou. Oxford: Oxford University Press, 1999.

Garsten, B. *Saving Persuasion: A Defense of Rhetoric and Judgment.* Cambridge, Mass.: Harvard University Press, 2006.

Geuss, R. *Public Goods, Private Goods.* Princeton: Princeton University Press, 2003.

Giddens, A. *A Contemporary Critique of Historical Materialism.* Vol. 2 of *The Nation-State and Violence.* Cambridge: Polity, 1987.

Gill, C. "Personhood and Personality: The Four-*Personae* Theory in Cicero, de Officiis I." *Oxford Studies in Ancient Philosophy* 6 (1988): 169–99.

Girardet, K. M. *Die Ordnung der Welt: Ein Beitrag zur philosophischen und politischen Interpretation von Cicero's Schrift De Legibus*. Wiesbaden: Franz Steiner, 1983.

Giuffrida P. "I due proemi del *De inventione* (I, 1–4, 5; II, 1–3, 10)." In *Lanx satura N. Terzaghi oblata*, 113–216. Genova: Fratelli Pagano, 1963.

Glucker, J. "Cicero's Philosophical Affiliations." In *The Question of "Eclecticism": Studies in Later Greek Philosophy*. Edited by J. M. Dillon and A. A. Long, 34–69. Berkeley and Los Angeles: University of California Press, 1988.

———. "Cicero's Philosophical Affiliations Again." *Liverpool Classical Monthly* 17 (1992): 134–38.

———. "The Philonian/Metrodoreans: Problems of Method in Ancient Philosophy." *Elenchos* 25 (2004): 99–152.

———. "*Probabile, Veri Simile*, and Related Terms." In *Cicero the Philosopher: Twelve Papers*. Edited by J. G. F. Powell, 115–44. Oxford: Clarendon, 1995.

Goodwin, J. "Cicero's Authority." *Philosophy and Rhetoric* 34, no. 1 (2001): 38–60.

Gordis, W. S. *The Estimates of Moral Values Expressed in Cicero's Letters: A Study of Motives Professed or Approved*. Chicago: University of Chicago Press (PhD thesis), 1905.

Görler, W. "Silencing the Troublemaker: *De Legibus* 1.39 and the Continuity of Cicero's Scepticism." In *Cicero the Philosopher*. Edited by J. G. F. Powell, 85–113. Oxford: Oxford University Press, 1995.

———. "Cicero's Philosophical Stance in the *Lucullus*." In *Assent and Argument: Studies in Cicero's Academic Books*. Edited by B. Inwood and J. Mansfeld, 36–57. Leiden: Brill, 1997.

Gorman, R. *The Socratic Method in the Dialogues of Cicero*. Stuttgart: Franz Steiner, 2005.

Graver, M. *Cicero on the Emotions: Tusculan Disputations 3–4*. Chicago: University of Chicago Press, 2002.

———. "Cicero's Philosophy of Religion." In *History of the Western Philosophy of Religion*. Edited by G. Oppy and N. Trakakis. Durham: Acumen, 2009.

———. *Stoicism and Emotion*. Chicago: University of Chicago Press, 2007.

Griffin, M. T., and E. M. Atkins, eds. *Cicero: On Duties*. Cambridge: Cambridge University Press, 1991.

Grilli, A. *Il problema della vita contemplativa nel mondo greco-romano*. Milan: Bocca, 1953.

Gruen, E. S. "The Exercise of Power in the Roman Republic." In *City States in Classical Antiquity and Medieval Italy*. Edited by J. Emlen, A. Molho, and K. Raaflaub, 251–67. Ann Arbor: University of Michigan Press, 1991.

Haakonsen, K. "Republicanism." In *A Companion to Contemporary Political Philosophy*. Edited by P. Pettit and R. E. Goodin, 568–74. Cambridge, Mass.: Blackwell, 1993.

Habermas, J. "The European Nation-State: On the Past and Future of Sovereignty and Citizenship." In *The Inclusion of the Other: Studies in Political Theory*. Edited by C. Cronin and P. D. Grieff, 105–27. Cambridge, Mass.: MIT Press, 1998.

Habicht, C. *Cicero the Politician*. Balitmore: Johns Hopkins University Press, 1990.

Habinek, T. *The Politics of Latin Literature*. Princeton: Princeton University Press, 1998.

———. "Towards a History of Friendly Advice: The Politics of Candor in Cicero's *de Amicitia*." *Apeiron* 24 (1991): 165–85.

Hall, U. "Greeks and Romans and the Secret Ballot." In *Owls to Athens: Essays on Classical Subjects Presented to Sir Kenneth Dover*. Edited by E. M. Craik, 191–99. Oxford: Clarendon, 1990.

Haskell, H. J. *This Was Cicero*. New York: Knopf, 1942.

Hathaway, R. F. "Cicero, *De Re Publica II*, and His Socratic View of History." *Journal of the History of Ideas* 29, no. 1 (1968): 3–12.

Heck, E. *Die Bezeugung von Ciceros Schrift De Republica*. Hildesheim: Olms, 1966.

Heinze, R. "Ciceros Staat als politische Tendenzschrift." *Hermes* 59 (1924): 73–94.

———. *Vom Geist des Römertums*. 3rd ed. Darmstadt: Wissenschaftliche Buchgesellschaft, 1960.

Hellegouarc'h, J. *Le vocabulaire latin des relations et des partis politiques sous la république*. Paris: Les Belles Lettres, 1963.

Holmes, T. R. *The Roman Republic and the Founder of the Empire*. Vol. 1 of *From the Origins to 58 B.C.* Oxford: Clarendon, 1923.

Holton, J. "Marcus Tullius Cicero." In *History of Political Philosophy*. Edited by Leo Strauss and Joseph Cropsey, 130–50. Chicago: Rand McNally, 1963.

Hume, D. *Essays: Moral, Political, and Literary*. Rev. ed. Edited by E. F. Miller. Indianapolis: Liberty Fund, 1987.

———. *Of the Standard of Taste and Other Essays*. Edited by J. W. Lenz. Indianapolis: Bobbs-Merrill, 1965.

Inwood, B. *Reading Seneca*. Oxford: Clarendon, 2005.

Jackson-McCabe, M. "The Stoic Theory of Implanted Conceptions." *Phronesis* 49 (2005): 323–47.

Jakobi, R., ed. *Grillius, Commentum in Ciceronis Rhetorica*. Munich and Leipzig: Saur, 2002.

Joly, R. *Le theme des genres de vie dans l'Antiquité classique*. Bruxelles: Palais des Académies, 1956.

Jonkers, E. J. *Social and Economic Commentary on Cicero's* De Lege Agraria Orationes Tres. Leiden: Brill, 1963.

Kaster, R. A. *Emotion, Restraint, and Community in Ancient Rome*. New York: Oxford University Press, 2005.

Kempshall, M. S. "*De Re Publica* I.39 in Medieval and Renaissance Political Thought." In *Cicero's Republic: Bulletin of the Institute of Classical Studies Supplement 76*. Edited by J. G. F. Powell and J. A. North, 99–135. London: Institute of Classical Studies, University of London, 2001.

Kendall, W. and F. D. Wilhelmsen. *Cicero and the Politics of the Public Orthodoxy*. Pamplona: Universidad De Navarra, 1965. Reprinted with additional notes and better editing in *The Intercollegiate Review*. 5:2 (1968–1969): 84–100.

Keyes, C. W., trans. *De Re Publica, De Legibus*, by Cicero. Cambridge, Mass.: Harvard University Press, 1928.

King, P., trans. *Against the Academics and the Teacher*, by St. Augustine. Indianapolis: Hackett, 1995.

Krarup, P. *Rector Rei Publicae: Bidrag til fortolkningen af Ciceros De Re Publica*. Copenhagen, 1956.

Kretschmar, M. *Otium, studia litterarum, Philosophie und* βίον θεορητικόν *im Leben und Denken Ciceros*. Diss. Leipzig, 1938.

Lacey, W. K. "Cicero, *Pro Sestio* 961–43." *Classical Quarterly*, N.S. 12, no. 1 (1962): 67–71.

———. *Cicero and the End of the Roman Republic*. London: Hodder and Stoughton, 1978.

———, and Wilson, B. W. J. C. *Res Publica*. London: Oxford University Press, 1970.

Lana, I. "La scuola dei Sestii." In *La langue latine, langue de la philosophie*. Edited by P. Grimal, 109–24. Rome: École Française de Rome, 1992.

Latham, R. E., trans. *On the Nature of the Universe*, by Lucretius. Baltimore: Penguin, 1951.

Leeman, A. D., H. Pinster, and J. Wisse. *M. Tullius Cicero*, De oratore libri III. Heidelberg: Winter, 1996.

Levine, P. "Cicero and the Literary Dialogue." *Classical Journal* 53 (1958): 146–51.

———. "The Original Design and the Publication of the *De natura deorum*." *Harvard Studies in Classical Philology* 62 (1957): 7–36.

Lévy, C. *Cicero Academicus*. Rome: École Française de Rome, 1992.

———. "L'âme et le moi dans les *Tusculanes*." *Revue des Etudes Latines* 80 (2002): 78–84.

———. "Le mythe de la naissance de la civilisation chez Cicéron." In *Mathesis e Philia: Studi in honore di Marcello Gigante*, 155–68. Napoli: Dip. Di Filologia Classica dell'Università degli Studi di Napoli, 1995.

Lintott, A. "Legal Procedure in Cicero's Time." In *Cicero the Advocate*. Edited by J. Powell and J. Paterson, 61–78. Oxford: Oxford University Press, 2004.

Locke, John. *Two Treatises of Government*. Edited by P. Laslett. Cambridge: Cambridge University Press, 1988.

Long, A. A., and D. N. Sedley. *The Hellenistic Philosophers*. 2 Vols. Cambridge: Cambridge University Press, 1987.

Long, A. A. "Carneades and the Stoic Telos." *Phronesis* 12 (1967): 59–90.

———. "Cicero's Plato and Aristotle." In *Cicero the Philosopher: Twelve Papers*. Edited by J. G. F. Powell, 37–61. New York: Oxford University Press, 1995.

———. "Cicero's Politics in *De Officiis*." In *Justice and Generosity: Studies in Hellenistic Social and Political Philosophy*. Edited by A. Laks and M. Schofield, 213–40. Cambridge: Cambridge University Press, 1995.

———. "Stoic Philosophers on Persons, Property-Ownership, and Community." In *Aristotle and After*. Edited by R. Sorabji, 13–31. London: Institute of Classical Studies, 1997.

Lord, C., trans. *Politics*, by Aristotle. Chicago: University of Chicago Press, 1984.

Luther, M. "An Open Letter to the Christian Nobility." In *Three Treatises*, 3–111. Philadelphia: Fortress, 1960.

MacKendrick, P. *The Philosophical Books of Cicero*. London: Duckworth, 1989.

Mackie, N. "*Popularis* Ideology and Popular Politics in the First Century B.C." *Rheinisches Museum für Philologie* 135, no. 1 (1992): 49–74.

Machiavelli, Niccolo. *The Prince*. Translated by H. C. Mansfield. Chicago: University of Chicago Press, 1985.

Mähly, J. "Zu Cicero de re publica." *Zeitschrift für das Gymnasialwesen* NS 1 (1867): 806–16.

Mansfeld, J. "Philo and Antiochus in the Lost *Catulus*." *Mnemosyne* 50, no. 1 (1997): 45–74.

Manuwald, G., ed. *Der Satiriker Lucilius und seine Zeit*. Zetemata 110. Munich: Beck, 2001.

Marquez, X., and W. Nicgorski. "La loi de la nature et la nature de la loi dans la pensée politique de Cicéron." In *Droit naturel: Relancer histoire*. Edited by Xavier Dijon et al., 157–91. Bruxelles: Bruylant, 2008.

May, J. M. *Trials of Character: The Eloquence of Ciceronian Ethos*. Chapel Hill: University of North Carolina Press, 1988.

Mayor, J. B. Introduction to *De natura deorum*, by M. Tulli Ciceronis. 3 Vols. Cambridge: Cambridge University Press, 1880–1885.

McDermott, W. C. "Cicero's Publication of His Consular Orations." *Philologus* 116 (1972): 277–84.

McKeon, R. "Introduction to the Philosophy of Cicero." In Poteat, H. M., trans, 1–65. *Brutus: On the Nature of the Gods, On Divination, On Duties*, by Cicero. Chicago: University of Chicago Press, 1950.

Meier, C. *Caesar*. Translated by D. McLintock. New York: Basic, 1995.

———. "Populares." *Paulys Realencyclopädie der Classischen Altertumswissenschaft*. Supplementband 10 (1965): 550–615.

Meyer, E. *Legitimacy and Law in the Roman World*. Cambridge: Cambridge University Press, 2004.

Millar, F. *The Roman Republic in Political Thought*. Hanover and London: Brandeis University Press, 2002.
Mitsis, P. 1994. "Natural Law and Natural Right in Post-Aristotelian Philosophy: The Stoics and Their Critics." *Aufstieg und Niedergang der römischen Welt* 2.36.7. 4812–50.
———. "The Stoics on Property and Politics." *Ancient Greek Ethics and Political Philosophy: Southern Journal of Philosophy* 43 (2005 supp.): 230–49.
Momigliano, A. "The Theological Efforts of the Roman Upper Classes in the First Century B.C." *Classical Philology* 79 (July 1984): 199–211.
Mommsen, T. *The History of Rome*. 5 vols. Translated by W. P. Dickson. New York: Scribner's Sons, 1905.
Montaigne, Michel de. *The Complete Essays of Montaigne*. Translated by D. M. Frame. Stanford: Stanford University Press, 1958, 1965.
Montesquieu. "Discourse on Cicero" [in French]. In *Oeuvres Complètes*. Vol. 1. Edited by Roger Caillois, 93–98. Paris: Gallimard, 1949.
Morstein-Marx, R. *Mass Oratory and Political Power in the Late Roman Republic*. Cambridge: Cambridge University Press, 2004.
Müller, R. "Βίος Θεωρητικός bei Antiochos von Askalon und Cicero." *Helikon* 8 (1968): 222–37.
———. "Das Problem Theorie-Praxis in der Peripatos-Rezeption von Ciceros Staatsschrift." In *Cicero's Knowledge of the Peripatos*. Edited by W. W. Fortenbaugh and P. Steinmetz, 101–13. New Brunswick: Transactions, 1989.
Muret, M-A. *Opera Omnia*. Edited by C. H. Frotscher. Lipse, 1841. Reprint, Geneva: Slatkine, 1971.
Nagle, D. B. *The Household as the Foundation of Aristotle's Polis*. New York: Cambridge University Press, 2006.
Narducci, E. *Cicerone e l'eloquenza romana*. Rome-Bari: Laterza, 1997.
———. *Modelli etici e società: un'idea di Cicerone*. Pisa: Giardini, 1989.
Nederman, C. J. "Nature, Sin, and the Origins of Society: The Ciceronian Tradition in Medieval Political Thought." *Journal of the History of Ideas* 49, no. 1 (January 1988): 3–26.
Nicgorski, W. "Cicero, Citizenship, and the Epicurean Temptation." In *Cultivating Citizens*. Edited by Dwight Allman and Michael Beatty, 3–28. Lanham, MD: Rowman & Littlefield, 2002.
———. "Cicero's Distinctive Voice on Friendship: *De Amicitia* and *De Re Publica*." In *Friendship and Politics: Essays in Political Thought*. Edited by John von Heyking and Richard Avramenko, 84–111. Notre Dame, Ind.: University of Notre Dame Press, 2008.
———. "Cicero's Focus: From the Best Regime To the Model Statesman," *Political Theory* 19 (May 1991): 230–51.
———. "Cicero's Paradoxes and His Idea of Utility." *Political Theory* 12 (November 1984): 557–78.

_____. "Cicero and the Rebirth of Political Philosophy." *Political Science Reviewer* 8 (Fall 1978): 63–101.

_____. "Cicero's Socrates: Assessment of 'the Socratic Turn.'" In *Law and Philosophy: The Practice of Theory*. Edited by J. Murley, R. Stone, and W. Braithwaite, 1:213–33. Athens: Ohio University Press, 1992.

———. "Nationalism and Transnationalism in Cicero." *History of European Ideas* 16 (1993): 785–91.

Nichols, M. P. *Citizens and Statesmen: A Study of Aristotle's Politics.* Lanham, MD: Rowman & Littlefield, 1992.

Nicolet, C. *Le métier de citoyen dans la Rome républicaine.* Paris: Gallimard, 1976.

Nussbaum, M. C. "Duties of Justice, Duties of Material Aid: Cicero's Problematic Legacy." *The Journal of Political Philosophy* 8 (2000): 176–206.

Pangle, T. L. "Socratic Cosmopolitanism: Cicero's Critique and Transformation of the Stoic Ideal." *Canadian Journal of Political Science* 31, no. 2 (1998): 235–62.

Pascal, B. *Pensées*. [no trans.]. New York: E. M. Dutton, 1958.

Pease, A. S. "The Conclusion of Cicero's De Natura Deorum." *Transactions and Proceedings of the American Philological Association* 44 (1913): 25–37.

———. Introduction to De natura deorum, by M. Tulli Ciceronis. 2 vols. Cambridge, Mass.: Harvard University Press, 1955–58.

———, ed. De divinatione, by M. Tulli Ciceronis. Darmstadt: Wissenschaftliche Buchgesellschaft, 1963.

Petersson, T. *Cicero: A Biography.* Berkeley: University of California Press, 1920. Reprint, New York: Biblo and Tannen, 1963.

Pettit, P. *Republicanism: A Theory of Freedom and Government.* Oxford: Clarendon, 1997.

Pocock, J. G. A. *The Machiavellian Moment.* Princeton: Princeton University Press, 1975.

Poteat, H. M., trans. *Brutus, On the Nature of the Gods, On Divination, On Duties,* by Cicero. Chicago: University of Chicago Press, 1950.

Powell, J. G. F. "Introduction: Cicero's Philosophical Works and their Background." In *Cicero the Philosopher*. Edited by J. G. F. Powell, 1–35. Oxford: Clarendon, 1995.

———. "The *rector rei publicae* of Cicero's De Republica." *Scripta Classica Israelica* 13 (1994): 19–29.

———. "Second Thoughts on the Dream of Scipio." *Proceedings of the Leeds International Latin Seminar* 9 (1996): 13–27.

———. "Were Cicero's Laws the Laws of Cicero's Republic?" In *Cicero's Republic: Bulletin of the Institute of Classical Studies Supplement 76.* Edited by J. G. F. Powell and J. A. North, 17–39. London: Institute of Classical Studies, University of London, 2001.

———. "Review of Zetzel, *Cicero De Re Publica, selections*, Cambridge 1995." *Classical Review* 46 (1996): 247–50.

———, and J. A. North, eds. *Cicero's Republic: Bulletin of the Institute of Classical Studies Supplement 76* (2001).

———, ed. *M. Tulli Ciceronis De Re Publica, De Legibus, Cato Maior de Senectute, Laelius de Amicitia*. Oxford Classical Texts. Oxford: Oxford University Press, 2006.

Price, J. V. "Sceptics in Cicero and Hume." *Journal of the History of Ideas* 25 (January–March 1964): 97–106.

Rackham, H. Introduction to and Translation of *De natura deorum, Academica*, by Cicero. Rev. ed. Loeb Classical Library. Cambridge, Mass.: Harvard University Press, 1951, 1994.

Radice, R. *Oikeiôsis*. Milan: Vita e pensiero, 2000.

Raphael, D. D. *Concepts of Justice*. Oxford: Oxford University Press, 2001.

Rawls, J. *A Theory of Justice*. Cambridge, Mass.: Harvard University Press, 1971.

Rawson, E. *Cicero: A Portrait*. London: Allen Lane, 1975, 1983.

———. "The Interpretation of Cicero's *De Legibus*." In *Roman Culture and Society*, 125–48. Oxford: Oxford University Press, 1991.

Reid, J. S., ed. *The Academica of Cicero*. London: Macmillan, 1885.

Reydams-Schils, G. *Demiurge and Providence: Stoic and Platonist Readings of Plato's Timaeus*. Turnhout: Brepols, 1999.

Robbins, Caroline. *The English Commonwealthman*. Cambridge, Mass.: Harvard University Press, 1959.

Robinson Jr., C. A., ed. *Eight Great Lives*, by Plutarch. Dryden translation revised by A. H. Clough. New York: Holt, Rinehart and Winston, 1960.

Ruch, M. *L'Hortensius de Cicéron*. Paris: Les Belles Lettres, 1958.

Rudd, N. and J. Powell, trans. *The Republic and the Laws*, by Cicero. Oxford: Oxford University Press, 1998.

Sabine, G. H., and S. B. Smith, trans. *On the Commonwealth*, by Cicero. Columbus: Ohio State University Press, 1929.

Sabine, G. H., and T. Thorson. *A History of Political Theory*. 4th ed. Hinsdale, Ill.: Dryden, 1973. Published in 1960 solely under Sabine's name.

Sagan, C. *Cosmos*. New York: Random, 1980.

Schlatter, R. *Private Property: The History of an Idea*. New Brunswick: Rutgers University Press, 1951.

Schmidt, P. L. "Cicero 'De re publica': Die Forschung der letzten fünf Dezennien." *Aufstieg und Niedergang der römischen Welt* I.4 (1973): 262–333.

Schmitz, S. "Rhetorik in Praxis und Theorie: Cicero: *Pro Sestio / De Inventione*." *Der Altsprachliche Unterricht* 38 (1995): 41–53.

Schofield, M. "Ariston of Chios and the Unity of Virtue." *Ancient Philosophy* 4 (1984): 83–96.

———. "Cicero's Definition of *Res Publica*." In *Cicero the Philosopher: Twelve Papers*. Edited by J. G. F. Powell, 63–81. New York: Oxford University Press, 1995.

———. "Cicero For and Against Divination." *Journal of Roman Studies* 76 (1986): 47–65.

———. "Epictetus on Cynicism." In *The Philosophy of Epictetus*. Edited by T. Scaltsas and A. S. Mason, 71–86. Oxford: Oxford University Press, 2007.

———. "Epicurean and Stoic Political Thought." In *The Cambridge History of Greek and Roman Political Thought*. Edited by Christopher Rowe and Malcolm Schofield, 435–56. Cambridge: Cambridge University Press, 2000.

———. "Morality and the Law: The Case of Diogenes of Babylon." In *Saving the City: Philosopher-Kings and Other Classical Paradigms*, 160–77. New York: Routledge, 1999.

———. "Plato on the Economy." In *Saving the City: Philosopher Kings and Other Classical Paradigms*, 69–81. New York: Routledge, 1999. Reprint from *The Ancient Greek City State*. Edited by M. H. Hansen, 1993.

———. *Saving the City: Philosopher-Kings and Other Classical Paradigms*. London: Routledge, 1999.

———. *The Stoic Idea of the City*. Cambridge: Cambridge University Press, 1991.

———. "Two Stoic Approaches to Justice." In *Justice and Generosity: Studies in Hellenistic Social and Political Philosophy*. Edited by A. Laks and M. Schofield, 191–212. Cambridge: Cambridge University Press, 1995.

Schulz, F. *History of Roman Legal Science*. Oxford: Oxford University Press, 1946.

Seager, R. "Cicero and the Word *Popularis*." *Classical Quarterly* 22, no. 2 (1972): 328–38.

Sedley, D. "Plato's *Auctoritas* and Rebirth of the Commentary Tradition." In *Philosophia Togata II: Plato and Aristotle at Rome*. Edited by J. Barnes and M. Griffin, 110–129. Oxford: Oxford University Press, 1997.

Shackleton Bailey, D. R., ed. *Cicero's Letters to Atticus*. Volumes 1–7. Cambridge: Cambridge University Press, 1965–1970.

———, trans. and ed. *Cicero's Letters to Atticus*. New York: Penguin, 1978.

Shuckburgh, E. S., trans. *The Letters of Cicero*. Vol. 1. London: George Bell, 1908.

Singer, P. *One World*. New Haven: Yale University Press, 2002.

Slaughter, M. S. "Cicero and His Critics." *Classical Journal* 3 (December 1921): 120–31.

Smith, A. D. *Nationalism*. Cambridge: Polity Press, 2001.

Solmsen, F. "New Fragments of Cicero's *De Re Publica*." *Classical Philology* 35 (1940): 423–24.

Soreth, M. "Die zweite Telosformel des Antipater von Tarsos." *Archiv für Geschichte der Philosophie* 50 (1968): 48–72.

Squires, S. *Asconius Pedianus, Quintus: Commentaries on Five Speeches of Cicero*. Bristol: Bristol Classical, 1990.

Stahl, W. H., R. Johnson, and E. L. Burge. *Martianus Capella and the Seven Liberal Arts.* New York: Columbia University Press, 1971.
de Ste. Croix, G. E. M. *The Class Struggle in the Ancient Greek World.* Ithaca: Cornell University Press, 1981.
Stahl, W. H. *Roman Science.* Madison: University of Wisconsin Press, 1962.
Steel, C. E. W. *Reading Cicero.* London: Duckworth, 2005.
Steinmetz, P. "Beobachtungen zu Ciceros philosophischem Standpunkt." In *Cicero's Knowledge of the Peripatos.* Edited by W. W. Fortenbaugh and P. Steinmetz, 1–22. New Brunswick: Transaction, 1989.
Stem, R. "Cicero as Orator and Philosopher: The Value of the *Pro Murena* for Ciceronian Political Thought." *Review of Politics* 68 (2006): 206–31.
Strauss, L. *The Argument and the Action of Plato's "Laws."* Chicago: University of Chicago Press, 1975.
———. *The City and Man.* Chicago: Rand McNally, 1964.
———, and Jacob Klein. "A Giving of Accounts." *The College* (St. John's College Magazine) 22, no. 1 (April, 1970): 1–5.
———. "Jerusalem and Athens: Some Introductory Reflections." *Commentary* 43, no. 6 (June, 1967): 45–57.
———. *Liberalism Ancient and Modern.* New York: Basic, 1968.
———. "Natural Law." *International Encyclopedia of the Social Sciences.* 2 vols. Macmillan, 1968, 80–90.
———. *Natural Right and History.* Chicago: University of Chicago Press, 1953.
———. *Persecution and the Art of Writing.* Glencoe, Ill.: Free Press, 1952.
———. "Plato." In *History of Political Philosophy.* Edited by Leo Strauss and Joseph Cropsey, 7–63. Chicago: Rand McNally, 1963.
———. "Political Philosophy and History," "Restatement on Xenophon's Hiero," "Criticism: Sixteen Appraisals." In *What Is Political Philosophy?* 56–77, 95–133, 261–311. Westport, Conn.: Greenwood Press, 1973.
———. *Political Philosophy: Six Essays by Leo Strauss.* Edited with an Introduction by Hilail Gildin. Indianapolis: Bobbs-Merrill, 1975.
———. *Thoughts on Machiavelli.* Glencoe, Ill.: Free Press, 1958.
Striker, G. "Sceptical Strategies." In *Doubt and Dogmatism.* Edited by M. Schofield, M. Burnyeat, and J. Barnes, 54–83. Oxford: Oxford University Press, 1980.
———. *Essays in Hellenistic Epistemology and Ethics.* Cambridge: Cambridge University Press, 1996.
Suerbaum, W. "Studienbibliographie zu Ciceros De re publica." *Gymnasium* 85 (1978): 59–88.
Sumner, G. V. "Cicero, Pompeius, and Rullus." *Transactions of the American Philological Association* (1966): 569–82.
Syme, R. *Sallust.* Berkeley: University of California Press, 1964.
Taran, L. "Cicero's Attitude towards Stoicism and Skepticism in the *De natura deorum.*" In *Florilegium Columbianum: Essays in Honor of Paul*

Oskar Kristeller. Edited by K.-L. Selig and R. Somerville, 1–22. New York: Italica, 1987.

Taylor, L. R. *Party Politics in the Age of Caesar*. Berkeley: University of California Press, 1949.

Tieleman, T. *Chrysippus' On Affections: Reconstruction and Interpretation*. Leiden: Brill, 2003.

Treggiari, S. "Ancestral Virtues and Vices: Cicero on Nature, Nurture and Presentation." In *Myth, History and Culture in Republican Rome: Studies in Honor of T. P. Wiseman*. Edited by D. Braund and C. Gill, 139–64. Exeter: University of Exeter Press, 2003.

Trollope, A. *The Life of Cicero*. 2 vols. 1880. Reprint of the first edition. New York: Arno, 1981.

Tyrrell, W. B. *A Legal and Historical Commentary to Cicero's* Oratio Pro C. Rabirio Perduellionis Reo. Amsterdam: Hakkert, 1978.

Vasaly, A. *Representations: Images of the World in Ciceronian Oratory*. Berkeley: University of California Press, 1993.

Viroli, M. *Republicanism*. 1st American ed. New York: Hill and Wang, 2002.

Voegelin, E. *Anamnesis*. Edited and translated by Gerhart Niemeyer. Notre Dame, Ind.: University of Notre Dame Press, 1978.

———. *The Ecumenic Age*. Baton Rouge: Louisiana State University Press, 1974.

———. *The New Science of Politics*. Chicago: University of Chicago Press, 1952.

———. "The Oxford Political Philosophers." *The Philosophical Quarterly* 3 (April 1953): 97–114.

———. *Plato and Aristotle*. Baton Rouge: Louisiana State University Press, 1957.

———. *The World of the Polis*. Baton Rouge: Louisiana State University Press, 1957.

Vivenza, G. "Renaissance Cicero: The 'Economic' Virtues of *De Officiis* I, 22 in Some Sixteenth-Century Commentaries." *European Journal of the History of Economic Thought* 11, no. 4 (2004): 507–23.

Walcot, P. "Cicero on Private Property: Theory and Practice." *Greece and Rome* 2nd ser. 22 (October 1975): 120–28.

Walsh, P. G. Introduction to *The Nature of the Gods*, by Cicero. Oxford: Oxford University Press, 1998.

Walzer, M. *What It Means to Be an American: Essays on the American Experience*. New York: Marsilio, 1996.

Waszink, J., ed. *Timaeus: A Calcidio translatus commentarioque instructus*. London: Warburg Institute, 1975.

Watson, A. *Roman Private Law*. Edinburgh: Edinburgh University Press, 1971.

Weber, M. *Economy and Society*. Translated by G. Roth and K. Wittich. 2 vols. Berkeley: University of California Press, 1978.

Winterbottom, M., ed. *M. Tulli Ciceronis De Officiis*. Oxford: Clarendon, 1994.
Wiseman, T. P. "The Necessary Lesson." *Times Literary Supplement* (June 15–21, 1990): 647–48.
———. *New Men in the Roman Senate, 139 B.C.–A.D. 14*. London: Oxford University Press, 1971.
Wistrand, M. *Cicero Imperator: Studies in Cicero's Correspondence, 51–47 BC*. Goteborg: Acta Universitatis Gothoburgensis, 1979.
Wood, N. *Cicero's Social and Political Thought*. Berkeley: University of California Press, 1988.
———. "The Economic Dimension of Cicero's Political Thought: Property and State." *Canadian Journal of Political Science* 16 (December 1983): 739–56.
Yack, B. "Popular Sovereignty and Nationalism." *Political Theory* 29 (2001): 517–36.
Yakobson, A. "Secret Ballot and its Effects in the Late Roman Republic." *Hermes* 123 (1995): 426–42.
Yonge, C. D., trans. *The Nature of the Gods and On Divination*, by Cicero. 1853. Reprint, Amherst: Prometheus, 1997.
Zerba, M. "The Frauds of Humanism: Cicero, Machiavelli, and the Rhetoric of Imposture." *Rhetorica* 22, no. 3 (2004): 215–40.
———. "Love, Envy, and Pantomimic Morality in Cicero's *De oratore*." *Classical Philology* 97, no. 4 (2002): 299–321.
Zetzel, J. E. G. "Citizen and Commonwealth in *De Re Publica*, Book 4." In *Cicero's Republic: Bulletin of the Institute of Classical Studies Supplement 76*. Edited by J. G. F. Powell and J. A. North, 83–97. London: Institute of Classical Studies, University of London, 2001.
———. ed. *Cicero: De Re Publica, Selections*. Cambridge: Cambridge University Press. 1995.
———, trans. *On the Commonwealth and On the Laws*, by Cicero. Cambridge: Cambridge University Press, 1999.
Ziegler, K., ed. *M. Tullius Cicero. Fasc. 39: De Re Publica*. 7th ed. Leipzig: Teubner, 1968.
Zucchelli, B. "L'independenza di Lucilio." Col. Univ. di ParMass. *Pubblicazioni dell'Instituto di Lingua e Lettere* 3, 81–141. Florence: Opus libri, 1977.

Index of Citations of Cicero

Acad. (Academica)
1.7	107n1
2.7	133
2.7–9	148n5
2.23	137–38
2.26	150n17
2.32	150n20
2.59	139, 140
2.60	150n20
2.66	139, 140, 141, 148n4
2.67	133, 139
2.69	150n20
2.76	150n20
2.78	133, 139, 140
2.84–87	135
2.88–91	135
2.99	141, 145, 146
2.99–104	141, 145
2.100	146
2.101	145
2.104	142, 145, 151n25
2.105	141
2.108	145
2.109	143
2.109–10	147
2.110	146, 151n22
2.113	133, 139
2.128	143
2.146	141
2.148	142, 151n23

Amic. (De Amicitia)
18	148n7
18–19	136
19	136, 148n9
61	83
91	83
105	84
140	84

Arch. (Pro Archia)
8	108n3
15	77n16

Att. (Epistulae ad Atticum)
1.17.1	76n5
1.17.5	76n4
1.17.7	76n7
1.18	148n10
1.19.8	90
1.20.2	90
2.1	148n10
2.1.8	148n6
2.3	110n26
2.4	110n26
2.5	77n20, 110n26
2.7	110n26
2.8.2	90
2.10	90
2.12.2	104
2.16	67

2.16.3	77n23	138	97
2.18	110n26	139	102
2.19	110n26	140	97, 102
3.9.2	96	142	97, 102
3.12.2	98	153	59
4.5.2	99		
5.11.5	89	*Corn. (Pro Cornelio de maiestate)*	
6.1.2	89	78	83
6.2.8	104–5		
6.2.9	105	*De Or. (De Oratore)*	
6.5	105	1.5	63, 279n7
6.16.3	89	2.156	73
6.20.6	89	2.184	95
7.1.6	148n6	3.94	76n10
8.15.2	91	3.78	178n30
8.16.1	91	3.107	63
9.1.2	91		
9.1.3	91	*Div. (De Divinatione)*	
9.1.4	91	1.1	168
9.7	239n25	1.5	169
9.10	239n25	1.7	169
10.7	239n25	1.8	169
12.3.1	109n16	1.9	170
12.5	109n16	2.1	145, 147n1
13.19.4	168	2.1–2	148n6
14.20.4	78n37	2.1–4	279n10
15.5.1	78n36	2.2	9, 279n12
		2.2.5	209n33
Brut. (Brutus)		2.4	8
9	78n31	2.8	170
31	8	2.17	170
103	86	2.28	172, 174
125	86	2.29	172
216–20	98	2.33	172
304–24	279	2.41	172
306	60, 76n8	2.48	172
		2.55	170
Cat. (In Catilinam)		2.60	170
1.1	206n11	2.61	148n7
2.27	82	2.70–71	172
		2.104	171
Clu. (Pro Cluentio)		2.124	171
136	102	2.126–27	171

Div. (De Divinatione) (cont.)
2.128   170
2.136   171
2.139   171
2.148   173, 174
2.149   172, 173
2.150   173, 174
3.14–16 148n7

Div. Caec. (Divinatio in Caecilium)
71   106
72   106

Dom. (De Domo sua)
34   104

Fam. (Epistulae ad Familiares)
3.3   109n14
4.7   111n45
5.7.3 109n14
7.3   111n45
9.2.5 71
9.16.7 74
11.5.1 111n41
14.3.1 96
14.4.6 111n37

Fin. (De Finibus)
1.10   148n6
1.11   8, 279n11
2.45–47 45
2.47   45, 52, 54
2.48–49 131n11
2.59   282n65
3.16–21 131n16
3.21   116
3.22   78n25
3.24   131n12
3.62–64 193
3.67   237n2
3.67–68 225, 240n34
4.14   9
4.61   148n10
4.65   134–35, 148n7
5.11   206n11
5.18   131n8

5.40   78n29
5.43   131n8
5.65   239n19
5.65–68 224

Inv. (De Inventione)
1.3   76n7, 76n14
1.4–5 279n7
1.5   76n15
1.8   65
1.24   76n7
1.55   76n7
1.56   76n7
1.70   76n7
1.92   76n7
1.102 76n7
2.4   76n7
2.9   148n5
2.24   76n7
2.35   76n7
2.52   76n7
2.64   76n7
2.67   76n7
2.90   76n7
2.92   76n7
2.94   76n7
2.96   76n7
2.97   76n7
2.99   76n7
2.101 76n7
2.105 76n7
2.107 76n7
2.137 76n7
2.139 76n7
2.140 76n7
2.143 76n7
2.145 76n7
2.161 76n7
2.163 76n7
2.166 76n7

Leg. (De Legibus)
1.3–4   210n42
1.5–6   197
1.16–19 130n1

1.18	132n27	1.2	157
1.24–25	103n1	1.6	154
1.27	117, 130n5	1.6–7	76n11
1.30	131n7	1.7	148n6
1.31–32	116, 129	1.10	155
1.33	129, 132n27	1.11	145, 147n1
1.36	128	1.12	153
1.38	128	1.13–14	159
1.47	118, 119, 129	1.15	159
2.5	199	1.17	156
2.31	172	1.44	159
2.32–33	179n74	1.49	161
3.20	206n11	1.60	160
3.29	211n48	1.61	160, 174
3.33–39	87	1.62	161
3.39	87	1.62–64	161
		1.66	163

Leg. Agr. (De Lege Agraria)

1.26	206n11	1.68	161
2.6.15	108n7	1.71	161
2.7	81	1.72	161
2.8.21	108n7	1.74–75	161
2.9	81	1.85	162
2.9.22	108n7	1.85–86	162
2.10.24	108n7	1.94	163
2.11.29	108n7	1.110	18
2.13.32	108n7	1.117	162
2.14.35	108n7	1.120	163
2.21.57	108n7	1.121	162
2.23.61	108n7	1.123	162
2.28.75	108n7	2.2	163
2.34.93	108n7	2.18	167
3.4	206n11	2.104–6	141
		3.3	162
		3.5	163

Leg. Man. (Pro Lege Manilia)

1	82	3.5–6	179n47
		3.6	164

Mil. (Pro Milone)

47	112n46	3.7	164, 174
		3.8	164
		3.9	164

Mur. (Pro Murena)

55	77n17	3.10	165
60–66	148n10	3.10–11	167
		3.11	167
		3.11–12	167

Nat. D. (De Natura Deorum)

1.1	154	3.14	165, 174
		3.14–15	167

Nat. D. (De Natura Deorum) (cont.)

3.15	165
3.26	167
3.26–28	175
3.27	167
3.28	167
3.44	164
3.65–85	167
3.79	148n7
3.95	155, 156, 168

Off. (De Officiis)

1.2	279n6
1.4–5	8
1.11–12	223, 226, 238n11, 240n34, 240n35
1.11–14	131n16
1.11–17	45, 48
1.12	223, 238n7
1.12–15	240n44
1.13	239n17
1.14	53
1.15	52
1.17	213
1.19	18, 78n39
1.21	225, 226, 233–35
1.21–22	238n11, 240n34, 240n35
1.22	240n42
1.23	231
1.25	220
1.26	239n26
1.50ff	240n48
1.51	225
1.51–55	240n34
1.53–55	226
1.53–57	95
1.57	197, 224, 227
1.61	238n17
1.65	131n11
1.66	238n17
1.85	239n25
1.93	43, 52, 53
1.93–94	48, 50
1.93–151	43, 53
1.96	48, 51, 54
1.97	49
1.97–98	48, 54
1.98	51, 54
1.99	51, 64, 233
1.100	51
1.100–121	46
1.103	54, 55, 233
1.107	48
1.108–9	46
1.110	49, 232–33
1.111	49, 93
1.111–14	49
1.112	148n10
1.113	49, 241n62
1.114	50, 94
1.119–21	46
1.121	195
1.122	47
1.122–24	46
1.124	47
1.125	47
1.126	233
1.126–51	54, 55
1.127	55
1.128	54, 55
1.130–33	46
1.133	49
1.141	55
1.143	54
1.145–46	46
1.148	54, 241n57
1.149	59
1.150	88
1.150–51	54
1.155	240n40
1.158	193, 227, 240n46, 240n48, 240n50
2.7	148n5
2.8	147n1
2.12–16	225
2.21–22	239n27
2.27–29	239n25
2.29	220
2.31	88
2.35	148n8

Index of Citations of Cicero   303

2.43	94	*Q. Fr. (Epistulae ad Quintum Fratrem)*	
2.44	95	3.5.1	25
2.51	110n24		
2.73	194, 213, 214, 226, 230, 238n7	*Rab. Post. (Pro Rabirio Postumo)*	
		14	85
2.73–79	234	18	86
2.74	241n65		
2.78	194, 214, 229, 230, 234	*Red. Pop. (Post reditum ad Populum)*	
2.79	240n32	1	82
2.81	195		
2.83–84	241n67	*Red. Sen. (Post reditum in Senatu)*	
2.84	241n65	7.16	206n11
3.7	43		
3.15–16	148n10	*Rep. (De Re Publica)*	
3.16	137	1.1	18
3.21–22	240n34	1.2	19, 78n26
3.28–32	233	1.2–3	130n1
3.31	137	1.3	19, 20, 131n8
3.32	234	1.4–8	20
3.33	137	1.9	20
3.41	210n42	1.10–12	21
3.52	241n58	1.18	282n65
3.53	241n58	1.18–19	22
3.57	241n60	1.23–25	23
3.61	137, 241n61	1.26–29	22
3.63	240n42	1.27	23, 213, 233, 237
3.83–85	239n29, 240n31	1.28	23
3.99–115	137	1.30	73, 282n66
		1.33	23, 282n66
Orat. (Orator ad Brutum)		1.36	23
70–74	46	1.39	192, 193, 214, 240n31, 240n48, 240n50
237	154		
		1.39–41	192
Phil. (Orationes Philippicae)		1.41	130n1, 131n8, 196, 228
2.2	46	1.42	24, 206n11
6.17	82	1.43	24, 204
7.9	92	1.45	25
7.12.2	78n35	1.49	24
		1.52	24
Prov. Cons. (De Provinciis Consularibus)		1.53	24
18	101	1.55	24
21	101	1.65	24
23	101	1.68	24, 240n31
38	82	1.69	25
41	101	2.2	201

Rep. (De Re Publica) (cont.)

2.4–5	210n42
2.16–17	172
2.17–20	210n42
2.20	210n42
2.21	202
2.22	210n43
2.26–27	27–28, 172
2.28–30	201
2.33	210n43
2.34	201
2.35	210n46
2.51	20, 279n8
2.57	210n42
2.64	200, 201
2.66	28
2.66–67	279n8
3.5	32
3.6	71
3.8–9	282n65
3.21b	208n25
3.24b	208n25
3.32–42	193
3.36	208n25
3.41	208n25
3.43ff	193
3.43–45	193
4	34
5	34, 35
Fr. 7	35
6	34
6.20	71
6.25	71
Fr. 1	35

Sest. (Pro Sestio)

23	69
96	78n24
99	70, 78n25
104	70
122	70

Sull. (Pro Sulla)

26	77n18
62	106
83	94, 106

Top. (Topica)

90	237n1

Tusc. (Tusculanae Disputationes)

1.40–42	130n1
1.109	131n13
1.109–10	131n11
1.7	72
2.1	73, 78n33
2.4	145, 147n1
2.10	78n32
2.44–46	149n11
2.48	149n11
2.51	149n11
2.63–64	131n11
3.2	131n8, 131n10
3.2–4	129
3.3	120
3.3–4	120–21
3.16–18	52, 54
3.17	45, 52
4.6	153
4.7	154
4.26–27	70
4.36	52
5.10–11	8
5.11	158
5.33	103, 144
31	103

Verr. (In Verrem)

2.2.179	110n24

General Index

Academy, 9, 74, 134, 146, 246
  Academic assent, 142–47
  Academic philosophy, 68, 134, 135, 141, 181, 192
  —and Cicero, 134, 140, 247, 252, 274
  Academic sage, 141–43
  Academic skepticism, 97, 102, 105, 160, 172, 174, 271
  Academic theology, 153–76
  New Academy, 247
  Old Academy, 67, 246–47
Achard, G., on date of *De Inventione*, 63
ambitio
  as part of *voluntas*, 59
American political philosophy, 244, 259–62
  republicanism in America, 261–62
amicus, 68, 83
André, J.-M.
  on "crisis of 59," 66
  on "impossible retirement," 58
Annas, J.
  on Aratus, 235
  on Diogenes/Antipater, 231
Anthony
  role model of Cicero, 62
  See also Antonius
Antiochus, 67, 68, 129, 146–47
  and the Old Academy, 246–47
Antipater, 231–32

Antonius
  in *De Oratore*, 95
  See also Anthony
Aratus of Sicyon, 235–37
aristocratic class, 216–17
aristocratic government, 24, 26, 28, 33
Aristotle, 21, 24, 40, 181, 264
  individualism, 263
  Nicomachean Ethics, 243
  political community, 188, 193, 195, 196
  political philosophy, 193–96, 199, 226–27
  Politics, 27, 188, 189, 198, 202, 226
  practical philosophy, 8
  property, 194
  wisdom, 269
assent, 135–47
  Clitomachus vs. Catulus (Philo), 143–44, 146
  dogmatic assent, 142–43, 146
  and *kataleptic* impressions, 135–36
  as part of knowledge, 141–43, 147
  passive assent, 144–45
  and the sage, 136, 138–39, 142
Athens, 28, 199–200
atomism, 153, 160, 161, 171
  social atomism, 215–16, 219
Atticus, 59, 60, 68–69, 95
  as Cicero's confidant, 88–92
  in *De Legibus*, 87
  on virtue, 103–5

Augustine
  and Antiochus, 67
  on Cicero's *De Natura Deorum*, 155
  Confessions, 5
  Contra Iulianum, 60
  De Civitate Dei Contra Paganos (CD),
    29, 33, 34, 38

Bailyn, Bernard, 262
Balbus, 156, 163–70, 175
Barlow, J. Jackson
  on role of justice with respect to
    property, 12
Beranger, Jean, on Cicero on Gracchi, 85
boni. See *optimates*
Büchner, Karl
  Books 5 and 6 of *De Re Publica*, 36

Caesar, 4, 7, 82, 91, 100, 237
  and Cicero's inconsistency, 99–101,
    104
  Cicero's written support, 99
  dictatorship, 75
  and *gloria*, 219–20
  and Pompey, 91, 248
  and property, 219–22, 237
Calcidius, 124–29
Carneades, 138–40, 143–44, 249–50
Catiline, 5, 82, 94, 106, 248
Cato, 64–65, 105
  in *De Legibus*, 197
  on property, 212
Catulus, 142–43
cave allegory, 122, 129
Chrysippus of Soli, 127–28, 166
  On Emotions, 123–24, 128
  perversion of will, 115, 123
cives, qualities of, 83
civilization, origins of, 30–32
civitas, 192–93, 197, 203–4, 275
Cleanthes, 122–23, 127
Clitomachus, 138–47
  definition of sage, 139
Cluentius, 97
Colburn, W. Trevor, 262

concordia, 29, 220, 235
consilium, 196, 203–4
consistency, 80–107
  difficulty during civil war, 92
  inward vs. outward, 101
  memory in writing vs. speech, 98
  and true character, 93
constantia, 11, 80–107. *See also*
  consistency
constitutions, 24–25
  mixed, 25, 261
  Polybian theory, 24–25, 250
  and virtue, 25
consul, 4, 20, 75, 81, 93, 248
Cornell, T. J., on *De Re Publica*, 2, 200
cosmic political community, 181–83,
  190–92
  and Stoicism, 190
Cotta
  as Academic, 155–68, 174–75
  dogmatic naturalism, 168
  and Epicureanism, 161–62
  skeptic, 167
  and Stoicism, 163
Crassus, 220
  role model of Cicero, 62
Cumming, Robert, 229, 253, 258, 261–65
  and the liberal tradition, 261–63

death, 116–17
deception, 95, 138
decorum, 43–56
  as fourth virtue, 52–53
  manifested in *verecundia*, 53
  and moderation, 51
  as order and consistency, 53
  related to *honestum*, 50
  related to *persona*, 46–50
decretum, 146–47
DeFilippo, Joseph G., on *De Natura*
  Deorum, 156
demes, 199–200
democracy, 24–26, 28, 33, 38
Demosthenes, 255
Dicaearchus, 67

Diodotus, 128, 246
Diogenes, 123–24, 231
disgrace, 117
divination, 165–67, 170–74
   political use, 169–73, 175
doctrina, 66
dogmatic naturalism, 167–68, 170, 172–73, 175
Douglas, A. E., 2, 253
Dream of Scipio, 18, 23, 37, 41
dreams, divine cause, 170–71, 173
Drumann, Wilhelm, 252
Dugan, John, 94–95, 98, 107
Dyck, Andrew R.
   definition of *verecundia*, 55
   on *De Natura Deorum*, 160–61
   translation of *De Officiis* 1.96 and 1.98, 51

eclecticism, 252–54
eloquence, 63–65
   paired with wisdom, 64
Ennius, 34, 73
Epictetus, 51
Epicurean theology, 153–54, 159–63, 266–68
   existence of gods, 154, 159–63, 171
Erskine, A., Stoic sympathy to democracy, 191
ethos, 106
exile, 96

fama, 83, 89
Fink, Zera, 260–62, 264
flattery, 83
fortitude, 17, 19
   and political life, 20
Fott, David
   dogmatic skepticism confronted, 11–12
frugalitas, as fourth virtue, 52

Galen, 123–24, 126
glory, 117, 120, 125–26
   and false glory, 120–22, 220–21
   and false praise, 121

Glucker, John, 147, 150–51
   on *De Natura Deorum*, 156
gods
   Epicurean, 159–60, 172
   existence, 153–75
   rest vs. motion, 163
good, the, 69, 119, 121, 125, 191, 236
good life, 198–200
Görler, Woldemar, continuity in the Academy, 134
Gracchi, 85–86, 220
Graver, Margaret, 11
   on Cicero's use of sources, 6
Grillius, 15–16, 35
   oratory and politics, 15

Habermas, J., 204
Habicht, Christian, 7, 99–100
Habinek, T., 82, 109n15
Heinze, Richard, on *rector rei publicae*, 15
Hermagoras, 65
Hirtius, 74–75
Holton, James, 253, 265, 271–72
homo novus, 80, 82, 85, 107, 216, 245
honestum, 10, 44, 69–71
   constitution of *officia*, 45
   related to *decorum*, 48–50
   shaped by reason, 45
honor, 116–17, 120
   natural human pursuit, 126
Hortensius, 247
human nature, conferred by divine, 113
Hume, D., 243

imagines, 94, 107
impression, 123–24, 145
   as cause of impulse, 145–46
   kataleptic impressions, 135–36, 139
impulse, 145
inconstantia, 99–105, 256–58
individualism, 226, 263–64
   economic, 215–17, 222, 225–26
   political, 215, 217, 225
injuria, 193

intellect, theoretical vs. practical, 22
iuris consensus, 193, 194, 196, 228
ius, 193–94, 214, 228

John of Salisbury, on two Ciceros, 257
Jonkers, E. J., on *De Lege Agraria*, 81
justice, 16, 17, 19, 27, 40, 222
   in *De Legibus*, 115
   in individual, 116
   in law, 33
   within the political community or state, 27–29, 33–34
   political vs. natural, 33
   and property in the polity, 214–37
   purpose of political community, 230
   and the statesman, 29

Kaster, Robert, on culture of the Roman republic, 55
kataleptic, 139
   true impression, 135–36
katēchēsis, 123–24
Kendall, W., Cicero and Voegelin, 276–77
Krarup, P., on *rector rei publicae*, 15

Lacey, W. K., on approaching the historical study of Cicero, 6
Lactantius, 32, 33
Laelius, 22, 65, 83, 136
   in *De Re Publica*, 32, 33, 37, 193, 201–3, 271, 274
   and Stoic natural law, 271
   and wisdom, 22–23
law, 19
   and nature, 198
   and reason, 191
   study of, 3
   tool of a statesman, 31
lawgiver. *See* statesman
Levine, Philip, on *De Natura Deorum*, 157–58
Lévy, Carlos, 36
   on Cicero's commitment to philosophy, 9–11

liberal tradition, 262–63
liberty, 263
life, 116–17
litterae, 65
Long, A. A., 222
Lucretius, 266–67
Luther, Martin, 243

Machiavelli, 95, 215, 221, 229, 262, 263
MacKendrick, Paul, 92
Macrobius, 37–38
   on the good statesman, 37
Mai, Cardinal Angelo
   De Re Publica manuscript, 10, 30
Marcus
   Cicero himself in *De Legibus*, 197
   Cicero's son as addressee of *De Officiis*, 219, 231–33
Marcus Antonius, 97, 102. *See also* Antonius
Marcus Crassus. *See* Crassus
Márquez, Xavier, special themes of his contribution, 12
May, James, importance of *ethos* in Roman oratory, 106
Mayor, Joseph B., on *De Natura Deorum*, 176
McKeon, Richard, 252–53
Meier, Christian, 219
mixed government, 25–26, 250, 261–62
moderatio, 38–39, 44, 55
   as fourth virtue, 10
   moderation, 50–54
Momigliano, Arnaldo, on *De Natura Deorum*, 155–56
Mommsen, Theodor
   critique of Cicero, 1–2, 7, 252, 254
monarchy, 24–25, 33, 38
Montaigne, 256
Montesquieu
   on Cicero's *De Natura Deorum*, 155
morality
   Cicero against relativism, 118
multitudo, 88
municipia, 199–200

Narducci, E., on Cicero's hiding true self, 95
natural law, 198
　in Laelius's speech, 33
　in political community, 191, 194, 195, 198
　and property, 212, 234
nature, 30–31, 113–19, 126
　divine cause, 170, 172
　and property, 227, 233, 236
Nicgorski, Walter, 175, 198
Nonius, 18, 35
Numa Pompilius, 201

officia, 43, 50–51, 88, 137
　as dictated by *persona*, *decorum*, 46–48
officium, 47, 48, 53, 69, 91, 105
oikeiōsis, 69–70
oikoi, 189
Oppicianus, 97, 102
optimates, 70–71, 84, 91
optimi, 31, 68–69
orator, 88
　and Cicero, 3, 95–98, 102, 245–46
　orator and ideal orator, 16–17, 62
oratory, 49
　and consistency, 88
　and politics, 15
otium, 64, 66, 68–72

paideia, 190–91
pain, 116–18, 124
Panaetius, 22, 94
　and Socrates, according to Scipio, 22
　source for *De Officiis*, 43–46, 92
　Stoicism, 59, 223–26
Pascal, 256
patria, 183, 197–200, 203–4
　created by will, 200
　historical nature, 197, 204
　and love, 197–201
　by nature and by law, 198
Pease, Arthur Stanley, 156–58

people, the, 186, 193
　in the ancient vs. modern state, 187
　in Cicero's political community, 196
persona, 43–56
　assigned by nature, 49
　common, human *persona*, 47
　definition, 48
　dictates *decorum*, 46–50
　dictates treatment of others, 47
　of individual nature, 49–50
　natural *personae* vs. circumstantial *personae*, 47
　used to determine *officium*, 47–48
persona theory, 47–48, 54
perversion, 113–30
　false values, 119
　general state, 116
　imitation of the Good, 119
　origin of, 120
　in Plato's *Republic*, 114
　pleasure vs. virtue, 125
　of will, 115
Petrarch, 257
Philo of Larissa, 60, 63, 65, 67, 72, 74, 246
　as an academic, 246
　anti-dogmatic skepticism, 79
　and Carneades, 138, 140, 143, 147
philosopher
　as statesman, 22–23
　vs. statesman, 20, 31
philosophical life, 154
　vs. practical life, 58–76, 248–51, 257–59
philosophical writings, 4, 249
　skewed or enhanced by political life, 258–59
philosophy, 246
　Cicero's approach, 252
　Greek vs. Roman, 246, 256
　and rhetoric, 65, 246
　Voegelin's view of Cicero as philosopher, 276
　See also Academy, Academic philosophy

Piso, L. Calpurnius, 52
pithanon, 144
Plato, 16, 21, 30, 40, 129–30, 181, 246, 277
    Academy, 153
    Apology of Socrates, 168
    Gorgias, 19
    guardians, *(phylakes)*, 20
    individualism, 215
    Laws, 188–89, 250
    natural law, 270
    perversion of will, 114
    political philosophy, 24–25, 28, 188, 202–3, 217, 263, 268
    property, 34, 194
    Protagoras, 30–31
    Republic, 17, 18, 27, 28, 30, 37, 114, 122, 129, 184, 188, 250, 272
    Timaeus, 124
Platonic virtues, 19, 24, 26, 37
pleasure, 116–18, 124
    and value, 126
    and virtue, 126
Pliny the Elder, 42n17
Plutarch, on reputation of Cicero, 61, 255
Pocock, J. G. A., 262
polis, 182, 188, 193
politeia, 190, 196
political community, 181, 184, 186–87
    Cicero's model, 183, 192–204
    creation of, 226
    and human nature, 228
    and justice, 230, 233
    and trust, 231–32
    urban vs. cosmic, 181–84, 188–92
political life, 20–23, 58–76, 248. *See also* practical life
political philosophy, 8, 11–13, 268
    of Cicero, 254, 266
    classical political philosophy, 266–69
    and human nature, 262, 268
    neglect of Cicero, 242–44
    and philosophy, 270
    revival, 1, 260
politician. *See* statesman

politics, 18–19, 21
    as science, 21, 31, 40
polity, 213–36, 273–75
Polybius, 22, 27, 40, 263
    Polybian theory, 24–25, 250, 261
Pompey, 90, 96, 100, 105
    and war with Caesar, 91–92, 248
popularis (*es*), 70–71, 81–84
    and the passions, 70
    and senate, 82
populus, 81–88, 203
populus Romanus, 81, 82, 84, 86
Posidonius, 247
Powell, J. G. F.
    Cicero as philosopher, 6
    Cicero the Philosopher, 1
    virtue in Cicero's writings, 10
practical life
    vs. philosophical life/theoretical life, 58–76, 248
    See also political life
practical philosophy, 8–11, 256–58, 273
praise, as testimony to virtue, 126–27
Price, John Valdimir, on *De Natura Deorum*, 158
probabilia, 142, 145–47
probable, as object of search and striving, 156, 158
property, 194, 212–37
    and goodness, value, 230
    and justice, 214–37
    private property, 214, 224
    redistribution, 221, 234, 237
    and republic, 218–19, 222–37
property rights, 222, 229, 236
    and justice, 236
    and nature, 236
    and self-ownership, 224
prudentia, 32–36, 39, 269
    innate vs. acquired through philosophy, 66

Quintus, 59, 87
    defense of divination, 169–71
    and Stoicism, 174

ratio, 60–61
  as part of *voluntas*, 59, 64
Rawson, Elizabeth, appreciating
  Cicero, 2
reason
  and community, 224
  human vs. divine, 167
  vs. pleasure, 61
rector rei publicae, 15, 36–37
Regulus, 137–38, 146
Reid, J. S., on unfair treatment of
  Cicero, 3
relativism, in morality, 118
Renaissance, political philosophy, 259–60
republic, meaning of, 34–35
republicanism, classical republicans, 261
reputation, and *constantia*, 89–90,
  105–6, 127
res publica, 21, 192–96, 204, 218–19, 225
  agreement on law and value, 193, 204
  Cicero's dedication to, 71–72, 75–76
  definition, 23, 228
  and justice, 33
  and property, 218–19
rhetoric
  Cicero's writings on, 3–4, 9
  and philosophy, 246
  populist rhetoric, 80–84
  in relation to consistency, 79–84,
    95–100
  as a tool for Cicero, 245–46
Robbins, Caroline, 261
Roman Republic, 40
  downfall, alluded to by Laelius, 22
Rome
  Cicero's judgment on, 274
  foundation, 199
  as political community, 182
  Roman history, 203, 244

Sabine, G. H., 252–53
Sagan, Carl, 152
sage, 136
  ideal vs. actual, 139
  Stoic ideal, 136

sapiens, 16, 20–21
sapientia, 65
  and *iustitia*, 33
  practical vs. theoretical, 19
  See also wisdom
Saturninus, 86
Schlatter, R., 213
Schofield, Malcolm, 12, 231
  definition of *res publica*, 23
  on *moderatio*, 10
Scipio, 65, 71, 192–93, 200, 202–3
  Panaetius and Socrates, 22
  on political virtue, 37
  and speculative philosophy, 271
Senate
  Cicero unpopular with, 90
  and defense of property, 216
Seneca, 53, 124
  Epistulae, 32
Septentriones, 141
Seven Sages, 21
Sextii, 74
Sextus Aelius Paetus Catus, 23
Sextus Empiricus, 143
  passive assent, 144
  Pyrrhonian view of assent, 144
Shackleton Bailey, D. R., 89, 92, 104–5
skepticism, 9–12, 80, 101, 103, 133–47, 174
  mitigated, 133, 146–47
  radical, 133
Social War, 199, 245
Socrates, 71, 94, 143, 236, 247, 249, 250,
  252
  corruption of nature, 114
  and divine, 167–68
  and knowledge, 269
  and Panaetius, according to Scipio,
    22
  philosophical life, 153, 158, 270
  practical philosophy, 8, 22–23
Solmsen, F., virtues of *rector*, 37
soothsaying, 171–72
sōphrosunē, 45–46
  dependent on other three virtues, 45
  as fourth virtue, 45

sōphrosunē (cont.)
  humans superior to animals, 48
  relation to *personae, decorum*, 47, 50
state, 25, 183, 185, 196
  harmony of, 28
  nation state, 184–85, 187
  order in, 34
  and property, 216
statesman, 15, 20, 88
  Cicero as, 243, 245
  in *De Oratore*, 250
  ideal, 26, 31–32
  vs. philosopher, 20
  qualities of, 16, 31–32, 250
  relationship to state, 25
  role of, 29, 31
  Scipio as enlightened example, 21–22, 31
  and wisdom, 29
statesmanship, 2–3, 5
Stoicism, 128, 270–72
  and Cicero, 274
  happiness, 217–18
  moral progress, 135
  natural law, 204, 270–74
  political community, 194
  property, 212
  theology, 153, 156–57, 163–68, 272
  and wealth, 220
Strauss, Leo, 5, 12, 259, 260, 264–73
  Cicero's philosophical works, 266
  Cicero vs. Catiline, Pompey, 5
striving as quest for probability, 158
Sulla, 220–21, 237
superstition and religion, 173–74
Sydney and republicanism, 261

telos, 69, 202
temperance, 16–17, 19, 34, 40
Theophrastus, 68
Thorsrud, Harald
  impact and consistency of Cicero's skepticism, 11
  nature of Cicero's philosophical interests, 9

Tiberius Gracchus, 85, 86
Tracy, Catherine
  importance of consistency, 2
  tension between skepticism and consistency, 11
truth
  Academic truth, 162
  attaining truth, 154, 176
  infallible vs. fallible, 146
  passive vs. active assent, 145
Tullia and Cicero's consistency, 90
"two Ciceros," 277

urban political community, 188–90
  political life = good life, 189

verecundia, 44, 53–55
  connection to *decorum*, 53
  definition, 54
  location of *temperantia et modestia*, 53
Velleius, 162
Verres, 90, 102, 106, 247
virtue, 7, 9–10, 12, 44–45
  four virtues, 16–18, 39, 44
  general, 18
  in individual, 27–28, 88
  natural endowment, 119
  perverted by pleasure, 125
  in politics, 18, 24–25
  Roman vs. Greek, 42n8
  in state, 26–28, 113
  summary of, 38–39
  understanding vs. acting, 44
  virtue ethics, 9
  virtuous action, 70–71
Voegelin, Eric, 264–65, 273–78
  renewed study of Cicero, 12, 260
Voltaire, on Cicero's *De Natura Deorum*, 155
voluntas, 59, 64, 66

Walsh, P. G., on Cicero and Roman piety, 156
Wilhelmsen, Frederick, Cicero and Voegelin, 276–77

Winterbottom, Michael
    translation of *De Officiis* 1.96 and 1.98, 51
wisdom, 16–17, 21, 33, 37
    Academic vs. Stoic definition, 140, 145
    and eloquence, 64–65
    in Greek theory, 24
    ideal and the attainable, 136
    in individual, 26–27, 29
    and justice, 33
    and oratory, 246
    and political wisdom, 23–24
    and politics, 20–21, 23–24, 26
    and the sage, 134–38
    in state, 29
    in statesman, 19
    Stoic ideal, 136

Wiseman, T. P.
    on allies over consistency, 104
    on Cicero over Caesar, 7
Wistrand, Magnus, on Cicero's Caesarian policies, 100
Wood, N., on Cicero on property, 213–30, 235
writing as commitment, 96–99

Xenocrates, 20

Zeno of Citium, 128
    in *De Natura Deorum*, 167
    Stoicism, 51
    virtue, 44
Zerba, Michelle, 88
    Cicero as Machiavellian, 95
Zetzel, J. E. G., on *De Re Publica*, 36, 193

www.ingramcontent.com/pod-product-compliance
Lightning Source LLC
Chambersburg PA
CBHW050619300426
44112CB00012B/1566